GERMAN
COASTAL FORCES
OF WORLD WAR TWO

Below: As completed, there was little to distinguish one F-boat from another.

GERMAN
COASTAL FORCES
OF WORLD WAR TWO

M. J. WHITLEY

ARMS AND
ARMOUR

Arms and Armour Press
A Cassell Imprint
Villiers House, 41-47 Strand, London WC2N 5JE.

Distributed in the USA by Sterling Publishing Co. Inc., 387 Park
Avenue South, New York, NY 10016-8810.

Distributed in Australia by Capricorn Link (Australia) Pty. Ltd,
P.O. Box 665, Lane Cove, New South Wales 2066.

British Library Cataloguing-in-Publication Data: a catalogue
record for this book is available from the British Library

ISBN 1-85409-085-2

Jacket illustration by Jim Mitchell.

Cartography by Anthony A. Evans.

Designed and edited by DAG Publications Ltd. Designed by
David Gibbons; edited by David Dorrell; layout by Anthony A.
Evans; thanks also to J. P. Allen; typeset by DAG, Typesetters
(Birmingham) Ltd and Ronset Typesetters; camerawork by M&E
Reproductions, North Fambridge, Essex; printed and bound in
Great Britain by The Bath Press, Avon.

CONTENTS

PREFACE

This volume covers the design and operation of S-boats, (Schnellboote) or, as they are more familiarly known in the UK and USA for no agreed reasons, 'E-boats'. These craft were active in all European theatres of war between 1939 and 1945, with their main campaign directed against the east coast shipping routes of the British Isles. Even if they were never the threat that the U-boats posed to the Atlantic convoys, the S-boats nevertheless made the east coast convoys a sometimes dangerous operation. The S-boats obtained their success with both torpedo and mine, as did their Allied adversaries, but the latter conducted a major mining offensive, predominantly aerial, against the German coastal convoy traffic between Brest and the Elbe as well as in the U-boat training areas in the Baltic. This resulted in the construction of a large programme of minesweepers by the Kriegsmarine whose role was an important if arduous and monotonous one. Their moments of action were few - clashes with Royal Navy coastal forces in the Channel, with Soviet light forces in the Baltic and Arctic, as well as with superior Allied naval forces in conjunction with Operation 'Overlord' in 1944. Above all, they were the frequent targets of air attack - reflected in the continuous upgrading of their anti-aircraft outfits. Space does not permit more than a study of their design and an even briefer consideration of their inshore counterparts, the R-boats (Raumboote). The large force of auxiliary and small number of specially built naval trawlers also used on minesweeping and escort tasks have had to be omitted altogether. This should not be taken as a reflection of their relative importance to the Axis war effort but rather the impossibility of dealing with such a large number of individual ships and designs in a limited space.

If the minesweepers' task was essentially defensive, there was another arm which complemented the offensive nature of the S-boat operations. This was the Kleinkampfverband, or Small Battle Unit Command, whose activities have not previously been described in detail, from such official records as remain of this somewhat shadowy organisation. Conceived in an air of some desperation and operated with a somewhat cavalier attitude to losses (although never a suicide group), the men of this command deserved better success for their bravery than their makeshift weapons would allow. In view of their relatively unknown activities, they have been included despite the 'surface ship' concept of this series.

Many of the smaller craft covered in this volume would have been unable to operate without the assistance - technical, material and human - provided by depot ships and support craft. Consequently the S-boat depot ships are also covered by this work, as are a number of other Kriegsmarine ships which, while not contributing greatly to the Axis war effort, are of interest to the naval enthusiast. These vessels - for example *Grille* and *Brummer* - would not otherwise receive attention in the press on their own merit.

The format of this volume follows that of the previous ones, modified only in the light of the sheer number of vessels included in the category 'coastal forces' which precludes a study of individual vessels and their careers. As usual, prime source official contemporary documents, both Allied and Axis, have been the basis for the technical and operational content.

Grateful thanks are also due to many individuals and organisations who have assisted the search for material used in this book. They include:

R.M. Coppock and A.J. Francis of the Naval Historical Branch, (Ministry of Defence); Herr Kästner and Frau Roschlau of the Bundesarchiv-Potsdam; Dr. Mäierhofer, Herr Jamans and the staff of the Bundesarchiv-Freiburg; Dr. Jurgen Rohwer of the Bibliothek für Zeitgeschichte, for his help and comments as well as the use of BfZ photographs; Paul Kemp of the Department of Photographs, Imperial War Museum; Colonel Hervé Monmarche and Contre-Amiral Kessler at the ECPA, France; Gerd-Dietrich Schneider, formerly of the 3rd Raumbootesflotille and 8th Artillerieträgerflotille; Gerhard Behrens, Germany; Captain S.Sandvold, Royal Norwegian Navy; P.J.V. Elliot, RAF Historical Branch; Herman Büchting formerly of the 1st S-Bootesflotille; Contre-Amiral Jacques Zang; Herr Bracke of the Frankfurter Allgemeine photo archive; Herr Wolff of Abeking & Rasmussen; Herr Knobloch and Herr Hoheisel of Germany; M. Bullen; David Ennor; and last but not least, my wife Rita for typing yet another manuscript!

M.J. Whitley, Wombourne 1991

INTRODUCTION

Naval powers have always required a wide range of ship types to fulfil the various duties and demands placed upon them by contemporary political, strategic and tactical situations. In the far off and simpler days of sail and cannon, the fleet ranged from the 1st rate 100-gun line-of-battle ship to the 6th rate of 20 guns, followed by sloops, brigs, cutters and other subsidiary classes mounting progressively fewer and lighter guns. Other 'coastal forces' included numbers of ships specially built for individual wars, such as the bomb vessels of the Crimean War. In general, none of the smaller vessels was a threat to any of the larger vessels on its own because of its inferiority in gun- and manpower, the deciding factors of the day. Certainly the 20-gun 6th rate had no possibility of defeating a 1st rate line-of-battle ship except under exceptional circumstances such as by fire and explosion, the most feared hazards of the time. Contemporary technology could not produce the mobility and firepower necessary; powerful weapons were large and cumbersome, needing equally large and cumbersome ships to carry them. Thus a sail-age frigate might well outpace a 1st rate but it had to approach very close to its adversary to deliver a broadside, when it would normally be overwhelmed by the latter's far heavier broadside. Even in the steam age, a minor warship approaching close to a battleship would stand a chance of annihilation, but now the differences in speed were far greater than in the sail age - manoeuvrability much more so - and new weapons allowed the smaller vessel the opportunity of dealing a mortal blow to the larger one.

The development of a fast craft of small size which was capable of delivering a lethal blow to a capital ship was impossible until the steam engine was combined with a self-propelled torpedo to produce the torpedo boat. This cheap and relatively simple vessel had immediate attractions for the minor, and some not so minor, powers of the late 19th century, who saw in it the means effectively to challenge the might of the premier sea power of the day, Great Britain. Steam had been the power behind the Industrial Revolution in Britain, being used initially to pump water from mines. Its potential soon became evident and it was then applied in factories and on tramways. At sea, steam was first employed for tugs to

manoeuvre the clumsy 'wooden walls' in and out of harbour and was gradually introduced - not it must be added without considerable opposition from the conservative minded seamen of the day - to progressively larger and more important fighting warships of the fleet. Propulsion was now independent of the vagaries of the wind and development could produce more and more powerful machinery with lower and lower weights. Speed was now regulated by engine power and a small vessel with a high power to weight ratio was a distinct possibility.

This was a considerable step forward but not the complete answer. The fast attacking vessel could now quickly close the enemy and also stand a chance of escaping from the encounter. But could it seriously damage or sink the capital ship? The answer was as yet no, because it was impossible to ship a large enough gun in sufficient numbers to do so. It was realized relatively early on that it made more sense to make a large hole in the target low down, in order to let the water in, rather than pepper the upperworks with shell holes to let the air in. The only means of achieving this objective was to use a large explosive charge placed in contact with the enemy hull. Such charges, credited to David Bushnell, an American engineer, appeared in the American Civil War; they were known then as 'torpedoes' but were actually employed in the manner of today's mines. It was but a short step to attach one of these charges on to a long boom or spar to produce the 'Spar torpedo boat', devised by Captain Hunter Davidson, a Confederate officer. The obvious drawback was the fact that to be effective, the attacker had virtually to ram the target and the resultant explosion usually destroyed both attacker and target. Despite this rather lethal shortcoming, large numbers of such craft were built, particularly by Russia, and did achieve some limited success. Conscious of the suicidal nature of the weapon, a number of solutions were tried, one being a towed version known as the Harvey torpedo, named after its inventor, Commander Harvey, R.N. but this proved ineffective. Much more promising was Count Luppi's idea of a self-propelled torpedo driven by clockwork, which had been envisaged by a fellow Austrian, Ffeiffer, as early as 1848. Their original ideas were not practical but the theme was further developed by Robert

Whitehead, an Englishman, who constructed a prototype driven by compressed air in 1869. Refined further by the addition of a gyroscope to aid course keeping, the locomotive torpedo (as it was originally known) now had the makings of a potent weapon. It was first used in action by the Russian Admiral Makarov in 1878 and thereafter was progressively improved through two World Wars.

The combination of the steam engine and self-propelled torpedo was to spawn huge numbers of torpedo boats which threatened the existence of the capital ship. In turn, destroyers (originally 'torpedo boat destroyers') were developed to counter the threat, and capital ships began to mount quick-firing guns, net defences and anti-torpedo protection schemes. Weapon always produces counter-weapon. From about 1880 until the end of the First World War, the steam-driven torpedo boat remained the 'hornet of the seas'. It was not altogether a perfect weapon because its small size reduced it in the main to coastal activities of a defensive nature. In time, its size was increased to improve seakeeping and to confer offensive ability, so that the distinction between torpedo boat and destroyer was becoming blurred even by the end of the first decade of this century. Great Britain ceased building true torpedo boats before the First World War but continental powers continued with both categories for considerably longer, to the end of World War Two in fact.

This situation was only changed by the appearance of a new invention, the internal combustion engine in self-propelled carriages ashore, soon known as motor cars. Early engines were cantankerous and unreliable but by the early years of the 20th century they were being used in fast racing boats, from which it was only a short step to develop armed versions for which the most obvious weapon was a torpedo. Now there was the possibility of a very fast, powerfully armed craft of low silhouette, cheap to man and without the tell-tale clouds of black smoke.

Boats driven by internal combustion engines appeared as early as 1883, while in Germany a 6-metre craft reached 5.5 knots with a 2hp engine built by Daimler. The last decade of the 19th century saw many further developments, including the use of naphtha fuel, which for a time rivalled the petrol- and oil-engined boats. Competitive events provided the impetus for experimentation in the same way as in the air, a race at Monaco being won at a speed of 18.9kt in 1903. By 1910 *Miranda IV* built by Thornycroft reached about 35kt on 1.27 tons displacement, while a year later the American boat *Dixie IV* achieved 38.8kt with 400hp. Clearly if these speeds could be harnessed to a robust load carrying hull, an effective weapon could be forged. By 1907 Yarrow had sketched a design for a 26kt motor launch armed with one torpedo tube and the Americans had produced a similar if slightly larger design, but little further development took place, mainly because of the lack of a suitable high performance engine of light weight.

It required the impetus of war to stimulate further development and in August 1914 the First World War broke out. At first the major powers saw no requirement for small attack craft, but the closure of the German Bight by minefields led to a suggestion from three officers of the Harwich destroyer force for the resurrection of the old idea of transporting torpedo boats on the davits of larger ships to the operational area, and then launching these shallow draft boats to slip in over the top of the mines in order to attack the German High Seas Fleet at its bases. Consideration of the lifting power of davits, the weights, space and manning demands and the size of the torpedo necessary to defeat modern armour constrained any design to a maximum hull weight of only 2.5 tons - a seemingly impossible design task. However, advances in aeroplane technology now made available high powered lightweight engines which could be adapted to marine use and these, allied to a stepped planing hull of modified *Miranda IV* lines, gave the basis of what was to become the British 40ft Coastal Motor Boat, or CMB. After intensive experimentation with hull forms and torpedo-launching methods, Thornycroft quickly developed a 'military design'. The hull was of single-step design and filled with compressed cork coated with paraffin wax to preserve buoyancy, with concave sections forward and hollow at the keel line aft, so that the water, after leaving the step, ran clear of the boat until shortly before the transom. The ideal length was quoted as five times the beam, and the structure was described as uniformly elastic as it was considered that a rigid bow striking seas at high speeds would soon be damaged. Power was provided by a 12 cylinder V form petrol engine (Y12) of approximately 250hp with a clutch but no reversing gear, giving a maximum speed of 33.5kt and a range of 160nm. The first service boats were commissioned in 1916 and eventually 39 of this type were completed, followed by 60ft and 70ft versions which were twin-screw designs.

Although never in fact used for raids into the Heligoland Bight, they were operationally successful in the southern North Sea and Dover Patrol areas, as for instance on 8 April 1917 when a force of four boats (*CMBs 4, 5, 6* and *9*) attacked German destroyers off Ostend. One torpedo hit *V81* but did not explode while a second hit and sank *G88*. In the confusion of a night action however, the Germans mistakenly believed that they had been attacked by submarines whose rounded hull and conning tower were similar to the silhouette of a CMB. At the end of the same month, *CMBs 7* and *13* had another engagement off Ostend, claiming a torpedo hit. Losses were also being incurred, *CMB1* being sunk by German destroyers but, worse still, *CMB33A* was captured virtually intact when it drifted ashore near Ostend after having been abandoned when damaged by shore batteries on 12/13 April 1918. This allowed the Kaiserliche Marine a leisurely examination of British design and construction methods.

On the German side, the idea of using fast motor boats for offensive purposes appears to have surfaced in both Baltic and Flanders commands at roughly the same time -

the summer of 1916. In the former theatre, the Imperial Russian Navy's ships presented a tempting but difficult target in the confined and shallow waters of the Gulf of Riga, while in the English Channel the British anti-submarine net defences were seriously hampering operations by the submarine and torpedo boat flotillas based in Flanders. During the summer of 1916 two boats (*F5* and *F6*) of the German Navy's 2nd Minesweeping Division were armed with one 45cm torpedo tube each, removed from the torpedo boat *S168* which had been damaged by a mine. These boats were capable only of 10kt and had a draft of 1.3m. They were of about 20 tonnes displacement, powered by a 120hp oil engine. Seventy five were constructed in various German yards between 1915 and 1919, among them Lürssen, Schlichting and Naglo, all of whom would play a part in later developments of fast torpedo attack craft. The purpose of their rearmament was to cover minelaying operations in the Gulf of Riga, but despite seeing numerous Russian destroyers and closing to within 100 metres without detection, they were unable to fire because of engine problems. Meanwhile, experiments were also under way in Flanders, using ex-civilian fast motor boats such as the 36kt *Boncourt* built by Lürssen in 1913, but she and others proved inadequate for the rigours of wartime service use. Lürssen had built its first fast motor boat as early as 1890, using a Daimler engine, and in the following years sold many of these craft for civilian pleasure purposes. By 1908 the motor boat *Donnerwetter*, fitted with a 30-40hp engine, had achieved 38kt and in 1911 the phenomenal speed of 50kt was reached by another Lürssen product, *Lürssen-Daimler* with a 102hp engine. Obviously, speed was the main requirement so it

was not altogether surprising that these craft were unsuitable for offensive service employment. On the basis of experience in the Baltic, a series of 22 boats were built to a new design, 26-27m in length, powered by two motors of 250/340hp to give a speed of 17-19kt. The bow was so designed that either a 35 or 45cm torpedo tube could be accommodated or a 5cm gun, but because of a shortage of torpedoes they were not used in this role and became the anti-submarine boats *UZ11-UZ22* instead. Prior to 1914 the Torpedo Inspectorate had been experimenting with a remote-controlled fast motor boat and examining the practicalities of fast torpedo craft. Although the boat was not a success, it did demonstrate the need for a larger craft and formed a basis for further development.

On the outbreak of the First World War, experiments with radio-controlled boats were resumed and in 1915 received further impetus from the situation on the Flanders coast. There, flotillas of German U-boats and torpedo boats based at Bruges, Zeebrugge and other ports were attempting to break through the British and French defences at the entrance to the Straits of Dover, the 'Dover Patrol'. It was a fairly lively theatre and the activities of the German forces drew counter-measures from the Royal Navy, one of which was to employ monitors to bombard the German bases. There were a number of these shallow draft, heavily armed ships ranging from the 15in-gun *Marshal Ney*, *Marshal Soult*, *Erebus* and *Terror* to the smaller 'M' class with 9.2, 7.5 or 6in guns, and they caused considerable nuisance to the Germans. Their activities made Ostend untenable as a destroyer base and Bruges had to be used instead, which considerably inconvenienced the Kaiserliche Marine as this port was

Right: *UZ33* seen in a disarmed state during Reichsmarine days. Note the tactical symbol on the mast.

eight miles inland and connected to the sea by a canal. To attack the monitors with torpedo boats or U-boats was impossible due to their shallow draft, shoaled waters and minefields, so the remote controlled boats provided an attractive alternative. Seventeen boats were built, *FL1-FL17*, the majority of which were sent to Flanders. They were of about 6 tonnes displacement with a length of 13m, capable of 30kt and armed with a 700kg charge. Guidance was by wire from a shore station, with or without seaplane spotting. Unfortunately, their existence was unnecessarily disclosed when *FL7* ran into the mole at Nieuport. Nevertheless, they were successfully employed against the British monitors, *FL12* hitting *Erebus* on 28 October 1917 and causing some casualties but little material damage. *FL8* was sunk by the monitor *M24* when attempting to attack and *FL4* was sunk by the destroyer *North Star* in November, being the last attack of this nature on the Patrol. Other boats operated in Baltic waters. However, despite the introduction of radio control in place of wire guidance, this technique was erratic and uncertain, there being no substitute for a human being on the spot for decision making. As the concept of manned suicide craft was unacceptable, the only answer was to use a small, fast torpedo armed craft.

This led to the specification for another craft capable of 30/40kt in sea state 3, with a range of 200/250nm armed with one torpedo tube, and having a crew of two to four men. Lürssen constructed a boat to this requirement, completing her on 1 April 1917. Built of oak, she was 11.2m long with a beam of 2.5m and powered by two 240hp Maybach airship engines. At 1,000rpm, 24kt was achieved and with 1,400rpm, 34.3kt; but at high speed the boat was three-fifths out of the water and the spray alongside made it impossible to see abeam. Even at 17kt, the boat was very wet; in fact this was her *minimum* speed because of engine cooling problems. The armament comprised one 35cm torpedo tube mounted in the bows, which was impossible to fire at speeds above 24kt. Despite a serious mishap in Kiel Bay on trials in the spring of 1917, the boat was sent to Windau (today Ventspils in Latvia) where she was accommodated aboard *Inkula*, the depot ship for the III Minesweeper Division. There she was intended for operational duties as the 'special command hydroplane'. On 24 August that year, this boat, under the command of Leutnant Peytsch, torpedoed and sank the 1,200-ton Russian minelayer *Penelope* off the Zerel peninsula; but this appears to have been the only success and on 10 October the boat failed to return from a sortie. The cause of her loss was never ascertained and could have been due to a mine or internal explosion. Following the construction of this boat, there were some experiments with shallow-draft craft driven by airscrew propellers, but by the spring of 1918 it had become apparent that their light construction negated any usefulness and they were not developed further.

Once again, however, the potential of a fast small torpedo armed craft had been demonstrated. It only remained to design a robust boat capable of operating under service conditions. The result was a specification which called for a speed of 31-32kt in sea state 3, low silhouette, good manoeuvrability and an armament of one 45 cm torpedo and one machine gun, with the ability to fire torpedoes at speeds of up to 20kt. A crew of six to eight men was envisaged. The main problem concerned the engines. To achieve the required speed, it was necessary to use three airship engines, of which there were a number of 'over-hours' spares available. These 210hp Maybach CX six cylinder engines were a mixture of right hand and left hand units and were non-reversible. No lightweight reversing gear was in existence, so the clutch arrangement used in the airship was used instead. An initial order for six boats was placed in 1917, of which the first four were intended for net cutting duties and were armed with one 3.7cm gun, while the other pair were to receive a stern torpedo tube for 45cm torpedoes and one machine gun. In the event, the stern torpedo was replaced by a bow tube once the problems of trim had been overcome. The first six boats were ordered from three different yards to allow development of ideas and to gain experience, Lürssen built *L1* and *L2*, Naglo in Berlin *L3* and *L4* and Max Oertz of Hamburg *L5* and *L6*. Further contracts were placed in the summer of 1917 with the same yards, Lürssen receiving *L7-L10*, Naglo *L11-L13* and Oertz *L14-L16*. A fourth yard, Roland-Werft at Hemelingen, contracted for *L17-L20*. However, in December 1917 all these boats were renumbered *LM1-LM20* to avoid confusion with the Zeppelins which also had 'L' numbers. From *LM14* onwards all were of round bilge design as this had proved more suitable to conditions in the shallow North and Baltic Seas.

By January 1918 there were 21 'LM' boats in service, one third of them in the Baltic, the remainder on the Flanders coast. For the moment no further boats were ordered, although the Austro-Hungarian Navy contracted for *LM24-LM33* which were intended to be transported to Pola by rail for operations in the Adriatic, but events overtook the plans and a number remained incomplete in November 1918. War service of the 'LM' boats is little documented but *LM1* was lost by petrol explosion at Bruges on 5 March 1918 and *LM2* by a motor explosion off Blankenberge on 17 April 1918. On the night of 22/23 August 1918 seven boats in two groups, *LM9*, *LM15*, *LM17* and *LM18* with *LM7*, *LM8* and *LM16* attacked ships off Dunkirk. *LM9* and *LM18* missed with their torpedoes while *LM15* and *LM17* claimed sinkings and both *LM8* and *LM16* claimed to have torpedoed and sunk a destroyer. However, there is no record of any British or French warship being sunk or damaged at that time and just who these boats attacked remains obscure. As was to become evident during the Second World War, the accurate assessment of results obtained during fast-moving confused night actions was difficult and both sides were frequently wildly optimistic as to both numbers and tonnage sunk.

1. THE DEVELOPMENT YEARS, 1920-1939

The Armistice of November 1918 brought to an end all development of fast torpedo craft by Germany and left many boats incomplete. Ignoring the 'UZ' boats (U-Boot Zerstörer or A/S boats), *LM19* and *LM22* to *LM33* remained incomplete and were either cancelled or sold for private use in the early 1920s. In fact, at least three boats (*LM20*, *LM22* and *LM23*) were the subject of bogus sales into private hands for the purpose of retaining the craft for later naval use. Eight other boats of an experimental series, by various yards to explore different aspects of construction and engine techniques, were also incomplete and of these only a couple were ever finished. One of these, however, ended up in the Colombian Navy, together with the former *LM16*, *LM23* and *LM28*, in which they served until after the Second World War.

In the years following 1918, the development of fast fighting boats such as CMBs was discontinued by all the belligerent powers, mainly because their need was purely a wartime one; they were of little use for routine peacetime tasks such as 'showing the flag'. Furthermore, funds were tight after the colossal expenditure incurred during the war years and additionally the 'war to end all wars' had also spawned the commendable but unrealistic desire to ignore all matters military. Britain, for example, had discarded all her boats rapidly so that by 1930 only a couple remained and then only in subsidiary duties. Nevertheless, Thornycroft continued to market similar craft and in the years up to the mid-1930s had exported over 30 boats, all of which were CMB stepped-hull designs. Interest at the British Admiralty did not reawaken until about 1935, when the British Power Boat Co. built *MTB1-MTB6* to a 22-ton hard-chine hull design which was now favoured over the old CMB round-bilge type. They did however retain the stern-launched torpedo, utilizing racks in the engine rooms and folding guide rails at the stern. The appearance of these boats heralded a slow and difficult rebirth of the type, now known as MTBs in the Royal Navy. Such well-known yards as J.Samuel White, Vosper and Thornycroft all joined the BPB with designs so that four or more different designs were available for evaluation and comparison. Much more important, however, was the eventual widespread distribution of contracts to small boatyards, to increase delivery rates. At least 34 yards in Great Britain and nine abroad built MTBs, while some of

Right: *S1* after receiving her torpedo tubes. The hull sheer line is of interest. (WZB)

Left: Speed was king and Germany was not alone in utilizing trials' results for advertising purposes, as with this Lürssen boat for China. (Author's Collection)

these and four other yards built MGBs. In striking contrast, this practice was never adopted by the Kriegsmarine, only two German yards being active in this field for most of the period. Not until 1944 was a third yard brought into the programme. On the other hand, British boats were forced to rely on marine adaptations of petrol aero engines throughout the war.

France during the inter-war period dabbled with MTB construction and purchased a couple of Thornycroft boats, but her efforts were largely unsuccessful and no operational craft were put into service. Similarly the USA, entering a period of isolationism, had little or no use for such craft and it was not until the realization that they might be useful for defensive purposes - in the Philippines, for example - that any effort was put into design work, the first contract for *PT-1* being placed as late as June 1939.

In the Soviet Union matters were different, for the revolution had virtually destroyed the Tsarist fleet and its remnants were largely ineffective. Design capability and shipyard skills had also disappeared. In this scenario, a cheap and simple defence deterrent had obvious appeal. The British raids on Kronstadt in 1919 had clearly demonstrated the possibilities of craft like CMBs and the Red Fleet quickly built up a force of MTBs for use in the shallow and island-studded Baltic. They assumed the role for which large numbers of torpedo boats had been built in the 1880s - ambush and coastal defence. By 1930 Russia had some 60 boats in service, which were of about 13 tonnes displacement, armed with two 45.7cm torpedoes

and powered by two 650hp petrol engines. Some Italian assistance was received but in the main development was along Russian lines. Of note was the widespread use of duralumin for hulls, but a return to wood was made prior to the Second World War. Large numbers were put in hand, so that in 1936, for example, 190 were in service and more than 40 under construction.

In contrast, it was not until about 1923 that an effort was made to rebuild a motor torpedo boat arm of the Reichsmarine and even then it was necessary to conduct this in utmost secrecy, for although these craft were not in fact specifically mentioned in the Treaty of Versailles, the total number of torpedo craft was limited. Moreover, Germany was in a state of political turmoil and economic chaos, while French troops had in January of that year occupied the Ruhr. Into this scene emerged a certain Kapitän zur See Lohmann who, having participated in the Armistice Commission deliberations, was made head of the Naval Sea Transport Division, a post for which he was outwardly suited since he was the son of a director of the Nord Deutscher Lloyd steamship line. He channelled his considerable efforts and intelligence into circumventing the intended restrictions placed on the German Navy by the Treaty of Versailles. These activities would eventually lead to political scandal, but Lohmann himself was concerned only with salvaging as much as possible out of the humiliation of Versailles. Much of his activity was centred around the covert maintenance and retention, not to say advancement, of U-boat technology but another

Right: In the summer of 1937 boats of the 1st Flotilla made a cruise up the Rhine to show the flag. (Author's Collection)

significant aspect concerned fast motor boats. In this respect he arranged the purchase and disappearance of several boats from the war period which should, under the terms of the treaty, have been destroyed. These included the aforementioned three 'LM' boats as well as others. Construction of new boats was impossible due to both political and economic restraints, so these refurbished old boats had to suffice. Recognizing that more than just material was required, Lohmann formed the Travemünde Yachthafen AG ('Trayag') in 1924 with the eventual object of constructing new boats. In 1925 he also became involved in the formation of Hochseesportsverband 'Hansa' (High Seas Sports Association) whose Hanseatic Yacht School in Neustadt on Lübeck Bay ran training courses in small boat seamanship for German youths. At about the same time or a little later the Neustädter Slip GmbH was incorporated as a repair yard for the boats of the yacht school and for the purpose of training motor mechanics. It would also serve as a reserve repair facility in the event of air raid damage. Finally, in order to secure as big a pool of suitable boats as possible for eventual naval use, Lohmann in 1926 financed the 'Motor Yacht Club of Germany' whose members were encouraged to purchase their boats from 'Trayag', thus stimulating further research and development. As early as 1924, however, the Navis GmbH (Lohmann's front organization) made available four boats for exercises which took place in August 1925. These boats, described as 'LM' boats, were named *Alma*, *Ruth*, *Lo* and *Liesel*, of which only the last-named can be

positively identified as having been built from materials assembled for the experimental wartime boats *Lüsi 1* and *Lüsi 2*. The exercises were to be held under the command of B.S.O., west of Fehmarn, with the 'LM' boats under the command of Korvetten Kapitän Anshütz. There had been considerable discussion earlier in the year as to how the boats were to be manned - with civilians or active officers. In the event, one reserve officer, Kapitän-Leutnant Ramien, and three retired officers, Kpt.Lt.(aD) Lange, Kpt.Lt.(aD) Rabe and Oberleutnant zur See (aD) Kaiser, took command of the four boats.

Lohmann himself attended the exercises, in which the veteran light cruisers *Nymphe* and *Amazone* also participated. The exercises investigated high speed attacks in daylight and darkness by boats singly, in pairs and by flotilla. They probed the manoeuvrability and seakeeping properties of the boats themselves, the reliability of the motors and the motormen tending them, as well as the visibility of the boats to the defending gunners. The question of motor noise was addressed, as was the best method of defence against such attacks. Although of short duration, the exercises demonstrated the potential of the 'LM' boat as a valuable weapon at night and in good weather conditions, provided that the proposed armament did not reduce the boats' performance significantly. (Treaty conditions still had to be observed and they were unarmed at this time). Any modifications for armament or operational reasons could not be allowed to enlarge the boats' silhouette, as a small silhouette was a distinct advantage. In this respect, although speed was required to be raised, it was not to be at the expense of height. More trials were obviously needed, especially in poor weather conditions, and more money was required for development. Interestingly, experiments had also been conducted to determine the best low-visibility paint scheme (found to be matt light brown and grey). In daylight, however, the high bow wave gave away the approaching boats and with their relatively low speed and manoeuvrability, the gunners were able to follow them easily. At night it was a different matter: an approach could be made undetected to within 400m, which was too late for defensive gunfire. Visibility from the air was also investigated.

Not surprisingly there were problems. Most boats were good for only about 26kt at best, their engines were in poor condition and difficulties were experienced in communications. Boats with low bows, such as the aptly named *Lo*, could only operate in conditions up to sea state 3, possibly less if trimmed down by the bows due to torpedo armament weights. On the other hand, *Alma* with raised bows could operate in force 4 conditions at high speed.

The potential of motor torpedo boats was obviously considerable, given certain conditions, and the achievements of the Royal and Italian Navies in 1916-1920 had not gone unnoticed. The former had scored some success at Kronstadt against Soviet forces in 1919,

Below: *S14* and *S15* lying at St. Goar on an idyllic summer's day during their Rhine cruise. (Author's Collection)

while the latter had sunk the Austrian battleships *Wien* at Trieste on 9 October 1917, *Szent Istvan* off Premuda on 10 June 1918, and *Viribus Unitis* at Pola on 10 October 1918. There had also been frequent incursions into Austrian harbours (no fewer than six times into Durazzo), resulting in the sinking of several transports.

For the Reichsmarine, faced with the might of the Royal Navy's battlefleet and hampered by the Versailles Treaty, the fast motor torpedo boat offered attractive possibilities, which the Germans were not slow to develop. However, it was obvious that the existing 'LM' design needed considerable improvement if it were to become an effective weapon.

One of the basic questions to be answered was how the torpedoes were to be shipped. There were two schools of thought: fired over the bow or launched tail first over the stern. This was examined in March 1926 by the TVA using the torpedo motor boat *Siegfried* (formerly *LM21*) when torpedoes were launched over the stern at boat speeds of 26kt. The torpedo speed in those days was 28.5kt and even with this low speed differential, it was clearly necessary for the boat to turn sharply to avoid being run down by its own torpedo. These trials were successful but it was demonstrated that for best results, bow launched torpedoes would be preferable.

In the meantime, the old wartime designed 'LM' boats were refurbished as far as funds would permit. Initially some were re-engined with new airship motors apparently bought from British sources! Later, from 1926, new Mercedes-Benz petrol engines became available and *LM11* and *LM13-LM16* received three new motors totalling 780hp; *LM17* one 260hp and two 210hp, while *LM20* was fitted with a 740hp powerplant on three shafts. This latter was subsequently altered to a twin shaft installation with one 500hp motor in each. At about this time the 'LM' designation was dropped and for subterfuge reasons the boats were renamed 'UZ (S)'...... (U-Boote Zerstörer (Schnell), or fast A/S boat). In the spring of 1927 it was decided to base these boats at Kiel, subject to suitable security arrangements to disguise their true role, and to commission a half-flotilla that year with the elderly *Nordsee* as tender. There remained the perennial problem of costs and personnel - should the boats be civilian or naval manned for example.

By the summer of 1927 the Torpedo and Mining Inspectorate had confirmed that the 'LM' type of small fast torpedo boat was especially valuable in the Baltic, emphasizing the need for speed and low silhouette; 40kt was considered the minimum speed requirement, as the boat's only defence was speed. Its main strength was seen as torpedo attack under cover of darkness, something which could not yet be performed by aircraft. As far as seaworthiness was concerned, *Siegfried* was considered generally satisfactory but her inability to run at less than 10kt was an obvious handicap. Bow torpedo armament was necessary; dropping gear, such as had been employed by the British, was only a second option.

Two other launching methods were also examined: the tail first stern-launched torpedo and the head first stern-launched torpedo. The latter was only of theoretical interest as it required high launching pressures and the torpedoes were not robust enough. Moreover, the boat had to complete a 180° turn between sighting the enemy and firing - an obvious tactical disadvantage. The prime requirement was for one or two bow tubes, without reduction in seaworthiness; they had therefore to be fabricated from light metal without a spoon but with guide rail and bow caps. Air ejection was needed and the tubes had to be removable to allow substitution by depth-charges. Director gear was to be as fitted in the new *Möwe*-class torpedo boats.

Some experimentation with new boat design had already been put in hand despite a shortage of funds. One such boat was known merely as *K* or *UZ(S)12*; she was built by Abeking & Rasmussen at Lemwerder in 1925/26. Displacing only 16 tonnes, powered by two 430hp motors and armed with two 45cm torpedoes, this boat achieved about 40kt. Based on the First World War Thornycroft type of round bilged CMB, she proved far too lightly built and was reconstructed in 1928 but was more or less a failure. It was this boat that tested the stern-launched head-first torpedo launch system described above, as well as side dropping gear. Lürssen also built an experimental boat at around the same time as a private venture. Named *Lür* (later *UZ(S)11*), she displaced around 23 tonnes and made 33.5kt with 1,350hp. She had in fact been built for the Deutsch Luftfahrt Industrie test centre. Constructed of mahogany, she was a round-bilge displacement design whose hull appearance already foreshadowed the subsequent S-boat hull design. She was unarmed although provision was made for tubes to be fitted later and was used for hull design proving trials. In 1930 she was passed over to the Luftwaffe who used her as an air-sea rescue boat, in which role she was still serving as late as June 1941. The third experimental boat was *Narwal*, later *UZ(S)18*, built by Trayag and completed in the autumn of 1926. This boat was also of the Thornycroft planing hull type but much more strongly built than *K*. She was designed to carry two bow torpedo tubes with mechanical discharge but these were not mounted and ballast weight was added to compensate. It was found on trials that although she performed better than *K*, she still slammed heavily in seas above state 3 and was very wet forward because of the turtle-back forecastle and powerful motors. She too was considered a failure. All the experiences with these experimental boats served to confirm to the Navy that the way forward lay through round-bilge displacement boats and not the stepped hull hydroplane. A close watch was also kept on foreign MTB development. Britain was inactive at this time but Italy was developing new designs powered by Isotta-Fraschini petrol engines and armed with 45cm torpedoes in side dropping gear. These were advertised as having achieved very high speeds, which in reality were attained in a very light load condition with no

armament aboard. The Reichsmarine was interested in these boats and in August 1928 Oberbaurat Burkhardt and Kpt.Lt. Bürkner travelled to Italy to discuss matters pertaining to fast torpedo boats.

By the end of the 1920s, sufficient design experience had been gained with experimental boats and operational experience with the old 'LM' boats to allow the Reichsmarine to formulate design parameters for future craft. In the spring of 1928 a discussion was held to establish future wartime needs in terms of boat types, construction times, numbers and manning. Kpt.z.S.(aD) von Koblinski summed up the needs: an effective boat in large numbers, cheaply and quickly built. A development of *Lür* was required but this was threatened to be delayed by other projects. It was high time progress was restarted as nothing concrete had been done since *Lür* in 1926; otherwise Germany would be overtaken by other nations. His view was echoed by the C-in-C (Fleet) but no further work was done because, as KIe stated in April 1929, 'The means were lacking and had been for years'. Delays were also caused by the investigations into diesel propulsion - the long-term aim of the Naval Staff. Diesels were twice as expensive as petrol boats, but should two less desirable petrol boats be built or one desirable diesel boat? According to Bürkner, by 1931 there were two design requirements, the first of which was a 20-tonne, 24kt boat powered by three Mercedes-Benz petrol motors of 140hp each. This was armed with one torpedo tube and one

machine-gun, being intended for deployment from larger ships, by davit or boom. Building time was estimated at three months for a cost of about 100,000RM per boat. Although projected in 1931, this design was in fact abandoned for other more important projects. Nevertheless, the idea of a 'portable' boat was to reappear later. A second project for a larger boat was based on Lürssen's commercial boat *Oheka II* in which a usable type for development was found. Powered by three airship petrol motors (of which there were about 36 available), this boat proved fast and robust. It was acknowledged that the use of high-octane petrol aboard boats, particularly wooden ones, was a dangerous practice, even more so for warships, but there was as yet no other choice.

The two alternatives, diesel and high-pressure steam, were both under consideration but neither had reached the state where front line use could be considered. Experience in several ships of the fleet had demonstrated the diesel's possibilities but there were teething troubles still to be overcome. High-pressure steam had been under development for some time and in 1930 had been installed in two 29m customs vessels, *Bremse* and *Brummer*. Five years earlier, an experimental plant had been installed in *UZ30* when in customs service. Attractive as the steam option was, it was not pursued, fortunately as it turned out because developments in diesel power produced better results. Had S-boats with steam propulsion been put into service, they would undoubtedly have suffered the same problems as the British Steam Gun Boats (SGBs), perhaps even more so because of the extremely high pressures adopted. Serious proposals for steam propulsion of S-boats at a later date appear to have resulted from work done by Macard-Fritsch between 1935-1938 in developing compact lightweight steam plants for aircraft (sic). This led in the autumn of 1938 to the examination of steam plant comprising two 3,000/3,300hp turbines combined with diesels for cruising. The higher powers available from steam propulsion and its greater reliability (sic) were quoted as salient advantages over diesels. This however was before the troubles associated with steam plants manifested themselves. The design quoted 1.90kg/hp (dry), 2.13kg/hp (operational), 50atm at 450° C, with plant dimensions of 5.25m long and 1.60m high.

The first militarized boat to be ordered was *UZ(S)16*, built by Lürssen as their yard number 12120. This was a 52-tonne displacement boat of composite mahogany/light metal construction powered by three 800/900hp Daimler-Benz BF2 12-cylinder 'V' engines with a 100hp Maybach cruising motor, and with this power the boat reached 34.2kt. Commissioned on 7 August 1930, she was not armed initially but had been designed to carry two 50cm (later 53.3cm) torpedo tubes and one machine gun.

Sea trials soon proved the worth of the design, which fulfilled all the specified requirements although it was unfortunate that petrol motors still had to be employed. Renumbered *W1* on 30 March 1931 and *S1* later on 16 March 1932, she was gradually modified in the light of service experience to form the basis for the design of all subsequent S-boats. She was paid off on 10 December 1936 and sold to Spain as a result of the latter's pleas for material aid after the outbreak of the Civil War.

Orders were placed with Lürssen for four similar 'replacement UZ boats', two on 28 April 1931 (*S2* and *S3*) and two on 16 July (*S4* and *S5*), also powered by petrol motors. These boats were built with oak keels and frames, with cedar decks and mahogany double-diagonal skin for maximum strength and elasticity. Their main engines developed 800/1,100hp each and were non-reversible. For manoeuvring purposes, a 100hp Maybach engine was installed, fitted with a chain drive to the centre shaft. This motor could also be used for silent attacks and could propel the boat at a maximum of 8.8kt. Maximum speed on main motors was 32kt with an emergency overload giving 34.5kt.

However, by means of the so-called 'Lürssen' effect, 36.5kt could be attained. This phenomenon was a result of the rudder arrangements on the vessels, which had a main rudder on the centre line and two independent auxiliary rudders in line with the outboard shafts.

It was discovered that if, at high speeds, the auxiliary rudders were turned outwards by about 30deg, critical flow changes took place in the region abaft the propellers which altered the boat's trim, reduced the stern wave and increased speed. Trials performed in 1943 with *S130* illustrate the effect:

Power	with effect	without effect
7,000hp	39.35kt	41.35kt
4,000hp	31.9kt	32.55kt

It has been suggested that it was this Lürssen 'Effekt' that led to these boats being known as E (=Effekt) boats in British parlance. This is somewhat unlikely as such an important design feature would not have been publicized and there is no evidence that it was known to the Admiralty before the war or indeed during it.

Maximum continuous speed was 32kt and range 350nm at 32kt, 800nm at 20kt and 2,000nm at 7kt. The hull was divided into eight watertight compartments and there were six fuel tanks for a total of 7,500 litres of petrol. Bunks were provided for eight junior rates, four senior rates and two officers, the normal ship's company being twelve. Armament comprised two 50cm torpedo tubes with two spares which could be reloaded in two minutes (53.3cm tubes were later specified). These torpedoes had a range of 11,300m at 28.5kt and 5,500m at 40kt. Electric firing was employed and the torpedoes could be launched at any speed. Other armament was limited to one 2cm Mg C/30 and one Mg 08. Alternatively, four mines or 36 explosive floats or six depth charges could be shipped.

The building of the four new boats was the result of the Naval Staff's decision in 1931 to form an S-boat half flotilla of four boats plus one reserve, the designation 'S-Boote' being promulgated in December 1931 as neither contrary to the Versailles Treaty nor the NIAC which allowed sixteen motor launches. In command of the 1st S-Bootes half flotilla was Kpt.Lt. Bey, who was to do much to develop tactics during the years leading up to the Second World War. Supporting the flotilla was the elderly tender *Nordsee*. While experience was being gained with the new petrol engined boats, work had been progressing on the design of a suitable diesel for S-boats, based on those used as generators in the 'K'- class cruisers and manufactured by MAN, Augsburg. On 28 August 1932, Lürssen received an order for another S-boat, *S6* of broadly similar design to her predecessors but powered by a diesel installation of three MAN L7 motors of 960/1,320hp each. This boat was commissioned in November 1937 but could not be considered a successful design because of problems with the engines (see Chapter 2). Nevertheless, she represented a great step forward since no other nation could power its MTBs with a lightweight, high-performance, low-fire-risk diesel engine. The diesel programme included Daimler-Benz as well as MAN and when engines of the former design became available, these were fitted to half the next series of boats to be built, *S7-S13*. They were somewhat larger than the earlier, petrol-driven boats because of the greater weight of the diesels. Thus displacement rose to 86 tonnes full load on a hull increased by about 4.5m in length and 0.6m in beam. *S7* to *S9* were powered by MAN 719/30 engines while *S10* to *S13* received the Daimler-Benz MB502 16-cylinder 'V' motors. Now referred to as

'Bewachungsfahrzeug' (or Guard boats), *S7* to *S9* were ordered on 1 July 1933 and *S10* to *S13* on 20 July. These entered service between August 1933 and March 1935.

In November 1932 the Fleet Command had acknowledged that S-boats would form a valuable asset in the Baltic to support the few German major units, but this resulted only in the call for an immediate strengthening of the S-Bootes half flotilla and provision for six boats to be fully fitted out in reserve at short notice. Then in March 1933 the Navy planned for three half flotillas but saw no urgency for their construction. Peacetime establishment was four boats per half flotilla, increased to six to eight in war from reserves. By May 1933 the completion of six boats was anticipated and more were to be ordered when means became available. The problem was not only financial but, more importantly, manpower. Thus between 1934 and 1936 it was impossible to form a second half-flotilla for this reason.

First trials of the diesel-engined *S6* had been disappointing because the heavier motors resulted in lower speeds, some 3kt slower at continuous speed and 2kt maximum than the petrol boats. In fact, in 1933 the S-boat programme appears to have been built around a reversion to petrol motors, only the Fleet Commander seeing the advantages of diesels outweighing the higher speed of petrol motors. Fortunately his views prevailed

and series construction of diesel motors was given a high priority. Even so it was still intended to order only two boats in 1934, instead of the four originally planned, and to delay even these orders as late as possible in order to get experience with the new Daimler-Benz motors in *S10-S13*. Then, during the latter half of 1934 and early 1935, the plans for S-boat construction were thrown into confusion over the question of action radius and the possibility of a war with France. It was stated that S-boats could play a major role against the French Channel ports but for this they would need an endurance of 900nm as compared with the current 700nm. In a memorandum from AI to AIV (Neu AIb 4154/34 dated 22 October 1934) it was noted that, although the newer diesel boats could, in theory, reach ports up to Boulogne from bases in Borkum, at a mean speed of 20kt and return, there was no margin for the inevitable high-speed manoeuvring during action. If passage speed were reduced to 12kt, a margin would exist but sortie times would be extended - hence the demand for 900nm. The question was posed as to what modifications could be made in boats already under construction, but in any event the matter had to be addressed in new designs. A further suggestion also emerged: could the boats be fitted with an electric motor for silent approach as apparently had been done in some First World War Italian designs? It was not possible to

Above: A contrast in lines between an early-type S-boat with the low forecastle and bridge forward of the wheelhouse and the later type with raised forecastle and bridge above the wheelhouse. (ECPA)

retrofit existing boats and in these silencing of the diesels would have to be improved. Finally, there was a request for a statement of current progress on designs of boats for transport aboard larger warships.

On 20 February 1935, AIV replied to the various points raised, stating that the demand of 900nm was not quite possible with existing boats, quoting as follows:

	7.8t fuel, 20kt, wing motors only	With full fuel load	
S6-S9	617nm	800nm	Full use
S10-S13	676nm(7.8 tonnes fuel)	878nm	of tanks
S14-S15	544nm(wing motors)	870nm	only 20kt

The question of deck tanks in place of the reserve torpedoes was considered, but if no extra weight were allowed then only an extra 2 tonnes of fuel could be accommodated. This would raise endurance to 960/1,050/1,060nm respectively but reduce offensive capacity and increase vulnerability. If the boats were fitted with minelaying gear, then the reserve torpedoes would not be carried anyway and extra fuel would be purely extra top-weight and stability would become a consideration. On the subject of electric motors, it was calculated that *S14/S15* could be fitted with motor and batteries sufficient for 3 hours at 8-9kt but at a weight penalty of 18.47 tonnes which was plainly impossible. In any case, AIV

doubted that a 120hp electric motor plus associated gearing and propeller would be completely silent. A silenced diesel was preferred and if this were not possible, the only alternative would be to fit a cruising diesel (weight 2 tonnes), resulting in a larger and slower boat. The Construction Office's proposal for increasing auxiliary diesel power to 60hp and using a chain drive to the wing shafts was not favoured either for noise reasons.

Finally, it was stated that the Construction Office had developed a design for a shipboard S-boat displacing 20 tonnes with a usable load capacity of 2-5 tonnes powered by two 1,200hp Daimler-Benz engines to give 40kt. AIV, however, considered this design to be too heavy for boom handling and as it could not run at less than 15kt, it was not feasible because this was too high in heavy seas. It was also very noisy. (This line of development seems to have led later to the LS-Boote.)

By May 1935, AIb considered that the *S14/S15* design had reached the limits for wooden construction but returned to the question of endurance for use against the French coast, 1,000nm at 20kt now being demanded. The arguments put forward by AIV were acknowledged but range had to be increased without deck tanks and the impossibility of electric power was accepted. On the subject of shipboard S-boats, AIV saw their use as very limited but questioned if a simple type could be developed for use aboard the Panzerschiffe (pocket battleships) and light cruisers.

Discussions continued, it being admitted that trials of the new diesels had not yet been completed because of problems, but the indications were that speeds exceeding 38kt were not expected. Power could only be increased by the use of steam, but it was stressed that it was necessary to prove the installations in the Geleitboote and Type 34 destroyers before this could be explored further for S-boats. Barely two months later, in July 1935, the subject of Russia as an enemy came up, requiring yet more range but not at the expense of speed.

While all this argument was going on, the building programme proceeded fitfully with *S14/S15* being ordered on 16 July 1934 and *S16/S17* on 5 November the following year. These boats all received the new MAN eleven cylinder engine and were of nearly 100 tonnes full load displacement as a consequence. Because the engines were basically unsatisfactory, these boats were a considerable embarrassment to the service.

The last five boats with petrol engines, *S1* to *S5*, were scheduled to be discarded from reserve status under the 1935 programme, leaving a total of fourteen diesel boats available by the end of 1937. These were to be formed into two half-flotillas of six boats each, the remainder in reserve, and with one depot ship. It was intended to commission the second half-flotilla on 1 October 1937, already delayed six months because of the aforementioned personnel difficulties. On 23 October 1936 K.Kpt. Schubert of AI issued a memorandum proposing a strong S-boat force and questioning if the existing type should be continued or should a completely new line be taken. His view was that the Anglo-German naval agreement made the possession of sufficient S-boats vital to Germany's security as they were classified as 'Exempt Ships' and were cheap with low manpower demands. In his opinion the S-boat was purely and simply a torpedo-carrier for nocturnal employment and its design should not be encumbered with equipment for subsidiary tasks. In summary the demands were:

Tactical	Operational
1) low silhouette	(1) large range
(2) high top speed	(2) adequate seaworthiness
(3) heavy torpedo armament	(3) high continuous speed
(4) good manoeuvrability	(4) sufficient accommodation
(5) silent running if possible	

Which or any of these demands were met by current designs? According to experience gained over the previous two years, boats the size of *S14* were the optimum and should not be exceeded. Paint schemes found best for low visibility at normal fighting ranges of 400-1,000 metres were white/light grey. The maximum speed of *S7*, 34.5kt, was not good enough, 40kt being demanded. *S14* had failed to reach this speed because of propeller problems.

Torpedo armament was considered good but the 50kt G6a (sic) torpedo was required urgently. On the other hand, manoeuvrability was less than desired on three motors and the turning circle too large. Performance was better in this respect on one engine but it was questionable if this feature could in fact be improved. As far as noise was concerned, this was satisfactory under normal operating conditions - i.e., versus a moving target - especially with the Daimler-Benz boats which had an underwater exhaust. If however the target was stopped or in harbour, then noise became a problem. Range was a matter for concern: for example, *S14* had the same range as *S7* despite more fuel because of her greater power. For a two-front war - i.e., against France and Russia - ranges would have to be decided from Pillau in East Prussia and Heligoland. Thus *S7* at 28kt could reach Moon Sound at the northern end of the Gulf of Riga from Pillau, or Dunkirk from Heligoland, in 13½ hours. But if Pillau were lost, the next available base was Swinemünde, adding 120nm to the sortie. Operations outside the range of S-boats were the responsibility of the Type 35/37 torpedo boats. 33/35kt was demanded for continuous passage, with 40kt maximum but it was stressed that the machinery must be reliable. This could only be achieved by heavier engines, especially in the MAN design, and ways must be sought to economize in weight by omitting such details as anchors and masts, etc. Under no circumstances should this economy be obtained by lighter hull construction. Seaworthiness was sufficient for the *S7* type in average weather conditions in the likely operational areas, but it would be advantageous for a meteorologist to be carried aboard the depot ship. In this respect it was also stressed that the improved seakeeping qualities of the larger *S7/S10* over the smaller *S2* should not lead to the conclusion that bigger boats inevitably meant better sea-boats because the heavier the hull, the greater the loads on it in a seaway. All the weight available must therefore be used for hull, weapons and machinery, with the minimum possible for fitting out and accommodation. *None* should be wasted for auxiliary tasks. Finally, the boats sailed on a single watch system in peacetime but it had to be recognized that extra men would be required in wartime. Summed up, the specification was as follows:

(a) Size as *S10-S14*
(b) Speed 40kt max. 33/35kt continuous
(c) Range 530nm at full speed
(d) Reliable machinery
(e) Armament: 2 x 53.3cm TT (4 x G6a torpedoes), 1x 2cm MG C/30
(f) Smoke generator
(g) Berths for one watch
(h) Radio outfit as previously
(i) Simple anchor for shallow water
(j) Small, lightweight mast
(k) Small gyro compass if possible
(l) No fitment for mines, depth-charges, etc

Kpt.Lt. Bey, senior officer of the 1st S-boat half-flotilla, was in the forefront of tactics development during the mid-1930s and was to play an important role in the forging of these boats into an effective fighting force. As early as October 1935 for example, he recognized that 'by day, aircraft were the most dangerous of the S-boats opponents' and that little could be expected of the 2cm defensive gun in a seaway against fighters. He was one of the many officers who pressed for the S boat arm to be expanded during the latter half of the 1930s but problems abounded, not least in yard capacity. Lürssen had monopolized boat construction since the commencement of the programme and there were only two builders of engines, one of which was proving unsuitable for S-boat propulsion.

As Germany's rearmament programme gathered pace, the problems increased. By May 1938 the programme envisaged the introduction of the Naglo yard in Berlin, when S20-S25 were to be ordered, with five boats going to Lürssen and one to the new yard. Subsequently, S26-S29 would go to Lürssen but thereafter six boats per year would be ordered (Lürssen five; Naglo one) until 1943, with the last completing in April 1945. Thus a total of 58 diesel engined boats would be available. However, Admiral Raeder considered building times too long and urged that ways be found to shorten them. It was for this reason that S26-S29 were to be ordered with MAN engines and also to have two groups of eight boats of the same type with similar engines (S14-17 and S26-S29 MAN and S18-S25 Daimler-Benz). Then on 24 August 1938, while steps were being taken to speed up S-boat production, Admiral Carls suddenly proposed that the programme should not go beyond S37. In his view exercises and experience gained over the previous ten years had demonstrated that S-boats had a much more restricted range of operational abilities than first envisaged. He went on to say that they were greatly affected by weather conditions, being only a weapon of opportunity, facts which he alleged had been proved many times in fleet exercises since 1937. Since construction began, displacement had been increased by 100 per cent, yet full seaworthiness had still not been achieved. His opinion was that the S-boat had reached the limit of its development potential and if building ceased with S37, thirty boats would be available, which appeared sufficient in comparison with other classes. He proposed to switch to a 'High Seas Torpedo boat' with stern launching tubes, capable of 40kt with 300-350nm radius and minelaying at 35kt and 300nm. This produced an immediate counter-attack from the proponents of S-boats: Bey, Boehm, Schubert, Conradi and Sturm.

Admiral Boehm, the Fleet Commander, stated that the S18 type, together with torpedo boats, formed an indispensable means of fighting the sea war. It was expected that the larger Daimler-Benz boats would be capable of operating up to the enemy coasts in the North Sea and Baltic in heavy weather conditions; moreover, they were especially suitable for minelaying. Because of their larger numbers and smaller size, they were actually a more potent weapon than the torpedo boats. Seaworthiness could be improved by a raised forecastle and moving the open bridge aft of the wheel-house. Radius could be improved by additional fuel stowage and speeds of up to 50kt were under consideration.

Konteradmiral Lütjens (FdT), who had had many years' experience in torpedo boats, stressed that the increase in displacement had not been due to any attempt to improve seaworthiness but rather as the consequence of the change from petrol to diesel engines. Diesels conferred a lower fire hazard, increased range from 650nm to 850nm at 20kt and simplified training because many other ships had diesels. The earlier boats, S1 to S5, could operate successfully in the northern and eastern Baltic up to force 4, and up to force 5 in the western and central Baltic. With reduced weapons load, performance was naturally better. He himself had experienced force 10 conditions in an S-boat without danger and in his opinion, these boats were surprisingly good for their size. The only defect, common to many German warships, was the fineness of the fore-ends. He also objected to the boats being described as weapons of opportunity; this applied equally to the torpedo boats, destroyers and aircraft. All were dependent on weather to greater or lesser extents. Actually, he argued, S-boats could be used on most days and nights in the North Sea and in the Baltic to the limit of their operational capability and range. Lütjens strongly disagreed that the limit of development had been reached and saw several improvements:

(a) Better seakeeping properties by employing higher and wider bows.
(b) Reduction in armament weight by the use of G6 tubes and G6a torpedoes.
(c) Further reduction in weight by reducing accommodation and auxiliary machinery.
(d) Increasing speed to 44/45kt, partly by the previous improvements but also by detailed propeller research, as was done in all navies and which had been started in Germany on the destroyers Z1 to Z7.

He considered, quite correctly, that numbers were essential and that to stop at thirty boats was nonsense. What was required were bases in Borkum, List, Heligoland, Kiel, Rügen and Pillau, each with three flotillas. Thus about 150 boats would be needed at about 1.2 million RM each - not excessive, he thought, and of inestimable value in peacetime for the training of young officers (he appears to have forgotten the manning crisis). Such a force would make an enemy very wary of approaching German coasts. Admiral Boehm's call for a 40kt torpedo carrier was not concurred with: S-boats could do the task and minelaying could be done by many vessels already.

Faced with such vociferous opposition, the SKL agreed

to the expansion of the S-boat force, Admiral Schniewind stating that the target was 75 boats in eight flotillas of eight boats (the remainder in reserve). This figure was to be reached by 1945. Carls remained unconvinced: perhaps 40-50 were necessary.

Meanwhile, the MAN engine had been abandoned for S-boats after *S17*, contrary to original intentions, because serviceability of this design remained a problem in flotilla operational employment. For this reason it had been impossible to use the 2nd Flotilla in the reoccupation of Memel in Lithuania (only *S9* managed to get as far even as Pillau). Since the flotilla had been commissioned in August 1938 it had been possible to stage only a single flotilla exercise of two hours' duration and only one practice night attack in the seven and a half months of the flotilla's existence. In the view of FdT, this confirmed all experiences since 1936 in that better accessibility and easier maintenance were of less importance than trouble-free running in wartime. MAN engines were henceforth used instead for R-boats. Further orders were placed on 21 December 1936 for *S18* and *S19*, which were based on the design and dimensions of *S14* but powered by the MB501 20-cylinder 'V' engine. These boats differed from *S14* only in detail but the longitudinals forward were strengthened and weight economies were made by the extensive use of light alloy and plywood.

The situation in Europe now looked more and more threatening with the possibility that Germany's expansion plans into the east and south-east would perhaps precipitate hostilities. As a consequence, the Naval Staff had to consider just what design they would opt for in the event of mobilization, a decision complicated by the fact that no active operational experience had been seen by any boat and the newer *S18/S19* had not even been completed (*S18* had been delayed by the late delivery of her engines while those of *S19* had been diverted to *Ludwig Preusser*, a fast target tug for S-boats). The question now was should the existing boats be continued, should a larger design be worked out, or indeed should a return be made to the dimensions of *S10/S15*?

The 1937 programme authorized a further six boats, *S20* to *S25*, to the same design as *S18* and powered by the MB501 engine. Five of these boats were ordered from Lürssen on 29 December that year and one, *S25*, from Naglo as their yard No. 1340. However this latter contract was subsequently switched to Lürssen and became their yard No. 12790. The following year saw contracts placed for a further twelve boats, *S26* to *S37* but of two different types. *S26* to *S29*, ordered from Lürssen on 2 August 1938, were powered by the standard 20-cylinder MB501 engine, but a shortage of crankshaft drop forging capacity forced a return to the shorter crankshaft 16-cylinder MB502 engine for *S30* to *S37*, for which contracts were placed on 9 August 1938. Two of these boats were originally ordered from Naglo (*S36* and *S37*) as their yard Nos. 1349 and 1350, but again these contracts were switched to Lürssen later, becoming yard Nos. 12829 and

12830. The shorter and less beamy hull of these boats was fortuitous, in that it allowed their transfer (with the exception of *S32*, lost in June 1940) through the French inland waterway system to the Mediterranean theatre in 1941-42. These were the final boats ordered before war broke out on 1 September 1939.

At the outbreak of hostilities seventeen boats had been completed and a further ten were under construction and on order. However, of the seventeen completed boats, seven had the unsatisfactory MAN engines and were far from reliable operationally; and of the boats under construction, over half would not be in service until 1940. New mobilization contracts were placed shortly after the beginning of the war when *S38* to *S53* were ordered from Lürssen on 23 September 1939; they were all of the large *S26* type with MB501 engines. The search for a suitable second yard for S-boat construction now finally reached fruition, for on 25 September Schlichting were awarded the contract for *S101* to *S108*, also to the larger design. In fact, according to pre-war plans, Stettiner Oderwerk were to be drawn into the S-boat programme, for in May 1939 contracts for *S44* and *S45* were scheduled for this yard, but in the event no boats were constructed there. The smaller *S30* type was also the subject of further orders when on 14 November 1939 Lürssen received contracts for *S54* to *S61* powered by the MB502 engine again, to utilize available crankshaft forging capacity. All these boats were destined to serve in the Mediterranean theatre also. They were the last 'small' type to be constructed and thereafter only the larger *S38* type was built, with minor variations as the war progressed. The pattern of orders placed during the war years was:

Contract Date	Boats	Builder	Total
4.6.40	S62-S69	Lürssen	17
	S109-S117	Schlichting	
26.8.40	S70-S73	Lürssen	4
12.40	S118-S125	Schlichting	8
3.1.41	S74-S89	Lürssen	16
18.9.41	S90-S100	Lürssen	
	S134-S138	Lürssen	24
	S126-S133	Schlichting	
24.2.42	S139-S150	Lürssen	
	S167-S170	Lürssen	32
	S161-S166	Gusto (Schiedam)	
15.1.43	S171-S186	Lürssen	
	S187-S194	Schlichting	24
7.5.43	S195-S218	Lürssen	
	S219-S230	Schlichting	35
4.12.43	S231-S260	Schlichting	
	S301-S425	Lürssen	280
	S701-S825	Danziger Waggon	

Danziger Waggonfabrik was brought into the programme at a very late stage when Germany's internal transport system was being paralyzed and engine deliveries could not keep up with hull construction. Hence this yard did not deliver its first boat until July 1944 and only completed nine boats altogether. They were not alone in this situation, for Schlichting completed none of the 1943 programme boats and Lürssen only five.

CONSTRUCTION

Experiments conducted to establish the best construction materials had shown that wood was best for displacements of from 50 to 100 tons, but that between 100 and 150 tons, steel and wood were of equal merit. Above 150 tons steel was the only option. Wood however had the advantage of localizing damage and of being easier to repair. Lürssen's experiences with *S1* had confirmed that wood was the best material, but that above 50 tons it was necessary to use light alloy for many components of the inner hull, frames, longitudinals, etc. Also, with the growing power and weight of diesel engines, steel had to be employed for motor foundations.

The following is a general description of the method of construction of *S90* to *S100*, and *S134* to *S138* but broadly applied to all S-boat construction with some variations.

The keel was of several lengths of oak, bolted together, under which was an additional protective layer, 23mm thick, screwed to the main member and extending between frames 10 to 58. Oregon or Scots pine was used for the 80mm x 45mm and 120mm x 45mm longitudinals

- except in the way of the main motors when it was replaced by oak - for almost the full length of the boat. These longitudinals were bolted to the light-alloy frames, but the Al-Cu-Mg (aluminium-copper-magnesium) alloy diagonal stringers were riveted to them. Transverse framing consisted of an Al-Cu-Mg 50mm x 50mm x 5mm angle at 575mm intervals on to which the wooden longitudinals were screwed, with bent oak frames being nailed to the latter.

Bulkheads were either of 3mm sheet steel below the waterline and 4mm Al-Cu-Mg alloy above or all light alloy, depending on their position. The collision bulkhead was of 3mm galvanized steel. All bulkheads were stiffened. Motor foundations were continuous St42 steel with lightening holes. Deck beams were 42mm x 36mm oak at 200mm spacings. Planking on the decks was 23mm Oregon or Scots pine, tongue and grooved, 23mm thick covered with sailcloth. Skin planking (double-diagonal) consisted of an inner white cedar or larch layer, 12mm thick, and an outer of 21mm mahogany, separated by muslin. Bulwarks and superstructure were of 2.5mm light alloy. Pre-war boats had only a 10mm inner planking and an 18mm outer with the inner being nailed to the frames and the outer riveted to the inner. From *S26* the outer planking was screwed to the inner and frames. Light metal diagonal stringers were introduced between the wooden longitudinals and the alloy frames as a result of damage experienced in *S14* to *S17*, especially in the fore ends.

Right: An unidentified S-boat captured by the Americans after running ashore in the summer of 1944 and slipped for examination. (BfZ)

SCHNELLBOOT GENERAL ARRANGEMENT

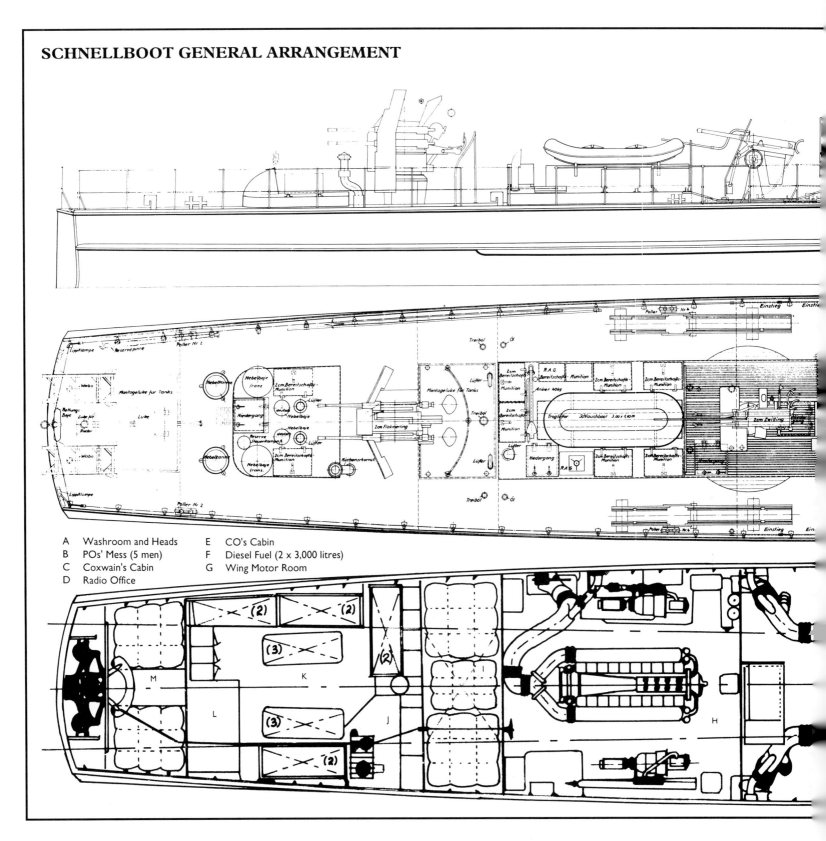

A   Washroom and Heads
B   POs' Mess (5 men)
C   Coxwain's Cabin
D   Radio Office
E   CO's Cabin
F   Diesel Fuel (2 x 3,000 litres)
G   Wing Motor Room

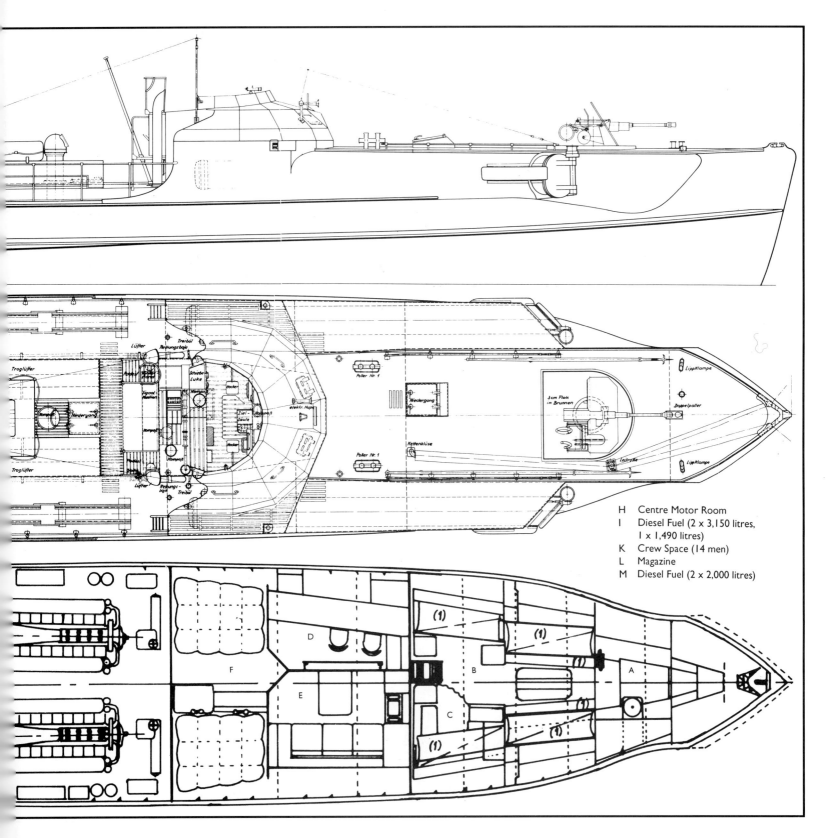

H   Centre Motor Room
I   Diesel Fuel (2 x 3,150 litres,
    1 x 1,490 litres)
K   Crew Space (14 men)
L   Magazine
M   Diesel Fuel (2 x 2,000 litres)

From *S205* a third skin was added because of the increase in weapons and weight of armour, and from *S330* a simplified form of construction was adopted.

SMALL S-BOATS

The quest for a small fast torpedo carrier suitable for use aboard auxiliary cruisers and the like during ocean deployments continued during the late 1930s. Furthermore, there was also a proposal for their use aboard specially constructed U-boats (the Type III). This latter project was later abandoned but the design of an S-boat for surface raider use continued and culminated in the ordering of two prototypes, *LS1* and *LS2*, in 1938. Various difficulties were encountered and the construction of both prototypes was stopped at the outbreak of war; in fact, *LS1* was never completed. In 1940, when disguised raiders were on the oceans, the project was reactivated and *LS2*, renamed *Meteorit*, was completed for service aboard raider 'HSK7' (*Komet*). She was however fitted as a minelayer with three TMB mines and not as a torpedo carrier. On 23 December 1940 *Meteorit* was lost from marine causes in the Bismarck Archipelago. *LS3-LS6* were also ordered as minelayers, from the Dornier yard in Friedrichshafen, and the first two received the lightweight diesels intended for *LS1* and *LS2*. *LS3* could carry four mines and was allocated to 'HSK8'(*Kormoran*), which was lost with her parent ship in the action against HMAS *Sydney* off Australia on 20 November 1941. *LS4* received

two 45cm stern torpedo tubes, was fully operationally fitted out (including sails) and embarked in 'HSK9' (*Michel*). She too was lost when the raider was sunk in the Yellow Sea in October 1943. *LS5* and *LS6* received Junkers diesels and were fitted only as anti-submarine vessels for the Mediterranean, but in 1942 they were refitted and equipped with two stern torpedo tubes. The main production series, *LS7-LS14*, was ordered from Dornier in 1940 and were similar to *LS3* and *LS4*. Of approximately 12 tons displacement with light metal hulls, they were powered by two Daimler-Benz MB507 12-cylinder diesels with a top speed of 38-40kt as designed. Construction proceeded only slowly: *LS7* was accepted on 8 October 1943, *LS8* on 20 December 1943 and *LS10* on 27 January 1944. *LS9* was commissioned at Kiel on 21 January 1944, *LS11* commissioned at Kiel on 18 May 1944 and *LS12* commissioned at Friedrichshafen on 14 July 1944. All were allocated to the 21st S-boat Flotilla and transferred to the Aegean, where *LS7-LS10* were relaunched at Piraeus on 2 May 1944. *LS12*, however, never reached the Aegean and was eventually used by the TVA, her passage south having been rescinded when she reached Yugoslavia. All the other boats were cancelled, as were *LS15-LS34*, because their intended use was no longer possible and, as a normal S-boat flotilla they were a disaster because of unreliable machinery and weak hulls.

The second type of craft to be considered is the Küstenminenleger (or coastal minelayer), intended to lay mines offensively in *enemy* coastal waters, thus requiring a

Left: One of the LS-boats. Note the aircraft-style gun turret and the twin tubes protruding from the transom. (BfZ)

small but fast boat. In conjunction with Lürssen, such a vessel was designed, employing off-cuts from normal S-boat production, with a double diagonal hard-chine hull. The boat displaced some 16 tons and was powered by two non-reversible BMW petrol motors for a top speed of 24kt (loaded). Four TMB mines could be accommodated in bottom traps under the hull; otherwise their sole armament was one or two 15mm machine-guns.

KM5-KM19 and *KM23* and *KM24* were ordered on 29 July 1940 from German yards, followed by *KM20* and *KM21* on 31 July. The Danish yard of Nordbjaerg & Wedell received orders for *KM1-KM4* on 26 August and *KM27-KM36* on 31 July, while the final orders, for *KM25* and *KM26*, were placed on 11 October. Two boats, *KM35* and *KM36* were burned out when the Danish yard was sabotaged on 6 May 1943, but the remainder were completed and had somewhat chequered careers.

As with the 'LS' boats, light construction and poor mechanical reliability severely restricted the usefulness of these craft. Certainly FdS did not want them for use in their designed role of minelaying in British coastal waters. However, war with the Soviet Union and the lack of German naval forces in remote areas, coupled with their transportable nature, led to their employment in areas far removed from those intended. Four boats, *KS3, KS4, KS8* and *KS22*, were sent to bolster Finnish forces on Lake Ladoga as part of the 31st Minesweeper Flotilla in 1942, which formation operated many of these craft in the Gulf of Finland during 1943-44. Four other boats *KM5, KM8, KM19* and *KM29* were sent to Lake Peipus in 1944 where they operated with the 4th Gun Carrier Flotilla. *KM1, KM2, KM4, KM9, KM10, KM12, KM22* and *KM26* were also sent to Lake Peipus. On 17 July 1942, *KM17* and *KM18, KM20* and *KM21* and *KM23* and *KM24* were commissioned for the Danube Flotilla and despatched to the Black Sea to escort convoys between Odessa, Sulina and Nikolaev. This was a task for which they were entirely unsuited and by October their serviceability and performance record was so poor that they were returned to Linz in Austria and all paid off on 20 January 1943. As a result of their general uselessness in their designed role, it was proposed that some be converted to carry torpedoes instead of mines. They were equipped with two 45cm stern tubes similar to those in the 'LS' boats and designated 'KS' boats. A total of 20 boats were converted, of which only nine (*KS11, KS17, KS18, KS20, KS21, KS23, KS24, KS31* and *KS32*) served with FdS. The remainder were allocated to the Lake Peipus flotilla and the 31st Minesweeper Flotilla in the Gulf of Finland, although a proposal by Gruppe Ost in June 1943 to fit two to four 'KM' boats with torpedoes for use in the Gulf of Finland had been vetoed by SKL. All torpedo armed 'KM' boats were destined for the Adriatic, Aegean and Black Sea theatres.

The boats controlled by FdS were formed into the 22nd S-Boat Flotilla whose career is described in Chapter 13.

HYDROFOILS

As the resistance of a hull being driven through water is high, ideas to reduce such resistance had been developed as early as the end of the 19th century in the case of hydrofoils, which employ 'skis' to raise the hull out of the water. By the use of such means, very high speeds became possible although there were a number of negative associated features, seaworthiness being one. During the lean years of the 1920s and 1930s, two German engineers were active in this field, Dr. Tietjens and Freiherr von Schertel, both of whom demonstrated successful prototypes in this period. The latter joined the boat builders Gebrüder Sachsenberg AG at Rosslau and developed his ideas to a pitch where they became potential war weapons. Ever interested in high speeds, the Kriegsmarine expressed the desire to develop hydrofoils towards the end of the 1930s and was able to earmark some funds for this purpose.

This led to the ordering of an experimental craft, *VS3* of 80 tonnes from Lürssen as their yard number 12816, on 3 August 1938. Orders for *VS2* followed on 3 September 1938 with the same yard and on 5 September for *VS1*, also with Lürssen. Unlike the other two, *VS1* was of only 30 tonnes. Both this boat and *VS2* were to be fitted with Mercedes-Benz MB588 motors, while *VS3* had MAN diesels. They were to employ the Tietjens system but the outbreak of war resulted in their cancellation. *VS1* was actually re-ordered in March 1942 but cancelled again a year later.

VS4 was the first Schertel boat, ordered from Sachsenberg, on 28 September 1938. Of 100 tonnes and armed with two torpedo tubes, she too was cancelled on the outbreak of war.

VS5 was a rather weird project, a semi-submersible S-boat, which was ordered from Deschimag, Bremen, as their yard number 1033. Being more submarine than S-boat, it is outside the scope of this volume and in any event was a complete failure. Construction of hydrofoils now lapsed until July 1940 when Sachsenberg were awarded another contract for an experimental boat, *VS6*. She was designed as a minelayer but was relatively small, displacing about 17 tonnes and could therefore accommodate only four TMB mines. Powered by two 700hp petrol engines, *VS6* was completed in the summer of 1942. Initial trials proved that the boat was not robust enough but following strengthening she was used for the rest of the war on trials duties. In Sachsenberg's opinion, *VS6* incorporated all the best up-to-date ideas of hydrofoil design but even so she was not truly fit for operational use. Some details of her trials are of interest. On 24-25 October 1944 when tested in Lübeck Bay, it was found that in relatively calm conditions she could come up onto the hydrofoils in about 6-10 seconds on all courses (installed power was 1,300hp). A second trial demonstrated her ability to become foil-borne from rest in 14 seconds. The following day both wind and seas had slightly increased (Sea 2, Wind NE force 2-3) and it was found that her engine power was sufficient to get foil-borne against and across the sea in 15 seconds. With the sea, it proved impossible however.

VS7 was built to compare the Tietjens system with that of Schertel used in VS6 but proved overweight and after rebuilding was used on trials in the Baltic.

The final hydrofoil boat to be constructed was perhaps the most interesting as it had its origins in an Army requirement for a fast transport capable of landing a Panzer Mk IV by means of a flooding pontoon. Taken over by the Kriegsmarine in 1941, VS8 was an impressive looking craft of 98 tonnes with a length of 31.9m designed to be powered by two supercharged MB511 diesels for a top speed of up to 45kt, although over 50kt was optimistically expected. She was ready for trials from the summer of 1943 but proved a disappointment because the hull was overweight and only non-supercharged MB501 engines were installed. Consequently, her speed did not exceed 37kt.

As yet there had been no real thought of using any of the 'VS' boats on offensive operations, but in April 1944 the possibility of their use as minelayers was actively pursued. At that time the only means of offensive minelaying was by means of the S-boats but their potential was limited by the small number of mines that could be accommodated. VS8 on the other hand was of a similar size to a normal S-boat but had been designed to carry heavy loads, actually tanks but equally could be mines. It was believed that the boat was capable of 50kt on two engines with a 20-tonne load and possibly more if a third engine were fitted. On foils, she would be immune to minefields, there was little danger from magnetic mines, less danger from acoustic mines and pressure mines would be totally ineffective. It was felt that the potential of this weapon could not be ignored. The reality was somewhat different because the boat did not perform well on trials off Danzig with the EKK in June and August 1944. In calm weather the boat could get foil-borne at 45kt but in the absence of the supercharged diesels, this was the maximum, in which case there was little advantage over the S-boats which were in any case far better sea boats. Eventually one of her engines failed during trials off Stolpmünde in September 1944 and, after the skis had been cut off, VS8 was towed into Swinemünde and laid up at the Naval Repair Yard there for the duration of the war, on the instructions of her builders.

By 1944, apart from a few small patrol craft (TS1-4) used for harbour defence duties in Norwegian waters, no usable hydrofoil craft had reached operational service. The reasons were many. The hydrofoils themselves were very sensitive to damage and the high silhouette was a disadvantage. Moreover, with the full hull clear of the water, the boats were very vulnerable and noisy. There were other problems associated with cooling the engines and propeller cavitation. Practically, when not foil-borne, the boats were slow, of deep draft and difficult to dock. All

things considered, to pursue development under the circumstances obtaining in late 1944 was unwarranted, a fact recognized by Dönitz when cancelling the whole programme on 7 November that year. VS6 and VS7 were turned over to the KdK (Small Battle Units Command) and the rest either scrapped or cancelled; some of them were very futuristic designs indeed.

DESIGN PROJECTS AND EXPERIMENTAL CRAFT

In 1942, with the problem of British MGBs becoming more serious, Bütow as FdT pressed for the development of a counter-measure, namely an S-boat with a purely gun armament. This led to some investigative design work by Lürssen who produced a modification of the standard S38/S100 type, armed with a twin 3.7cm M42 forward, a single stabilized 2cm Mg C38 in a cupola on the bridge and a 2cm vierling amidships over the engine room. An alternative project envisaged a 120 ton displacement steel boat armed with a twin 3.7cm M42 fore and aft together with the single 2cm and two MG34 on the bridge. However, when Petersen assumed command as FdS, his views were different. In his opinion, what was required was a heavier armament in existing boats, if necessary at the expense of half the torpedo outfit. In January 1944 SKL agreed that a new design was not feasible and MOK (Nord) concurred with Petersen that the best interim solution was to rearm the existing boats. Perhaps in the long term a 'Gun' boat might be possible, which could be given one 2cm forward, one 3cm amidships and either a 7.5cm or 5.5cm gun aft. It was felt that the R-boat provided a good convoy defence vessel as experience had demonstrated that they could successfully fight off MGBs. The idea of a pure MGB type was therefore shelved.

However, the idea of a combined R- and S-boat was not new, having been proposed as early as November 1940 by Gruppe (West). This was vetoed by SKL in March the following year as the displacement would be over 120 tonnes, thereby necessitating steel construction. In addition, to achieve the demanded speed, 400hp would be required. The only suitable engine was the 1,400hp Germania U-boat engine, but using three of these resulted in a displacement of 236 tonnes and a maximum speed of only 22.5kt, much below that required. Use of three 2,100hp Germania engines gave a growth in displacement to 300 tonnes with a speed of 23.9kt. S-boat engines were ruled out because they were designed for high speed running and were not therefore suitable for escort work. In any event, there was already a shortage of these engines for S-boats. A torpedo armament for R-boats was finally vetoed by the K.Amt. on 28 February 1942, despite the fact that Gruppe (Nord) saw good use for such craft in the Baltic and Norwegian areas as well as on the east coast of Great Britain.

The suspension of the Escort R-boat or Geleit Raumboote, remained a bone of contention with Gruppe (West) and others, so SKL felt it necessary to detail the reasons: (a) shortages of raw materials; and (b) construction would be at the expense of normal R-boats.

The solution proposed was similar to that for the S-boats: i.e., rearm existing boats with three 2cm and one 3.7cm, which could begin in the summer of 1942. This would entail a slight loss of speed but was considered the best method. Gruppe (West) agreed but with some reluctance because of the drop in speed. There the matter

Below: As the danger of air attack from fighters increased, a new-style bridge, known as the Kalottenbrücke (`Skullcap'), was introduced and armour progressively fitted. (WZB)

appeared to rest but quite soon was resurrected because such a boat was designed in 1942 and twenty of this type were ordered from Abeking & Rasmussen as *R301-R320*. These were armed with one 3.7cm and up to seven 2cm guns and carried two 53.3cm torpedoes. However, they failed to meet their designed speed and could only achieve 23.5kt maximum. Only twelve were completed, serving with the 21st R-boat Flotilla in Norwegian waters. There they were well placed as they provided torpedo-armed coastal craft available for use against infrequent Allied incursions into these waters, an area in which the stationing of a pure S-boat flotilla would be a waste of scarce resources.

The continued perception of a requirement for a combined R/S-boat for escort duties (i.e., a multi-purpose vessel) eventually led to the design of just such a ship, known as an 'MZ' boat (Mehrzweckboot or multi-purpose vessel) described later.

ARMOURED S-BOATS

FdS's requests for better armour protection presented problems in that securing the protective plating to curved hull lines would be difficult, there would probably be corrosion and rot problems between steel and wood interfaces and the hull weight would be increased dramatically. A better solution appeared to be the development of a completely new design, intended from the outset as an armoured S-boat. This would of necessity have to be of steel construction, which in the long term would also be cheaper. Side armour was to be 12mm with 8mm decks and the hull was of hard-chine construction, displacing about 113 tonnes. Dimensions were 34.8m length and 5.4m beam. The superstructure was wooden with armour plating. It is believed that *S231* was to be the prototype of such a boat. A second design was also prepared, this being a round bilge displacement hull of slightly less speed than the hard-chine project. Endurance and weapons - three 3cm guns, two machine-guns and four torpedo tubes (two bow, two stern) - would be identical to those of the other project. Opinion of such a design within the Fleet was mixed and in March 1944 FdS stated that he was against such a craft because at best it could only be used as a convoy escort. Hitherto only the R-boats and 'MZ' boats had been considered for this role, which was to give protection against light surface forces and fighter-bombers. An armoured S-boat was probably best employed against the first wave of an enemy landing force.

Such a view is surprising, for if all the specified parameters had been met, such a well armed and protected craft with a speed of 44kt would have presented a formidable means of waging the East Coast Convoy war. As it was, faced with Petersen's views, Dönitz decided not to build an armoured boat, no doubt also influenced by the effect of its steel construction on available materials and shipyard capacity.

2. MAIN MACHINERY

The first diesel engines available were produced by MAN, being their type L7 Zn 19/30, a seven-cylinder in-line, double-acting two-stroke non-reversing design. This developed 1,200/1,320hp at 1,000/1,050 rpm. Engines of this type were installed in *S6* to *S9* and because of their novelty required a considerable period of time before they could be regarded as fit for service operational use. They were certainly a step forward from the BF2 petrol engines but despite much attention from MAN they were not considered satisfactory, and there is no doubt that installation should not have gone beyond *S6* until the design was properly proved for service use. As it was, the service commands had the task of running four essentially experimental boats to the detriment of operational employment, which greatly stretched the Reichsmarine's meagre resources.

The motor casing of this design was of welded sheet and plate, which was considered strong and sound with good accessibility. However, the exhaust system drew adverse comment due to oil fumes permeating the motor room spaces and this was a weak point in the design. *S6* had welded cylinders while the remainder employed cast ones. Early experience did not reveal any great advantage of one over the other, but *S6* did have to have two motors removed for cylinder repairs. This boat experienced other problems, in particular failures of the connecting rods, manufactured from chrome-nickel steel, but a change to a silico-manganese steel and some detail design modifications reduced the tendency to failure. There were also piston rod failures similar to those experienced in *Bremse*, for which the reason could not be precisely ascertained, but it was not simply a case of the wrong material being specified; however, nitrided piston rods fared better. Other problems included trouble with the piston rings, which was solved, but the most serious and persistent trouble concerned the geared drive, *S6* experiencing such a failure on trials after commissioning.

The next four boats, *S10* to *S13*, received diesel engines of Daimler-Benz design, type BOF6 (MB502), a 16-cylinder 'V' four-stroke design of 1,200/1,300hp at 1,550/1,650rpm. This was much faster running than the MAN type and 2 : 1 reduction gearing was employed. Like the MAN engine, it too was based on the BF2 petrol

engine and was similar to those used aboard the airship *Hindenburg*. This engine differed from the MAN design in many respects, not least in the use of an aluminium-silicon alloy casting for the cylinder casing. This was something of a mixed blessing as an engine failure often destroyed the casting, necessitating a good reserve of spare engines because a lead time of four weeks was required for a new casting. Accessibility was also poorer and it was found advisable to remove the engine from the boat for repairs whereas the MAN engine could be dealt with in situ. The weights of the two designs were almost the same, but the MAN type had a higher centre of gravity. In terms of space requirements, the Daimler-Benz engine was lower and had smaller exhaust trunkings but the lengths were similar. The MAN diesel was found easier and better at starting and ran considerably slower at 140rpm minimum, compared with 400rpm (minimum) for the Daimler-Benz. This in turn affected propeller design for the two types of boat. In operation, fuel consumption was found to be about 10 per cent lower in the Daimler-Benz engines with better combustion efficiency, leading to almost invisible exhausts, whereas the MAN type at 900rpm produced a very dark exhaust. The latter was also more prone to fuel impurity problems. Noise reduction was an important factor for operational reasons; it was found that the Daimler-Benz type was the quieter of the two and was better suited to underwater exhaust venting. Vibration was a feature of the MAN motors which could be reduced by wider engine foundations.

MAN developed their engine further by increasing the number of cylinders to nine, the motor now being designated L9 Zn 19/301, which produced 1,320/1,700hp. It was proposed that these be retrospectively installed in *S6* to *S9* but there was insufficient space and, in the meantime, development had further progressed to an eleven-cylinder model. Twenty sets of the nine-cylinder design were ordered in case of war, four of which were later sold to the Luftwaffe and used in the air-sea rescue boats *FLS11* and *FLS12*. With their maximum power reduced to 1,500hp, they proved satisfactory in service. The remainder were held for possible future use in S-boats.

The eleven-cylinder L11 Zn 19/30 engine was specified

for four boats, *S14* to *S17*, three per boat, of which *S14* had been provisionally accepted by the Navy on 9 June 1936. The acceptance of *S15* depended on the progress of trials with *S14*. Unfortunately, despite successful shop trials at the manufacturer's works, shipboard trials proved less successful, delaying full acceptance of *S14* by four months.

Initial trials showed the propellers to be unsatisfactory - only 850rpm could be achieved. After three different sets of propellers had been tried, the revolutions were pushed up to 1,000rpm, but the boat was still 2kt short of contract full speed. Exhaust temperatures were very high and severe vibration was experienced. The poor performance could not be explained as the poor output of the engines could not be measured. Because of the size of the new engines, the boat's hull had to be increased in size by 25 per cent (displacement) and it was considered that it would have been prudent to have increased power only so far as to be able to retain the previous boat's displacement. Motors were on order for *S16* and *S17* (three each) with three spares for a total of nine, but by this time the continuance of the MAN design was under question and the following boats, *S18* and *S19*, were to receive Daimler-Benz BOF 8 (MB501) diesels. As a result of the unreliabilty of the MAN L11 engines, *S14* to *S17* were to prove liabilities throughout their service life, which was in fact relatively short in their designed role. As early as August 1940 they had been relegated to a fast A/S-boat role but were somewhat of a liability even in this task. A major problem with this engine was its length and insufficiently robust foundations, and the continuous working of a light wooden hull in a seaway at speed led to cracking problems. The use of MAN engines was therefore discontinued in S-boats, although six- or eight-cylinder MAN diesels were retained for use in R-boats.

The MB501 engine specified for *S18* onwards was merely an uprated version of the older type installed in *S10* to *S13*. Now it was enlarged to twenty cylinders and developed 2,050hp. It was anticipated that further increases in power could be obtained by supercharging, but there was some concern that this might adversely affect the engine's life; already the superchargers fitted to *S1-S5* were no longer used.

The intention to standardize on the MB501 was soon thwarted by lack of building capacity. Yet again dreams were being brought to earth by reality; Germany's industry was just not capable of matching the huge rearmament demands being placed upon it in the late 1930s. There was only one source of supply for Daimler-Benz engines, the factory at Untertürkenheim where there was a shortage of crankshaft forging capacity, particularly for the twenty-cylinder engine. As a result, a series of fifteen boats (*S30-S37* and *S54-S61*) had to be ordered with the sixteen-cylinder MB502. The production bottleneck was recognized and in January 1940 Daimler-Benz were ordered to build a second factory at Marienfelde, but with wartime conditions now prevailing this could not be ready

until May 1941 at the earliest, and even then output would be low. At the same time, steps were taken to expand the Untertürkenheim works and alleviate the shortage of specialists and machine tools, in particular crankshaft forging. All this was in the future however, for by 1940 serious problems were being experienced in boat and engine availability. An added burden on availability was the OKM's decision - based on wartime experience so far (i.e., before the fall of France), which indicated that the operational possibilities were distinctly limited (see Chapter 4) - that no more than 50 S-boats were required.

At the outbreak of war Daimler-Benz were producing six engines a month, which rate by 1940 had only risen to nine. This led to a conflict between putting new boats into commission or building up a reserve of spare engines. Usually the former course prevailed and its effect on operations had not been foreseen. Misuse of S-boats on tasks for which they had not been designed - e.g., despatch duties, convoy escort and supply carrying - led to excessive engine wear and overloaded the repair shops. Engines were normally returned to Untertürkenheim for major repairs and overhaul, but it was intended that the facilities at Wilhelmshaven dockyard, where most of the S-boat refits were carried out, would be equipped with engine repair and overhaul shops as soon as possible. Deutsche Werft at Kiel, Stettiner Oderwerk and Deutsche Werft, Gotenhafen (Gdynia), were also to be given these facilities but the full programme was not expected to be complete until the summer of 1942. By 1941 raw material shortages began to be felt; a shortage of copper in particular affected the production of oil coolers. In the autumn of that year, the effect on S-boat operations was becoming serious enough for Führer der Torpedoboote to inform the OKM that unless urgent measures were taken, the S-boat arm might well be reduced to ineffectiveness. So far, 34 boats were available fitted with this engine, making a total of 102 engines, but there were only nine spares. Of these 34 boats, twelve were in the yards for engine changes, some having been there for several months. *S103* had no engines at all while *S21*, *S24* and *S25* had been laid up since June 1941. The more new boats that were commissioned, the more boats lay in the yards awaiting engine replacement. Although turn-round time for engine overhaul had been reduced to about eight weeks, there had been no significant effect on boat availability. More boats of the new *S26* type were needed, together with spare engines. Of the older type (*S18*) used for the important task of training, four were already without engines, further disrupting S-boat activities. Bütow pressed for a solution to the various engine technical problems and an increase in the supply of engines and spares.

Two months later Admiral Kranke at OKM informed Bütow that measures had already been taken to increase engine production and that from January 1942 the output was expected to be twelve engines per month while the current four spare engines would rise to the desired number by the summer of 1942. The problem caused by inadequate roller-bearing rings, which led to bearing damage, was being rectified by a new design tried in *S25* in November and all new engines would be fitted with this type. On the question of supercharging of the MB501, Kranke had to report that this was still not in a state for operational use but tests and trials were continuing with extreme urgency. He requested Bütow to give a further situation report in January 1942.

The engine position had become so acute that Daimler-Benz themselves were being criticized for their part in the matter, which stung the company into producing a hard-backed voluminous report detailing their version of events. In their defence they reminded the Kriegsmarine that 900, 1,200, and 1,320hp motors had been developed by their company at the request of the Navy. They had developed successively higher-powered engines rapidly, and mostly without the benefit of shipboard trials results being available because of the pace of new construction demands. When the larger MB501 twenty-cylinder engine appeared, six trial engines and 25 production ones had been delivered by 1938/39, but overall the volume of orders was not sufficient to warrant an increase in production capacity. At the beginning of the war the following orders had been executed:

42 x MB501, 32 x MB501, 30 x MB502, plus 3 x MB588 for an unnamed experimental boat, 6 x BOM 805 for MR-boats and 4 x MB507 for LS-boats.

Not until the outbreak of war was a bulk order for 72 MB501s received for delivery at the rate of three per month from the tenth month of the war and at six per month from the twelfth war month.It was also pointed out that as early as December 1938 the OKM had discussed the expansion of the Untertürkenheim works and a year later had also considered equipping the Marienfelde works. According to the Daimler-Benz report, engine deliveries up to the end of 1941 were as follows:

	MB501	MB502	MB500	MB507
1939				
September	-	2	-	-
October	2	3	-	-
November	2	1	-	-
December	1	1	-	-
1940				
January	-	4	-	-
February	1	4	-	-
March	1	4	-	-
April	1	2	-	-
May	2	5	-	-
June	5	3	-	-
July	3	2	-	1
August	3	3	-	1
September	3	1	-	-
October	6	5	-	1
November	2	4	-	1
December	6	2	-	-

	MB501	MB502	MB500	MB507
1941				
January	6	5	3	-
February	8+1*	3	3	-
March	8	3	2	-
April	9	3	2	-
May	7+1	3	2	-
June	10+1	3	-	-
July	13+3	3	-	-
August	5+3	-	2	-
September	4+3	-	-	-
October	6+3	-	2	-
November	7+4	-	-	-
December	6+5	-	2	-
Totals	127+24	54	20	4

* Marienfelde works

Major Overhauls:

	MB501	MB502
1939	6	1
1940	26	23
1941	27	7
Totals	59	31

Other Overhauls: 56

Obviously, Daimler-Benz considered that they had played their part and that had the Navy been better prepared this bottleneck would not have arisen.

After the command organization for S-boats was changed in April 1942, Kpt.z.S. Petersen assumed the post of Flag Officer (S-boats), or FdS. He issued an appreciation of the S-boat war on 9 October 1942, in which, among other issues, he addressed the question of engines. Since Bütow's report in December 1941, the position had improved somewhat, especially in terms of reserve engines, since deliveries from Daimler-Benz were now running at about eighteen a month, of which nine were allocated to new boats and nine to the reserve stock. At this rate, the target of 50 per cent spares would be reached by 1 November 1942, assuming that the three reserve boats of the 1st Flotilla currently without engines (*S40*, *S47* and *S52*) remained in this state. If, however, they were brought forward for service, the spares target would not be reached until 1 March 1943. From that time on, four instead of three new boats per month could be commissioned. The spares situation for the MB502 engines had improved but for the wrong reasons - four boats had been lost. Technical problems referred to by Bütow had to some extent been overcome, in particular a reduction in the high incidence of crankshaft bearing damage experienced during the summer of 1941 on MB501 engines with relatively low hours. Bearing life had improved and engine life now averaged 400 hours, but it was not known what Daimler-Benz had done to achieve this. A second measure was aimed at reducing connecting rod failures by substituting plain bearings for the roller pattern; at the same time the exhaust valve seatings were re-cut 2mm lower to reduce carbonizing and valve damage. The first modified engines had been installed in *S25* in November 1941 and arrangements were in hand to fit *S69* and *S111* similarly before completion of trials by *S25*. To date the hours to basic overhaul had been extended from 275 to 350, but the final target was 510 service hours in *S25* and 420 hours in the operational boats. A disadvantage of the plain bearings was the lack of pre-warning of failure, which was one of the factors in deciding to leave roller-bearing engines in the 1st Flotilla (Black Sea) because of the distance from repair facilities - pre-warning would prevent catastrophic motor failure.

The position with regard to supercharging had also improved in that modifications to the MB502 had been completed and refitted units with mechanical superchargers were now available. In addition, the first new MB501 with superchargers was complete. In supercharged form, these engines were designated MB512 and MB511 respectively. It was anticipated that the MB512 would produce about 25 per cent more power; this had been borne out by the trial installation in *S56*, one of the Mediterranean boats. The top speed of these boats with a full war load was now expected to be about 36.6kt, while the boats fitted with the MB511 type were expected to reach 42kt. The latter engine was fitted in *S84* and *S85*. Two more MB502s were currently being converted at Untertürkenheim and more would be put in hand as soon as *S56* had reached 300 hours. Six MB511s were aboard *S84* and *S85* with six more in the shop at Mercedes Benz as spares. However, due to the supply position it was not expected that more operational boats could be fitted until August 1943 at the earliest. The engine situation at this date, October 1942, could be summarized as follows:

	Installed	Reserve	%	
MB500	24	7	29	
MB501	177*	85	48	
*of which	114	21	18.4	Plain Bearings
	63	64	101	Roller Bearings
MB502	36	24	66.6	

(These figures include the few MB511 and MB512 engines).

The improvement in engine delivery was due in part to the Marienfelde works coming on stream, where it was intended to produce ten engines per month with the parent works contributing twelve. Crankshaft production remained a major bottleneck, for at the beginning of the war there had been only one forge-master (in Württemberg) with a large enough steam hammer. Krupps built a second but a third was much delayed. Thus the plan to produce 22 engines in a single shift and twice that number on double shifting was aimed at the completion of eleven S-boats per month, with the remainder as spares. This plan soon came to nought for in 1942 Albert Speer transferred the Marienfelde works to Luftwaffe production, and in 1942-43 the sole manufacturer at Untertürkenheim could deliver only sufficient engines for three boats a month. Given the deployment of S-boats to new theatres such as the Mediterranean and Black Sea, this decision seriously affected S-boat production and operation. Engine production thereafter dictated the S-boat programme. During the night of 1/2 March 1944, more than 400 Lancaster bombers raided Stuttgart, followed by over 600 on the night of 15/16 March. The results of these raids stopped production entirely, but only for a month. Nevertheless, this disruption in the programme was considerable and Daimler-Benz delivered only one engine in October 1944 for example. Unrealistic promises continued to be made for production programmes which, under the prevailing circumstances, were little more than figments of the imagination. Thus the plans in 1944 called for an increase to 150 boats per annum increasing to 25 boats per month by January 1945!

Further development by Daimler-Benz to increase engine output led to the introduction of the even more powerful MB518, which was first installed for evaluation in *S170*, commissioned in February 1944. This engine was essentially a development of the MB511 with a maximum rating of 3,000hp at 1,720rpm for 30 minutes. Its dimensions were virtually the same as those of the MB511 and its weight increased by less than 2 per cent. On trials, *S170* reached 43.5kt fully loaded, but considerable teething troubles were encountered with the starter and pistons. Despite her commissioning in early 1944, *S170* remained on engine trials until at least the end of January 1945 and it is doubtful if any operational activity was engaged in by this boat or any others of the 11th Flotilla. A complete switch of production to this new engine totally disrupted the construction programme, with the result that out of a series of boats *S301* to *S425*, only those up to and including *S307* entered service, while about twenty or so more remained incomplete at the end of the war, were broken up or scuttled. Many were awaiting engines. In fact, of the 292 S-boats listed as on order or under construction in November 1944, 138 were listed as delayed by engine installation and these represented all those actively in work. The remainder were orders that had not yet been started. After that date only nineteen of these 292 boats were completed.

3. ARMAMENT

The S-boat's main armament was always the torpedo which, apart from the early days when 50cm weapons were used, was the standard 53.3cm G7a, a conventional wet-heater compressed-air torpedo with a maximum range of 14,000m at 30kt or 6,000m at 44kt. In fact, this torpedo was too powerful for the S-boats to use to its full capabilities as, for example, it was seldom fired at ranges exceeding 3,000m. The boats were therefore carrying a much heavier torpedo than was required, and its weight could have been put to better use without sacrificing offensive properties, if a lighter weight special S-boat torpedo had been available. By the time that this had become fully appreciated during the war, there was no chance of putting such a specialized weapon into production, although early documents relating to S-boat development refer to a G6a torpedo which may have been this lightweight mark. Few references to this torpedo have survived, but it appears to have had a length of approximately 6,422mm (as opposed to the G7a at 7,186mm) and a total weight of possibly 1,374kg (G7a, 1,528kg). The electric G7e was shorter in range and slower but also heavier than the G7a. Its use aboard S-boats was proposed by FdT in November 1940, but because operations were invariably in darkness, when trackless running was not important (and all supplies were in any case being claimed by the U-boat arm), few if any reached the S-boats. All S-boats, except for a few of the later ones, were equipped with two torpedo tubes and could carry two spare torpedoes as re-loads. Whether or not these were carried depended on the operation concerned and prevailing weather conditions.

Both contact and magnetic pistols had been developed; the latter was tested aboard *S22* in September 1939 for use in angled shots, the pistol being cleared for use up to red/green 40deg angles. In December 1939 the Torpedo Inspectorate ordered the equipping of all surface ships, including S-boats, with the Pi.A magnetic pistol. *S22* was fitted with an experimental torpedo director type RZA5 which allowed angle firing, whereas the RZA3 pattern fitted in *S20-S29* did not. Supply difficulties prevented these boats receiving the RZA5 but it was expected that it would be fitted from *S30* on. In March 1940 the Torpedo Inspectorate ordered all G7a-equipped vessels to use a modified pistol, Pi.A & B, but the torpedo scandal was about to break and on 23 May Flag Officer U-boats banned its use. A similar ban was enforced for surface vessels on 29 May 1940.

After the Allied invasion of Europe in June 1944, S-boats operated for a while using T3d 'Dackel' long-range torpedoes. The defensive ring around the invasion beachhead was so strong that the S-boats were unable to achieve any noteworthy success and this seemed an ideal opportunity for the 'Dackel' which could be used at a range of up to 57,000m. It had a speed of only 9kt, a reduced warhead of 281kg and was intended to pattern or circle run in crowded anchorages after an initial straight approach. It was first employed at the beginning of August 1944 against shipping concentrations off the Normandy beachhead.

In March 1944 the employment of T5 homing torpedoes for S-boats for use against destroyers was mooted. Dönitz was sceptical but ordered that the matter be investigated. The result was the T5a which was actually used by S-boats from July 1944 in the Normandy area but with no known success. One destroyer was claimed sunk by the 8th Flotilla but evidence was lacking; in fact the destroyer concerned, HMS *Cattistock* (in company with the frigate *Retalick*), was actually badly damaged by *gunfire*.

For self defence, S-boats relied initially on a single 2cm MG C/30 cannon on a circular platform aft but later boats were equipped with a second such mounting forward, in a well between the torpedo tubes. This gun was the standard Kriegsmarine light flak weapon and suffered from a poor rate of fire; this was improved with the C38 model with which boats were fitted as it became available. As in coastal forces everywhere, light machine-guns were added as and when the crews could obtain them but the S-boats normally carried a pair of MG34 7.92mm machine-guns on the bridge. Six depth charges and two chemical smoke generators completed the armament.

Under the stimulus of hostilities, this armament was augmented initially and most notably by mines, although the use of this weapon had been foreseen in pre-war days. However, the breaking loose of mines aboard the destroyer *Wolfgang Zenker* in heavy seas in January 1940 led the

SKL to reconsider if it was safe for S-boats to act in the minelaying role. The SKL was especially concerned with EMC and EMD mines which had a high centre of gravity (850mm above deck level), as opposed to the same weight at only 436mm for RMA mines. When the K Amt reported that there was no way to lower the centre of gravity, SKL vetoed the use of EMA, EMC and EMD mines aboard S-boats. Towards the end of March 1940 some experiments were conducted by the 2nd S-boat Flotilla out of Wilhelmshaven. *S14*, *S15* and *S16* were given loads of four or six RMA or RMB mines and their effect on speed and seakeeping was assessed. It was found that while the speed of *S14* dropped by 3kt, that of *S15* and *S16* fell by only half that; furthermore, they were dry whereas the older boat was found to be very wet. From these experiments it could be expected that operationally the boats would employ RM type ground mines. However, this was not the case, for when the first minelaying sorties were launched early in July 1940 by the 2nd Flotilla EMC mines were used, despite the SKL's veto. Also used on these early sorties were Soviet MO8 mines (captured in Poland and presumably dating from before the First World War when Poland was part of Russia). Not listed in many documents, this was a moored contact mine weighing 550kg with a 120kg trotyl charge, less than half that of the standard EMC mine. As the war progressed, other types of mine were used, including the torpedo tube launched TMB/S adapted from the U-boat version, and the LMB/S or LMF/S type mines, all of which were influence mines with either acoustic or magnetic firing (or both). In fact, the S-boats gained the majority of their successes with the mine and they remained a serious threat throughout the war.

By 1942 war experience had shown that a heavier gun armament was required if the S-boats were to defend themselves successfully against the ever-increasing number of MGBs being employed by the Royal Navy in the Channel. Although it was the destroyers of the convoy escort which were the most feared opponents, it was acknowledged that an S-boat could not, and should not, trade fire with these adversaries. However the MGBs were a different matter. In the early years of the war the S-boats' British counterpart, the MTB, was as weakly armed as themselves, perhaps even more so, and actions between the two were mostly indecisive. But when it was found that the expected U-boat threat in coastal waters had failed to materialize, fifteen Motor Anti-Submarine Boats (MASBs) became surplus to requirements and were converted to MGBs to counter the S-boat menace. Armed initially with only one 20mm gun, this was nevertheless a beginning and as the war progressed MGBs shipped progressively heavier armaments, including ultimately 6pdr (57mm) weapons. Some idea of the coming threat posed by the MGB was gleaned when *MGB 335* was captured. Documents obtained from her suggested that twelve MGB flotillas of six boats each were in service. More importantly, the fitting of radar was evident - something the S-boats were never to get on a production basis. It soon became essential, therefore, for something to be done to augment the S-boats' relatively puny self-defence. The first step was usually to fit 2cm guns forward and aft, but a heavier weapon was needed, and here there was not a lot of choice. The standard 3.7cm SKC/30 semi-automatic weapon found in all ships of the Kriegsmarine had far too slow a rate of fire to be of much use in a fast-moving night action, despite its designed flak role. The only other alternative was the 4cm Flak 28 (Bofors), numbers of which had been captured in Poland. Even so, by October 1942 there were only ten boats fitted with this gun, three in each of the 2nd and 4th Flotillas, two in each of the 5th and 6th Flotillas (*S29*, *S39*, *S42*, *S44-S46*, *S81-S83* and *S117*). It displaced the after 2cm. Pleas for a 4cm in the bows could not be met due to lack of space between the tubes. At that time, the autumn of 1942, Flag Officer (S-boats) stressed that, although he was not in favour of an MGB type (because without tubes it could not sink tonnage), there was an urgent need to augment further the armour and armament of the standard *S38*-type boat. What he wanted was two 3cm MK103s plus a triaxial 2cm C/38, the former being a Luftwaffe weapon. Alternatively a 3cm MK103 in a triaxial mounting in place of the after 2cm C/38 was requested. Nothing like this was available and other fully automatic weapons between the 3.7cm Flak 36 and the 5cm Flak 41M were either too heavy or required too many crew for use aboard S-boats. Much therefore depended on the 3cm MK103 trials. In addition, the MG34 needed to be replaced with some other weapon operated by a single crewman, possibly the MG15. The interim solution was the fitting of ten 4cm guns.

By 1943 the situation was becoming more acute and there was a demand for more 4cm guns, but the lack of an armour-piercing shell for this weapon was seen as a drawback, it being stated that the S-boats were deployed against a 'well armoured enemy'. The high explosive 4cm round was not as effective as the existing 2cm AP, so, as an alternative the 3.7cm M42 was suggested , as this had an AP round. If this was not possible, then could a 4cm AP round be developed quickly? The answer was no and in any event it is difficult to grasp just who or what this well armoured enemy was. British coastal forces were comprised almost wholly of wooden boats driven by petrol motors - a good target for HE cannon fire. The only minor exception was a group of nine steam gunboats which were very heavily armed but protected only by limited areas of 19mm armour. However, it may well be that these few boats made a greater impression than perhaps they warranted.

The numerous engagements that took place during and after the Allied invasion of Europe in June 1944 led to renewed discussion of S-boat armament during a conference held on 29 September. It was also evident at that time that the forays into Norwegian waters by heavily

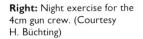

Right: Night exercise for the 4cm gun crew. (Courtesy H. Büchting)

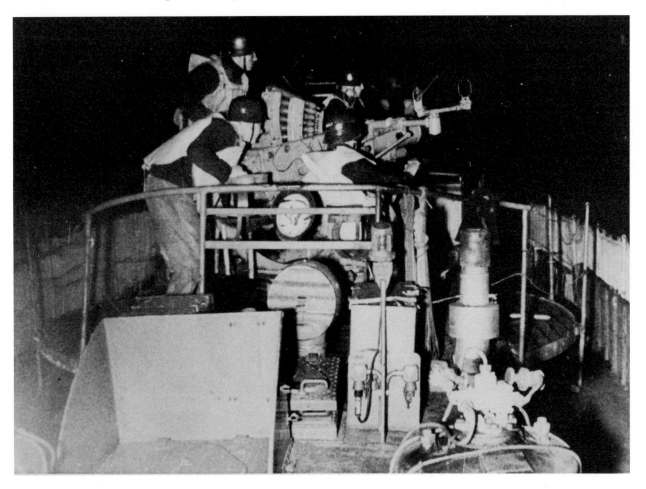

armed Fairmile 'D' boats were becoming a serious threat. The older type S-boats were by now fitted with one 2cm single forward, an LM44 2cm twin amidships with a 4cm aft. New types were to have either a single 2cm or 3cm forward, one twin LM44 amidships and either a 3cm or 3.7cm aft. All boats should have received a 3cm Flak M44 forward, but despite demands for several years no guns had appeared.

Air attack was also becoming a serious menace, so it was proposed that 8.6cm RAG M42 outfits be fitted to S-boats. Flag Officer (S-boats) already had twenty sets and these would be installed.

With the non-appearance of the 3cm gun, armament in late 1944 was as follows :

1 - 2cm C/38 forward (1,000rpg)
2 - 2cm LM44 twin amidships (1,500rpg)
1 - 4cm Flak 28 or 3.7cm (500rpg)
1 - MG151 (1,500rpg)
8 - MG15 (9,000rpg)
1 - RAG M42 (30 R Sprgr 800 and 60 RLg)
30 hand grenades
6 depth charges and two DC rails, or
2 - 65cm TM rails or 2 - 80cm mine rails,
4cm /3.7cm boats - 4 LMB or LMF mines
2cm only boats - 6 LMB or LMF mines, or
alternative loads of BRB(S), UMB, RB, etc.

There were also some local augmentations of armament and several boats ,including S65, received a 2cm vierling aft, first mentioned in July 1944 in the Invasion Front area. There is also mention of a 4cm twin but this is a puzzle because as far as is known none was available to the Kriegsmarine, excepting perhaps the Dutch weapon which was too heavy for S-boats.

The smaller survivors of the S30-S54 series were armed with one 2cm LM44 twin (1,500rpg), one MG151 (1,500rpg), eight MG15s (9,000rpg) and one RAG M42 with 30 R.Sprgr 800 and 60 Rhg. They were not officially fitted for minelaying but carried four scare bombs.

Following the D-Day landings, and the appearance of destroyers and frigates leading hunting groups of MTBs, there came a demand for stern tubes to be fitted to the S-boats. This was presumably intended to deter chases on retirement from action and would not necessarily reduce the boat's offensive power against merchant vessels. FdS however reported that this would not be possible for existing boats and could only be done in the new boats with the MB518 engine. This step was in fact adopted from S701 upwards, but these boats were ordered so late in the war that few ever entered service.

A potentially disturbing development in the S-boats' armoury took place in the autumn of 1942 when boats of the Training Flotilla - S20, S22, and S103 (28/29 August) and S24, S50 and S103 (6/7 October) - took part in poison

Below and opposite page: Two boats of the same flotilla showing the different bridge styles and armaments at different periods. The picture on the opposite page was taken after the surrender. (WZB)

38 ARMAMENT

gas experiments off the island of Bornholm . There is little information available on this trial except the comment that only two consecutive test runs could be made at a time as the test personnel needed time to recover. It was not mentioned just who these persons were.

The main mode of S-boat operation from the type's conception to the final surrender was nocturnal attack. Training and equipment for this role were of vital importance, but while the former was generally maintained to a high standard, it was in the field of equipment where the serious omissions lay, or rather in one specific area - radar. By the outbreak of war in 1939, the general principles of radar were well understood and at that time the Germans were arguably ahead of the British. However, this lead was allowed to slip away for various technical and political reasons. Suffice it to say, that whereas the Royal Navy could rely on radar warning from at least 1941 onwards and could even begin fitting MTBs and coastal forces craft from about 1942, the Kriegsmarine lacked any suitable set for use in small craft. This deficiency was not remedied before the end of hostilities and became a grave handicap to operations. Darkness was no longer a cover and eventually PPI radar displays disclosed every move the S-boats made. The situation was compounded by the introduction of 'Headache' by the British - a code-name for eavesdropping on the short wave R/T sets used by the Kriegsmarine, using German speaking personnel. This further removed the veil over S-boat operations and intentions.

FdS was able to obtain five Luftwaffe FuG202 Lichtenstein B/C night fighter radar sets as 'cast-offs' in the summer of 1942. These were modified and given a new designation, FuM071, or with a rotating aerial FuM072. The first set was fitted in *S112* (5th Flotilla) at the beginning of August, with the other sets going to *S86* (2nd Flotilla), *S87* (4th Flotilla) and one set to a boat of the 6th Flotilla. The fifth set was intended for the 3rd Flotilla in the Mediterranean. One S-boat, possibly *S87*, was fitted experimentally with a radar mast to give increased range, but the size of this aerial rendered the boat highly conspicuous and it is not certain how long it remained aboard.The Lichtenstein apparatus did not achieve the expected performance - i.e., the detection of a destroyer at 10km - and it was hoped that the Hohentweil FuMO 62 would be an improvement; one of these sets was reportedly in a boat by the end of 1943. In the event, there was no large-scale fitment of radar to S-boats despite the fact that one boat had received an experimental Berlin set for trials in February 1944, while in November both *S122* and *S127* of the 3rd S-boat Training Flotilla were running special trials with this equipment out of Swinemunde. This set was a development of the Rotterdam apparatus, operating on a 9cm wavelength, a peak power of 20kW and having a PPI display. Thus radar

remained a rarity in the S-boat flotillas, and apart from the boats mentioned above only *S130* and *S701* are known to have been so fitted.

There was little that the Germans could do to alleviate the absence of radar, other than to fit passive receivers (which detected enemy radar transmissions). The first of these, the crude 'Biscay Cross', had been developed as a result of devastating U-boat losses off western France. A range of such instruments was put into production but U-boats had priority. A few sets became available towards the end of 1942 when *S70*, for example, was one boat so fitted. FuMB 4, Samos, followed this early crude set and an improved version, Naxos I, which became standard, was fitted in *S127* for trials in February 1944. In the Mediterranean, boats were exchanging their Metox sets for Samos as late as June 1944, while even in the important Channel and North Sea areas, by late 1944 only one in three boats per flotilla were scheduled for the fitment of FuMB 9 (Cypern II), FuMB10 (Borkum) or FuMB24 and FuMz6 or FuMz7. In the absence of adequate radar, the S-boats made great use of this passive detection equipment in their operations.

S-boats used Thetis radar decoy buoys both in the Channel and in the Adriatic from 1944 and also Aphrodite balloons for similar purposes. Great ingenuity was exercised in the search for a defence against radar, as exemplified by the 'Netzhemd' (or, in translation, 'String vest'). An early example of 'Stealth' technology, this was anti-radar netting consisting of a steel wire mesh that surrounded the boat from the waterline to the topmost part of the superstructure. It was supported by stanchions that held it about one foot away from the boat's side. Its presence did not apparently inhibit the firing of the boat's guns or torpedoes. *S147* was so fitted for trials while at Travemünde in late December 1943, these being conducted off Pelzerhaken near Neustad between 1 and 15 January 1944.

Seehund infra-red emission detectors, developed as a result of reports that British warships were employing red searchlights (which was believed to be some sort of IR sensor) were also experimented with in the Mediterranean.

Finally, another handicap to fast-moving night action was the fact that the Kriegsmarine never perfected a reliable IFF device, the FuKG experimental equipment having been found unsatisfactory during trials with Mammut radar installations.

Below: *S142* with the positions of the 2cm and 4cm guns clearly shown. (WZB)

4. AT WAR AGAIN: HOME WATERS, 1939-40

The available strength of the S-boat force at the outbreak of war had been reduced by the sale of the decommissioned petrol-engined boats *S1* to *S5* to Spain during the Civil War, although these vessels had in fact been promised to China. The latter country agreed to relinquish the boats and was offered new construction in lieu. *S6* was later also sold to Spain. The transfer to Spain did not proceed smoothly as a report from the German liaison team in El Ferrol on 26 November 1936 shows. The boats had been shipped from the Weser to Spain aboard the Hansa Line's *Uhenfels* but tug crews in Germany were unco-operative, causing delays. When the boats finally arrived it was found that not only had they been badly prepared for the journey, but that some 26 cases of spares were missing. First trials could not be run until the end of November 1936 and the transfer was not facilitated by the fact that the Spanish Navy had drafted stokers and not motor mechanics to the boats. When they eventually entered service they were renamed *Falange*, *Oviedo*, *Requeté*, and *Toledo*. One boat, either *S3* or *S5*, is reported to have been damaged on unloading in Spain and was not commissioned, hence only four names. (The report mentioned above suggests that *S5* ran trials on 26 November 1936 so the damaged boat must have been *S3*, but the dates in Gröner do not agree).

When hostilities with Poland were opened on 1 September 1939, the 1st Flotilla (Kpt.Lt. Sturm) was operating off Kahlberg in company with the destroyer *Leberecht Maass*, stopping and searching merchant vessels for contraband and also being used as fast despatch vessels. *Tsingtau* supported the flotilla which comprised *S19*, *S20*, *S21* and *S23*, all Daimler-Benz boats. The flotilla had moved into a waiting zone towards the end of August in anticipation of the war with Poland, their task being to blockade the Bay of Danzig. Merchant vessels were sent out for them to lie alongside while on station. However, such was the success of the German blitzkrieg that the Polish Navy was destroyed in harbour, or at least that part which had not been previously sent out of the Baltic to England, such as the destroyers. In consequence, the 1st Flotilla was underemployed and was ordered to Sassnitz on 3 September in preparation for a move to the west because of the threat that was now posed by the

declaration of war on Germany by the British and French.

The 2nd Flotilla (Kpt.Lt. Petersen), comprising *S10-S17* and subordinated to Seebefehlshaber West, was hardly fit for operations because most of its boats had MAN engines which had proved a liability in service. It was intended, however, that on formation of the 3rd Flotilla, these old and unreliable boats would be passed on to the new unit for training purposes and the 2nd Flotilla would be re-equipped. For the present, though, the flotilla was saddled with these boats and operated as best it could from Heligoland where its depot ship *Tanga* lay. Apart from the questionable engines, the flotilla's main enemy was in fact the weather, for autumnal storms resulted in damage to several boats.

S17 in particular was so badly damaged by heavy seas, on 4 September, that her keel was fractured and the boat was paid off on 8 September. Her engines were removed for use as spares, the vessel never again becoming operational.

The 2nd Flotilla was replaced in Heligoland by the 1st Flotilla, which arrived at the island on 8 September. This flotilla had no more luck with the weather than did the 2nd, for frequent winter storms interrupted exercises and operations. Boats were sometimes unable to leave the harbour in Heligoland for days. By that time the 1st Flotilla was due for refit (as in peacetime, refits were still done by flotilla not by boat) and ordered to Kiel on 29 November. Kpt.Lt. Birnbacher relieved Sturm on 1 December. At the same time, the 2nd Flotilla, based at Kiel-Wik, also went into dockyard hands, SKL having been requested to transfer it back to the west as no useful tasks remained in the Baltic.

Meanwhile, the staff organization had changed, with the creation of the post of Flag Officer (Destroyers). These vessels now left the control of Flag Officer (Torpedo boats) who henceforth would administer the large Type 23, 24 and 35 torpedo boats, as well as the S-boats. Appointed to this post was Kpt.z.S. Bütow, formerly in command of the Danube Flotilla. Thus ended the first four months of S-boat operations, which cannot have been claimed successful. Poor weather, frequent breakdowns and employment on tasks for which they had not been designed all conspired to leave the impression in certain

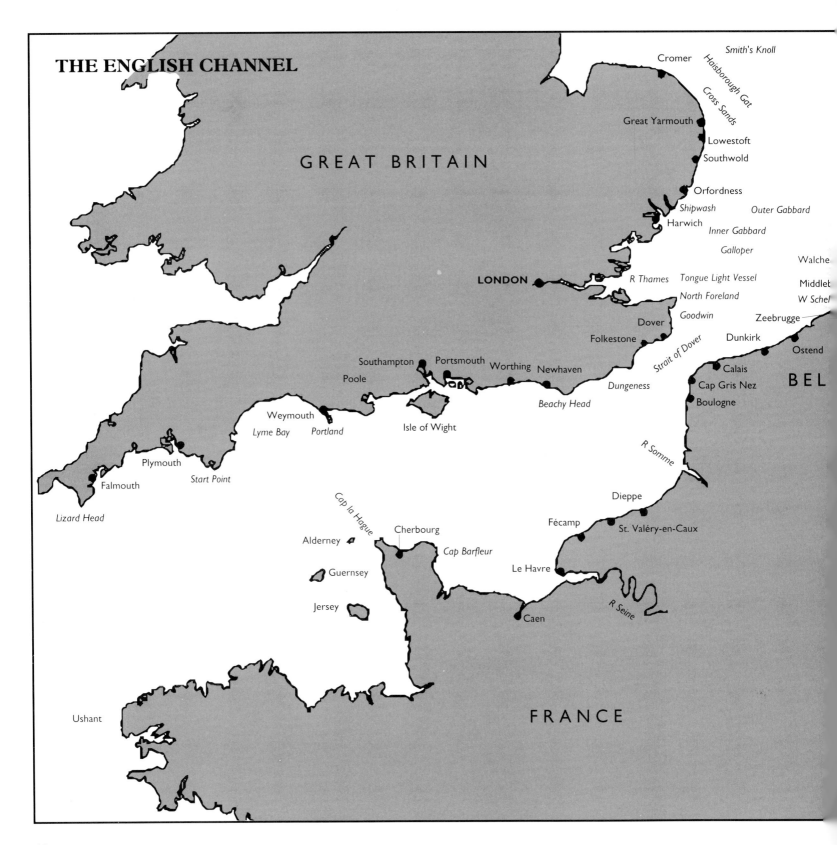

THE ENGLISH CHANNEL

GREAT BRITAIN

Cromer

Smith's Knoll

Haisborough Gat

Cross Sands

Great Yarmouth

Lowestoft

Southwold

Orfordness

Shipwash

Outer Gabbard

Harwich

Inner Gabbard

Galloper

Walche-

LONDON

R Thames

Tongue Light Vessel

Middlet

North Foreland

W Schel

Dover

Goodwin

Zeebrugge

Folkestone

Strait of Dover

Dunkirk

Ostend

Southampton Portsmouth

Worthing Newhaven

Calais

Poole

Dungeness

Cap Gris Nez

BEL

Beachy Head

Boulogne

Weymouth

Lyme Bay *Portland*

Isle of Wight

R Somme

Plymouth

Falmouth *Start Point*

Cap la Hague

Dieppe

Lizard Head

Cherbourg

Fécamp

St. Valéry-en-Caux

Alderney

Cap Barfleur

Guernsey

Le Havre

Jersey

R Seine

Caen

Ushant

FRANCE

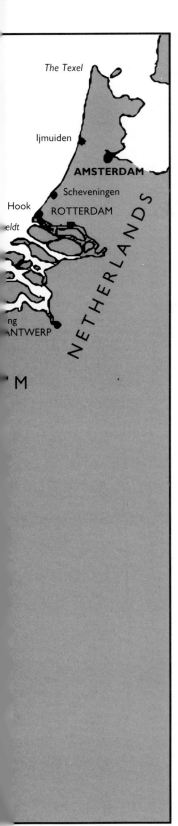

quarters of high command that S-boats were a bad bargain, not capable of fulfilling the tasks for which they had been designed. Fleet Command had originally projected an S-boat force of five or six flotillas, each of eight boats plus two reserves, which made a total of 50 boats. Now the Construction Office required confirmation of this requirement, pointing out the current yard overloading and the manning difficulties, in the face of increasing demands for U-boat construction. It is probable then that the perceived poor performance in the first few months of the war led to the decision to defer construction of further S-boats for the present.

In February 1940 *Tanga* sailed for Wilhelmshaven where, with the assistance of *Hessen* as a makeshift ice-breaker, she arrived on the 19th. This ice however was sufficient to trap her flotilla in Kiel until March. *S9, S14, S15* and *S16* commissioned at Kiel on 12 March and over the next week or so these boats sailed individually to Wilhelmshaven. This flotilla was now a very mixed one, comprising *S30* to *S31*, all new Daimler-Benz boats, and *S14-S16*, older MAN boats, which made for operational problems. Experiments in mine-carrying abilities were conducted with *S14-S16* in March when four to six RMA mines were shipped. It was found that while *S14* suffered a drop in speed of 3kt, her sisters lost only $1\frac{1}{2}$-2kt. However, *S15* rammed *S32* and badly damaged herself, necessitating some three months' repairs.

In Kiel, the 1st Flotilla was continuing its refit and on 10 January was joined by its new depot ship, *Carl Peters*, to which Birnbacher and his staff transferred immediately. The S-boat crews on the other hand remained in *Tsingtau* because the new ship still had her sea trials to finish. The extremely harsh winter of 1939/40 contributed to the delays in the refit programme, as did late delivery of motors from Daimler-Benz and material shortages, so that it was not until March that the refits were finished. In the meantime, on 12 February, *Tsingtau* had been re-rated as a Cadet Training Ship and on 14 March *Carl Peters* sailed for Cuxhaven to work up. Ice prevented her boats from sailing and a request from Birnbacher that they be put into a floating dock and towed to Wilhelmshaven was turned down on the grounds of a shortage of docks. Not until 25 March did the flotilla leave Kiel, reaching Wilhelmshaven on the 26th, where *S18-S24* secured alongside *Carl Peters*. It was intended to bring the flotilla up to a strength of twelve 'long' Mercedes boats as soon as possible. This flotilla was henceforth to refit by boat (i.e., continuously), whereas the 2nd Flotilla would still refit as a flotilla, due to its mixture of equipment.

Leberecht Maass had been withdrawn from FdT early in January 1940, leaving Bütow without a tender, which fact he bemoaned considerably until *F3* re-commissioned on 5 March at his disposal. Unfortunately, she too was withdrawn (on 18 April) and despite a lively correspondence, Bütow failed to get a replacement of sufficient performance to allow him to accompany torpedo boats on operations. He was not impressed by the allocation to him of the elderly *Jagd* and none of the larger torpedo boats were fitted with the necessary accommodation, so FdT and his successor FdS were to remain shore-based to the end of the war.

The forces committed to the invasion of Norway and Denmark (Operation 'Weserübung') included all available S-boats of the 1st and 2nd Flotillas, fourteen boats in all. The 1st Flotilla, *S18-S24*, with *Carl Peters*, were allocated to Group 3 and tasked with the occupation of Bergen under the command of Konteradmiral Schmundt; while the 2nd Flotilla (*S9, S14, S16* and *S30-S33*) with *Tsingtau* were part of Group 4 (Kpt.z.S. Rieve in the cruiser *Karlsruhe*), tasked with securing Kristiansand (S).

The boats of the 1st Flotilla sailed from Heligoland to join Group 3. Only five were operational, *S19, S21-S24*, and of these *S19* and *S21* collided on passage, damaging the former so that she had to be detached, escorted by *Wolf*. At dawn on 9 April, the four remaining boats took on troops from the cruisers *Köln* and *Königsberg* and landed them as ordered, while the cruisers engaged the shore batteries. By midday, the town was secure in German hands. In the weeks that followed, the S-boats were employed in securing the remote villages and settlements in and around Sognefjord and Hardangerfjord, as well as rounding up vessels of the Royal Norwegian Navy, the old torpedo boat *Sael* being sunk on 18 April near Anuglo. However, most of the work was mundane, routine and not what the boats were designed for. Propellers were frequently damaged in the poorly charted waters.

The 2nd Flotilla's participation in the capture of Kristiansand went according to plan and they, together with *Tsingtau* (the latter as a W/T station), remained in southern Norway at the disposal of Admiral (South Norwegian Coast). The S-boats were employed on escort and A/S patrol duties in the Skaggerak and along the Norwegian coast where they found, like the 1st Flotilla, that their design was ill-suited to these duties. They could not proceed slowly enough on two engines, could not steer on one and in consequence the centre engine did all the work and soon ran up the hours. *S9, S14* and *S16* proved particularly unreliable and useless.

By May it had become clear that no British counter-attack was likely against occupied Norway so the S-boats could now be withdrawn to a potentially more profitable theatre since the ground and air offensive in the west had begun. The 2nd Flotilla, previously engaged on escort duties between Stavanger and Wilhelmshaven, were by 9 May 1940 distributed between these two ports, *S30, S32* and *S33* at the latter and *S34* and *S31* in the former.

A chain of circumstances now led to the first success by the S-boats in their designed role. On 9 May the torpedo boat *Möwe*, en route to escort *Scharnhorst* home from Norway, was torpedoed and badly damaged by the submarine HMS *Taku*. In consequence, all available S-boats were sailed from Wilhelmshaven and Stavanger to assist covering both her and *Scharnhorst*. At the same time, a force of minelayers - *Roland*, *Cobra*, *Preussen* and *Kaiser* - escorted by three destroyers and a torpedo boat were engaged on a sortie to 57°N, 3°E. This force had been reported to the British and a squadron comprising the light cruiser *Birmingham* and seven destroyers sailed to intercept it. In turn the British ships had been found by Dornier Do 18 'L' of 2.Staffel, Küstenfliegergruppe 406 and identified as a battleship and six destroyers steaming north about half way between the Firth of Forth and the entrance to the Skaggerak. When received by Group West that evening, the respective positions of the two forces were only 85nm apart and the information was passed to the S-boats. Then at 2025 another report was received - this time from Do 18 'A' of 2./Küflgr. 406 - of three, later corrected to five, destroyers in Q4527. After due consideration of these reports, together with the news that the first group was now steaming east, Admiral Saalwachter ordered the minelayers to abandon their sortie. At the same time, since the S-boats appeared to have the best chance of interception, he ordered Petersen to act as he saw fit. At 1935, *S32* made contact with the British force and she and her consorts, *S31*, *S34* and *S33* were engaged by the destroyers. A confused night action then ensued but at 2333, *S31* (Ob.Lt.z.S. Opdenhoff) fired two torpedoes at a destroyer which turned out to be *Kelly*, claiming two hits. Although not sunk as Opdenhoff believed, *Kelly* was badly damaged, the torpedo which hit having struck No.1 Boiler Room and opened the hull from keel to upper deck. Both boiler rooms flooded but the bulkheads held and with her upper deck awash, *Kelly* was eventually docked on the Tyne after a tow of 91 hours. The action itself continued into the early hours of 10 May, the success slightly marred by the fact that *S33* rammed one of the destroyers, damaging her bows so badly that scuttling arrangements were made. Fortunately it was found that the boat could be saved but she was out of action until August.

The 1st Flotilla was also withdrawn from Bergen in mid-May and moved to Wilhelmshaven in preparation for operations in the southern North Sea.

THE CHANNEL 1940

While the success of *S31* pointed the way to better things, it was the Army's blitzkrieg against the Allies in the west that allowed the S-boats the opportunities they had been waiting for. The overrunning of Holland, followed by the collapse of Belgium and France within a few weeks in the spring of 1940, brought the possibilities of bases for S-boat operations within easy range of British coastal convoy traffic. Bütow claimed to have recognized the importance of such moves as early as December 1939 and forecast that bases at Borkum initially, and later Dutch and Belgian harbours, would provide the necessary support for these S-boat operations. He had been against the employment of S-boats in the invasion itself because he saw their use mainly as being against convoy traffic and wished to spare

their engine hours for just such operations. Group West did not agree and S-boats were to be used on sorties against the Dutch, Belgian and finally French ports. In fact, because of the operations in Norway, no S-boats were used against traffic fleeing from Dutch ports. Not until 19 May was a force available in Borkum, by which time the coast as far as the Scheldt Estuary was in German hands and a golden opportunity had been lost.

The first sortie from Borkum was launched on the afternoon of 20 May 1940, when the 1st Flotilla (*S22*, *S23*, *S24* and *S25*) and *S13*, *S30*, *S31*, *S32* and *S34* of the 2nd Flotilla sailed to attack shipping off Nieuport. Under less than ideal conditions, with a full moon, the flotillas steamed on, surviving concentrated attacks by RAF 'Ansons' (probably Hudsons) en route. Various boats reported torpedo attacks on several different targets, ranging from destroyers to patrol craft and auxiliary cruisers, but no success was actually scored. This was the first war operation by the S-boats in their designed role. In a second sortie by the combined flotillas on 22 May, it was planned that the 1st Flotilla would operate against targets off Calais and Dunkerque, while the 2nd Flotilla would strike against shipping in the Downs. The latter operation was abandoned because of the light night but the 1st Flotilla proceeded with theirs. *S21* and *S23* attacked a steamer each, unsuccessfully, and then saw a destroyer off the starboard bow steaming slowly eastwards. The S-boats stopped and over the short wave radio decided on a combined attack. One of the torpedoes struck this target in the bows, the second amidships but despite this, the destroyer, actually the French *Jaguar*, was not sunk directly. She ran aground, only to be destroyed subsequently by the Luftwaffe.

After this sortie, the boats returned to their new base, Den Helder in Holland, from where the first sortie was mounted on 26 May, with *S25*, *S24*, *S30* and *S13*, although the last was forced to return with engine trouble. En route home, she depth-charged a suspected submarine, erroneously claiming success. According to her report, she saw an oil trail off the entrance to Den Helder and dropped depth charges. She reported three torpedoes fired at her and fired one herself in return without effect. Hammocks and newspapers came to the surface, causing *S13* to believe that she had sunk a Dutch submarine. It is more probable, however, that an older wreck was the source of the debris.

Her flotilla-mates continued their sortie, making attacks on shipping and destroyers off Dunkerque. *S30* claimed a destroyer sunk but this ship, HMS *Vega*, was not hit at all. Many were the erroneous claims of success made by light surface forces, both German and Allied, in the course of confused night actions at close quarters. However, in the early hours of 29 May, during a sortie by *S24*, *S30* and *S36*, the destroyer HMS *Wakeful*, packed with evacuated troops, was torpedoed by *S30*. She broke in two and sank in 15 seconds with very heavy casualties among the many aboard. The 2nd Flotilla, operating off Westhinder, had a small success in the sinking of the 694-ton *Abukir*, but had *S32* damaged by a mine.

On 30 May *S24*, *S30*, *S23* and *S26* sailed from Den Helder just before midday for another sortie to the north of Ruytingen light vessel. *S26* sighted and reported a destroyer which both she and *S23* attacked successfully, sinking the French *Siroco*, again with heavy casualties. *S24* hit another French destroyer, *Cyclone*, blowing off her bows but not sinking her; although her repairs were never completed and the ship was scuttled in Brest upon that port's occupation.

On 1 June 1940, two boats of the 3rd Flotilla arrived at Rotterdam for operations, unknown to FdT. As these boats were *S11* and *S12*, previously withdrawn from service to form a training flotilla, Bütow was not best pleased on hearing of their arrival. They had had machinery breakdowns already on passage, so that their reinforcement was questionable. The first operation, on 3/4 June, was abortive but on 6 June the first attack into the Downs anchorage was planned, in which all three flotillas were to participate. Diversionary air support was requested but failed to materialize. Nine boats sailed, working in three groups, but found targets scarce. Unfortunately, even the few ships found at anchor were missed, for which failure the torpedoes themselves were probably responsible. Further operations on the nights of

9/10 and 10/11 June produced no success either, all the torpedoes being out-manoeuvred, missing or running amok.

SKL was now pressing for operations to be mounted from Boulogne because a good deal of evacuation traffic was still using Le Havre, but Bütow was most reluctant to move until the necessary base facilities were available in Boulogne. Flak defence was inadequate and a torpedo depot needed to be established before such a move could be contemplated. However, he did agree to use the port as a 'jumping off' point until the facilities were available. Thus on 11 June the 2nd Flotilla, comprising *S35*, *S31*, *S34*, *S30* and the new (ex-Bulgarian) *S1*, were ordered to Boulogne by Bütow. They were not expected at that port but extemporized camouflage and berthed in the Loubet Basin. During the afternoon and evening two air raids were made by six and five Fleet Air Arm Skuas respectively. No damage was done to the boats but a number of men were killed, including the CO of *S35*, and several were wounded. The result of this experience was that the boats were ordered back to Rotterdam. Most of the 1st Flotilla (*S21-S25*) was sent on to Wilhelmshaven for engine overhauls, leaving only *S19* and *S26* in Rotterdam, with *S31*, *S35*, *S19* and *S1* of the 2nd Flotilla. By 16 June, however, Bütow could report that twelve heavy and twenty-three, 2cm flak guns plus eight

Right: The French destroyer *Cyclone* explodes after being hit by torpedoes. (Courtesy G. Behrens)

searchlights were in position in Boulogne but that no fighter defences were yet available. Consequently four boats (*S31*, *S35*, *S19* and *S1*) returned to Boulogne that day, having survived an attack by RAF Hudsons en route. The flotillas scored their first success when, on the night of 19/20 June, five boats in two groups attacked the convoy routes off Dungeness and Beachy Head. *S19* and *S26* torpedoed and sank the 3,103-ton *Roseburn* off Dungeness.

On the political front, the most important event yet was the Armistice with France, signed on 21 June. This meant, as far as the Kriegsmarine was concerned, that the whole of the French Channel and Atlantic coastlines were now available to them. Operations continued from Boulogne for the moment and late on 21 June a new sortie was launched by *S19*, *S26*, *S32*, *S31* and *S35* under the command of the 2nd Flotilla. This was a strike against the convoy route south of Dungeness and it led to the first S-boat loss of the war when *S32* struck a drifting mine 30nm west of Boulogne in the early hours of 22 June; it destroyed all of the boat forward of the wheelhouse. The stricken boat foundered with the loss of seven men, including her CO. *S31* and *S35* brought in the survivors, while the other boats carried out a fruitless patrol.

By now, Bütow had laid plans to establish a further base at Cherbourg, in addition to those at Boulogne and Rotterdam. Boats operating from this new base were to attack shipping off the Isle of Wight and as far east as Brighton, the intention being to force the British to so time their convoy sailings that they would pass the Dover Straits in early evening and allow the S-boats operating out of Rotterdam to attack this traffic between the North Goodwins and Smiths Knoll.

In continued operations out of Boulogne, six boats sailed on the night of 23 June, again for the area south-west of Dungeness. These were *S35*, *S36*, *S31*, *S1*, *S19* and *S26*, of which *S36* torpedoed and sank the 3,477-ton *Albuera* and *S19* the 276-ton *Kingfisher*. Cherbourg was opened for use and on the night of 27 June the 1st Flotilla was transferred there, arriving the following morning. The situation in Cherbourg was not ideal as yet, for the crews' quarters were some distance away in Urville, whence it was necessary to ferry them to and fro by car. The 1st Flotilla was chosen for this because of their higher speed; a considerable amount of daylight running would be necessary from this base.

The bases at Cherbourg and Boulogne were complete with a torpedo servicing depot, W/T station and base personnel, but at Rotterdam only the torpedo servicing depot was ready. This base was also used as a transit station for boats sailing west from Germany, because as yet there were insufficient boats to operate from three main bases. Bütow commanded operations at Cherbourg and his staff officer at Boulogne. Flag Officer Torpedo boats was fully aware of the need for good reconnaissance in the successful pursuance of S-boat operations. Some intelligence could be gleaned via the B Dienst and coastal radar stations but co-operation with the Luftwaffe was vital. To this end he sought good liaison between his forces and General Sperrle's VIII Fliegerkorps.

1ST FLOTILLA AT CHERBOURG

The first operation was launched on the night of 29 June by *S24*, *S26* and *S19* into the area to the west of the Isle of Wight. Nothing was sighted but on the return journey, a steamer was attacked and missed by *six* torpedoes, off St. Catherine's point. Actually there were at least two ships present, of which *Clan Ogilvy* (979 tons) and *Helder* (979 tons) were damaged in a brief exchange of gunfire. No attempt was made to finish off the merchantmen, which drew criticism from Bütow later. The 1st Flotilla operations continued with an attack on the night of 4/5 July against the remnants of convoy OA178, from which several ships had already been sunk by Junkers Ju 87 dive-bombers of St.G.2 south of Portland. Four boats (*S24*, *S20*, *S19* and *S26*) sailed from Cherbourg for the attack, making contact with enemy shipping a couple of minutes after midnight. Working in pairs ('Rotte'), *S24/S20* and *S19/S26* attacked several vessels in the darkness. *S24* (carrying only two torpedoes) missed her target, *S20* had two misses against a tanker then reloaded and made single torpedo attacks on two separate ships, claiming both sunk. *S26* fired torpedoes against a tanker and a merchant ship, claiming both sunk. *S19* was driven off by the escort. Actual loss and damage incurred that night were: *Elmcrest* (4,343 tons) sunk, *British Corporal* (6,972 tons) and *Hartlepool* (5,500tons) damaged; *S20* was also damaged.

A follow up operation on the night of 5/6 July by the same four boats was aimed at a crippled ship under tow, reported 30 miles north of Cherbourg, escorted by a cruiser and two destroyers. This force was not located but *S19* claimed the sinking of a loaded 6,000-ton steamer off the Isle of Wight, the identity of which cannot be confirmed. However, during subsequent operations, *S36* sank the armed trawler *Cayton Wyke* off Dover on 8 July and *S26* sank the General Steam Navigation's diminutive *Mallard* (352 tons) on the night of 10/11 July. A tragic incident occurred on the night of 24/25 July, when four boats sailed for a strike, *S19/S27* south west of Portland Bill and *S26/S20* east of the Isle of Wight. Shortly before midnight *S19* sighted a large merchant vessel steaming west with her navigation lights on. Her torpedoes missed, as did three of the four fired by *S27*. The one which did hit was a surface runner and it struck the merchantman towards the stern, whereupon she slowly sank. Unfortunately, this ship was the 6,127 ton *Meknès*, carrying some 1,100 French officers and men being repatriated to France. By some oversight, her sailing had not been reported and as a result of her sinking, some four hundred men were lost.

The flotilla's next sortie was made on the night of 25/26 July, when three boats, *S19*, *S20* and *S27*, sailed to attack convoy CW8. This had already suffered from the attention of the Luftwaffe, which had sunk five out of the convoy's 21 ships. The S-boats made contact with the convoy off Brighton and, in the course of their attacks, claimed three ships totalling 29,000 tons sunk, one 5,000-ton ship capsized while avoiding torpedoes and another of 2,000 tons set on fire. The reality was a little different, for once again the tonnage of the ships in question were greatly overestimated; for the three vessels actually sunk were *Broadhurst* (1,013 tons), *London Trader* (646 tons) and *Lulonga* (821 tons).

Further sorties by the flotilla during the remainder of July were fruitless, despite close co-operation with Luftwaffe reconnaissance aircraft, because the heavy losses sustained by CW8 forced the Admiralty to suspend further convoys for the present. When they were restarted, their cover was to be a combined naval/air operation and barrage balloon defences were provided for the ships themselves. Furthermore, the convoys were reduced in size from about 25 ships to twelve, while the new 'Hunt'-class destroyers began to be allocated to the escort. Thus in August, following an unsuccessful sortie to the Isle of Wight, four boats (*S20*, *S21*, *S25* and *S27*), attacked convoy CW9 off Newhaven, the first west-bound convoy since the new arrangements had come into effect. Its opposite number, CE8 from Falmouth, had passed unscathed, sailing mostly at night, but CW9 was not so lucky. Despite intentions, this was a large group of ships, 25 in fact, when it passed Dover. Off Newhaven it lost two ships to the torpedoes of the 1st Flotilla - *Holme Force* of 1,216 tons and *Fife Coast*, 367 tons. In addition, *Ouse* (1,004 tons) sank as a result of a collision while avoiding torpedoes and two others, *Polly M* (380 tons) and *John M* (500 tons), were damaged by gunfire. Fifty per cent of the attacker's torpedoes missed however.

Operations now became affected by the major Luftwaffe bombing offensive against Britain, for Group West ordered that air-sea rescue operations had to take precedence during major air raids. In the event the raids were scaled down and spread over longer periods with smaller forces, so that the S-boats were able to continue their offensive at the same time. No success was achieved, however, and by mid-August it was planned to move the flotilla's base to Rotterdam as soon as *Tsingtau* arrived for use as a depot ship. Until that time, minelaying sorties were to be carried out from either Cherbourg or Boulogne. The first such operation from Boulogne on 20 August had to be abandoned because of heavy seas, but a second on 25 August was carried through when six boats mined the Spithead area. Unfortunately, this was ineffective because the mine delay clocks had not been set. On the following day, the flotilla was ordered to join *Tsingtau* at Rotterdam and arrived there without incident. *Tsingtau*, however, had only 24 torpedoes available. Two more boats, *S22* and *S19*, were en route from Cuxhaven to join the flotilla at Rotterdam but *S19* struck a mine and was badly damaged at the stern. Fortunately she could be towed into Calais but required full repairs in Germany.

Initial operations from the new base were fruitless, but on the evening of 4 September five boats sailed on a sortie to the north-west of Smiths Knoll, where experience had shown that convoy traffic could be expected at night. This was an accurate estimation for the four boats which reached the east coast (*S25* having returned early with engine problems) did encounter a convoy, from which they sank: *Corbrook* (1,729 tons) and *New Lamton* (2,709 tons) by *S21*; *Joseph Swan* (1,571 tons) and *Newland* (1,075 tons) by *S18*; and *Fulham V* (1,562 tons) by *S22*. In addition, *S54* torpedoed and damaged *Ewell* (1,350 tons), which was recorded as an 'I'-class destroyer. Even if this bag was nowhere near the 39,000 tons claimed, it was nevertheless a significant success for the flotilla, which returned to Cherbourg shortly after the sortie. Subsequent operations proved unsuccessful, including one against Plymouth on 25/26 September in conjunction with a Stuka attack on the dockyard.

By this time, experience had demonstrated the value of the high forecastle in improving seaworthiness and as the 1st Flotilla was the most experienced, Bütow proposed fully to re-equip the flotilla with this type at the expense of the 4th Flotilla which would receive the 1st Flotilla's cast-offs. Even so, the poor winter weather had greatly affected the boats' operational chances and many sorties were abandoned because of it. On 10 October the flotilla was ordered to Rotterdam where *Carl Peters* was to join it as a depot ship while *Tsingtau* was to be withdrawn to the Baltic to support the 4th Flotilla. After delays because of poor weather, the 1st Flotilla arrived in Rotterdam late on 14 October, from where their first sortie by six boats was launched on 15/16 October, against a convoy off Lowestoft. As a result of the lightness of the night however, this attack was easily detected and the boats were driven off, but a later sortie on 17/18 October was more successful. In this attack, by *S27*, *S18* and *S24*, north-east of Cromer, *Hauxley* (1,361 tons) was sunk and *PLM14* (3,754 tons) and *Gasfire* (2,972 tons) damaged. Again the tonnage claimed, 33,000 tons, greatly exceeded fact. *S28* and *S20* operating as a second group to the south failed to make contact with the enemy. This was the last success achieved by the flotilla in the North Sea theatre, for on 26 October it was ordered back to Germany with *Carl Peters*.

2ND FLOTILLA AT OSTEND

After a small success on 8 July, when the armed trawler *Cayton Wyke* (550 tons) was sunk by *S34* and *S36* off Dover, the 2nd Flotilla began a concentrated period of minelaying against the Thames Estuary. The first sortie took place on 10/11 July when the gap between the North and South Falls was mined. Seven boats participated, of which three carried mines (4 EMCs each), two explosive floats (12 each) and the remainder acted as escort. On the following night, however, in the course of a sortie against a convoy reported off Smiths Knoll, *S23* struck a mine, losing 8 metres from her stern. She was taken in tow and

the operation abandoned but the stricken boat foundered four hours later north of Ruytingen shoal. Bütow later criticized the abandoning of the operation, maintaining that only two boats should have stood by the casualty and the remainder should have continued. In all, between 10 July and 7 August, the 2nd Flotilla conducted eleven minelaying sorties, laying a total of 130 mines, over half of which were elderly ex-Polish MO8 units. Laying areas included Shipwash, Galloper, Kentish Knock and Gabbard, as well as off Orfordness and Aldeburgh.

On 8 August K.Kpt. Petersen travelled to Paris where he received his Ritterkreuz, awarded for his flotilla's performance in the war effort. A week later the torpedo depot at Ostend blew up in a spectacular explosion, as forty-two torpedoes and a dozen depth-charges detonated. The depot was all but destroyed and three boats, *S31*, *S24* and *S35*, were badly damaged with *S37* less so. Sabotage was suspected but never proved. The damaged boats were all made fit for return to Germany over the next few days, where full repairs were to be carried out. To replace the damaged craft, *S33*, *S36*, *S37* and *S55* sailed from Wilhelmshaven on 1 September bound for Ostend and *S201*, the first ex-Dutch boat, was accepted at Gusto, Schiedam, on 20 August. The new boats began torpedo sorties almost immediately but their only success was the

sinking of the Dutch *Stad Almaer* (5,750 tons) from the south bound convoy FS273 off Lowestoft on the night of 6/7 September. *S33* was the boat responsible.

Misfortune struck again, however, when on 7 September, after the boats had returned to Ostend following their success against FS273, an RAF air raid left *S36* badly damaged by splinters while *S33* and *S37* were also damaged. Now the flotilla had only *S55* operational. Bütow expected that the British would now launch operations to blockade both Calais and Boulogne and sent what boats were available out to defend these ports (Calais was in fact bombarded by the monitor HMS *Erebus* on 30 September). The forces available amounted only to *S33*, *S54* and *S55*, which ran into three destroyers approaching Boulogne. In a confused close quarters engagement, *S55* was badly shot up but the boats thwarted a bombardment of Boulogne.

On 10 September the 3rd Flotilla arrived at Vlissingen (Flushing) with *Adolph Lüderitz*, *S1*, *S10*, *S11* and *S13*. During an air raid on that port the next day all except *S11* and *S13* were damaged, so these two boats were temporarily attached to the 2nd Flotilla.

Operations against the East Coast Convoy routes were not particularly fruitful and in September the 2nd Flotilla only managed to sink the diminutive *Continental Coaster*

(555 tons) on the 24th, the successful boat being *S30*. Once again the escort managed to drive off the attackers with relative ease, as the night was quite light. Further minelaying sorties continued and in the course of one on 11/12 October by six boats, with Bütow embarked in *S36*, *S37* steaming third in line off the Nord Hinder struck a mine. The explosion, under the radio office, blew the boat in two, killing her CO, Ob.Lt.z.S. Schultze-Jena, and a dozen of his crew. Bütow considered it possible that the British had deduced the S-boats' approach routes to the east coast and taken appropriate counter-measures by laying mines to catch shallow draft vessels. Minelaying was in fact the main preoccupation of the Skl at that time, for an increase in such operations was ordered. The target area was defined as 52°10′ N (i.e., Aldeburgh, northern limit), the British declared mine area as the eastern, 51°25′ N (i.e., North Foreland) as the southern limit and bounded to the west by 1°40′E. The latter limit was not to be crossed during torpedo sorties. Minelaying sorties were begun by the 2nd Flotilla on 15 October, although in fact the first fell victim to bad weather. Later, mines were laid in the vicinity of Galloper Bank in two operations.

The employment of the S-boat flotillas at that time was the subject of some discussion between SKL, Flottenkommando, Group West and Flag Officer - Torpedo boats. The capabilities and limitations of the boats were not fully appreciated in higher circles, so much so, that Bütow had to travel to Berlin personally to enlighten the high command. Flottenkommando considered that S-boats were basically unsuited to long range operations and minelaying, believing that their true use was strikes against British Channel convoy traffic. Group West generally agreed, but pointed out that S-boats were in fact the only way of mining the shallow waters of the Thames Estuary. Aircraft could also be used but they were few in number and the only available type then was the Heinkel He 115 Seaplane which could carry but one LMA or two LMB mines. Bütow also pointed out that the withdrawal of the 1st Flotilla had had a major effect on operations for the 3rd Flotilla, which comprised only a few older and unreliable boats no longer suited to front-line operations. In fact, with the departure of the 1st Flotilla to Bergen, the dispositions of the remaining boats on 1 November was:

2nd Flotilla (5 boats)	based at Ostend
3rd Flotilla (2 boats)	based at Rotterdam

Some light appeared on the horizon however, for on 13 November the first of the war-construction programme boats, *S38*, arrived at Rotterdam. She was soon despatched on operations when three boats of the 3rd Flotilla (*S54*, *S57* and *S38*) put out from Rotterdam and six boats (*S34*, *S30*, *S33*, *S36*, *S55* and *S56*) of the 2nd Flotilla from Ostend to ambush convoy traffic off East Anglia on the evening of 19 November. The 2nd Flotilla's operation was thwarted by fog and the 3rd Flotilla ran into

a destroyer patrol consisting of *Campbell* and *Garth* off Southwold. In this engagement the unfortunate new *S38* was sunk by the destroyers.

A shortage of operational boats continued to plague Bütow, while the autumnal weather frequently affected such operations as could be launched. As a result, it was decided to attack with all available boats when the next favourable opportunity arose, at the expense of a second attack the following night. As far as the enemy was concerned, convoys were now more heavily escorted, with destroyers being especially keen, but no specific anti-S-boat tactics could yet be discerned. Some reinforcement arrived in mid-December when *Carl Peters* and four boats of the 1st Flotilla arrived back at Rotterdam where there were now eight boats (1st and 3rd Flotillas) with three boats of the 2nd Flotilla at Ostend.

Operations in December bore little fruit, the only success being the sinking of the 2,301 ton Danish vessel *N.C. Monkberg* east of Yarmouth by *S58* on 15 December. On the 21st an air attack on Ostend resulted in three boats of the 2nd Flotilla being damaged, one seriously. Finally, on the night of 23/24 December it was possible to launch a massed attack against the East Coast Convoy traffic. At 1530/23, the 3rd Flotilla sailed from Rotterdam with *S59*, *S54*, *S58* and *S57* followed half-an-hour later by the 1st Flotilla (*S27*, *S26*, *S101*, *S28* and *S29*) and another half-an-hour later the 2nd Flotilla put out from Ostend with two boats, *S34* and *S56*. No specific target had been sighted but after the boats had sailed, Bütow signalled that a seven-ship convoy with one destroyer escort was thought to be north bound but no position was available - not especially useful intelligence. However, at 2150, *S28* found and reported a convoy but most of her signal was corrupt. In the attack which followed, *S26* and *S29* missed with their torpedoes, *S59* sank the Dutch freighter *Stad Maastricht* (6,552 tons) and *S28* the trawler *Pelton* (358 tons). Several boats made no attack and in the course of the sortie *S28* rammed *S29*, damaging the latter badly. It proved a poor return for such a large operation, the final one of 1940. At that time the forces available were pitifully small, for the operational strength was limited to two boats of the 1st Flotilla at Rotterdam, two of the 2nd Flotilla at Ostend and four boats of the 3rd Flotilla at Boulogne/Ostend - eight in all.

The Royal Navy's light forces opposing them across the water were, in the Nore Command, the 1st MTB Flotilla (*MTB14* and *MTB18*); 4th MTB Flotilla (*MTBs 22, 29, 30, 31, 32* and *34*) and 10th Flotilla (*MTBs 67, 68, 104* and *107*); while at Dover was stationed the 11th MTB Flotilla (*MTBs 5, 69, 70* and *72*). A far greater threat to the S-boats, however, were the destroyers of the 16th Flotilla at Harwich (*Cotswold, Eglinton, Exmoor, Quorn* and *Southdown*) as well as those of the 21st Flotilla at Sheerness (*Cattistock, Garth, Holderness, Pytchley, Hambledon* and *Mendip*). There were also a number of 'V & W'-class destroyers, '*Kingfisher*'- class sloops and many auxiliary escorts.

5. THE CHANNEL, 1941

By the end of the first week of January 1941, operational strength at the forward bases had improved somewhat, with a total of twelve boats from the three flotillas sailing on a sortie on 11 January. It was thwarted by fog. A second sortie by the combined flotillas on 16 January was no more successful because of the prevailing weather conditions. The problem of good intelligence remained acute for reports from the coastal radar stations were distrusted. However, good relations existed with Fliegerkorps II and effective co-operation was arranged with the long-range reconnaissance Staffel 1.(F)/122, which was to shadow convoys after dark and transmit radio bearings on the S-boat net. Major successes continued to be elusive. No ships were sunk in January and the following month only the 501-ton *Angularity* fell victim to a sortie by four boats of the 2nd Flotilla to the east coast convoy route on 6 February. Her survivors, of which two were picked up by the Germans, disclosed a number of details about the way the convoys were composed and routed. In a later sortie on 18/19 February by twelve boats of the three flotillas off Great Yarmouth, the 1st Flotilla (*S28*, *S101* and *S102*) claimed two ships of 6,000 and 4,000 tons sunk, but in fact the only loss was *Algarve* (1,355 tons). A total of fifteen boats, the largest sortie yet, sailed on 25 February for positions off Cromer, Great Yarmouth and Lowestoft. This resulted in the sinking of the 'Hunt'-class destroyer *Exmoor* by *S30* from the north-bound FN417 and the 1,123-ton *Minorca* by *S28* on 26 February.

Operations continued to be concentrated against the east coast traffic, with the 1st Flotilla of seven boats being based at Ijmuiden, the 2nd of four boats at Ostend and the 3rd Flotilla of six boats at Rotterdam. The formation of new flotillas continued, a 4th Flotilla having been raised on 1 October 1940 and the 6th Flotilla officially on 1 March, but neither of these had yet reached operational status.

The first fruits of the Luftwaffe co-operation came on 7/8 March when, as a result of shadowing reports, a force of seventeen boats was sailed to attack convoys off Cromer and Southwold. Boats involved were: 1st Flotilla (*S26*, *S27*, *S28*, *S29*, *S39*, *S101* and *S102*); 2nd Flotilla and 3rd Flotilla (*S31*, *S57*, *S59*, *S60* and *S61*). Sinking claims amounted to nine merchantmen (30,000 tons+) and two destroyers. Actual results were lower but nevertheless substantial, amounting to *Dotterell* (1,385 tons), *Corduff* (2,345 tons), *Rye* (1,048 tons), *Togston* (1,547 tons) and *Norman Queen* (957 tons) by the 1st Flotilla and *Kenton* (1,047 tons) and *Boulderpool* (4,805 tons) by the 3rd Flotilla. In all, a total of 13,134 tons was sunk - a success which Bütow unhesitatingly ascribed to good co-operation with the Luftwaffe. A subsequent sortie by the combined flotillas with sixteen boats on 9/10 March was driven off by the escorts.

Bütow varied his tactics to keep the British guessing. He now decided to make the next strike using only the 1st Flotilla, the object being to prevent the enemy making use of the fact that massed attacks were only possible on alternate nights. In this sortie on 11/12 March, six boats sailed of which *S28* torpedoed and sank the 5,257-ton *Trevethoe* off Orfordness, although believing it to be a destroyer.

The combined flotillas sortied once more with sixteen boats on 14/15 March, despite bright moonlight, just to make the British insecure in these conditions, but the S-boats were driven off by the escort. In a further change of tactics, Bütow now launched a strike to the Humber light-vessel in order to stretch the Royal Navy's defences northwards. Six boats of the 1st Flotilla (*S26*, *S29*, *S39*, *S55*, *S101* and *S102*) sailed for the Humber while the 2nd Flotilla with four boats sailed for the convoy routes, on the night of 17/18 March. Bright moonlight and communications failures prevented major success but two vessels totalling 10,000 tons were claimed by the 1st Flotilla. The 2nd Flotilla was repulsed by the escorts. The only actual success was the sinking of the French *Daphne II* (1,970 tons) by *S102*. Subsequent attacks during the month were driven off by intense destroyer counter-attacks and on several occasions the boats' C.O.s claimed radar-directed gunfire as being responsible. Bütow however did not believe that escorts had radar, choosing instead to attribute their accuracy to hydrophone plots.

Possibly as a result of disappointing returns from torpedo attacks in the recent period, it was now proposed to recommence minelaying operations against the south-east coast of England, using TMA and TMB mines.

Because these mines were ineffective in depths over 11 fathoms, the areas selected for mining were: Cross Sand, the banks between Haisborough Sand and Smiths Knoll, the coast between Cromer and Blankney, as well as the fairway between Sheringham and the Outer Dowsing. Most of these areas were not actually on the convoy routes but it was hoped that these operations would force convoy traffic onto the outer routes. A mixture of mine types, firing mechanisms and delays would be employed to make sweeping a difficult task. A period of poor weather set in so the first operation could not be mounted until 16 April, when eight boats of the 1st Flotilla laid 42 mines between Cromer and Blankeney, four boats from the 2nd Flotilla laid 26 mines on Cross Sand and six boats of the 3rd Flotilla laid 32 TMB mines between Haisborough Sand and Smiths Knoll. After minelaying, the 2nd Flotilla attacked a south bound convoy with torpedoes, claiming three ships (10,000 tons) sunk and one 3,000-ton ship damaged. They escaped a concerted counter-attack by destroyers and aircraft without damage. In an engagement with MTBs however, the 3rd Flotilla had *S58* damaged. Actual successes amounted to *Effra* (1,446 tons) and *Nereus* (1,298 tons) sunk with *Ethel Radcliffe* (5,673 tons) damaged; she was later sunk by aircraft on 16 May. All these were victims of the 2nd Flotilla. In a further operation on 28/29 April, seven boats of the 1st Flotilla intended to mine the area north of Cromer but only one could do so as destroyer patrols and escorts drove them off. In a second attack, *Ambrose Fleming* (1,555 tons) was torpedoed and sunk by *S29*. The 2nd Flotilla was also prevented from reaching its main objective and laid mines east of Yarmouth instead. The 3rd Flotilla laid their mines in the Thames Estuary but encountered some of the MGBs of the newly formed 6th MGB Flotilla, which had recently arrived at Felixstowe. These were converted MA/SBs and were intended to counter the S-boat menace. Two boats on patrol off Brown Ridge buoy fought an inconclusive action for 25 minutes as they pursued the retiring S-boats. It was the first encounter between MGBs and the elusive S-boats.

By the beginning of May weather conditions were once again affecting operations, as were mechanical problems, for many boats were overdue for refits or replacement engines. Only four boats of the 2nd Flotilla and two of the 3rd Flotilla were operational. No sorties were possible during the first half of May.

Greater events now had a critical effect on North Sea operations, for on 17 May Bütow and his staff transferred their headquarters to Swinemünde. Ostensibly this was to supervise the refit and work-up of the flotillas being transferred to the Baltic for overhaul, but in reality it was in preparation for the invasion of Russia, Operation 'Barbarossa'. All three western flotillas were earmarked to participate in the invasion, while the 4th Flotilla (Kpt.Lt. Bätge) had been ordered to the North Sea to cover their withdrawal. By 1 June five boats (*S19*, *S20*, *S22*, *S24* and *S25*) lay at Rotterdam ready for operations, the first torpedo sortie being launched on 3 June, when all five sailed for a position off the Wash. One ship of 6,000 tons was claimed sunk but this remains unidentified.

The 4th Flotilla was now employed mainly on minelaying operations and during the course of one on 20/21 June, *S22*, *S24* and *S20* were hotly engaged by boats of the 6th MGB Flotilla off Brown Bank and on the way home. This action demonstrated both the unreliability of the German 2cm MgC/30 and the disadvantage of the British MGBs' 20mm gun being sited aft where it was useless in a chase. In consequence, another inconclusive action resulted. The German boats also used depth charges for the first time as a deterrent. This was the last North Sea operation for some time as Group West had decided to transfer the 4th Flotilla to Cherbourg for offensive operations in the Channel and as a defence against possible British landings on the French coast in the wake of the invasion of Russia. This transfer duly took place when the flotilla arrived at Cherbourg on 25 June.

4TH FLOTILLA OPERATIONS JULY TO DECEMBER 1941

The initial task of the 4th Flotilla was minelaying and on three consecutive nights starting on 6 July, small fields of 18, 24 and 16 TMA mines were laid off Durston Head, the Isle of Wight and Portland Bill respectively. On the last two nights, coastal batteries engaged the S-boats without effect but the lays had obviously not gone unnoticed, which minimized their effectiveness. Torpedo operations were thwarted by the absence of targets; five special air reconnaissance patrols in the area between Portland Bill and the Isle of Wight had detected no enemy ships. Because TMA mines had to be laid in shallow waters, with the consequent need to approach close inshore, sorties were being detected by the British quite easily. Bütow therefore decided that the use of aerial mines might be more profitable. These mines could be laid in up to 20 metres of water. Moreover, the Straits of Dover/Dungeness appeared a more attractive mining area because of the greater concentration of shipping. Nevertheless, during the remainder of July, five more minelaying sorties were carried out using TMA mines between Portland and the Isle of Wight. On several occasions, the boats were again engaged by coastal batteries and on two of these destroyers also attacked the S-boats. British defensive measures were noted as increasing. Bütow also believed that the British were able to D/F the boats' VHF radio transmissions from ashore, but was not certain whether this could be done aboard ships. Radio silence was ordered but radio had to be used to direct torpedo attacks and minelaying.

As the central Channel area had so far proved fruitless, the flotilla was transferred to Boulogne, where four boats arrived on 1 August. There it was intended to attack the convoy routes once more, in co-operation with intelligence from Luftwaffe coastal radar stations. The first attack took place on 6 August when four boats attacked a convoy south-east of Hastings, claiming hits on a large steamer which sank off Folkestone, but the full moon made attack conditions difficult. No success was actually achieved by the attackers. In a later attack on the night of 10/11 August, three boats attacked a convoy off Dover, claiming the sinking of two ships totalling 10,000 tons, but the sole success was the 1,548-ton *Sir Russell*, torpedoed and sunk by *S49*. Targets in the Dover area now became sparse and as a result of five consecutive nights without convoy traffic being reported, the flotilla was ordered to Rotterdam. *S48*, *S49*, *S20* and *S51* transferred to the new base on 16 August, while *S50* and *S107* went to Schiedam for overhaul at the Wilton yard.

The four available boats attacked convoy FN507 on the night of 19/20 August, when *S48* sank the Polish *Czentochowa* (1,971 tons) and damaged the tanker *Dalewood* (9,274 tons). *S49* and *S20* encountered a destroyer but their torpedoes missed. Later sorties produced no results, lack of air reconnaissance being blamed for these fruitless journeys. In future two TMA mines were to be carried by each boat so that the sorties would not be completely wasted. On 6/7 September six boats sailed to attack a south-bound convoy reported by aircraft, expected to be off Haisborough between 0200 and 0300/7. One boat dropped out due to engine problems and the remainder (*S48*, *S49*, *S50*, *S52* and *S107*) were diverted to attack a north-bound convoy detected by the

German radio intelligence service, off the Cross Sands. This was duly attacked, claims being made for three ships of 7,500 tons sunk and two others of 3,000 tons hit but not seen to sink. Actual losses were *Duncarron* (478 tons) and *Eikhaug* (1,436 tons).

The policy of shipping a few mines on sorties paid off. For example, after a sortie on 9/10 September, the 8,290-ton tanker *Pontfield* was damaged by one such mine. Torpedo successes remained sporadic, although *Teddington* (4,762 tons) was sunk and *Tetela* (5,389 tons) damaged during an attack on a convoy off Cromer on 16/17 September. All subsequent sorties during September were fruitless, either sighting nothing or being driven off by escorting destroyers. On 3/4 October *S107* was damaged during an RAF air raid on Rotterdam and *S51* and *S52* received splinter damage. Reinforcements in the shape of four boats of the 2nd Flotilla arrived at Rotterdam on 5 October as the focus of S-boat operations moved once more to the western theatre, following the end of the first phase of the naval war in the Baltic.

THE NEW OFFENSIVE BEGINS

By the second week of October Bütow had shifted his H.Q. to Scheveningen, under the command of Group West. In Rotterdam he had available the 2nd Flotilla (six boats) and the 4th Flotilla (three boats) while more boats were expected during the month. This base was chosen because the shelter at Ijmuiden was not yet complete. That in Rotterdam could accommodate sixteen boats. The task was to attack convoys off the south-east coast of Britain with torpedoes and to mine the various east coast convoy routes and focal points for shipping. Of the other flotillas, the 1st remained in the Gulf of Finland for the present, the 3rd was preparing to move to the Mediterranean, the 5th was working up in the Baltic and the 6th was employed with BSO in the Skaggerak.

For the minelaying offensive, LMB mines were now available and would be laid mixed with TMA mines. The use of EMA, EMC and EMD types had been forbidden by SKL on stability grounds. Nevertheless, even with the other types, full loads could only be used in favourable weather conditions to avoid overstressing hulls and engines. The maximum load was to be six TMA, TMB or LMB mines. It was with the torpedo, however, that the first success of the new offensive was achieved, by boats of the 2nd Flotilla. Six boats (*S41*, *S47*, *S53*, *S62*, *S104* and *S105*) attacked a convoy north of Cromer in two groups on 12/13 October, sinking *Chevington* (1,537 tons) and *Roy* (1,768 tons). However, the build-up of forces in the North Sea, already affected by the need to transfer boats to the Mediterranean now became influenced by events in the Arctic. There on the front line around the Finnish-Soviet border the German and Finnish advance towards Murmansk had become bogged down and the light forces of the Red Fleet were beginning to attack German convoys around North Cape. These were of vital importance in view of the paucity of road communications in the area. Destroyers had been sent to the area (6th Flotilla) at the start of 'Barbarossa' but had not proved particularly effective. Now Hitler ordered an S-boat flotilla to be sent as well as a new destroyer flotilla (the 8th). The directive regarding the S-boats was received by Bütow on 18 October from SKL, who ordered the transfer of four refitted craft of the 2nd Flotilla together with the depot ship *Adolph Lüderitz*. These refitted craft were to form the new 8th Flotilla (K.Kpt. Petersen) while the rest of the 2nd Flotilla would remain in the west.

At the end of October preparations were begun to base two flotillas on Cherbourg, but for the present the 2nd and 4th Flotillas still operated from Rotterdam. On 19/20 November both flotillas operated off the east coast, the 4th (five boats) off Sheringham, the 2nd (six boats) north of Cromer. The latter flotilla successfully attacked a convoy, sinking *War Mehtar* (5,502 tons, by *S104*), *Aruba* (1,159 tons, by *S105*) and *Waldinge* (2,462 tons, by *S41*). Due to a signalling error, *S41* and *S47* collided and were so badly damaged that *S41* had to be underslung to prevent her sinking and *S47* had to be towed. While making their way home the group of cripples was attacked by MGBs of Lieutenant-Commander Hitchen's 6th Flotilla which had sailed on receipt of information that S-boats were active that night. Three boats sailed, but one broke down and one of the other two had engine trouble, so they lay in wait for the returning enemy west of the Hook of Holland. In the brisk close-quarters action, *S41* was cast away and abandoned while the remainder of the German boats disengaged from the two MGBs (*MGB 63* and *MGB 64*). Derelict and adrift, *S41* was later chanced upon by the MGBs who boarded her in the hope of towing her in. This proved impossible as she was foundering and after removing as much as possible from her, she was left to sink. In their report, the 2nd Flotilla estimated some fourteen MGBs present. All the German boats had been damaged by gunfire, especially in the tanks which were time-consuming to repair.

This action left the 4th Flotilla to conduct the offensive alone for a while and on 23/24 November they attacked convoy FS654 east of Orford Ness, when their torpedoes accounted for *Virgilia* (5,723 tons, by *S109*), *Groenlo* (1,984 tons, by *S52*) sunk and *Blairnevis* (4,155 tons, by *S51*) damaged. Later, on 28/29 November, three boats attacked a convoy north-west of Cromer, having previously laid six LMB mines. *S51* sank *Cormarsh* (2,848 tons), *S52* sank *Empire Newcomen* (2,840 tons) and *S64* accounted for *Asperity* (699 tons). On their return, there was another action with a small group of MGBs, during which *MGB 89* was damaged. The successful convoy attack was attributed to air reconnaissance and good radio interception reports. The 2nd Flotilla rejoined operations on 4 December and the two flotillas were fully extended on torpedo and minelaying sorties until the turn of the year. Well over one hundred mines were laid, but all the torpedo attacks were driven off by the escorting destroyers.

6. BUILD-UP IN THE WEST, 1942

At the beginning of January 1942 Bütow had the following forces at his disposal:

1st Flotilla - under refit at Kiel
2nd Flotilla - 4 boats (plus 1 of 1st Flotilla) operational, Rotterdam
3rd Flotilla - 5 boats in Sicily, 5 en route
4th Flotilla - 6 boats operational, Rotterdam
5th Flotilla - trials and refits
6th Flotilla - 1 boat attached to 2nd Flotilla, Rotterdam
8th Flotilla - 2 boats operational, Norway

The new year saw the continuance of minelaying operations. Between 29 November 1941 and 1 January 1942, 246 LMBs had been laid in six operations and a further 42 were laid in January. Torpedo attacks were fruitless and there was now concrete evidence that the short-wave net used by the S-boats for orders and manoeuvring was being listened-in to by the British. Measures had to be taken to restrict its use and change code words more frequently, but the British continued to make use of it. Their code word for this technique was 'Headache' and it was to prove more and more valuable in the combating of the S-boat menace.

At the end of January the flotillas received a secret order, which was brought into effect on 8 February, under which the boats were to augment crews and armament, increase W/T personnel, take on smoke floats and paint the decks yellow. The 2nd Flotilla (six boats) was ordered to Ijmuiden, the 4th (ten boats) to Boulogne and the 6th (five boats) to Ostend. All this was in preparation for Operation 'Cerberus', the break-out of the Brest Squadron. Boats of the 6th Flotilla were to make a diversionary attack on Dungeness/Beachy Head while the other flotillas were to form part of the local escort. In the event, the 6th Flotilla's sortie encountered nothing and bad weather forced the other boats into harbour, playing no effective role in 'Cerberus' although they assisted in repelling an attack by MTBs and had S64 shot up by Spitfires.

After this diversion, the flotillas returned to their main task, the trade war. On 19/20 February, after laying mines, eight boats of the 2nd Flotilla were engaged off the east coast by *ML 185* and *ML 224* as well as *MGB 329* and *MGB 319* and the destroyer *Holderness*. Later both *Mendip* and *Pytchley*, close escort to convoy FS29, also became embroiled, claiming (incorrectly) one sunk and one damaged. *S39* and *S53* collided during this action, the former being badly damaged. Some time later *S53* was chanced upon by *Holderness* which went alongside and sent across a boarding party. Just as this was being done, the S-boat's captain detonated scuttling charges, blowing himself up at the same time and the boat sank. Survivors were picked up by the British ship. Bütow remarked after the operation that the British destroyer C.O.s on the east coast knew their job and only the best and most experienced officers should be given command of S-boats in this area. All S-boat C.O.s should have had comprehensive destroyer or torpedo boat training prior to appointment but this was not yet possible. He considered the loss of *S53* to have been due to the weakness of her C.O. and that he should have been replaced, as had the C.O. of *S109* in December - perhaps an unfair statement in view of the man's sacrifice.

Mines were also laid in the Straits of Dover but Bütow commented that operations in this area were difficult because the boats were always picked up by British radar and the lack of good reconnaissance meant that attacks were often made into thin air. German radar only detected convoys when they were in the Straits - too late for the boats to attack. However, because the nights were now becoming progressively lighter and shorter, activity would have to be concentrated in the Straits. There were certain prerequisites for success: (a) an extension of German radar coverage; (b) jamming of British radar stations; and (c) special moored mines with long time settings.

Off the east coast, six boats of the 2nd Flotilla attacked a convoy on 10/11 March but their only success was the sinking of the small vessel *Horseferry* (951 tons). On 14 March both the 2nd and 4th Flotillas were ordered to immediate notice for a torpedo operation and sailed with seven boats that evening. *S70* soon had to return because of engine trouble. A north-bound convoy was expected in the vicinity of 54F buoy and a south bound convoy had been reported off Whitby by aircraft that morning. The 4th Flotilla, disposed in two groups, was to operate against the former convoy while the 2nd Flotilla was to attack the latter. The destroyer *Wallace*, part of the escort to the north-bound convoy FN55 (41 ships), had a brief exchange of fire with some S-boats, as did *Holderness* on patrol 'M'. After a trawler escorting the south-bound FS49 reported an underwater explosion another escort, *Guillemot*, engaged some S-boats, as did MGBs. The assailants were one group of the 2nd Flotilla which had succeeded in making contact with the enemy, and *S104* torpedoed the destroyer *Vortigern*. Struck by two torpedoes on the port side, one forward, one abreast the after boiler room, the ship went down on two minutes with heavy loss of life. The remainder of this flotilla failed to find targets in the darkness, hampered by heavy rain and low clouds. *S111* lost contact with her consort in the inky blackness and while making her way home alone fell in with three MGBs (*MGB 87, 88* and *91*) of the 7th MGB Flotilla out of Lowestoft on an anti-E-boat patrol 20 miles off the Dutch coast. After a brief action at close quarters, when depth charges were used by the British boats to disable the enemy, *S111* surrendered and was boarded by the British. However, their intention to capture the enemy vessel was thwarted by the arrival of three S-boats (*S104, S62* and *S29*) which had sailed from Ijmuiden to search for and support the missing boat. Their intervention drove off the MGBs, badly damaging *MGB 91* in the process. *S111* was repossessed but was in extremis, with some nine of her crew dead aboard, the remainder having been taken prisoner. Nevertheless, she was taken in tow but around midday a heavy attack by Spitfires wounded many and at 1400 *S111* finally foundered. Most of the other boats were damaged, *S105* having been hit some 80 times with machine-gun fire, while *S104* had taken a direct hit from a 4.7in shell through the bridge, but this had failed to detonate.

The last torpedo attacks had been detected by the British so Bütow now ordered a reversion to minelaying and during the remainder of March five minelaying sorties were successfully completed. April saw both minelaying and torpedo sorties, with UMB mines being used for the first time. The torpedo sorties were without result but the mining sortie on the night of 18/19 April by *S67, S108, S82* and *S70* (2nd Flotilla) with 24 UMB mines out of Ijmuiden and *S51, S52, S63, S64* and *S109* of the 4th Flotilla out of Ostend with 30 UMB mines proved most successful. Two 'Hunt'-class destroyers, *Cotswold* and *Quorn* were badly damaged by these mines and two merchantmen, *Plawsworth* (1,498 tons) and the Belgian *Vae Vectis* (1,829 tons) were sunk. *Cotswold* was towed in by *Leeds* and beached at Shotley Spit but was out of action for twelve months. *Quorn* was towed in by *Shearwater* and took four months to repair.

In April 1942 the command structure was once again revised, with the post of Führer der Torpedoboote being abolished when Kpt.z.S. Bütow was posted away on the 7th, the command being officially dissolved on 19 April. At this juncture, the Type 23, 24, 35, 37 and 39 torpedo boats were transferred to the control of Führer der Zerstörer and a new command was created purely for the S-boats, Führer der S-Boote or FdS. The first and in fact only incumbent was K.Kpt. Petersen, who was eventually promoted Kpt.z.S. and Kommodore. At the time of the formation of this new command, the S-boat arm was organised and disposed as follows:

HQ FdS (Schveningen)

1st Flotilla	6 boats (between Hamburg and Ingolstadt en route for the Black Sea)
2nd Flotilla	3 boats (operational, Ijmuiden)
	3 boats (unserviceable, Ijmuiden)
	2 boats (unserviceable, Rotterdam)
	1 boat (working up with 5th Flotilla)
3rd Flotilla	10 boats (operational, Mediterranean)
	4 boats (en route south)
4th Flotilla	5 boats (operational, Ostend)
	3 boats (unserviceable, Rotterdam)
	2 boats (unserviceable, home ports)
5th Flotilla	Training duties, home waters (4 crews steaming 3rd Flotilla boats to Mediterranean)
6th Flotilla	4 boats (operational Kristiansand (S))
	1 boat (unserviceable Kristiansand (S))
	1 boat (trials, Kiel)
7th Flotilla	Crews in Swinemünde. First boat (*S153*) still in Rotterdam
8th Flotilla	4 boats (operational, Arctic Norway)

On the night of 21/22 April another minelaying sortie was made by the 2nd and 4th Flotillas off the East Dudgeon and a few days later claimed the 2,768-ton *Chatwood* sailing with convoy FS83. On their return the 4th Flotilla had an engagement with four boats of the 6th MGB Flotilla when both *S52* and *MGB 64* were damaged.

The weather condition in late April and early May was so bad that no operations were conducted for three weeks. When conditions did improve, both the 2nd and 4th Flotillas carried out a series of minelaying sorties off the Suffolk coast and off Cromer. Most of the mines, however, were quickly located and swept. Combined operations with Luftwaffe minelaying squadrons were also subject to some discussion, the main concern being the types of mine to be used and the possible dangers to S-boats operating in those waters.

Extending the minelaying sorties into the southern exits to the Downs and off Dover by boats operating from Boulogne or Ostend was also discussed with Group West, and early in June the first LMB mines were laid. However, by mid-June the operational state of the flotillas was poor, only three boats of the 3rd Flotilla and four of the 4th being serviceable. With this force it was proposed to continue the minelaying into the Dover area, using four boats until the middle of the month when it was hoped that more would be available and allow torpedo sorties of eight boats, using radar jamming. Later, when the 5th Flotilla arrived at the front, two flotillas were to be transferred to Cherbourg for operations between Start Point and Portland. This latter flotilla was expected to complete its work-up training by mid-July and to be operational with six boats from 25 July.

At this time Petersen was proposing that, in the light of the increased menace from MGBs, the armament of S-boats be augmented by 4cm guns.

The minelaying continued. Since 4 June 155 mines had been laid on the convoy routes between Dover and Dungeness in six sorties. Some surprise was expressed at the lack of reaction from the British, despite the S-boats having been detected on occasions. By 20 June FdS was ready to try a torpedo operation by the combined 2nd and 4th Flotillas using the jamming system for the first time. Eighteen naval and ten Luftwaffe jamming stations were to be employed. Seven boats under the command of the 4th Flotilla duly sailed from Boulogne on 21 June to attack a convoy off Folkestone. They failed to find it, the jamming system did not appear to work and in fact the only contact with the enemy was an exchange of fire with the Polish MTB *53*. Actually it is believed that the jamming was highly effective but the British, expecting such a move, continued to operate their radar, thus giving the Germans the impression that they were wasting their time. Consequently, no further faith was placed in jamming by the German radar technicians, and the British were given a free hand.

CHANNEL OPERATIONS

The intended switch of operations to Cherbourg took place when eight boats of the 2nd and 4th Flotillas arrived there on 28 June. This switch had been precipitated by both a lack of success in torpedo sorties off the east coast and the approach of the short summer nights. The first sortie had to be cancelled because of a lack of intelligence regarding convoy movements. A short period of bad weather followed. Then, when eight boats of the 2nd Flotilla sailed on the night of 6/7 July, no convoy could be found. It was a different matter on the night of 8/9 July, when eight boats found convoy WP183 in Lyme Bay. HMS *Brocklesby* (Senior Officer - Escort) failed to pick up any radar contact and the first indication of an attack was the explosion of a torpedo on the A/S trawler *Manor*. In the attack that followed, five other ships were also sunk: *Pomella* (6,766 tons), *Kongshaugh* (1,156 tons), *Rosten* (726 tons), *Bokn* (698 tons) and *Reggestroom* (2,836 tons). It was a conspicuous success and an unpleasant shock to the British Command.

Some reinforcement of the western flotillas was now possible, due to the dissolution of the 8th Flotilla (see Chapter 8). Establishment of the 2nd and 4th Flotillas was now eleven and twelve boats respectively but only fourteen were serviceable at the time. Towards the end of the month, the command was informed that it was also

intended to withdraw the 6th Flotilla from Arctic waters for transfer into the Channel theatre.

Another torpedo operation was launched on 3/4 August when a total of nineteen boats sailed to attack a convoy off Start Point. This was in fact PW196, S.O. escort in *Tynedale*, later *Blencathra*. Only sixteen boats reached the operational area, claiming two ships sunk and one damaged, a bag which caused Admiral Saalwachter at Group West to comment on its small size for the number of boats involved. In fact, no ship was sunk from this convoy. FdS, while pleased with the result of his earlier convoy attack, considered that time was needed to deduce the convoy pattern and assess defensive measures - which had already been done on the east coast. Consequently he now intended to transfer the flotillas back to the southern North Sea, massed attacks with all available forces being his main aim. Thus the 2nd and 4th Flotillas would return to Rotterdam or Ijmuiden, while the 5th Flotilla would be based at Boulogne or Cherbourg according to the situation. This was incomprehensible to Saalwachter, coming so soon after the success against WP183; he required a flotilla each at Cherbourg and Boulogne until at least mid-September but did agree to transfer one flotilla to Ijmuiden. Petersen was actually the better judge of the situation because, unknown to him, the attacks on WP183 and PW196 had caused the Royal Navy to alter the convoy schedule so that no convoy would be at sea at night between Lands End and Portsmouth. Thus targets would in any event be lacking.

In mid-May, prior to the appearance of S-boats at Cherbourg, the Royal Navy had altered the sailing arrangements for Channel convoys, commencing with CW81. The cycle time was to be two days, the maximum number of ships fourteen, the minimum ten, and the escort reduced by half - i.e., it would henceforth consist of one destroyer, three to four balloon vessels, two or three trawlers and four MLs.

The 5th Flotilla had also reached Cherbourg by the end of July and together with the 4th Flotilla conducted a number of minelaying sorties off the Isle of Wight and Lyme Bay in the first half of August. Operations in the Channel, both torpedo and mining, were made difficult by a number of factors. First, there were the convoy cycle changes which meant that the possible attack area for west-bound convoys was the Eddystone and that for the east-bound was Portland Bill. This gave the boats little time to operate and was an expected area of attack. Moreover, because of the defensive minefields, they could not approach closer to the coast than four miles and the convoys were inside this. Lastly, the number of night fighter patrols had increased markedly (actually these were Coastal Command aircraft). Fighter Command had also operated specific 'anti-E-Boat' patrols from January 1942 and the two commands had, by the autumn of 1942, made 187 direct attacks but not sunk any boats. Nevertheless, their activities were clearly recognized as a danger by FdS and forced him to operate only at night.

Mid-August saw only units of the 5th Flotilla remaining at Cherbourg, with the other two now operating in the North Sea. On 27 August SKL ordered the 6th Flotilla to Ijmuiden, reiterating that the 5th Flotilla must remain in the Channel for defensive tasks, a decision undoubtedly taken because of the Dieppe raid. Apart from the odd minelaying operation, the 5th Flotilla was not particularly active during the first half of September, but on the night of the 16th/17th six boats sailed to attack a west-bound convoy off the Eddystone. This was PW219 of nine ships in two columns, Senior Officer (Escort) *Cleveland*, with the trawlers *Olvina* and *Fir*. Only four boats attacked but unsuccessfully, although *Cleveland* was narrowly missed by torpedoes. Another west-bound convoy was attacked on the night of 1/2 October, this being PW226, when *S112* used her 'Lichtenstein' radar for the first time. Again only four boats attacked, *S112* sinking the A/S trawler *Lord Stonehaven*, while the Polish destroyer *Kujawiak* (S.O.Escort) was slightly damaged during the encounter. Subsequent sorties in October were fruitless, as was a search for survivors from the raider *Komet*, but there was more action in November. On the night of 18/19 November, eight boats sailed to attack a convoy reported off Bigbury Bay and made contact with PW250 (Senior Officer (Escort) *Brocklesby*). From this convoy their torpedoes sank the A/S trawler *Ullswater* and the merchantmen *Birgette* (1,595 tons), *Yew Forest* (815 tons) and the Norwegian *Lab* (1,118 tons). PW256 was the next victim on the night of 30 November/1 December. This consisted of only four merchant vessels, plus one tug and tow, escorted by the destroyers *Glaisdale* and *Tyndale*, the trawlers *Cornelean*, *Jasper* and *Ellesmere* plus three MLs.

The trawler *Jasper* was sunk and *Cornelien* and *ML184* were damaged. The final success of the year was an attack on 2/3 December by six boats on PW257 which consisted of seven ships escorted by *Penylan* with the trawlers *Pearl*, *La Nantaise*, *Ensay*, *Vardo* and *Mandal* with three MLs. Contact was made with the convoy off Start Point when the 383-ton *Gatinais* and the destroyer *Penylan* were torpedoed, the latter attributed to *S115*. On the flotilla's return, *S116* and *S82* were attacked between Cap de la Hague and Cherbourg by about ten Spitfires, both boats being badly damaged and suffering casualties.

Admiral Marschall, who had succeeded Saalwachter at Group West, now proposed that a further flotilla be transferred to the Channel because he did not wish the boats stationed in Dutch waters to lie idle during the bad weather period. Petersen was unenthusiastic because Channel convoys were making more use of the relative security of Lyme Bay, where there was good radar coverage; and in any event these convoys consisted of only eight or nine vessels, sailing every two days. In addition, because of the limited reconnaissance facilities, the time and zone of attack were very restricted. On the other hand, the east-coast convoys consisted of 25-30 ships sailing daily. In the face of this argument and the successful attack on FN89 on 12/13 December, Marschall was forced to agree that prospects were better on the east coast.

EAST COAST OPERATIONS

Returning now to August 1942, the 2nd Flotilla was operating from Ijmuiden and the 4th from the Hook of Holland. In an unsuccessful sortie against a north-bound convoy on 19/20 August by both flotillas (six boats each), action was joined with *Mallard* and *Hambledon* which forced the S-boats to retire without having seen any sign of a convoy. Their next sortie was a minelaying operation on the night of 24/25 August, when a force of eleven boats of the combined flotillas mined the swept channels off Lowestoft about two hours before the arrival of a south-bound convoy. This was diverted but the 2,830-ton *Kyloe* was mined and had to be beached. After completing their lay, the German force was engaged indecisively by *Cattistock* and *Mendip* as well as two MGBs. The final sortie of the month was a mining operation by nine boats of the two flotillas, this time to the convoy route east and south-west of Orfordness. Thirty LMB and 24 UMB mines were successfully laid and the boats of the 2nd Flotilla had an indecisive encounter with *Pytchley* and *Cottesmore*. A period of poor autumnal weather followed and prevented any operations being launched. Things improved somewhat by the night of 7/8 September when a total of fourteen boats of the 2nd, 4th and now 6th Flotillas sailed for a torpedo strike into the vicinity of Smiths Knoll. The 2nd Flotilla made no contact with enemy forces, while boats of the 4th Flotilla encountered the escort vessel *Shearwater* as well as the *MGBs 319, 315* and *327,* but no significant damage was incurred by either

Below: *Hambledon*, a 'Hunt'-class destroyer, seen here with 2pdr bow-chaser for anti-E-boat work. (Author's Collection)

side. A couple of nights later, after a torpedo sortie against a suspected north-bound convoy had failed to find it, boats of all three flotillas were intercepted on their return by a force of MGBs stationed for that purpose off the Dutch coast. Three 70ft MGBs and four Fairmile 'C' boats of the 16th MGB Flotilla were involved. The latter, *MGBs 325, 327, 334* and *335*, were badly shot up by the S-boats. *MGB 335* was seriously hit and set on fire. Although all but two of her crew were taken off by one of her consorts, the Germans drove off the British boats and captured *MGB 335*. Confidential books and equipment fell into German hands as a result of this action, including radar and IFF sets - something that FdS had been asking for for years. It was a valuable prize but it did not, in the event, bring radar equipment to the S-boat command any quicker.

The inevitable bad weather of the period continued to disrupt operational planning, as did the lack of consistent and regular air reconnaissance over the east coast convoy routes. Thus the only major operation during the latter half of September was a minelaying sortie into the Humber, where no mines had been laid since December 1941. Due to a navigational error, the field was badly placed. Minelaying continued in October with a force of seventeen boats of the 2nd, 4th and 6th Flotillas laying some 90 LMB mines on the convoy routes east of the Humber, on 1/2 October. This was followed on the night of 6/7 October by a torpedo sortie against the convoy routes off Great Yarmouth. Fourteen boats of the 2nd and 6th Flotillas sailed from Ijmuiden and three of the 4th Flotilla from the Hook. As a result of air reconnaissance reports, they were diverted to Cromer where the 6th Flotilla patrolled the inner routes and the remainder the outer. Although the 6th saw nothing, the 2nd and 4th Flotillas found and attacked convoy FN32, from which their torpedoes sank *Ilse* (2,874 tons), *Jessie Maersk* (1,972 tons), the tug *Caroline Moller* (444 tons) and the motor launch *ML 339*. Also hit was *Shearwater* (2,730 tons) which was badly damaged and taken in tow by *Sheldrake* but later foundered. To add to the destruction, the collier *Ightham* (1,337 tons) struck a mine and sank and the Norwegian *Varoy* (1,531 tons) was lost during the night, although from what cause is not clear.

The next major attack against the east coast routes was made on 13/14 October when seventeen boats, the largest strike yet launched, sailed to attack a north-bound convoy of 22 ships reported off Cromer by air reconnaissance. Eight boats of the 6th Flotilla, four of the 2nd Flotilla and five of the 4th Flotilla were involved. Only the 6th Flotilla made contact, the target in fact being FN38 (Senior

Officer (Escort) *Westminster*). This was also escorted by *Vanity*, HM Tug *Champion* and *ML196* and *ML197*. In addition, *Whitshed* was on patrol between 56 and 57F Buoys. *S74*, *S75*, *S71* and *S69* fired torpedoes and claimed several hits. Two ships were hit but not sunk: *George Balfour* (1,570 tons) and the Norwegian *Lysland* (1,335 tons), both of which were towed into port. On their return, *S69* and *S71* were attacked by Whirlwind fighter-bombers and themselves damaged.

November opened with a torpedo sortie by 24 boats of all three flotillas against a north-bound convoy of 26 ships reported east of Haisborough Gap, this in fact being FN54 whose destroyer escort included *Mendip*, *Lauderdale* and *Campbell*. Bad weather forced a premature abandonment of this operation and curtailed operations for the following week, in fact until the afternoon of 9 November, when Petersen saw a chance for a torpedo attack into the southern North Sea. Orders were therefore issued for a sortie by all three North Sea flotillas with Petersen himself commanding the operation aboard the leader of the 2nd Flotilla. His intention was to make a surprise attack by the combined flotillas as far south as possible against a north-bound convoy. Things did not go entirely according to plan for delays were experienced and the reconnaissance sortie flown by 3.(F)/122 was made outside the convoy

route in poor visibility and hence sighted nothing. As a result, B-Dienst reports had to be employed to plan the strike. Twenty-three boats sailed, the 2nd and 6th Flotillas at Ijmuiden providing eight and seven boats respectively and the 4th Flotilla sailed from the Hook with eight boats. Petersen was embarked in *S29*. The convoy, FN61, was encountered off 3C Buoy between Lowestoft and Great Yarmouth. In the action which followed, the 1,843-ton *Fidelio* was torpedoed and sunk, while *Wandle* (1,482 tons) had her bows blown off but was towed into port. On the German side, *S113* was heavily hit by gunfire about the bows and had to be towed home stern first with two other boats alongside.

The invasion of North Africa at the beginning of November now had repercussions within the S-boat force because contingency plans for the occupation of the Iberian peninsula and of Vichy France were reactivated and preparations were made for the movement of German troops into northern Spain to relieve Spanish units which were to be sent to the south on the Mediterranean coast. Naval forces were also earmarked to assist and FdS was instructed to prepare to send two flotillas from Holland to the French south-west Atlantic coast if required. Petersen proposed sending the 2nd and 4th Flotillas as the S-Boats Division (South) under the command of K.Kpt. Max

Schultz with their base at Bayonne. This would leave only the 6th Flotilla to fight the trade war, reinforced by a number of boats from the two other flotillas. In the event, Operation 'Gisela' was never launched and no S-boats operated on the south-west Atlantic coast.

Back in the North Sea, winter weather continued to be unkind and December sorties were few. On the night of 12/13 of December, however, a total of seventeen boats of the three flotillas sailed to attack a north bound convoy whose position was not accurately known. Consequently, none of the 6th Flotilla and most of the 2nd Flotilla failed to make contact with any convoy. Only one 'Rotte' (*S70/S80*) of the 2nd Flotilla and two 'Rotte' (*S117/S63* and *S48/S110*) of the 4th Flotilla got into action. Of these, *S80* fired only one torpedo and missed before both she and her consort were driven off by the escort. The other four boats fired a total of eleven torpedoes, sinking *Avonwood* (1,056 tons), *Marianne* (1,915 tons), *Knitsley* (2,272 tons), *Lindisfarne* (999 tons) and *Glentilt* (817 tons). The destroyers *Mendip* and *Meynell* engaged many of the boats of the three flotillas, damaging *S105* and *S114*.

This was a signal success for the S-boat force and encouraged Petersen to fight any moves to divert boats to other theatres. Bad weather prevented any further operations during the month. At the end of 1942, the nominal strength of the S-boat force in the North Sea was:

2nd Flotilla:	*S29, S62★, S67★, S70, S80, S83, S86, S89★, S104*
4th Flotilla:	*S42★, S48, S63★, S78, S88★, S109★, S110★, S117, S120*
6th Flotilla:	*S39, S71, S74★, S75★, S76, S91★, S113, S114, S119*

Several of these boats were non-operational, or not with their flotillas in the war zone (★), thus leaving only a total of sixteen operational boats. In comparison, the Royal Navy's light forces on the east coast at the same time were:

Sheerness:	105th ML Flotilla (8 boats)
Harwich:	16th Destroyer Flotilla (5 Hunts, 2 Montrose, 3 V & W)
	21st Destroyer Flotilla (7 Hunts, 1 Montrose, 1 V & W)
	1st & 2nd A/S Striking forces, (7 Kingfisher)
Felixstowe:	4th & 21st MTB Flotillas (17 boats)
	6th & 7th MGB Flotillas (16 boats)
	6th & 51st ML Flotillas (12 boats)
Lowestoft:	22nd MTB Flotilla (7 boats)
	1st, 5th & 7th MGB Flotillas (25 boats)
	13th ML Flotilla (8 boats)
Yarmouth:	31st MTB Flotilla (8 boats)
	12th, 16th & 17th MGB Flotillas (20 boats)
	1st ML Flotilla (7 boats)
Grimsby:	24th ML Flotilla (8 boats)

It should be noted that these figures are establishment totals and the vessels actually on station and operational would have been much fewer. Even so, they were more numerous than the forces available to Führer der Schnellboote.

Below: *ML 354*, typical of the lightly armed MLs which were used on the East Coast convoys. (Author's Collection)

7. WESTERN AREA, 1943

NORTH SEA OPERATIONS

The new year brought, once again, a period of bad weather but on 5 January the 4th Flotilla (four boats), 6th Flotilla (five) and 2nd Flotilla (seven) sailed to attack the convoy routes off the east coast. Both a southern convoy (code-named 'Status', FS4) and a north-bound one ('Agent') were expected. Rain and poor visibility resulted in *S116* and *S82* ramming one another, as did *S119* and *S76*, whereupon the operation was abandoned. In any event, the sortie had become known to the British who diverted the target convoys out of trouble.

The next sortie was sailed on the night of 8/9 January with ten boats of the combined flotillas, but on the outward passage *S104* struck a mine which blew off all forward of the bridge although the rest remained afloat. Because it was out of the question to tow the casualty home, her crew were taken off and the wreck sunk. As a result, the remainder of the 2nd Flotilla abandoned their sortie because of time lost. The 4th Flotilla followed suit, leaving only the 6th Flotilla to conduct a fruitless patrol

before returning to Ijmuiden. When weather conditions next permitted an operation, it was a minelaying sortie north of Cromer but on return *S109* struck a mine and lost her bows, although it proved possible to bring her safely into Ijmuiden.

On 24 January eighteen boats of the flotillas under the command of Senior Officer 6th Flotilla sailed to attack a north-bound convoy off Lowestoft but were detected by *MGB 88* and MLs, thus forewarning the defences. After a brief engagement with ships of the 21st Destroyer Flotilla, *Mendip* and *Windsor*, the attack was abandoned and the S-boats returned to base. Lack of effective reconnaissance was largely blamed for this abortive mission, but concern was expressed as to the possibility of the 'Lichtenstein' radar set giving away the Germans' position. In fact, it was the weather at this time of the year that was mainly responsible for the lack of success, although it was true that escort forces were becoming stronger, MGBs more numerous and better armed. It was not until 18 February that the next major operation was launched, a two-pronged assault against the convoy routes. The first phase

Below: As the war progressed special bunkers had to be provided for protection against air raids. (ECPA)

was aimed at mining the channel off Sheringham ahead of a north-bound convoy, the second a mining off Great Yarmouth. In the course of the northern sortie, by the 6th Flotilla, action was joined with the destroyers *Montrose* and *Garth* when *S71* was badly hit and stopped; she was finally rammed by *Garth*. The 2nd and 4th Flotillas carrying out the southern task were ineffectively engaged by *Kittiwake*. Overall it was an unsatisfactory operation since it was obvious to the British that the intention was minelaying, so the minesweepers were soon at work nullifying the Germans efforts. The disappearance of *S71* incidentally led to a rebuke for Petersen from Admiral Marschall because he had sailed no fewer than seventeen boats to search for the missing vessel. Group West rightly considered this number not only excessive but risky, pointing out the dangers of air attack in the growing daylight. *S110* and others were lucky to escape attack without damage on this occasion.

Aircraft had been foreseen as the major threat to S-boat operations before the war, but until 1943 this threat had failed to materialize. There were several reasons for this, one being the fact that until January 1942 attacks by RAF Fighter Command were carried out on a purely fortuitous basis - no specific 'anti-E-boat' patrols were flown. Another was that Coastal Command possessed no suitable aircraft or armament capable of dealing with a small and highly manoeuvrable craft moving at high speed. Nevertheless, the existence of these air patrols forced the Germans more and more towards nocturnal operation, which in itself demanded certain special abilities of an aircraft. Fortunately for the British, while the individual services had their rivalries, they were seldom so bigoted as to work to the detriment of the nation - unlike the case in Germany. As a result, the Admiralty, which had a vested interest admittedly, decided in the late summer of 1942 to put No. 823 Squadron with its ASV Mk II equipped Albacores under the control of Coastal Command. This was in addition to some Swordfish of Nos. 812 and 819 Squadrons already with Coastal Command. Throughout the winter of 1942/43 the 'anti-E-boat' campaign was maintained largely by these naval biplanes, but despite their ability to detect and attack they had so far been unable to sink any of these elusive craft.

The ideal aircraft for dealing with the S-boat menace was one which was comparatively slow, had a good view ahead, with reasonable endurance and bomb capacity as well as being fitted with radar. Fast single seat cannon-armed fighters had not so far proved satisfactory in this role and rocket projectiles (RPs) had not yet been used successfully at night. Another problem was the vectoring and control of the aircraft. All things considered, the lumbering Swordfish and Albacores fitted the requirements best, although Whirlwinds and 'Hurribombers' packed the biggest punch.

At 1 March 1943, the main S-boat operating bases were Ijmuiden, Rotterdam, Ostend, Boulogne and Cherbourg, with the numbers and dispositions varying with operational requirements. Petersen as FdS had permanent battle H.Q.s in bunkers at Wimereaux, near Boulogne and at Scheveningen in Holland. Although losses in boats had so far been light, replacement crews could no longer be trained 'on the job' in operational flotillas and it was fortunate that with new construction now reaching three boats per month, a training flotilla could be formed to take over this task. One of the most serious shortages was in officers and as a result senior rates were eventually posted to command some boats.

Tactics too had been altered in the face of increased convoy defence, MGB patrols, aircraft and above all radar, for it was no longer possible to ambush convoys by laying in wait on dark nights - radar made night into day. The tactic now was for concerted attacks by all available boats acting in pairs ('Rotte') and all firing their torpedoes, still the main weapon, together. Such a technique required adequate and timely reconnaissance, which only the Luftwaffe could provide. Hitherto this had been barely sufficient but with the diversion of aircraft to other tasks and the absence of a dedicated maritime air command in the Luftwaffe, matters deteriorated considerably. In the short term, co-operation did improve temporarily in two ways. One was by means of bomber attacks on the convoys a few hours before the S-boats were due to attack, thus giving up-to-date information as to position and strength, etc. The other was by using fighters to drop flares over the convoy and illuminate it. Neither method proved entirely satisfactory.

Mining sorties were carried out when torpedo operations were unfavourable, especially on moonlit nights, the most favourable area being that between Cromer and the Humber. In the Channel, mining had been carried out in the Straits of Dover, Brighton Bay and to the east and west of the Isle of Wight, but west of St. Albans Head the water was too deep for ground mines.

Returning now to operational activities, 21 boats sailed on 27 February to attack a south-bound convoy which had been reported by a Junkers Ju 88. A follow-up flight in the afternoon was driven off without having sighted the convoy, and as a result the S-boat sortie failed to find it either. Some boats encountered British patrols and *S110* received some inconsequential hits. Ominously too, attacks were also experienced from aircraft during the night, part of the British measures described earlier. After this operation, poor weather interrupted operations until, on the evening of 4 March, B-Dienst interceptions reported that British MTBs and MGBs were being sent out to attack a German convoy off Texel. To Petersen this indicated an improvement in the weather from the west and he alerted the S-boat flotillas accordingly. This caused some surprise in the flotillas who had been given leave and had to recall men urgently; even so, only half the boats were available. These boats, fifteen in all, sailed before midnight with orders to attack a south-bound convoy in borderline conditions. This convoy, code-named 'Result', had been reported leaving the Firth of Forth on the

Above: S-boats in a bunker. (WZB)

afternoon of 3 March. In the early hours of 5 March, *S70* struck a mine which simultaneously detonated the starboard reserve torpedo, whereupon the boat sank. After rescuing survivors, the remaining three boats of the 2nd Flotilla broke off their sortie and returned to Ijmuiden. Meanwhile the other two flotillas pressed on; having been reported by British Coastal Forces units, there was no chance of surprise. They were intercepted off Lowestoft and driven off by the patrolling destroyers *Windsor* and *Southdown* together with the corvette *Sheldrake*. While returning to base, two boats of the 6th Flotilla, *S74* and *S75*, were attacked by four Spitfires (of No.118 Squadron) and two Typhoons (No.56 Squadron). *S75* was badly hit and set on fire by the first pass. She sank shortly afterwards with heavy casualties. Her consort was also badly damaged with a number of casualties, but with the survivors of *S75* aboard, managed to limp home on one engine. All in all, it was a most unsatisfactory operation and worse was to come.

An abatement of the weather allowed another sortie to be launched on 7 March, once more against a south-bound convoy. Located by reconnaissance that evening, it was reported to consist of twenty ships. In the event, the 4th Flotilla, tasked with detecting the convoy by use of their FuMB sets, failed to find it, whereupon Petersen ordered the attack to be switched to the north-bound convoy which was expected to stand off Great Yarmouth by about 2300. Before they could make contact with this, however, they fell in with the destroyer *Mackay* which took them under heavy fire. While taking avoiding action, *S114* was rammed by *S119*, the former having her fore-ends badly damaged, the latter being opened up from bow to bridge. After firing off her torpedoes, *S119* regained some degree of trim and both casualties began a limping journey

home, only to be intercepted by three MTBs, *MTB 17*, *MTB 20* and *MTB 21*. In the quarter of an hour's action which followed, the two German boats became separated but managed to join up again. *S114* then lay alongside her now-derelict mate and took off the crew before *MTB 20* returned to sink the wreck.

This latest loss left the S-boat force in a parlous state, with only thirteen operational boats in Holland and four at Cherbourg. The remainder, 21 in total, were all unserviceable or under repair. This situation did not help Admiral Marschall at Group West for he had always to be aware of the possibility of an Allied landing on the French coast; Dieppe and the numerous Commando raids had had a greater effect than perhaps the British realized. Thus in mid-March at the period of a full moon, the 4th Flotilla transferred from Rotterdam to Boulogne while the 2nd Flotilla moved to Ostend so that, by 19 March, the dispositions were as follows:

Ostend	2nd Flotilla (6 boats)
Boulogne	4th Flotilla (5 boats)
Cherbourg	5th Flotilla (5 boats)
	6th Flotilla (2 boats)

F.Kpt. Petersen commented bitterly in his war diary that another bloody encounter with British defensive forces had been experienced and that operational strength was so depleted by loss and damage that the prospects of success were now very low. Only by an attack in overwhelming numbers were the British defences likely to be breached.

Of the boats remaining in Holland, the 2nd Flotilla with *S92*, *S76*, *S29*, *S86* and *S89* laid a field of 26 UMB mines off the east coast. Although their purpose was known and sweepers were quickly despatched to clear the mines, the minesweeper *Moravia* fell victim to one of them.

Towards the end of March, when the danger of a full moon had passed, the boats at Ostend, Boulogne and Cherbourg returned to their normal bases in Holland, leaving only the usual 5th Flotilla resident in Cherbourg for operations against the WP/PW convoys. The lamentable operational state referred to earlier was now compounded by the OKM's decision to allow six new boats to be sold to Spain, giving Petersen further cause for concern. This decision did not of course immediately affect operations but it was bound to later. Meanwhile, a force of seven boats under the command of the S.O. 2nd Flotilla sailed from Ijmuiden and seven more of the 4th Flotilla from the Hook for a torpedo sortie against a south-bound convoy (actually FS1074). On the outward passage, the 2nd Flotilla was intercepted near Smiths Knoll by two 'C'-class MGBs, Nos. *321* and *333*, and brought to action. The two 2pdr (40mm) guns carried aboard each of these MGBs wrought havoc with the closest S-boat, *S29*, completely disabling her, whereupon one of the MGBs rammed her, further damaging the boat.

When the MGBs departed the remainder of the flotilla rejoined the casualty but, mindful of the loss of *S75*, Petersen, after consultation with Marschall, ordered her to be scuttled. Another boat had been lost for no return. Aircraft of No. 841 Squadron claimed an attack on 'E-boat' targets that night but it seems to have gone unnoticed. *S29*, incidentally, was one of those which had not yet been fitted with bridge armour, thus accounting for the casualties. The 4th Flotilla was equally unsuccessful but succeeded in disengaging from *Blencathra* and *Windsor* without loss or damage.

April storms interrupted all operations for the first half of that month, with winds gusting up to 140km/hr as a deep low hung over the area. By 12 April these winds had abated somewhat and fog banks had formed, so that on the 14th a minelaying sortie by fifteen boats of the 2nd, 4th and 6th Flotillas with a mixed load of UMB and LMB types could be launched. Barely two hours after sailing, the force was detected and shadowed by aircraft, thus alerting the British patrols, one of the several handicaps which the S-boats were to experience more and more in their pursuance of the trade war. The northern group (2nd and 6th Flotillas) out-manoeuvred British coastal forces and laid its mines successfully but then fought an engagement with 'destroyers' standing to the north and south, these being *Westminster* and the corvette *Widgeon*. Light forces including *MGBs 88* and *91* also joined in but the only damage caused was a 40mm hit on *S83*, although the British forces claimed two sunk and four damaged - yet another example of over-optimistic claims in night actions. The 4th Flotilla had not completed laying their mines before they were intercepted by two trawlers, *Milford Prince* and *Adonis*, but the latter was sunk by a torpedo and the S-boats withdrew. On the way home they were found by a Swordfish and two Albacores of No.841 Squadron which attacked them unsuccessfully, after which the boats regained base. Most of the mines were swept during the following days.

In contrast to the stormy weather with which the month had opened, there now followed a period with clear moonlit nights, equally unsuitable for operations. It was expected, too, that the number of suitable operating nights would fall as summer approached. Petersen therefore advised Group West that he intended to take this opportunity to put the boats in hand for fitting armour and rebuilding their bridges. Consequently, until about August, only about half the boats currently in the area would be operational at any one time (an average of five per flotilla). Strong winds returned towards the end of the month, by which time FdS had decided upon yet another change in the direction of his attacks - back to the Channel in fact.

To take advantage of the coming new moon period, all flotillas were being transferred to Cherbourg for massed torpedo attacks against the PW/WP convoys. Petersen himself intended moving with his operational staff to Boulogne for closer co-operation with the 2nd Sicherungsdivision and the coastal radar station network. As an interim move, the 2nd Flotilla transferred to Ostend on 30 April, while the 4th and 6th Flotillas moved to Boulogne. Yet again the weather was not favourable as a deep low hung over the British Isles, moving slowly south-west, right across the intended area of operations. Despite the weather, however, ten boats of the 4th and 6th Flotillas carried out a mining sortie from Boulogne on the night of 30 April / 1 May.

The transfer to Cherbourg was completed by 6 May. It was intended to launch sorties of twenty boats against convoys in Lyme Bay and off Plymouth using Cherbourg, St. Peter Port and L'Aberwrach as bases. Nature intervened once more, preventing any operations from the new base for the first half of May, except for one minelaying sortie by the 5th Flotilla. In fact, it was not until 23 May that another operation could be launched, again a minelaying sortie by nineteen boats of all flotillas between Portland and the Isle of Wight. This was detected and destroyers sailed to intercept, but only the Albacores of No. 823 Squadron were able to attack the 5th Flotilla and their bombs missed. In another operation on 28/29 May, to Lyme Bay, the German force was detected in the early hours off Cherbourg by an Albacore and then engaged by MGBs, coastal batteries and destroyers, as well as Albacores from Tangmere. The latter claimed four boats sunk and two damaged, but again no losses were actually incurred. Other minelaying operations took place on 30/31 May, 5/6 June and 6/7 June. In total, during 77 sorties, 321 mines and 84 protection floats were laid, but because of British intelligence successes most of these were quickly swept and the results were therefore few, if any.

FdS was by now increasingly concerned about the threat of air attack. In the Channel, for example, in the course of three operations, sixteen attacks were experienced, even on the darkest night. Obviously the aircraft were fitted with radar and until the Luftwaffe could deploy night fighters and force the British to withdraw the slow Swordfish and Albacores, they would remain a serious problem.

Partly for the reasons mentioned earlier, operations during June, July and August were few. No torpedo sorties were carried out during the first two months and minelaying became the main activity. By July, the 2nd and 6th Flotillas had returned to the North Sea and the intention was to have one task force of four to six boats of the 2nd/6th Flotillas at Ostend and a second of five or six boats of the 4th/5th Flotillas at St. Peter Port. The remainder of the boats were undergoing urgent overhaul and rearmament, the completion of which was scheduled for 22 August.

On 24 July *S68* and *S77* were ordered to move from Boulogne to Ostend but were detected by the British who vectored MGBs out of Ramsgate and intercepted them off Dunkirk just after midnight. *S77* took the brunt of their attack and both 2cm guns were quickly knocked out. A hit on her starboard reserve torpedo detonated it with the result that the boat quickly sank. *S68* failed to give any support to her wingman and her C.O., Ob.Lt.z.S. Moritzen, was court-martialled for his feeble performance and relieved of his command. Further loss occurred the following night when four boats were being transferred from the Hook to Boulogne; one of them, *S88*, was en route for repair at Cherbourg. On passage, this boat was damaged by a mine but was brought safely into Dunkerque. Then on 25 July, B-17 Fortresses of the USAAF's 8th Air Force raided Kiel with over one hundred aircraft. Among their victims were *S44* and *S68* of the 8th Flotilla sunk. In a follow-up raid on 29 July by 139 aircraft, *S135* and *S137* were hit, the latter so badly that she had to be paid off; the damage to *S135* was only minor. Thus the sinking of the trawler *Red Gauntlet* southeast of Orfordness by *S86* on 5 August during a strike by seven boats against the patrol lines was of small consolation. *Lord Melchet*, *Hornbeam* and *Mary Haistie* were also engaged, the latter being narrowly missed by a torpedo.

There were no torpedo attacks on coastal convoys during September but three minelaying sorties were carried out and three diversionary operations on other nights. Increased Allied sea and air activity in the Channel, especially in the area of Boulogne, again raised fears of a landing and as a result much of the S-boat activity at that time was directed towards defensive tasks. By the end of September the 8th Flotilla had arrived to reinforce the boats in the North Sea and on the 24th/25th they were among the 29 boats of all flotillas that carried out a mining operation centred on the Sunk lightship. This was the first of the planned combined operations with Luftwaffe minelaying aircraft, when each employed different mine-firing methods to confuse the minesweepers. The naval operation did not begin well as *S39* and *S90* collided off the Hook, necessitating both boats plus one other to return. As the remainder laid their mines, patrol trawlers arrived on the scene but were missed by *S69*'s torpedoes. Another group of boats was attacked inconclusively by MGBs, although *S68* received some damage. The 4th Flotilla also ran into trawlers of the patrol line, one of which, *Franc Tireur*, was sunk by a torpedo from *S96* (*S88* having missed). After laying their mines a group of three boats encountered *ML 150* and *ML 145*. These slow MLs could not hope to engage in a running fight, so *ML 150* opted to ram one of the enemy, *S96*, as did *ML 145*. Severely damaged, *S96* was scuttled while *ML 150* with all gone forward of the bridge and the lesser damaged *ML 145* struggled home. In a confused night of engagements, *Puffin* and *Pytchley* also got into action, as did the trawlers *Donna Nook* and *Stella Rigel*, but the two trawlers collided with the loss of the former. Petersen was not entirely happy with the results of this night's work and felt that the standard of training left a lot to be desired. This was not surprising as there had been few operations of late and the 8th Flotilla was new to operations in any case.

Another major minelaying task was planned in October using all operational boats of the 2nd, 4th, 6th and 8th Flotillas, all except the latter carrying mines. This took place on 7/8 October without incident. No further operations of note occurred until the night of 24/25 October when a torpedo strike was launched against a north-bound convoy, actually FN1160 off Cromer. No fewer than 32 boats of the North Sea flotillas put out for this operation. The attack was designed to cover the whole of the convoy route from 57B buoy in the north to 54 buoy in the south. As usual, the British had forewarning of the attack and were on alert. The night engagement therefore developed into a confused series of separate encounters between British and German forces.

A little before midnight the 1st Group of the 6th Flotilla were surprised by the destroyer *Pytchley* and several boats were damaged and suffered casualties. Then as a result of a signalling error, this group moved north and later, not having sighted the convoy, retired to base on account of the damage received. The second group of the 6th Flotilla encountered the trawler *William Stephen* which was missed by both torpedoes from *S79* before she was sunk by two torpedoes from *S74*. They then came under fire from *Worcester* and, having evaded her, ran into MGBs when both *S73* and *S74* as well as one or more of the MGBs were damaged. Finally the German boats managed to disengage and return to base without further loss.

The second group of the 4th Flotilla (*S120*, *S122*, *S87* and *S89*) encountered the destroyer *Worcester*, which damaged several boats before they succeeded in eluding her. They subsequently came under fire from both destroyers and MGBs and, unable to break through the defensive ring, retired eastwards. In doing so they were in action with *MGBs 439* and *442* which had sailed from Yarmouth on receipt of news of the attack. *MGB 442* was damaged in the encounter.

The first group (*S88*, *S63*, *S110* and *S117*) were engaged by *Mackay* which hit *S62* in the side engine room. She was however able to maintain speed for the moment and keep up with her consorts. As this group disengaged from the destroyer, they encountered the two Fairmile 'D' boats of unit Y (*MGBs 607* and *610*). A fierce action ensued in which *S88* (S.O. 6th Flotilla) valiantly attempted to protect the damaged *S63* and in doing so received terrible punishment from the 'Dog' boats' 2pdrs and Oerlikons. Many of her crew were killed and the boat was set on fire. *MGB 607* then attacked *S63* which had stopped due to a misunderstanding between her C.O. and engineer officer. The German poured a devastating fire into the MGB but could not avoid the latter's ramming tactics. *S63* sank shortly after and, as *MGB 610* came to the assistance of her damaged mate, *S88* exploded and sank. Nineteen survivors were rescued by British forces. On the way home, the remnants of this flotilla joined up with the 6th Flotilla and reached Ijmuiden without further incident.

The 2nd Flotilla also failed to make contact with the convoy or any other enemy vessels except for a brief

Above: An *S38*-type boat before armament and bridge alterations. Note that a canvas dodger was frequently used aft. (WZB)

exchange of fire with MGBs just before dawn, while retiring to base. The 8th Flotilla appears also to have been engaged briefly by *Pytchley* before midnight and thereafter managed to evade contact with several destroyers seen, but at the same time also failed to find the convoy.

It was a most unsatisfactory operation considering the number of boats involved but the lessons were quite clear: close co-operation between the British destroyers and MGBs, and air reconnaissance, would stand a good chance of driving off an attacking force of S-boats, especially when the latter had no radar, no central control and whose VHF radio net was being listened in to. Petersen once again cited the destroyer as being the main threat and, to make his firepower more effective against these ships, demanded faster but shorter-ranged torpedoes, the possibility of deflection shots up to 180deg or stern tubes and the issue of acoustic types to S-boats. What he did not know was that No. 415 Squadron, RCAF, had become operational on 3 November with a strength of 8 + 2 Wellington Mk XIIIs and 8 + 2 Albacores (the latter ex-naval aircraft), both equipped with ASV Mk II and IFF Mk III. This squadron assumed full

responsibility for anti-E-boat operations from No. 841 Squadron, FAA, on 2 December. It was controlled by No. 12 Group from Coltishall. The technique developed was to patrol so as to give half to three-quarters of an hour's notice of S-boats approaching the 'Z' line (the defensive patrol line to seaward of the convoy routes where MGB groups were stationed), then shadow and switch on their homing beacons. Coastal Forces HQ would then maintain a plot from the aircraft position. This procedure was adopted because there was no suitable Type 271 radar in the Nore Command with a range good enough for use against S-boats. As a result, the aircraft could not be vectored out under 'Chain Home Low' radar control as was used elsewhere. Already the writing was on the wall as far as the S-boat menace was concerned but they were to have quite a few stings left.

On the night of 4/5 November eighteen boats of the 2nd, 6th and 8th Flotillas carried out a minelaying sortie off Smiths Knoll and the Humber Estuary. After laying their mines, the 2nd Flotilla encountered convoy FN1170 between Cromer and Yarmouth. *S94* missed a destroyer with two torpedoes, *S80* claimed hits on a ship in the

convoy, as did *S89* and *S62* before the destroyers *Vega*, *Eglinton* and *Fernie* drove them off. The second group of this flotilla was also driven off without obtaining a success. None of the other flotillas attacked the convoy, which had both *Firelight* (2,820 tons) and *British Progress* (4,581 tons) damaged. The former had her bows blown off while the latter became a total loss after having been towed into the Tyne by *Superman*. On their return, the 6th Flotilla were attacked by six Beaufighters of No.254 Squadron which sank *S74* and damaged *S61* and *S116*. One aircraft was shot down.

Victims of the minelaying campaign included *Cormount* (2,841 tons) and *Morar* (1,507 tons) sunk off the Humber as well as the destroyers *Holderness* and *Worcester* damaged; the former required six months' repair while the latter was declared a 'constructional total loss' (CTL).

No further operations of note occurred off the east coast in 1943. In mid-November the 9th Flotilla became operational and moved to Rotterdam with four boats (*S130*, *S145*, *S144* and *S146*), all with the new supercharged engines, the first flotilla to be so equipped.

CHANNEL OPERATIONS

The first success by the 5th Flotilla stationed in Cherbourg was an attack on the west-bound convoy WP300 while in Lyme Bay on 27/28 February. This convoy was reported to consist of ten ships with a number of trawlers as escort. Four boats participated (*S65*, *S68*, *S81* and *S85*) and they sank the 4,858-ton *Moldavia* as well as the naval trawlers *Lord Hailsham* and *Harstad*. In addition, *LCT 381* was badly damaged, boarded and a dozen prisoners taken before she was sunk. A later attack on Lyme Bay convoys, this time on the night of 4/5 March, was less successful. Six boats sailed from Cherbourg intending to attack convoys WP303 and PW303 but they were twice driven off by the Polish destroyer *Krakowiak*, although without damage. After an operation in support of the movement of the 8th Destroyer Flotilla to Brest, two further fruitless torpedo sorties against the east-west Channel convoys followed. At that time St. Peter Port was being used as a forward base from which the sorties were despatched, although the main base remained Cherbourg. Thus seven boats laid fourteen LMF mines off the Eddystone on 3/4 April and on the following night the same boats attempted to attack a convoy reported off Start Point, using St. Peter Port as a base. Both this latter sortie and one on the night of 9/10 April were unable to find a convoy to attack. What was of increasing concern was the almost continual shadowing and sometimes attack by prowling aircraft. Success finally came with an attack on convoy PW323 by eight boats of the 5th Flotilla operating from L'Aberwrach on the night of 13/14 April. Two boats had to be detached but the remaining six (*S81/S82*, *S90/S121* and *S112/S65*) found and attacked the convoy. This comprised six merchant ships, escorted by the Norwegian-manned destroyers

Eskdale and *Glaisdale* and five trawlers. *S90* torpedoed *Eskdale*, which was later finished off by *S112* and *S65*. *S121* torpedoed *Stanlake* (1,742 tons), which in turn was finally sunk by *S90* and *S82*. The convoy took shelter in Falmouth and two Beaufighters were scrambled to attack the S-boats but failed to find them. It was perhaps significant that on the previous night Nos. 833 and 834 Squadrons, FAA, based at Exeter had been stood down in preparation for their return to duties aboard aircraft-carriers; so on this night none of the prowling naval biplanes was airborne.

The summer months saw the main thrust of S-boat operations switched to the shorter-ranged attacks on east-west Channel convoys and a minelaying campaign in the Channel as described earlier. By August, of the North Sea flotillas temporarily detached to the Channel, only the 4th Flotilla remained. On 11 August seven boats of this flotilla were lying to buoys in L'Aberwrach Bay preparatory to launching a torpedo sortie to Plymouth Bay. That afternoon eight Whirlwinds of No. 263 Squadron escorted by twenty Spitfires attacked the boats, sinking *S121* and damaging all the others to varying degrees. A second attack that evening further damaged *S117*. These attacks were made by cannon fire but FdS noted in his war diary for the second half of August that rocket projectiles had been employed for the first time.

In September the first Hohentweil-equipped Ju 88s reached the Luftwaffe's Channel reconnaissance squadrons and it was anticipated that their appearance would boost the S-boats' success rate. However, the first such combined sortie on 2/3 September by nine boats of the 4th and 5th Flotillas against an east-bound convoy in Lyme Bay failed because the aircraft was driven off by night fighters. The 4th Flotilla returned to the North Sea early in September, leaving only the 5th Flotilla at Cherbourg. The strength of this formation naturally fluctuated but on 15 September consisted of five operational boats at Cherbourg and four more non-operational either there or in Germany. Operational activities during September and October were few, mainly escort and minelaying tasks in conjunction with torpedo boat operations or the movement of blockade-runners.

On 25/26 October the flotilla transferred to Boulogne to make a surprise attack on an expected west-bound Channel convoy (no S-boat attacks had been made in this area against convoys for some eighteen months). Intelligence (B-Dienst) reports had established that the CW convoys operated a four-day cycle and often contained large ships; significantly, too, landing craft were often included in the average strength of fifteen ships. On 2 November such a convoy was reported having passed the Thames Boom at midday, which had been sighted from Cap Griz Nez early the same evening. Nine boats sailed to attack the convoy (CW221), working in four groups, between Dungeness and Beachy Head. *Dona Isabel* (1,179 tons) was sunk by *S146*, *Foam Queen* (811 tons) by *S100* and *Storaa* (1,967 tons) by *S138*. The destroyer *Whitshed*, on patrol, engaged the S-boats intermittently for a couple of hours and some RN coastal forces also got into action, but only *S141* was damaged slightly. In total, 23 torpedoes were fired of which, at most, four hit, this low number being attributed by Petersen to the fact that the flotilla had not fired torpedoes since February and also because of the sea conditions. Many of the C.O.s were in fact firing their first live torpedoes. The remainder of November was beset by poor weather, the flotilla undertaking only a couple of tasks, one of which was providing flank escort to the destroyers *Z27* and *ZH1* in their move to Brest, made in conjunction with the flotilla's return to Cherbourg on the 2nd. Apart from this, there was a minelaying sortie on 26/27 November, when 54 mines were laid to the east and west of the Isle of Wight.

December opened with an attack by nine boats on an east-bound convoy of five ships south of Selsey Bill. Eight torpedoes were fired of which only one from *S142* sank a ship. Although claimed as 1,000 tons, this was in fact the escort trawler *Avanturine* (196 tons), which was under tow at the time and was lost with all hands. A subsequent sortie to Lyme Bay on 3/4 December had to be abandoned because of heavy weather which curtailed operations almost until the end of the month. Then a sweep was launched between the Needles and Portland Bill without reconnaissance in the hope of chancing upon one of the regular convoys. This took place on 23/24 December by nine boats which fell in with convoy WP450 consisting of six merchant ships and four US Navy LSTs (*LST 369, 388, 392* and *393*). Their escort included the destroyers *Bleasdale* and *Glaisdale* (which had just joined) with five trawlers and *BYMS 2036*. The destroyers drove off the S-boats, once again making use of 'Headache' and the SGBs *Grey Wolf* (*SGB 8*) and *Grey Shark* (*SGB 6*) on patrol south of the convoy had a brief engagement as the enemy retired. Only one torpedo was fired in this sortie, by *S140*, which missed one of the destroyers. This was the final operation in the Channel during 1943.

The results obtained in 1943 were disappointing for the Germans: sixteen ships totalling 26,024 tons gross sunk, compared with 28 ships of 38,397 tons in 1942; but even so, in view of the vast tonnages moved on the coastal convoys, these were in reality mere pinpricks, although a great nuisance.

Left: S-boats in dry dock. Note the different configurations. (BfZ)

8. THE INVASION YEAR, 1944

When the New Year opened, the forces at the disposal of FdS for employment in the west were as follows:

2nd Flotilla	Ijmuiden	*S62, 67, 80, 83, 86, 89, 92, 94* and *98*
4th Flotilla	Rotterdam	*S48, 87, 99, 117, 120* and *122*
5th Flotilla	Cherbourg	*S84, 100, 112, 136, 138, 139, 140, 141, 142* and *143*
6th Flotilla	Ijmuiden	*S39, 76, 79, 90, 91, 97, 114, 128* and *135*
8th Flotilla	Ijmuiden	*S64, 65, 68, 69, 85, 93, 127* and *129*
9th Flotilla	Rotterdam	*S130, 144, 145, 146* and *150*

Another 22 boats were allocated to the S-boat Training Division in the Baltic.

NORTH SEA OPERATIONS TO MAY 1944

Weather conditions in the southern North Sea prevented all operations during January except for one minelaying sortie off Orfordness by the 4th Flotilla on the night of the 20th/21st. The North Sea forces were then at rather a low ebb as the 9th Flotilla had been transferred to the Channel theatre because the 5th Flotilla were refitting with 4cm guns. At the same time fears of an Allied invasion of the Iberian peninsula prompted plans to despatch both flotillas to the Biscay coast, but yet again this came to nought, fortunately for Petersen, because his forces were already sparsely spread out. In the first half of February, three minelaying sorties were carried out by the 2nd and 8th Flotillas. During one of these sorties on 13 February, the minesweeping trawler *Cap d'Antifer* was torpedoed and sunk by *S99* and *S65*. On the night of 14 February there was an indecisive clash between boats of the 2nd and 8th Flotillas and the corvettes *Mallard* and *Shearwater*. Interestingly, the 8th Flotilla's task had been to attempt to capture and bring home an MGB. During the second half of the month, three torpedo attacks were made against south-bound convoys and one minelaying sortie carried out. On 22/23 February fifteen boats of the two flotillas sailed for a torpedo attack but were driven off by the destroyers *Garth* and *Southdown*. In the ensuing mêlée, six torpedoes were fired, unsuccessfully, at the destroyers and two boats of the 2nd Flotilla (*S94* and *S128*) collided. However, *S80*, *S92* and *S135* were able to prevent the destroyers from intervening further by counter-attacking with four more torpedoes while the damaged boats were scuttled. The only success of the month came in the course of a combined minelaying and strike on 24/25 February when convoy FS1371 was encountered. Only one ship was torpedoed, *Phillip M* (2,085 tons), before the destroyers *Vivien* and *Eglinton* drove off the attackers. A sortie the following night was even less successful as *Meynell* forced away the S-boats without their sinking or damaging anything. These results were disappointing, especially as the weather in the area was more favourable than in the Channel, in contrast to recent months. What concerned Petersen most, however, was the fact that the newly installed 'Naxos' FuMB sets had revealed that all radar-equipped enemy vessels had centimetric radar.

The first half of March was a complete blank for operations due to a combination of heavy weather and bright moonlit nights. Nor was there much improvement in the S-boats' fortunes in the latter half when five further torpedo attacks were launched. *S67* and *S64* were both damaged in encounters with escorts and on 26 March there was a daylight raid by USAAF Marauders on Ijmuiden when 594 tons of bombs were dropped. The old S-boat bunker was hit but barely damaged and the new bunker, which had received its 70cm interim roof but was not complete, was also damaged. However, *S93* and *S129* lying outside the bunkers were both destroyed. A small recompense for this loss was the sinking of *MTB 241* by S-boats off Den Helder on 30/31 March. FdS was forced to admit that not one of the month's sorties had brought the expected success and cited poor reconnaissance, strong defences, radar and poor visibility as the main reasons for this.

In April there were only five minelaying sorties, of which two were broken off, and in the first half of May there were no operations at all because of the moon phase and weather conditions. The second half of the month saw three further minelaying operations when new-type firing mechanisms were employed. In one of these, a field laid by the 8th Flotilla on 18/19 May accounted for the minesweepers *Wyoming* and *MMS 227* but on return, a Swordfish of No. 819 Squadron bombed *S87* which caught fire and sank while being towed by *S83*.

Even the minelaying proved disappointing. Intelligence reports indicated that, for example, of a field of 31 mines laid on one occasion, 27-29 had been swept within six hours. This was not altogether surprising as radar prevented much chance of unseen lays and the experienced minesweeping commands soon surmounted all new firing devices.

CHANNEL OPERATIONS TO 1 JUNE 1944

After the almost obligatory week of bad weather, the 5th Flotilla was able to mount a torpedo sortie on 5/6 January but the North Sea flotillas remained weathered in. The attack in the Channel was further west than had so far been attempted by the S-boats - off Lands End in fact. Seven boats sailed from Cherbourg and attacked the Bristol Channel-Portsmouth convoy WP457 escorted by four trawlers and the destroyers *Talybont* and *Melbreak* (which had only joined at the Lizard). Twenty-three torpedoes were fired, sinking *Polperro* (403 tons), *Underwood* (1,990 tons) and *Solstad* (1,408 tons) as well as the escorting trawler *Wallasea* (545 tons) although the tonnage claimed was 12,500, plus the trawler. The S-boats disengaged without damage. This action was interesting in that TZ3 magnetic pistols were used for the first time but FdS, while pleased with their performance, felt that too many shots had been wasted by firing singletons from excessive ranges. Two further sorties, on 15/16 January against convoy PW461 and on 20/21 January, were unsuccessful as they were driven off by the escort in the former case (*Brissenden* and *Talybont*) and bad weather plus attacks by Beaufighters of Fighter Command in the latter. However, in an attack on CW243, consisting of 21 ships escorted by *Quorn* and *Albrighton*, three minesweeping trawlers and six MLs, the 5th Flotilla's torpedoes sank *Emerald* (806 tons), *Caleb Spragge* (1,813 tons) and the trawler *Pine*. All these vessels were sunk by *S142* and *S138*, mostly the former as the other boats had been driven off by the escort.

By the middle of February the 9th Flotilla had arrived at Cherbourg to reinforce the 5th Flotilla and on 15/16 February twelve boats of the combined flotillas under the command of S.O. 9th Flotilla attempted to locate a westbound convoy off Beachy Head. They were detected by British radar stations and the sortie was abandoned. Sorties on 27/28 and 28/29 February were also abandoned. March saw no improvement in the fortunes of the Channel flotillas for on the 15th/16th of that month a sortie by seven boats of the combined flotillas which intended to intercept convoy WP492 off Lands End was itself detected by Halifax 'J' of No. 502 Squadron on an anti-submarine patrol between Ushant and Lands End. The aircraft made a bombing attack, as did Wellingtons of Nos. 172 and 612 Squadrons, using depth charges but to no effect. Their reports called up Force 115, *Brissenden* and *Melbreak*, which intercepted and engaged the retiring S-boats, claiming one sunk and several damaged (*S143* was hit on the forecastle but, after jettisoning her torpedoes, got home safely). Three further attempts to find PW convoys between Portland and Plymouth during the latter half of March were equally unsuccessful.

April saw a number of unsuccessful attempts by boats of the 5th and 9th Flotillas to attack the Channel convoys. Minelaying operations were also carried out around the Isle of Wight. The sortie on 21/22 April is of interest as it is recorded as the first successful shore-controlled

interception of an S-boat strike by naval forces. Ten boats had sailed to attack a convoy off Dungeness, but as a result of their detection Force 113 (*Volunteer* and *Middleton*) plus MTBs were sailed to intercept them. In the brief action that followed, both *S167* and *MTB 416* were damaged. Not until towards the end of the month did a small success come the Germans' way when *S100* sank the tug *Roode Zee* with all hands while on passage to Portsmouth on 23/24 April.

During the next operation, on 25/26 April, which was a sortie to attack the convoy route off Selsey Bill, twelve boats put out from Boulogne, six each from the 5th and 9th Flotillas. Although one group of the 5th Flotilla approached as close as ten miles south of the Nab Tower, when they were engaged by the shore batteries on Culver Cliffs, no convoy was found and the sortie was effectively broken up by two destroyer patrols, *Stevenstone/Seymore* and *La Combattante/Rowley*. The latter pair of destroyers intercepted the first group of the 9th Flotilla (*S167*, *S146* and *S147*) and sank *S147*. *S167* was also damaged but returned to base safely.

One of the S-boats' most damaging attacks was made on the following night, which involved US forces for the first time. Both east- and west-bound convoys had been reported west of Portland Bill, so six boats of the 5th Flotilla and three of the 9th sailed from Cherbourg for an attack. The convoys had in fact passed out of the danger area and instead the S-boats encountered a group of eight USN LSTs on 'Exercise Tiger', designated convoy T4. These were steaming at $3^{1}/_{2}$ knots in line ahead across Lyme Bay, some thirty miles off Slapton Sands, escorted only by the corvette *Azalea*, despite Plymouth Command having received warning that S-boats were at sea a couple of hours earlier. The destroyer *Scimitar* should also have been part of the escort but she had been in collision with

LCI(L)324 the previous night and had been detached to Plymouth for repair. By an oversight, the destroyer *Saladin*, while ordered to replace her, had not yet joined the convoy. The first indication of something amiss did not come until the S-boats were on the convoy. As it broke up in confusion, *LST507* and *LST531* were torpedoed and sunk with tragically heavy loss of life among the American troops, *LST289* was damaged by another torpedo. The destroyers *Onslow*, *Offa* and *Orwell* sailed to intercept the German force but had only a fleeting glance of the enemy who escaped unscathed. It was a most embarrassing incident for the Allies. No shore radar contact had been obtained until the boats were some ten miles inside the distance at which contact was normally expected; and when warning was broadcast, why was T4 allowed to steam into the enemy's path? C-in-C Plymouth accepted failure to provide sufficient escort but *Azalea*'s C.O. was censured for taking no steps to avoid the enemy once contact had been made. There was little excuse for continuing to steam at $3^{1}/_{2}$ kt in line ahead some two hours after initial enemy reports. The corvette was actually under the orders of USN officers but it was considered that her captain could and should have taken steps to defend the convoy. Her best position would have been to seaward, not at the head of the column, but it was believed that the absence of *Scimitar*, although unfortunate, was not critical once the enemy had got inside the screen. There were more than five hundred US casualties in this fiasco.

It was obvious to the Germans that the increasing numbers of landing craft being concentrated in the Channel presaged an invasion, but the question was when, and equally important where? In May Petersen considered that, based on his information gained from S-boat operations and despite a lively increase in Allied naval and air activity, including practice landings such as Operation

'Tiger', there had so far been no indication that a landing was imminent. However SKL ordered a stepping up of minelaying around the Isle of Wight and the transfer of a third flotilla into the Channel. It was soon realized that Allied defences would greatly restrict minelaying operations and the 4th Flotilla would therefore remain at Boulogne.

April and May saw frequent clashes between the S-boats and the Royal Navy's light forces of destroyers, destroyer escorts, corvettes and coastal forces as well as RAF and USAAF aircraft. Most of the S-boat operations were of a mining nature and in the course of one such mission on 12/13 May *La Combattante* shelled and sank *S141*; two other S-boats were damaged. On 23/24 May *Vanquisher* damaged *S112* while defending convoy WP526. Success was now hard to come by, especially in the Channel where the Allied naval build-up for 'Overlord' meant that huge numbers of destroyers and smaller craft were available, not only for convoy escort but also to form hunter groups to combat the S-boats' activities. Moreover, it was now seldom possible to leave Cherbourg undetected by British radar. On 1 June, the eve of 'Overlord', the strength and disposition of the S-boat forces were as follows:

2nd Flotilla (Ostend)	5 boats operational
	5 boats unserviceable
4th Flotilla (Boulogne)	8 boats operational
5th Flotilla (Cherbourg)	5 boats operational
	4 boats unserviceable
8th Flotilla (Ijmuiden)	4 boats operational
9th Flotilla (Cherbourg)	7 boats operational

Thus in the Channel there were 20 + 4 boats and in the North Sea 9 + 5 boats - not a great number to face the might of Allied seapower.

THE INVASION BEACHHEADS, JUNE TO AUGUST 1944

At midday on 3 June Boulogne suffered an air raid in which the S-boat bunker was hit by four bombs but not severely damaged. *S172* and *S174* were however trapped by some wreckage for a period. The fact that the invasion must be close was reinforced by the capture at Morlaix the same day of people who ventured the information that the Allied landings would take place on the night of 3/4 June. Leaflets with similar information were also found. As a result, all forces were brought to short notice but stood down again when no landing took place. The final alert did not come until the early hours of 6 June, when paratroops began dropping in France, at which point Group West ordered all flotillas to immediate notice. Then when it became clear that an invasion was in progress from the sea, the 5th and 9th Flotillas sailed from Cherbourg and the 4th from Boulogne on reconnaissance missions but failed to make contact with enemy forces.

That afternoon Group West ordered the Cherbourg flotillas to attack the invading forces that night and the 4th Flotilla to patrol from Boulogne. This latter flotilla saw only a lone destroyer which *S172* missed with her torpedoes. The 5th Flotilla saw and attacked a couple of destroyers but missed, then lost *S139* on a mine laid by the 64th MTB Flotilla. Off St. Vaast, one group, having evaded the destroyers, torpedoed and sank *LST 715*, after which, with all their torpedoes expended, they withdrew to the last known position of *S139* but found no survivors. Part of the 9th Flotilla now joined up but *S140* was mined and sunk by the same field that had caught *S139*.

The second group of the 9th Flotilla fired five torpedoes at a couple of destroyers and missed. Then the first group fired six into a group of landing craft, sinking one LCT before joining up with the 5th Flotilla. A dozen more torpedoes were fired, including eight by *S130* and *S145* at a destroyer, all of which missed. It was a small return for the torpedo expenditure and caused Petersen to remind the flotillas that invasion craft and not the destroyers were the main target.

The following night there was a repeat sortie when the 4th Flotilla encountered a convoy of landing craft escorted by the destroyer *Beagle* and fired torpedoes, sinking *LST 376* and *LST 314* and probably an LCT. The 9th Flotilla attacked a group of landing craft escorted by *ML 903*, sinking *LC(I) 105* and *LCT 875* with six torpedoes. They then fired another six at an American cruiser (perhaps *Tuscaloosa*) before encountering some MGBs, when *S145* and *S168* were damaged; the latter had to be towed in. Of the five boats of the 5th Flotilla, *S100*, *S138* and *S84* unsuccessfully attacked a group of landing craft, then fired torpedoes at a cruiser and destroyer group, claiming hits on both a cruiser and destroyer. They were then driven off by the frigates *Retalick* and *Stayner*, when *S84* was badly hit as well as *S138* and *S142* (of the second group) which had joined up again. No losses were actually caused to the Allies by the 5th Flotilla that night. Nor were they any more successful on the night of 8/9 June when the 5th and 9th Flotillas left Cherbourg to lay mines and, having done so, were taken under radar-directed gunfire by the US destroyer *Frankford*, east of the Cotentin peninsula in the early hours of the 9th. The 9th Flotilla claimed to have sunk two LSTs before two more US destroyers, *Hambleton* and *Baldwin*, intervened and drove them off. No damage appears to have been inflicted by either side. During the same night the 4th Flotilla sortied from Le Havre, also on a minelaying task, but broke off, missed a destroyer with three torpedoes and then returned to Le Havre, a performance which incurred some comment from FdS. The supply of torpedoes at Le Havre was now a matter of some concern as there were only thirty available, all needing regulating, and of these, seventeen had been given to the 5th Torpedo boat Flotilla. More had been demanded but if they did not arrive, the 4th Flotilla would have to go to Boulogne to replenish, which was undesirably far from the beachhead.

Sorties against the invasion shipping were now being made nightly by the 5th and 9th Flotillas from Cherbourg, the 4th Flotilla from Le Havre and the 2nd Flotilla from Boulogne, using both mine and torpedo, but the results remained meagre in comparison with the effort expended. There were frequent skirmishes with US destroyers on the 'Dixie' patrol line at the western extremity of the beachhead and with RN forces further east. On 10/11 June boats of the 5th Flotilla were in action against the frigates *Stayner* and *Halstead* as well as units of the 35th MTB Flotilla. *Halstead* was hit by a torpedo in the bows and damaged so badly that she was declared a constructional total loss. *MTB 448* was also sunk that night, as was *S136*. The 9th Flotilla came into action with the SGBs *Grey Wolf* and *Grey Goose* but were able to sink the US tug *Partridge* and *LST 496*, as well as damaging *LST 538*. On their return, *S130* was badly damaged by splinters during an attack by aircraft. Six boats of the 4th Flotilla laid mines west of Le Havre, then evaded several destroyer and MGB groups before putting into Boulogne. The 2nd Flotilla, also operating from Le Havre with four boats, encountered a convoy south of the Isle of Wight, after having laid mines. *S177* and *S178* sank three ships between them, *Dungrange* (621 tons), *Ashanti* (534 tons) and *Brackenfield* (657 tons). After this night's operations, FdS commented that the enemy's defences north of Barfleur were becoming stronger and it would therefore be more difficult to break into the invasion area and return to Cherbourg afterwards. In an effort to ease the situation, the 4th Gun Carrier Flotilla was ordered to draw off the destroyer patrols north of Barfleur during the following night's sorties. Furthermore, Cherbourg itself was becoming difficult to operate from and on 11 June orders were given to transfer as many boats as possible to either Le Havre or St. Malo. Petersen, however, did not consider St. Malo particularly suitable, well defended or secure, while a transfer to Le Havre could only be done in groups of three boats at full speed. At the same time SKL ordered the 6th Flotilla out of the Gulf of Finland to the invasion area with all despatch.

The night of 11/12 June saw yet another series of engagements between the S-boats and Allied warships. Coastal batteries and the deployment of the 4th Gun Carrier Flotilla facilitated the passage of the Cherbourg boats into the invasion zone, but the US destroyers *Somers*, *Laffey* and *Nelson* engaged *S150*, *S160*, *S138* and *S142* before they could get at the supply chain itself. *Nelson*, with only half her machinery operational, was anchored on the 'Dixie' line screen and in the early hours of 12 June gained radar contact with enemy vessels. After her challenge went unanswered and the anchor heaved in, she fired about ten salvoes in full radar control before a torpedo from *S138* blew off the stern including the after gun. Despite casualties and the damage incurred, *Nelson* was towed safely to Portsmouth. Meanwhile, *Laffey*, ahead of *Nelson* and *Somers*, hunted the S-boats and drove them off with radar-controlled gunfire. The 2nd Flotilla had

engagements with a frigate and the 29th (Canadian) MTB flotilla which prevented their reaching the invasion area, and both *S181* and *S179* were damaged by mines when returning to Le Havre. The 4th Flotilla, working out of Boulogne, encountered a destroyer patrol (*Onslow*, *Offa*, *Onslaught* and *Oribi*) and MTBs when *S171* sank *MGB 17*. They too were prevented from attacking the important landing craft and finally put into Le Havre.

Le Havre, despite the critical shortage of torpedoes there, was in fact the best placed base for operations; Boulogne was too distant and the problems at Cherbourg have already been outlined. Nevertheless, boats were ordered to return to Le Havre only in an emergency until the torpedo situation improved. Dispositions of boats on 12 June were as follows :

Cherbourg:	*S138*, *S142* operational (5th Flotilla)
	S112 semi-operational (5th Flotilla)
	S150, *S167* operational (9th Flotilla)
	130, *S145* semi-operational (9th Flotilla)
Boulogne:	*S175* operational (4th Flotilla)
	S177 operational (2nd Flotilla)
	S174 non-operational (4th Flotilla)
Ostend:	*S83*, *S127*, *S133* operational (8th Flotilla)
	S117 non-operational (8th Flotilla)
Le Havre:	*S84*, *S100*, *S143* operational (5th Flotilla)
	S144, *S146* operational (9th Flotilla)
	S178, *S179*, *S181*, *S189* operational (2nd Flotilla)
	S172, *S169*, *S171*, *S173*, *S187*, *S188* operational (4th Flotilla)

That night the four operational boats at Cherbourg, under the command of the 9th Flotilla, succeeded in transferring to Le Havre despite an engagement with a patrol consisting of *Glaisdale*, *Stevenstone* and *Isis*, in which *S138* was damaged. 'Aphrodite' decoys were used in this sortie. The 4th Flotilla sailed from Le Havre on a sortie but *S169* was mined outside the harbour, after which her group of two boats returned. The second group of three boats suffered air attack and was engaged by three Canadian corvettes, which damaged *S188*; the sortie was then called off. It was the 2nd Flotilla that suffered most that night. Just before midnight four boats sailed from Le Havre and were immediately engaged by destroyer and MGB patrols which completely prevented their breakthrough to the west despite several attempts to do so. Eventually visibility deteriorated and the sortie was broken off. The flotilla then headed for Boulogne, but before they could reach this haven, they were set upon by Beaufighters of Nos. 143 and 236 Squadrons, which sank *S178* and damaged *S179* and *S189*. The latter, on fire and unable to stop her engines, was also sunk soon after. *S181* rescued the survivors of *S178* and attempted to tow the crippled

S179 to Boulogne. Two miles from the port, most of *S179*'s people were taken off, when the 8th R-boat Flotilla arrived to assist. *S179* was then attacked again and both she and *R97* alongside were sunk. Several other vessels were also damaged.

The position at Cherbourg now led Petersen to request the removal of as much equipment and stores for use elsewhere. Group West agreed but advised that the use of Cherbourg as a base some time later was still to be considered. A period of bad weather interrupted operations for a few days and then on 14/15 June a major blow fell when a large force of RAF Lancaster bombers raided Le Havre. Quite apart from the damage and loss inflicted on other Kriegsmarine units, a total of fourteen S-boats (*S169*, *S171*, *S172*, *S173*, *S187* and *S188* of the 4th Flotilla; *S84*, *S100*, *S138*, *S142* and *S43* of the 5th Flotilla; *S146* and *S150* of the 9th Flotilla) were destroyed and heavy casualties incurred. Only *S167* remained fully operational, with *S144* in a damaged condition. In the invasion area there now remained only these two boats, plus three of the 9th Flotilla at Cherbourg, two of the 2nd Flotilla and two of the 4th at Boulogne. At Ostend there were two more 2nd Flotilla boats and three of the 8th - a total of thirteen operational boats. The following night there was a large air raid on Boulogne: none of the S-boats suffered but the R-boats *R81*, *R92*, *R93*, *R125*, *R129*, *R130* and *R232* were sunk and three more badly damaged.

The surviving S-boats continued their attempts to interdict the beachhead area but, as before, were driven off by superior forces and on several occasions attacked by aircraft, when a number of boats suffered damage. On 23 June *S190* had to be sunk after being seriously damaged by destroyers during a sortie by the 2nd Flotilla from Le Havre. The following night both *S175* and *S181* were damaged in action with Allied forces, when Cherbourg was evacuated. Mines and torpedoes were employed on many sorties from Le Havre but the torpedo depot there blew up in the early hours of 5 July. Three boats of the 6th Flotilla arrived in Le Havre as reinforcements that day but *S90* and *S135* had been damaged by aircraft en route. They returned to Boulogne later in the month, from where the flotilla launched the first successful attack against a convoy for some time. Eight boats in two groups sailed in the early hours of 27 July to attack a west-bound convoy reported off Dover. The first group (*S97*, *S114*, *S90* and *S91*) located the convoy and damaged two ships, *Fort Perrot* (7,171 tons) and *Empire Beatrice* (7,046 tons), before being chased off by the destroyers *Obedient*, *Savage* and *Opportune* and MTBs. On the other hand, during a sortie the same night from Le Havre by the 9th Flotilla, there was an engagement with *Retalick* and coastal forces. This led to *MTB 430*'s being rammed and sunk by *S182* and *MTB 412* sinking as a result of striking the wreck of her consort; *S182* had also to be scuttled. On 29 July part of the 6th Flotilla transferred to Le Havre and part to Dieppe. It was from the latter port that three boats (*S97*, *S114* and *S91*) sailed at 2300 hours on 30 July to attack an

east-bound convoy east of Eastbourne. This convoy was FTM53 and consisted of eleven merchant ships, eight LSTs and a trawler, escorted by *Campbell*, *Poppy*, *Kingcup* and *Pickle* with *ML 595*. In addition, the anti-E-boat patrols consisted of three groups of three MTBs, the destroyers *Obedient*, *Savage* and *Opportune* as well as MLs. *Opportune*'s radar failed although *Pickle* and *Kingcup* gained contact by radar but not visually, causing *Campbell*'s C.O. to remark that it was incredible that the enemy passed so close unseen. As the convoy approached Dungeness at 9kt, five ships were torpedoed, starting from the centre and finishing with the Vice-Commodore and Commodore. This was a superb performance as only six FAT torpedoes had been fired. Unfortunately for the Germans, of the five ships hit, only one, *Samwake* (7,219 tons) sank; the remainder, *Fort Dearborne* (7,160 tons), *Ocean Volga* (7,174 tons), *Fort Kaskaskia* (7,180 tons) and *Ocean Courier* (7,178 tons) were all damaged.

At the beginning of August Petersen anticipated the arrival of the newly worked-up 10th Flotilla (six boats) and a strengthening of the 8th Flotilla by the arrival of six new boats. These two flotillas were to be employed in the Dover Straits (8th) and southern North Sea (10th). Operations against the Allied supply routes to France would be maintained by the boats at Le Havre. However, because of the strength of the Allied defences, a new means of attack was to be employed, the T3d Dackel long-range running torpedoes. Eight such operations were carried out, on 4/5, 5/6, 6/7, 8/9, 9/10, 10/11, 14/15 and 17/18 August, when 24, 12, 9, 10, 11, 10, 8 and 7 Dackels respectively were fired - a total of 91. The results were meagre: the freighter *Iddesleigh* (5,208 tons) sunk, and the elderly cruiser *Frobisher*, the repair ship *Albatross* and a minesweeper damaged. Further operations were curtailed because of a torpedo shortage. In any event, FdS was sceptical about their usefulness and because of a similar lack of success with T5 acoustic types, ordered a return to normal torpedo operations. This effectively brought to an end sorties aimed specifically at the invasion beachhead and led to a gradual retreat of the S-boat force into the North Sea. Some strikes were carried out in August against the south coast convoy routes, such as that by the 8th Flotilla against FTM70 escorted by *Fitzroy*, *Rutherford* and *Vestal* plus *ML 587* and *593* off Dungeness on 17/18 August. Patrolling destroyers *Walpole* and *Opportune* drove off the S-boats without damage and once again the T5 torpedoes were a complete failure. Only *Fort Gloucester* (7,127 tons) was damaged.

The evacuation of Le Havre was begun on the night of 23/24 August and the S-boats covered the nightly evacuation convoys, many of which were decimated by Allied light forces. On 3/4 September the last operational boats were withdrawn to Rotterdam and Ijmuiden, thirteen in all, of which one, *S184*, was sunk by the Dover shore batteries en route. Le Havre surrendered on 12 September leaving only two boats, *S145* and *S112*, in the area, trapped in Brest, where they remained until 1945.

9. NORTH SEA, 1944-45

With the evacuation of Boulogne, the harbour was mined and the last S-boats departed for Dutch harbours where they arrived on 5 September. Administration of the S-boat Command was now vested in Group (North) with FdS's headquarters being at Scheveningen. The flotillas themselves were based at Ijmuiden and Rotterdam, their primary task being minelaying sorties along the Flanders and Norfolk coasts. Two sorties to the former on the 8th and 10th were uneventful but one on 12/13 September was detected, shadowed and bombed soon after leaving Rotterdam by Wellingtons of No. 524 Squadron although no hits were scored (No. 524 Squadron was re-formed in April 1944 for anti-E-boat duties in the Channel and moved to East Anglia in July, when No. 415 Squadron, RCAF, returned to Bomber Command). Surprise being lost, the sortie was called off but another on 16/17 September was carried out successfully. On 18/19 September four boats successfully ran deck cargoes into the besieged port of Dunkerque where a German garrison was still holding out and evacuated General von Klug and his staff. Three other boats (*S183*, *S200* and *S702*) stationed to seaward as flank defence were intercepted by the frigate *Stayner* and *MTBs 724* and *728, and* all three S-boats were sunk. Bad weather prevented any further operations during September and on 1 October the forces available for operations consisted only of:

4th Flotilla (Rotterdam)   *S201, S202* and *S219*
8th Flotilla (Rotterdam)   *S198* and *S199*
10th Flotilla (Ijmuiden)   *S185, S186, S191* and *S192*

During October their tasks consisted mainly of minelaying in the western Scheldt and its approaches. From about 5 October some reinforcements arrived: the 9th Flotilla returned re-equipped while other refitted boats of the 4th, 8th and 10th Flotillas trickled back to the operational bases, bringing the number of serviceable boats up to twenty. On the night of 10 October fourteen of these boats laid 25 LMB and 31 UMB mines (the former pressure-activated), west of Walcheren, but the concentration of boats was shortlived, for on 19 October SKL ordered the 4th Flotilla home via the canals to refit at Swinemünde for service in Norway. Weather conditions as winter approached now became the deciding influence on many operations and the number of sorties declined. A minelaying sortie by the 8th and 10th Flotillas off Ostend on 31 October/1 November led to the sinking of *LCT 420*, and in a torpedo sortie to the same area on 2 November, four boats of the 9th Flotilla (*S175, S167, S168* and *S207*) sank the tanker *Rio Bravo* and possibly the 'Isles'-class naval trawler *Colsay*, although the latter may well have been a victim of the Kleinkampfverband. On 15/16 November a group of boats laid mines off the Humber unopposed and a second operated in the Scheldt approaches where there was an engagement with RN forces. *S168* was set on fire but regained port and *MTB 742* was damaged. The final operation of the month was one by eight boats on 29/30 November when mines were laid in the Scheldt approaches and off Dunkerque.

No more S-boat sorties took place until the latter half of December, but in anticipation of their reappearance the RAF strengthened its forces by the transfer of No. 612 Squadron with Leigh-Light Wellingtons to No.16 Group on 19 December. It was the RAF in fact who struck the next major blow against the S-boats when, on 15 December, No. 617 Squadron with seventeen Lancasters dropped 'Tallboy' bombs on the shelters at Ijmuiden. Two of the 12,000lb bombs penetrated the roof, destroying *S198* and damaging half-a-dozen others. Six of the pens were unusable and the 8th Flotilla was put out of action until the end of the month. As Petersen remarked bitterly, the bunkers could no longer afford the desired protection in their current form and because of their conspicuousness, they were no longer to be fully used and the boats dispersed about the harbours instead.

The 2nd Flotilla was immediately moved from Germany to Den Helder to replace the 8th Flotilla and, with the other flotillas, carried out three minelaying sorties off the Flanders coast on 18/19, 22/23 and 24/25 December. Unsuccessful air attacks were made on them but naval forces summoned to the scene on 22/23 December sank *S185* off Dunkerque and off Ostend *Walpole, Curzon* and *Torrington* with *Kittiwake* and MTBs sank *S192*. Another blow by the RAF aimed at the bunkers on 29 December failed however because of the measures taken by FdS as a result of the Ijmuiden raid.

On 1 January 1945 the organization of the flotillas in the western theatre was:

FdS H.Q.	Wilhelmshaven/Sengwarden
2nd Flotilla:	7 boats operational at Den Helder
4th Flotilla:	4 boats operational at Rotterdam
6th Flotilla:	6 boats operational at Rotterdam
8th Flotilla:	5 boats operational at Ijmuiden
9th Flotilla:	4 boats operational at Rotterdam
Total:	26

Of the other flotillas in home waters, the re-formed 1st Flotilla was working up with three new boats, the 5th Flotilla was under refit at Wilhelmshaven, the 10th non-operational and the 11th Flotilla, whose boats were fitted with MB518 engines, was beset with teething problems as a result. A further 38 boats were serving with the S-boat Training Division of which about a third were unserviceable. The main operational task was the offensive against the Allied supply traffic between the Thames and the Scheldt, which was shared, not always satisfactorily, with the Small Battle Units (see Chapter 15). If, however, there were insufficient opportunities there, then a secondary target was the old favourite, the Thames-Humber convoy routes. Mining operations were restricted by the need to operate 'Seehund', 'Biber' and 'Molch' midget underwater craft against the Thames-Scheldt convoys. 'Linsen' were to be used in the outer Scheldt area.

Allied defensive measures at the end of 1944 included, on the air side, nightly anti-E-boat patrols close off Den Helder, Ijmuiden and the Hook, plus a patrol in depth against boats leaving the Hook for east coast convoy attacks. In addition, there was a patrol designed to detect both S-boats and 'Biber' off the Hook and a daylight patrol line off Walcheren for anti-midget submarine purposes. This latter patrol was undertaken by the Albacores of No. 119 Squadron operating from Knocke near Zeebrugge while the day patrols were carried out by Wellingtons of Nos. 512 and 612 Squadrons as well as naval Swordfish of No. 819 Squadron. All aircraft on patrol now had the capability to attack (as opposed to shadowing) and carried 250lb MC bombs fused to burst in the air just above the surface.

On the naval side, the Royal Navy maintained a continuous patrol line from the Dudgeon Shoal (53°20′N, 1°00′E) and the Thornton Ridge (51°35′N, 3°00′E) using twelve to fourteen destroyers and 'Captain'-class frigates (DEs) with up to fifty MTBs and MGBs. All the larger surface units had radar, of which the 'Captains'' SL with continuous rotation was the best. That in the destroyers, 271Q, did not rotate, while the 'Hunts' had their 271Q aft, which was not best placed. The 291 radar in the

Below: A Fairey Albacore of No. 415 Squadron, RCAF, tasked with anti-E-boat work and seen bombed-up on a Continental airfield in 1945.

MTBs was considered poor in 1945 but nevertheless this was better than anything the S-boats had, which was nothing. Other innovations also assisted in the fight: 'Headache', flashless cordite, rocket flares detection using asdic, white camouflage, etc. The frigates which controlled groups of MTBs, MGBs and MLs were intended to have a VHF link between a shore control at Ostend and with aircraft, but the former was abandoned and the direct link to aircraft did not become operational until March and April. This first tie-up was the means by which the S-boat menace was eventually defeated.

On 13 January the S-boat strength at the front was reinforced by the arrival at Den Helder of the 5th Flotilla with eight boats, but the bad weather that had prevented all operations in January forced an abandonment of a planned minelaying sortie by boats from all three main bases on 9/10 January. Thus it was not until 14/15 January that the first sortie of the year was undertaken. Eight boats of the 2nd Flotilla sailed from Den Helder to lay mines around No. 14 buoy off the Humber but half had to return because of engine defects, leaving only *S176*, *S210*, *S174* and *S209* to continue and lay a total of twenty mines. The 5th Flotilla sailed with six boats, also bound for the Humber, where nineteen mines were laid in the Outer Dowsing channel. Both sorties were detected and attacked by air patrols but without success. The 4th, 6th, 8th, and 9th Flotillas, intending a torpedo sortie against the convoy routes off the South Falls, had to break off because of thick fog. *S180*, one of the 2nd Flotilla released because of engine defects, lost her way in the murk and ran into a 'friendly' minefield off Texel before midnight on the 14th and sank. It is probable that *Dalemoor* (5,835 tons) was a victim of these mines and it was also claimed from B-Dienst reports that *Grainton* (6,341 tons), *St. Nicholas*, *Empire Milner*, *Leaside Park* and *Carrier* (3,036 tons) were all damaged, but this has not been confirmed.

There was a major effort the next night when nine boats of the 2nd and 5th Flotillas carried out a torpedo sweep north of Cromer but sighted nothing. The 5th Flotilla was then inconclusively engaged by the destroyer *Farndale*. Nine other boats of the 6th and 9th Flotillas attacked an east-bound convoy in the western Scheldt but were driven off by *Cotswold*, *Curzon* and *Seymour* without damage to either side. The 4th Flotilla with three boats operated unsuccessfully off Margate and was briefly taken under fire by *Guillemot*; while the 8th Flotilla, also in the Margate area, attacked convoy TAL97 with eight LUT and FAT torpedoes, sinking *LST 415* with one of the former. Gunfire from the Tongue Sand Fort and MTBs finally drove off the S-boats. Nine bombing attacks were made on various groups of boats that night by the RAF but without effect.

On 22/23 January two dozen boats from the Rotterdam and Ijmuiden flotillas attacked the Thames-Scheldt routes again when three boats of the 9th Flotilla found convoy TAC14 to the north of Dunkerque. The straggler *Halo* (2,365 tons) was sunk by *S168* and *S175* which were then

damaged in action with MTBs. The 4th and 6th Flotillas were driven off empty-handed by the MTBs, while the 8th Flotilla, which had sortied towards the Thames end of the route, was engaged by *Seymour* and *Guillemot* as well as coastal forces craft. *S199* was sunk by the guns of the Tongue Sand Fort and *S701* collided with *MTB 495*. Neither boat was sunk but the former was considered irreparable.

The Den Helder flotillas laid mines in the Humber area the next night and on 24/25 January up to eighteen boats operated off Orfordness where mines were again laid. Fog over the East Anglian airfields prevented all air patrols at that time. The bad weather persisted until 29/30 January when both Den Helder flotillas sailed again but only the 2nd Flotilla laid their mines off the Humber, where the boats were inconclusively engaged by *Cubitt* and *Wolfhound* early on 30 January. Fog yet again had grounded the air patrols. February was notable for a resumption in bombing raids against the S-boat bunkers at Ijmuiden on the 3rd and 8th of the month by the RAF and by the USAAF on the 10th. In both the RAF attacks, by Nos. 9 and 617 Squadrons respectively, the 'Tallboy' bombs shattered the structures but lessons had been learned and the boats were too widely dispersed to suffer any damage. In the USAAF raid by nine B-17s of the 92nd Bomb Group, Royal Navy rocket bombs were employed for the first time. Much damage was done to the port installations but only one boat, *S193*, was sunk.

On 12 February complaints were made to Berlin that the restrictions placed on minelaying by the S-boats due to 'Seehund' operations were depriving them of their most effective weapon. Moreover, the 'Seehund', in whose favour this restriction had been made, were proving less successful than anticipated. Petersen argued that it would be far more profitable for his boats to mine the Scheldt estuary, an argument he finally won, subject to some provisos.

The middle of February was marked by frequent fogs which completely grounded night air patrols between the 15th and 18th, so that a sortie by the Den Helder boats on the night of 17/18 February, when mines were laid in the Wash and Humber, went undetected by both sea and air patrols. The Free French destroyer *La Combattante* and the trawler *Aquarius* (187 tons) were sunk by these mines (recent research by Contre-Amiral Zang has proved that *La Combattante* was mined and not sunk by a 'Seehund' as had previously been suggested). *City of London* (8,039 tons) and *Cydonia* (3,517 tons) were probably damaged by these mines off the Humber.

Activity increased towards the end of the month when boats from Ijmuiden and Rotterdam operated on 20/21 February against the Thames/Scheldt traffic with torpedoes and mines but without success. They were engaged by surface forces and attacked no fewer than thirteen times by aircraft - all unsuccessfully. The following night, boats of all six flotillas, 22 in all, sailed for a torpedo attack on the east coast convoy routes. Sixteen air attacks were made off the Dutch ports as they sailed, all without effect, and shadowing aircraft reports enabled surface forces to drive off boats of the 4th, 6th and 9th Flotillas. However, this allowed boats of the 2nd and 5th Flotillas to attack the convoy, FS1734, 23 miles north-east of Great Yarmouth. *Goodwood* (2,780 tons) and *Blacktoft* (1,109 tons) were sunk and *Skjold* (1,345 tons) damaged by gunfire. The 8th Flotilla found a convoy of landing craft in the Thames estuary from which *LCP707* was sunk. *S193* was however sunk in turn by the escort and, on the return journey, *S167* of the 9th Flotilla was lost following a collision.

On the third consecutive night, the Rotterdam boats operated mainly with mines against the Thames/Scheldt route but were engaged by surface forces before reaching the swept channel. The Ijmuiden Flotilla was shadowed and attacked by Wellingtons almost half way to the east coast before they abandoned their mission. On the fourth night, 24/25 February, minelaying was again the task. Boats from Ijmuiden were attacked and shadowed continuously, but shot down two Wellingtons, 'A' of No. 612 Squadron and 'B' of No.524, in the process. The final operation of the month was a combined minelaying and torpedo sortie to the Thames/Scheldt and East Anglia areas. Once again, Wellingtons shadowed the S-boats and attacked but without result. Clashes with surface forces occurred on both sides of the North Sea but off Ostend after mines had been laid, *S220* was sunk in action with *Cotswold* and *Seymour*; 26 survivors were rescued. No torpedo attacks were made. As a result of these mining operations, known losses were *Auretta* (4,571 tons), *Sampa* (7,219 tons) and *Robert L. Vann* (7,176 tons). Allied casualties (number of ships and tonnage) in the southern North Sea for January and February due to S-boat activities were:

	January	February
Torpedo:		
Sunk	2=5,115 tons	2=3,889 tons
Damaged	–	1=1345 tons
Mine:		
Sunk	5=16,361 tons	10=19,551 tons
Damaged	1=1,100 tons	3=11,956 tons

The 8th Flotilla left Ijmuiden at the end of February to refit in Germany and was not replaced. The remaining flotillas were now concentrated on Rotterdam and Den Helder, probably because of the destruction caused by air raids on Ijmuiden. The nominal strength was about 40 boats of which no more than 25 to 30 were operational at any one time. No operations took place until 9/10 March when three flotillas laid mines in the Scheldt approaches. They were detected but escaped, shooting down Swordfish, 'G' of No. 119 Squadron. On 11/12 March a combined operation with 'Biber', 'Molch' and 'Linsen' took place, when the S-boats of the Rotterdam flotillas were used to transport 'Linsen'. The Den Helder flotillas

laid mines off the Wash the same night. Poor weather and incessant harrying by aircraft prevented further operations until a large minelaying operation was carried out against Ostend and East Anglia. There was one naval interception when two MTBs were damaged.

The following night, all the flotillas were at sea again, some 25 boats, directed against the east coast convoy routes between the Humber and Orfordness. Aircraft shadowed the boats across the North Sea, enabling Royal Navy forces to intercept six boats of the 5th Flotilla; two were damaged by destroyers before withdrawing empty-handed. The 2nd Flotilla's six boats were also intercepted by MTBs and withdrew when all their boats were damaged. The 9th Flotilla (five boats) was engaged by destroyers off Southwold and driven off but the 4th and 6th Flotillas succeeded in laying their mines. While these two flotillas were withdrawing, they came across convoy FS1759 off Lowestoft. In the ensuing attack, *Crichtown* (1,097 tons) and *Rogate* (2,871 tons) were torpedoed and sunk. In addition, the mines accounted for *LST80*, *Samselbu* (7,253 tons) and *Empire Blessing* (7,062 tons) as well as a trawler. *Hadley F. Brown* (7,176 tons) was damaged.

In another sortie on 20/21 March, by 20 boats against the east coast convoy routes, the 2nd Flotilla was attacked by Coastal Command Beaufighters as soon as it left Den Helder. Beaufighter 'G' of No. 236 Squadron sank *S181* whose casualties included the flotilla commander and the boat's C.O., whereupon the remaining boats aborted the mission. One aircraft, 'J' of No. 236 Squadron was shot down. The other boats continued the sortie despite air and sea attacks but returned to base afterwards. Other minelaying sorties took place on 22/23 and 25/26 March during which there were frequent engagements with surface and air patrols. In the last, the Norwegian destroyer *Arendal*, the Polish *Krakowiak* and RN *Riou* came into action but did not succeed in sinking any boat. The mines laid accounted for *Eleftheria* (7,247 tons), *Charles D. McIver* (7,176 tons), *ML466* and *LCP840*.

A critical point had now been reached in the war in the North Sea. On the Allied side, co-operation between sea and air forces had improved vastly with direct VHF R/T between aircraft and the destroyers/frigates. Flares could be requested from shadowing aircraft by surface vessels or, if no naval units were present, Beaufighter strike forces could be called up instead. It had reached the point where the threat of torpedo attack had been reduced to nil and greatly limited the extent of minelaying opportunities. On the German side, the significant feature was fuel, or lack of it; it had been with great difficulty that the last operation had been mounted at all. Furthermore, on 26 March the 5th Flotilla was ordered to the Baltic, leaving only four flotillas in Holland.

As a result of the lack of diesel fuel, no further sorties took place until 5/6 April, when eighteen boats made an unsuccessful sortie against the Thames/Scheldt convoy routes. On the following night, six boats of the 2nd Flotilla left Den Helder to lay mines off the east coast. They were, as was usual now, shadowed continuously and intercepted in the early hours of the 7th off Smiths Knoll. In an hour and a half's close engagement, *S176* and *S177* were rammed and sunk by *MTBs 494* and *493* (not necessarily respectively) and *MTB 5001* was sunk by gunfire. *MTB 494* sank as a result of her damage and *MTB 493* could only make harbour stern first. No more success was achieved the following night when a dozen boats of the 4th and 6th Flotillas sailed to attack the Thames/Scheldt route again. The alerted defences were ready for them and engaged in the early hours north-west of Ostend. In the action that followed, *S202* and *S703* collided at high speed and sank, some 40 survivors being rescued by the pursuing frigate *Rutherford* and *MTBs 482* and *454*. Shortly afterwards, *S223* detonated a mine about 30 miles north of Ostend and sank.

Such heavy losses in so short a period were a serious blow and no further sorties could be mounted until 12/13 April when twelve boats of the 4th and 9th Flotillas sailed to lay mines in the Scheldt approaches again. Although duly shadowed and reported, the mines were laid before they were brought to action by a surface patrol consisting of the frigate *Ekins* and *MTBs 797* and *746*. *S205* was badly damaged by gunfire and both MTBs suffered light damage. The mines later claimed *Gold Shell* (8,208 tons) sunk while *Conakrian* (4,876 tons), *Benjamin H. Bristow* (7,191 tons) and *Horace Binney* (7,191 tons) were all damaged.

This proved to be the last operation of the war in the North Sea by the S-boats. Fuel was in desperately short supply (the transfer of the 1st Flotilla from the Baltic was vetoed because of it) but the Allied counter-measures were now so tight that success was virtually impossible. Mines could continue to sink ships but the attrition rate of the boats was likely to be so great as to be totally unacceptable. The S-boat menace had finally been defeated.

Below: Two type 35/37 torpedo boats and an S-boat at Brunsbüttel in 1945. (Author's Collection)

10. BALTIC AND NORWAY-OPERATIONS, 1941-45

It was anticipated that the launching of Operation 'Barbarossa' would provide ideal opportunities for the offensive use of S-boats against the Red Fleet. To this end virtually the whole of the operational S-boat force had been withdrawn from the important Channel theatre and deployed eastwards. SKL wished to take advantage of Finland's long coastline on the north side of the Gulf of Finland, in order to harass Soviet traffic which was expected to be retreating towards Leningrad. This proved difficult because the inhospitable and sparsely populated coast offered few ideal or even acceptable locations for operational bases. After great difficulty, the island of Suomenlinna was selected for the 1st Flotilla and the island of Pensar for the 2nd Flotilla. No base could at first be found for the 5th Flotilla and conditions in the Turku area were so difficult that without the assistance of *Carl Peters* and *Tsingtau* bases could not be established. Plans for another base further east at Kotka were shelved until those at Turku and Helsinki were ready. By 17 June the two depot ships had reached Pensar and the following day six boats of the 2nd Flotilla had arrived at Suomenlinna. Operations commenced on 21 June, by which time the 2nd Flotilla's strength had reached eight boats. The first sortie was to cover minelaying operations and then to attack Soviet warships in the Gulf. This proved uneventful. Boats of the 1st Flotilla covered the laying of the 'Corbetha' barrage, while others of the 2nd Flotilla laid mines in Moon Sound.

Further south in the Baltic itself, boats of the 3rd Flotilla laid mines off Libau (now Liepaja in Latvia) and Windau (Ventspils), while the 5th Flotilla mined the western approaches to the Irben Straits at the entrance to the Gulf of Riga. Early successes included the sinking of the Latvian steamer *Gaisma* (3,077 tons) by *S59* and *S60* and the capture of 1,181-ton steamer *Estonia* by boats of the 1st Flotilla, the latter being sent into Uto with a prize crew. On the debit side, *S39* and *S103* were damaged while returning from operations.

The following nights saw further operations during which *S43* sank the 780-ton *Luesa* and *S44* claimed the sinking of a coastal patrol vessel of 400 tons (*MO-238*, actually about 60 tons). A much more important success was the sinking of the Soviet submarine *S3* off the Latvian

coast by depth charges and hand grenades from *S35* after her torpedoes had missed the submarine.

On 25 June the 3rd Flotilla came close to another success when it encountered the submarine *S7* in the Irben Straits. Despite the S-boat attack, *S7* escaped. That night five boats of the 1st Flotilla, accompanied by six of the 2nd Flotilla and a single 5th Flotilla boat, sailed to escort the minelayer *Brummer* which was to lay a field to the north of Moon Sound. This was accomplished but on return, in the early hours of 27 June, the S-boats ran onto a Soviet mine barrage and lost both *S43* and *S106*.

Meanwhile the 3rd Flotilla, still off the Latvian coast, fought an action with Soviet light forces consisting of destroyers supported by the cruiser *Kirov* and minesweepers in the Irben Straits. The Russian squadron, based near Riga, had been engaged on minelaying at the entrance to the Gulf of Riga. One such sortie on 24/25 June had been successfully completed but that on 26/27 June encountered the 3rd Flotilla. In the action that ensued, the German force claimed 2 'G'-class destroyers and one torpedo boat sunk, but Soviet losses in fact appear to have been the destroyer *Storozhevoi* badly damaged by *S59* and *S31*, the submarine *S10* (?) damaged by *S59* and *S60* and the minesweeper *T208* sunk by *S35* and *S60*.

The first week of Baltic operations was now complete and the experiences were assessed critically. Opportunities were limited because intelligence and reconnaissance reports did not reach the boats in time for them to put to sea. They were in any case forbidden to sink merchant ships. On the other hand, the 3rd Flotilla's successes were very encouraging but the best opportunity for the boats' employment was seen as minelaying. Boats were only to be used offensively against worthwhile targets, such as destroyers. On 1 July the flotilla strengths in the Gulf of Finland were:

1st Flotilla (Helsinki)	7 boats
2nd Flotilla (Turku)	4 boats
5th Flotilla (Turku)	3 boats

At that time it was decided to dissolve the 5th Flotilla and transfer its boats to the 1st (*S28*) and 2nd (*S41* and

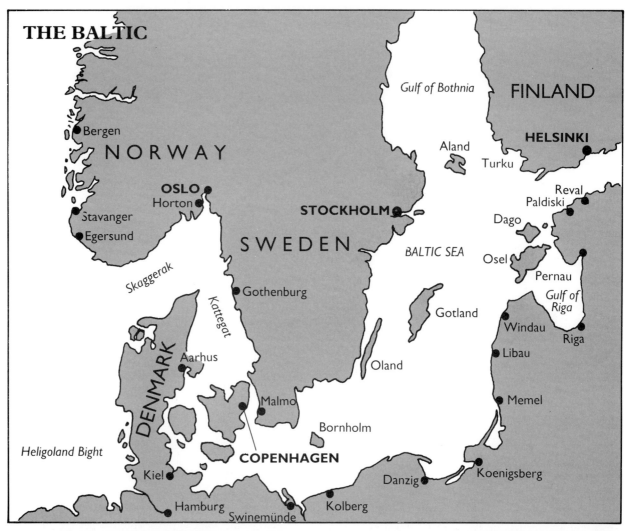

THE BALTIC

FINLAND

Gulf of Bothnia

Bergen

N O R W A Y

Aland

HELSINKI

Turku

OSLO
Horton

STOCKHOLM

Reval
Paldiski

Stavanger
Egersund

Dago

Skaggerak

S W E D E N

BALTIC SEA

Osel

Pernau

Kattegat

Gulf of Riga

Gothenburg

Gotland

Windau

Riga

Aarhus

DENMARK

Oland

Libau

Malmo

Memel

Bornholm

Heligoland Bight

COPENHAGEN

Kiel

Danzig

Koenigsberg

Hamburg

Swinemünde

Kolberg

THE GULF OF FINLAND

Viborg

FINLAND

Kotka

Biorko

HELSINKI

Kronstad

Suersaari

Lavansaari

Porkkala

Leningrad

Cape Juminda

Gulf of Narva

Reval

Narva

Above and opposite page:
The Schnellbooteslehrdivision on exercises in the Baltic in 1943. (Courtesy H. Büchting)

S46) Flotillas. Mining and patrol sorties continued in the western end of the Gulf of Finland during the course of which *S102* and *S103* were themselves badly damaged by mines. Attempts were also made by the 1st Flotilla to intercept convoy traffic between Reval (now Tallinn in Estonia) and Hango but without success. On 10 July six boats operated against a convoy reported by the Finns when *S28* and *S26* torpedoed a stationary steamer near Eckholm; this was the 3,204-ton *Rasma* which had been beached after being mined five days earlier.

The 3rd Flotilla continued operations in the Gulf of Riga, unsuccessfully engaging a destroyer on 15 July and again on 18 July, but on 22 July sank the torpedo cutter *TKA-71* and a tug off Oesel. A few days later *S55* and *S54* encountered the lone Soviet destroyer *Smely* in the northern Gulf of Riga and *S54*'s torpedoes sank her. Other boats were unsuccessful against minesweepers off Oesel but on 28 July the 253-ton ice-breaker *Lachplesis* was sunk by gunfire off Arensberg. On 2 August *S55* and *S58* attacked and missed the destroyer *Artem* in the Gulf of Riga.

In the Gulf of Finland, the boats of the 1st and 2nd Flotillas had no noteworthy success and were used mainly on minelaying and patrol duties. It was intended to use S- and R-boats to mine the approaches to Leningrad and the 1st Flotilla was therefore ordered to Kotka where it arrived on 3 September. After only a couple of operations, however, Bütow recalled the flotilla to Helsinki on 14

September. It returned to Kotka on 23 September (four boats) but the opportunities for action were now few with the rout of the Soviet naval forces complete and because of the extreme cold weather. On 15 October the boats were recalled to Helsinki and the Kotka base was closed down the following day. *Carl Peters* left for Germany the same day and as *Tsingtau* had returned home in mid-August, support for the flotillas was now limited. Towards the end of November, the S-boats too were withdrawn for refit in Germany.

From the end of 1941 until early 1944, the Baltic was mainly a training ground for the Kriegsmarine, with only the S- and U-boat training flotillas using these waters. As the situation in the east deteriorated in the winter of 1943/44, SKL ordered the transfer of an operational flotilla of S-boats from the Channel to the Gulf of Finland on 4 February 1944. To operate under the command of FdM (Ost), their base would be Reval. FdS selected the 6th Flotilla (K.Kpt. Obermaier) for this task, with the depot ship *Carl Peters*, the latter having to disembark the 21st Flotilla staff and base personnel precipitately at Kiel on 5 February, while eight boats of the flotilla left Ijmuiden for the Elbe the following day. About ten days later *Carl Peters* and her flotilla (*S39, S76, S90, S91, S114* and *S132*) arrived in Reval but premature freezing-up of the Gulf of Finland made operations temporarily impossible and the flotilla was therefore ordered to Libau. On 7 March FdM (Ost) ordered the flotilla, now

reinforced by *S79*, back to Reval. During the month only two reconnaissance patrols were made, which were considered a waste of fuel and engine hours by FdS, as the boats had been sent for offensive duties. Icing continued to be a problem so it was decided to transfer the flotilla to Helsinki from about the beginning of May, for operations among the islands under the coast. There were now nine boats operational, *S135* having rejoined. Suitable targets for torpedo attack were elusive, only small patrol vessels being encountered, and these were engaged by gunfire. *M0122* was sunk on 14 May in such an encounter, while during the second half of the month a sortie to Kronstadt Bay claimed the sinking of a patrol vessel. Operations in the Gulf of Finland were brought to an abrupt halt when the Allies invaded Europe on 6 June 1944 because the flotilla was immediately ordered to the west, arriving in Brunsbüttel on 18 June en route for Ijmuiden. Plans remained to operate S-boats in the Gulf of Finland however, but SKL's intentions were difficult to execute because FdS still had to keep forces in reserve in case the Allies also attempted a landing in Denmark, for whose defence contingency plans ('Wallenstein') had been made. Petersen proposed that if boats had to be sent to the Gulf of Finland, a new flotilla should be formed using eight suitable craft that were currently part of the S-Booteslehrdivision, but he pointed out that if these boats were required for more than three months, the training programme would be seriously affected.

The boats concerned (of which *S65*, *S67* and *S80* had reached Helsinki by the end of July) formed the reconstituted 5th Flotilla, which had lost all its boats during the disastrous air attack on Le Havre on the night of 14/15 June. In command of the new flotilla was Kpt.Lt. Holzapfel. The remainder of his boats (*S68*, *S85*, *S110*, *S116* and *S120*) were having their armament augmented before sailing for Helsinki. Their depot ship was to be *Hermann von Wismann*. No significant actions occurred and on 1 September *S80* was mined and sunk in Viborg Bay. By now Kotka was being used as a base for four boats (*S65*, *S68*, *S85* and *S120*) because of the Soviet offensive in Karelia. The political situation forced the next redeployment when, on 2 September, the Finns asked for an Armistice with the Soviet Union and on 4 September a cease-fire came into force. On 14 September a major and futile German operation was launched to capture the island of Suursaari from the Finns. Even if it succeeded initially, it could never have been held, and it resulted in heavy German losses. The 5th Flotilla took part in these operations.

As a result of the Finnish collapse and after evacuating island garrisons, the 5th Flotilla was withdrawn to Windau later in September. At the same time OKM ordered a second flotilla into the Gulf of Finland because of the seriousness of the situation. This demand could only be accomplished by despatching the 2nd Training Flotilla, whose five boats (*S64*, *S69*, *S81*, *S117* and *S99*) also now arrived in Windau; three of them had been intended for

transfer to Finland. From Windau, the boats of both flotillas operated to the entrance of the Gulf of Finland, into the Gulf of Riga and around the Baltic islands. Their task was to disrupt Soviet landing attempts against the islands and to support the German forces in the Sworbe peninsula. Many mining operations were carried out during this period and the 2nd Training Flotilla particularly distinguished itself in engaging enemy landing forces.

By the beginning of November, however, the 5th Flotilla had only one boat operational at Windau and the 2nd Training Flotilla six. Both Windau and Libau had now been properly equipped as S-boat bases, thus eliminating the necessity of depot ships, in particular *Tsingtau* whose presence invited air attack. These bases, or at least that at Libau, had been taken over from the 25th U-boat Flotilla. *Tsingtau* finally sailed for Gotenhafen on 18 November. The boats belonging to the 5th Flotilla were well worn and weakly armed and in response to Holzapfel's complaints, FdS promised that the four boats despatched to Romania, which had MB501 engines, would be allocated to the 5th Flotilla on their return, although Petersen himself doubted if he would see them again. By 1 March 1945 this flotilla was ordered to remain in the Baltic, subordinated to 9 Sicherungsdivision. In the face of overwhelming Soviet might, the German forces were forced back inside their own borders. The S-boat base at Stettin was closed down on 6 March and the S-boats participated in the last desperate struggles to evacuate as many troops and refugees as possible from areas of Soviet invasion. In this task, the newly re-formed 1st Flotilla (*S216-218*, *S225*, *S226*, *S707* and *S708*) operated during the final two months. Surprisingly, considering the overwhelming Soviet air superiority, not one boat was lost in 1945 during Baltic operations.

In 1941 Operation 'Barbarossa' had opened up a new front not only in central and southern Europe but also in the Arctic. Although occupied Norway had no direct frontier with the USSR, Germany's ally Finland did and the distance between the frontier and Norway was only a few miles. In addition, the poor or non-existent road system along the Arctic front made the coastal shipping routes of vital importance to the maintenance and supply of the German Army in this theatre. The threat to this supply line posed by the Soviet Northern Fleet was obvious, and to counter this the 6th Destroyer Flotilla had been ordered to the Arctic late in June. Their experiences were not encouraging: there were few targets, air attack was a constant threat and the weather conditions were often severe. D(6), Schulze-Hinrichs, believed that S-boats would be more effective than destroyers as they were in less danger from mines and could seek out targets inshore. Whether these comments precipitated the despatch of S-boats to the Arctic is not clear but when the 6th Flotilla was ordered home in November 1941 it was replaced not only by the 8th Destroyer Flotilla but also by a flotilla of S-boats.

FdT, Kpt.z.S. Bütow, ordered the formation of a new S-boat flotilla, the 8th, on 19 October 1941 'for a special operation'. In command was to be Kpt.Lt. Christiansen, with the boats *S42, S44, S45* and *S46*, all of which had been completed in the spring of 1941. The deployment of S-boats to such a far-flung and inhospitable theatre demanded considerable organization and preparation, which soon absorbed all the attention of the newly formed flotilla staff. Many problems had to be solved, not least the maintenance and operation of torpedoes, torpedo tubes and weapons in temperatures far below zero. There were no recognized naval bases in the far north so the flotilla had to take with it everything required to maintain operational readiness under isolated and adverse conditions. A spare parts reserve was built up at Trondheim and the steamer *Hernösand*, which had previously been supporting the 6th S-boat Flotilla in the Gulf of Finland, was commandeered for the 8th Flotilla. When she sailed north, her cargo included 50 torpedoes, 100 depth charges, 50 TMA and 25 TMB mines, two portable barracks and consumables for six months. *Tanga*, with Admiral (Nordmeer), had a further twelve torpedoes and 72 depth-charges. However, the depot ship detailed to administer the 8th Flotilla was *Adolf Lüderitz* (Kpt.z.S. Erasmi), formerly with the 3rd Flotilla which arrived in Kiel from Wilhelmshaven on 5 November. Preparations continued apace until on 18 November the flotilla sailed for Arctic Norway. Part of the passage was made with the S-boats in tow to conserve engine hours and it was not until 3 December that Trondheim was reached. The passage to Bodø - made under very poor weather

conditions with east-south-east gales, 7-8 gusting 9 and temperatures down to -10°C - gave a portent of Arctic operations. Icing rendered guns and depth-charges unusable while watch-keeping on the small craft became a nightmare.

Reaching Tromsø on 15 December, the flotilla remained there until 24 December when reports of a British force consisting of a light cruiser and three destroyers in Westfjord precipitated their first operational sortie. Unfortunately the flotilla was unprepared, with some of the crews on leave, so that it was not until 1440 hours that all four boats sailed. Visibility was poor with thick fog and on 26 December the flotilla was recalled without having made contact with the enemy. The latter was in fact a force under the command of Rear Admiral Hamilton with the cruiser *Arethusa* and some eight destroyers which, together with the landing ship *Prince Albert*, was engaged on a Commando raid in the Lofoten Islands (Operation 'Anklet'). This achieved some success but from the German point of view it was unfortunate that the S-boats had got as far as the entrance to Ofotfjord before their recall. In fact, this recall was premature and reflected the uncertainty in the German mind as to what was going on in Westfjord. Had the flotilla continued, they may well have encountered British forces or, at the very least, helped clarify the situation. Equally, had the flotilla been able to sail on receipt of the first signal, the outcome may well have been different. As it was, a valuable two and a half hours were lost. It was an opportunity that was never to come again.

As a result of the British raid, the flotilla was ordered to

Below: *K2* was a well-armed gunboat captured incomplete in Holland and commissioned by the Kriegsmarine in November 1942. Armed with four 12cm guns, she was eventually sunk off Egersund on 28 September 1944. Although raised and later towed to Holland, she was never again operational, either in the Kriegsmarine or the Royal Netherlands Navy.

Left and right: Many hundreds of these Kreigsfischküter were built all over Europe and Scandinavia, being used in all war theatres for patrol, A/S and M/S work. *KFK202* and *KFK203*, however, were allocated to the Kleinkampfverband and sent out on Operation 'Panama', a saboteur frogman operation to the Indian Ocean and Persian Gulf. They sailed from Norway in January 1945 and were last heard of off West Africa, but their final fate is not known.

Narvik for local defence but on the last day of the year it was sent back to Tromsø en route for the far north. Bad weather thwarted sailing until 3 January 1942 and the flotilla eventually arrived in Vardø four days later. It was immediately obvious that Vardø was not particularly suited as an S-boat base as there was always a heavy swell in the harbour. Nevertheless, on 13 January the first sortie was made by *S46* and *S44*, a strike towards Kola Inlet, which had to be abandoned after ten hours at sea because of the bright Northern Lights. Apart from the unwelcome light, little other experience was gained because the weather was unusually fair. A second sortie by all four boats on 15 January was also aborted because of thick fog, as was a third on 22 January by three boats because of heavy seas. The omens for successful S-boat operations were far from favourable. Ice, extreme cold (now down to -18°C), fog, heavy seas, and a complete lack of air reconnaissance all combined to render operations futile. It also soon became evident that the boats had to be able to lie alongside *Lüderitz* at all times, so that they and the torpedoes could be supplied with heat, which it was impossible to do in Vardø. Under the prevailing conditions problems abounded; for example, fenders became solid blocks of ice and instead of preventing damage to the fragile S-boats, promoted it. Thus, after only a brief stay at Vardø, on 27 January the flotilla shifted to Kirkenes, where an ideal base was established in the narrow Semskefjord the following day.

Kpt.Lt. Christiansen's views on his flotilla's usefulness in Arctic waters were recognized by Admiral (Nordmeer) who nevertheless thought that, despite all the drawbacks, the flotilla was needed for offensive and indeed defensive tasks in inshore waters, at least until the threat of a Soviet landing behind German lines was over. Admiral (Norway) concurred so the flotilla remained in the inhospitable north for the time being.

Bad weather prevented any sorties during the first half of February and not only was *Lüderitz* overdue for refit but the non-arrival of *Hernösand* with all the flotilla's stores was also creating problems. She eventually arrived on 25 February having taken two months for the passage from Germany. In the meantime, on 19 February, the full flotilla had sailed for a sortie to the west coast of Kildin Island and a sweep along the Murmansk coast. Yet again bad weather forced the sortie to be aborted

By the beginning of March the flotilla had organized quite a cosy little base in Semskefjord; the barracks brought up by *Hernösand* were being erected, a defensive minefield had been laid across the entrance to the fjord and guns mounted on the cliffs. Cold and inactivity remained a serious problem; snow, some 7cm deep, lay on the frozen sea. Two sorties, on 19 March and 2 April, to escort minelaying operations ('Bantos' and 'Saft') fell victim yet again to weather conditions, as did another on 4 March.

The position was now giving concern, not least from

the point of view of morale. While there was no direct reference to problems from this aspect, the fact remained that since the flotilla reached Tromsø in December, not one shot had been fired in anger. Only one unsuccessful sortie had been completed and six broken off due to weather conditions. Admiral (Nordmeer) saw no prospect for success in the long daylight months for torpedo attacks and the boats themselves would be very exposed to counter-attacks. Minelaying was not a viable alternative because the EMC mines available were unsuitable for S-boat use, the TMA mines were unreliable and the TMB type could only be used in certain restricted areas. MOK (Nord) agreed with these comments but reported that UMB mines were en route to the Arctic and observed that until the threat of a landing in the Petsamo region had receded, the flotilla could be of decisive value in an opportunist engagement. Requests by the flotilla captain that the older S-boats (currently used as a fast 'UJ' group in the south) could do his task in Kirkenes just as well were vetoed on the grounds that no more older boats were available.

The UMB mines finally reached Kirkenes on 6 June, all 24 of them, but once again the weather intervened. Not until 13 June did conditions abate sufficiently for each boat to be loaded with six mines and then only with difficulty. The next day all four sailed for the task, the boats working very hard in the steep seas. It can hardly have been a surprise that the heavy seas and poor visibility

forced the abandonment of yet another operation.

Relief was at hand, however, for in the forenoon of 23 June *Tsingtau* (Kpt.Lt. Freyer) secured alongside *Lüderitz*, having brought her 6th Flotilla (Kpt.Lt. Obermaier) up from Germany. It must have been hard for *Lüderitz*'s ship's company to hear that they were not going to be going home just yet. With the departure of *Tanga* for Narvik on 11 May, Admiral (Nordmeer) required *Lüderitz* in her place as a W/T repeating station for U-boats; *Tsingtau*'s W/T equipment was not powerful enough. Thus on 24 June the staffs of the 6th and 8th Flotillas transferred depot ships and all superfluous munitions, stores and equipment were transhipped to *Tsingtau*. Finally at midday *Tsingtau*, *S42*, *S44*, *S45* and *S46* sailed from Kirkenes into a freshening north-east breeze bound for Tromsø and home. On the evening of 27 June the Polar Circle was crossed and on 5 July the flotilla reached Kiel. The following day the ships passed into dockyard hands for refit and on 10 July the flotilla was formally disbanded, its boats going to the 2nd and 4th Flotillas while *Tsingtau* came directly under the orders of FdS.

The 6th Flotilla comprised eight boats (*S69*, *S71*, *S73 - S76*, *S113* and *S114*) of which two were stationed at Narvik, the remainder in Semskefjord. Their first sortie from there was on 30 June when five boats set out on a minelaying sortie which, like all previous attempts, was abandoned in the face of the poor weather conditions. This sortie was intended to mine the approaches to Kola

Inlet in anticipation of convoy PQ17's arrival. On 4 July the flotilla was ordered at short notice in support of 'Rösselsprung', the Kriegsmarine's strike against PQ17 itself. Again the intention was to mine the approaches to Kola Inlet. The following day Gruppe (Nord) ordered the flotilla to one hour's notice for either a minelaying sortie or a torpedo strike, but Admiral (Nordmeer) ordered preparations for a torpedo sortie as the likely time scale prohibited a change from mines to torpedoes at short notice. Reference to the other volumes in this series will show that the Kriegsmarine's attempt to interdict PQ17 with its surface forces came to nought because of Hitler's fear of carrier air power and even the S-boats were never sent into action against the survivors of the decimated convoy.

Eventually, FdS's views about S-boat employment and the realization that such craft were unsuited to Arctic employment prevailed and the 6th Flotilla's stay in Northern waters was brief. They were ordered home and at the beginning of August most were sent to Rotterdam in preparation for operational employment in the English Channel. *Adolf Lüderitz* remained unlucky for despite badly needing a refit, her services as a W/T repeater were of pressing importance and she was not sent home. The elderly *Meteor* was earmarked as her relief but needed a major refit herself. Thus, although *Lüderitz* returned to FdS control officially on 4 September 1942, she remained at Kirkenes. It was not until 4 January 1942 that *Meteor* relieved her and on 9 January *Lüderitz* finally sailed for home. She reached Kiel for refit on 7 February after an attempted torpedo attack on her off Alesund on 17 January by the Norwegian submarine *Uredd* had failed.

Although the main focus of S-boat operations was seen to be in the Channel and North Sea, the Führer's preoccupation with Norway continued to dictate naval deployments, aided it must be said by British raids along the coast. Consequently, only a few months were to pass before S-boats were sent to Norwegian waters again. Thus on 1 December 1942 the 8th Flotilla re-formed under the command of Kpt.Lt. Zymalkowski with *S44*, *S64*, *S66*, *S69*, *S108* and *S118*, supported this time by the depot ship *Carl Peters* (Ob.Lt.z.S. Reuthal). The orders specified a rapid deployment for several months in Northern waters to strengthen coastal defence in the area between Narvik and Trondheim. Once again the steamer *Hernösand* would take all the flotilla spares and stores. Under the operational command of Admiral (Nordmeer), the flotilla was to be based at Bodø. *Carl Peters* sailed from Kiel on 17 December, followed by her flotilla the next day. Passage northwards was again affected by bad weather and Trondheim was not reached until 31 December. Much of the early part of January 1943 was taken up with repairs at Trondheim, so it was not until 19 January that the flotilla finally reached its new base of Bodø. Training and working up the newly formed flotilla now took precedence but long spells of bad weather, sometimes with hurricane force winds, occurred during much of February and

March. For torpedo training, the flotilla moved temporarily south to the Narvik fjords but fuel for *Carl Peters* was, as usual, scarce. *Hernösand*, however, never arrived, thus severely affecting the flotilla's operational abilities. At the end of May the OKM informed the flotilla that it was to return home for refit at Deutschewerk, Kiel. The flotilla sailed from Bodø on 10 June and arrived at Kiel on 18 June.

So ended the last deployment in northern Norwegian waters, which became the only theatre where S-boats saw no action at all. In the Arctic, employed more aggressively, they might have scored success in the Kola Inlet/Murmansk regions but the weather was always against them. Added to which, boats were never properly 'arcticised' for operations in the prevailing conditions which undoubtedly reduced their efficiency. In the far north, with air co-operation, there was a chance of finding targets but later deployment to the west coast of Norway deprived them of targets altogether, except perhaps the occasional raid by Royal Navy forces. Reduced to coastal defence tasks, the S-boats' attributes were wasted and they could have been replaced to advantage by other types of vessel.

Some eighteen months were to pass before S-boats reappeared in Norwegian waters, which in the eyes of FdS were very much a backwater. In October 1944, however, the SKL ordered Petersen to deploy a flotilla to arctic Norway (Admiral, Polarküste), much against his wishes. The 4th Flotilla (K.Kpt. Fimmen) was selected and on the 19th of that month received orders to proceed to Germany via the inland waterways to refit at Swinemünde. At the same time *Hermann von Wissmann* received orders to disembark all 5th Flotilla personnel to Gotenhafen and sail with all despatch to Swinemünde to fit out and augment her flak armament. The flotilla comprised *S201 - S205*, and *S219 - S221*. Its initial destination was the south west coast of Norway, but on relief by the 1st S-Boat Training Flotilla it would move to polar waters. All eight boats and their depot ship arrived in Kristiansand on 9 November. Unfortunately, while moving on to Bergen that day, *S203* was rammed by *R220* and so badly damaged that she had to be sunk by a minesweeper. She was replaced by *S703*. From 17 November the flotilla was operationally subordinated to Admiral (Norwegian West Coast) and based at Egersund with the task of defending convoys between Kristiansand (South) and Stavanger from attacks by Allied surface forces. No operations were carried out because in mid-December, SKL ordered the reinforcement of the western flotillas by all available means, including the withdrawal of boats from Norway and the Baltic. Thus on 17 December the 4th flotilla received orders to move provisionally into the German Bight for eventual deployment to Holland. They were to be replaced in Norway by one of the training flotillas. By 1 January 1945 only one boat remained in Norway, non-operational at Bergen; most of the others were at Rotterdam.

11.WESTERN MEDITERRANEAN, 1941-45

After the Baltic Sea had been secured in the autumn of 1941, the S-boats in that theatre could be redeployed to other operational areas. One of these, currently of great strategic importance, was the Mediterranean where Rommel's Afrika Korps was locked in combat with British and Empire forces contesting the North African coast. Malta remained the lynchpin in the Allied hold over the whole theatre and its capture (Operation 'Herkules') figured strongly in Axis planning, because of its stranglehold over the supply routes from Italy to the African coast. Events in this area were of great concern to Hitler who in his Directive No. 38 issued orders for the strengthening of the German presence in the region. A complete Air Corps (Fliegerkorps II) released from operations in Russia was to be sent and a new command C-in-C South established. Grand Admiral Raeder was ordered to send U-boats from the Atlantic into the Mediterranean against his wishes and also to despatch such light forces as were available to him. In practice the latter could only comprise vessels which could make the journey by way of inland waterways and rivers. The only units of any offensive potential that could fulfil these requirements were S-boats, and then not all available types. Preparations for the move of a flotilla to the south had in fact already been put in train by the Navy before Directive No. 38 was issued, the chosen formation being the 3rd Flotilla.

This flotilla was selected because its boats were of the smaller *S30* type, with a beam of only 5m compared with the larger *S38* type's 5.28m, an important factor in view of the need to transit the lock system of the canal network across Europe. After refit at Wilhelmshaven, the flotilla began its journey on 7 October, sailing for Rotterdam and the first stage of its passage, the journey up the Rhine. For the passage, the flotilla was organized into two groups, *S55*, *S35*, *S61*, *S31* and *S34* and *S56*, *S54*, *S57*, *S58* and *S59*. From the Rhine, the boats made for Strasbourg on the canal system, then via the Rhine/Rhône canal and its 167 locks down to the River Doubs. Joining the Saône at St. Sinforien, passage was continued down this river until it converged with the Rhône at Lyons. From there the journey was comparatively simple and on reaching the open sea, the boats traversed the Golfe de Lion and the

Ligurian Sea, arriving at La Spezia on 18 November 1941. The first group then moved up to its forward base, Augusta in Sicily, where it arrived on 1 December. This passage across Europe demanded much ingenuity and effort because even though the smaller 16-cylinder craft had been selected, clearances on bridges and in locks was still marginal. Deckhouses and bridges had to be cut down and a dummy funnel added to disguise the true nature of the vessels. Painted black and wearing the State Service flag, they were intended to appear as air-sea rescue craft.

Their first sortie was launched on 12 December, a torpedo patrol off Valletta, Malta, which, apart from being attacked three times by Luftwaffe aircraft, was relatively uneventful. A second sortie the following night was equally unsuccessful, which caused K.Kpt. Kemnade, the flotilla commander, to think that perhaps traffic did not leave Valletta at night and that minelaying might be a better option. Following this conclusion, the flotilla laid 73 mines off the entrance to Grand Harbour in four sorties between 16 and 30 December, these fields being designated MT1 to MT4. The TMA mines, however, proved liable to premature detonation.

On 14 January 1942 the second group arrived at La Spezia having had a much more difficult passage than the first. Low water levels on the Rhône had delayed their passage by six weeks. Base and staff facilities followed by rail. Minelaying operations continued with MT5 on 14 January but by now Kemnade had reservations about the effectiveness of this work because of the increasing number of premature explosions of the TMA mines. So he requested permission to conduct torpedo sorties in the Sicilian Straits but C-in-C, Italy vetoed this idea while at the same time agreeing that the TMA mines were useless. As luck would have it, the next sortie was a torpedo strike for on 18 January a convoy (MW8) had been reported proceeding to Malta from the east. It consisted of four merchantmen heavily escorted by cruisers and destroyers, but the S-boats narrowly missed it in the darkness, leaving Kemnade to complain bitterly about the lack of radar available to him.

On 5 February the second group finally joined up with the rest of the flotilla at Augusta and during the next day seven boats moved to a new base at Porto Empedocle,

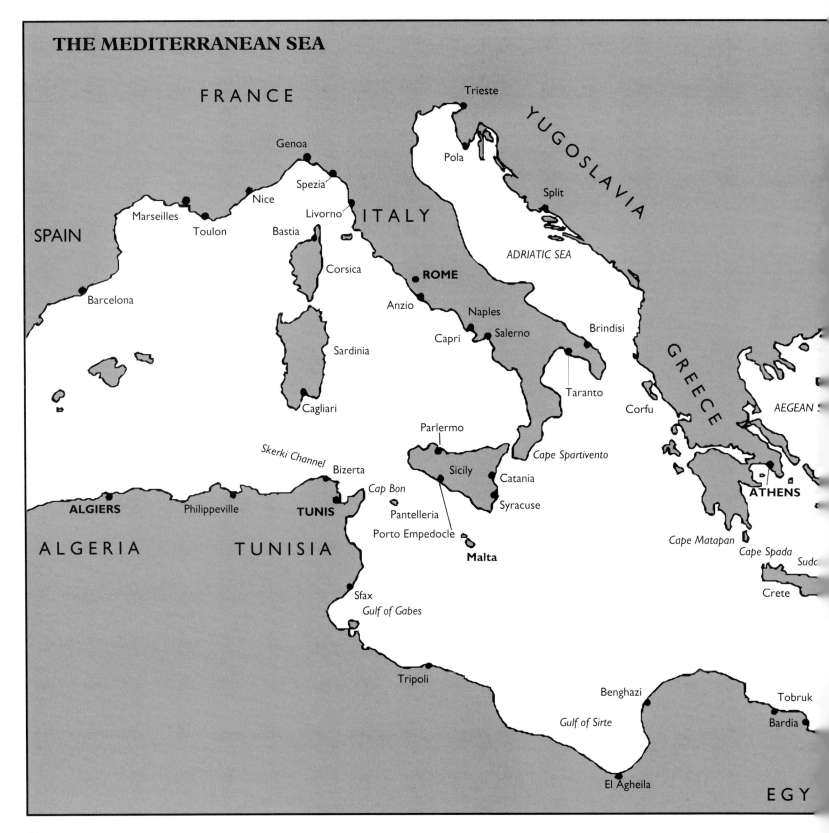

THE MEDITERRANEAN SEA

FRANCE

Trieste

YUGOSLAVIA

Genoa

Pola

Spezia

Nice

ITALY

Split

Marseilles

Livorno

Toulon

Bastia

ADRIATIC SEA

SPAIN

Corsica

ROME

Anzio

Naples

Brindisi

Barcelona

Capri

Salerno

GREECE

Sardinia

Taranto

Corfu

AEGEAN S

Cagliari

Parlermo

Cape Spartivento

Skerki Channel

Sicily

Catania

ATHENS

Bizerta

Cap Bon

Syracuse

ALGIERS

Philippeville

TUNIS

Pantelleria

Cape Matapan

Porto Empedocle

Cape Spada

Suda

ALGERIA

TUNISIA

Malta

Crete

Sfax

Gulf of Gabes

Tripoli

Benghazi

Tobruk

Gulf of Sirte

Bardia

El Agheila

EGY

increased to nine boats by 14 February. This port lay on the southern coast of Sicily and was judged a better base for offensive sorties against Malta and its convoys. The first attack, on 14 February by eight boats against west-bound convoys MW9A and MW9B, was a failure despite visual contact with enemy forces. Poor W/T conditions were judged responsible. Later in the month seven boats were moved to Pantelleria in an attempt to intercept *Ulster Monarch* which was expected to break through to Malta. Bad weather and the poor harbour on the island defeated this intention. Then during the first week of March, a new directive was received from SKL which attached special importance to attacks on the enemy's supply traffic along the African coast. Boats were to commence attacks in the Tobruk area from bases in Suda Bay, Crete, forthwith. Forward bases were to be established at Derna and other suitable bays where spares and munitions were to be stored in schooners. In accordance with this directive, five boats moved from Porto Empedocle to Augusta on 9 March, but on 14 March SKL postponed the Tobruk operations and minelaying off Malta was recommenced. There, between 14 March and 16 May 1942, fields MT6 to MT24 were laid. The 'Hunt'-class destroyers *Southwold* and *Kujawiak* were sunk by these mines, and possibly also the 154-ton tug *C308,* while *Badsworth, Matchless, Hebe* and the merchantman *Orari* (10,350 tons) were damaged. In addition, during the sortie of 6/7 May, *S61, S34* and *S31,* having laid their FMC mines comprising field MT19, encountered the lone *ML130.* In the action which ensued, the British ML was damaged, set on fire and boarded by the Germans. Eleven of her crew, including her C.O., Lt. D.R.H. Jolly, were taken prisoner and items of equipment captured before the crippled boat was scuttled. *S61* also received some damage in this action. *ML130* was one of the first two boats of the 3rd ML Flotilla which sailed unescorted from Gibraltar and had only been at Malta since mid-March. Her survivors led the Germans to understand that the cruiser *Aurora* had been mined off La Valletta before Christmas but in fact this ship had actually been damaged by a mine off Tobruk earlier. The minelaying offensive saw the laying of 133 TMA, 8 LMF, 4 UMA, 216 UMB and 196 FMC mines, as well as 308 explosive floats and 108 cutter floats. The effort involved can hardly have justified the returns however. On the debit side, *S31* had been sunk by a mine off Malta on 10 May with the loss of nine of her crew. This loss was at the time believed to have been due to one of the FMC mines laid previously. Then in the course of the final minelaying operation, coastal batteries engaged the S-boats, obtaining a direct hit in the engine room of *S34.* Confidential books were taken off and scuttling charges fixed, but the boat remained afloat and had to be sunk by the Luftwaffe the following morning.

The move to Derna, via Suda Bay, was finally begun on 21 May when five boats left Augusta and by the end of the month seven boats were available at Derna. The first operation was an armed reconnaissance into the approaches to Tobruk by four boats. They encountered an enemy group reported as consisting of two destroyers and a merchant vessel, and expended fifteen torpedoes against them. Only one hit was claimed, on a destroyer which was believed to have sunk. However, this large expenditure of torpedoes claimed only the A/S whaler *Cocker.* Patrols off Tobruk continued and on occasion torpedoes were fired into the harbour itself. More important targets now came into prospect as a west-bound convoy had been reported off Alexandria on 11 June.

Receipt of this report led to the sailing of six boats for a position off Ras Azzaz, but on 13 June further intelligence was received to the effect that the convoy had put about. In fact, this was a diversionary convoy sailed from Alexandria in an attempt to draw the enemy fleet (i.e., the Italians) prematurely to the south. The real convoy was Operation 'Vigorous' and included, according to Luftwaffe air reconnaissance, about ten merchant ships and a heavy escort among which was a King George V-class battleship and eight cruisers. (The former was actually the dummy warship *Centurion* disguised as a 'KGV'). The German naval plan was to attack with three boats from the north and three from the south between Derna and Crete. Six boats duly sailed from Derna and were homed onto the convoy by D/F signals from a shadowing aircraft. After the two groups had separated, the northernmost one was first attacked by Ju 88 aircraft and then embarrassed by flares dropped by aircraft, which led to their being attacked by destroyers. Despite signals from the flotilla, flares continued to be dropped, destroying the cloak of darkness under which they preferred to operate. In the early hours of 15 June, *S59* fired two torpedoes at destroyers and missed, as did *S58* with another two torpedoes. At 0227 hours *S56* was equally unsuccessful with her first salvo, also aimed at destroyers, but having reloaded she made contact with a cruiser escorted by five destroyers. She succeeded in penetrating this screen and fired her last two torpedoes at the cruiser at close range, claiming one hit forward and one amidships, before being chased off by destroyers. The victim was *Newcastle,* struck by a single torpedo on the starboard side abreast the cable locker, making a hole 10m x 4m. No major damage was caused and the ship was able to make Alexandria at reduced speed. Full repairs were eventually made in the USA and at Plymouth but the ship was out of action until March 1943. The only other success was the torpedoing of the destroyer *Hasty,* probably by *S55,* necessitating the scuttling of the badly damaged ship. Further searches for stragglers the following night were to no avail.

British fortunes on the North African coast had now taken a turn for the worse and by mid-June the fall of Tobruk was anticipated by the Germans. In the expectation of this event, the 3rd Flotilla was ordered to attack all vessels attempting to leave the port and to cover the 6th R-boat Flotilla, tasked with clearing a passage in. In the ensuing exodus from Tobruk, boats of the flotilla claimed a number of successes, including the capture of

Above: An *S30*-type boat, disguised and disarmed, makes her way south to the Mediterranean through the French canal system. (USN)

LCT150 and two smaller landing craft, the trawler *Parktown* and the tug *Alaisia* sunk, as well as a schooner and a merchant ship. Many prisoners were taken but *S58* was damaged and her C.O. killed. *S36* was also damaged by German fighters (Messerschmitt Bf 109s) which mistook her identity. Following the fall of Tobruk, the flotilla transferred to Mersa Matruh on 1 July from where patrols were made off Alexandria but without success. During the month British naval forces bombarded the port on a couple of occasions and there were indecisive skirmishes between destroyers and S-boats. By 11 August, however, there remained only two boats at Mersa Matruh with another pair at Suda Bay, Crete. Three more were in reserve at Augusta, Sicily.

This was the situation when an east-bound convoy to Malta was reported between Cartagena and Oran, expected to pass the Sicilian Narrows on the night of 12/13 August. The convoy, Operation 'Pedestal' comprised fourteen merchantmen escorted by three aircraft-carriers, two battleships, seven cruisers and two dozen destroyers. To attack this target, the 3rd Flotilla intended to sail three boats from Augusta to rendezvous with the two from Suda Bay at Porto Empedocle with all despatch. The boats at Mersa Matruh were too far away to participate. In the event, only *S36* and *S30* sailed from Augusta and *S58* and *S59* from Porto Empedocle, this latter group making contact with 'Pedestal' forces just after midnight on 12 August off Cape Bon. They were immediately engaged, *S58* receiving a 4in shell hit which completely disabled the boat but she managed to disengage successfully. *S59* claimed torpedo hits on a merchant vessel, *S30* hits on two tankers and *S36* on an 8,000-ton merchant vessel. Establishing who sank what on this occasion is complicated because Italian MS and MAS boats were also operating at the same time (*MS26* and *31*, *MAS552*, *553*, *554*, *556*, *557* and *564*). Merchant vessels sunk by surface craft torpedoes were *Glenorchy* (8,982 tons), *Almeria Lykes* (7,773 tons), *Santa Elisa* (8,379 tons) and *Wairangi* (12,436 tons); the latter was probably a victim of *S30* and *S36*. The following day the flotilla was ordered out again to attack a damaged aircraft-carrier (possibly *Eagle*) between Bizerta and Cape Farina. *S35* and *S59* sailed from Porto Empedocle but were forced to return with engine trouble.

By October eight boats were operational at Porto Empedocle, Augusta having been vacated in the expectation of the arrival of the 7th Flotilla. Serviceability was a problem for it was found that serious barnacle growths in cooling water circuits, on rudders and propellers necessitated six boats being despatched to Augusta and Palermo for docking. Towards the end of November, German Naval Command, Italy ordered a new minelaying offensive against Malta. The new fields, MT25 and MT26, were laid on 2 and 3 November in accordance with this directive. The first was detected and the boats were engaged by shore batteries so that the field's value was questionable. After a third operation on 5 November (MT27), minelaying sorties were cancelled and the flotilla was ordered to prepare for torpedo attacks, almost certainly as a result of the landings under way against North Africa - Operation 'Torch'. Ten boats transferred to Trapani on 8 November and from there six of them proceeded to La Goulette, Tunis, to attack the Allied supply lines, but on 10 November they were ordered to Bizerta. Uneventful patrol and escort duties ensued until on 7 December the flotilla was ordered to take over French naval vessels in the Lac de Bizerte to prevent them from being scuttled. This was accomplished the following day when a miscellaneous collection of some twenty warships were captured. During December and January 1943 a number of minelaying sorties were carried out, mostly off Bone. On one of these on 6 January, the naval trawler *Horatio* was torpedoed and sunk by *S58*.

The Mediterranean S-boats had by now been reinforced by the arrival of the 7th S-boat Flotilla which consisted of Gusto, Schiedam-built boats (*S151* to *S158*); these were smaller than the *S38* type, and were able to pass through inland waterways to the south. The flotilla had been formed as early as 1 October 1941, but had only just reached operational status and was now commanded by K.Kpt. Trummer. All eight boats reached La Spezia by 8 October 1942 and had been transferred to Augusta by 6 December. Seven of the boats arrived at Bizerta on 7 January 1943.

January and February saw combined operations by the two flotillas with several minelaying sorties to Bone and Philippeville, Algeria, when action was inconclusively joined with MTBs on occasions. The 'Isles'-class trawler *Stronsay* was probably a victim of the minefield laid on 4 February. On 28 February *S35* failed to return from a patrol north-west of Bizerta and it is believed that she was a mine victim. Both the 3rd and 7th Flotillas continued their minelaying sorties during March, again in the Bone

and Philippeville areas. On the night of 12/13 March three boats of the 3rd Flotilla sailed from Bizerta to lay mines off Philippeville, while a similar number of the 7th Flotilla patrolled to screen a Sicily-Bizerta convoy. The mining operation was cancelled and while returning, the 3rd Flotilla detected enemy contacts by means of their FuMB sets. At 2156 hours the 7th Flotilla also made contact with four destroyers and later attacked with torpedoes, claiming three hits. One survivor was picked up. The enemy was Force 'Q', consisting of destroyers, of which *Lightning* was sunk; 170 of her survivors were rescued by *Legion*. Further skirmishes took place during the night between destroyers and S-boats but no vessel was sunk although *S158* was damaged. Boats of the 3rd Flotilla also fired torpedoes and claimed hits, but it seems doubtful that *S55* was in fact the boat that sank *Lightning*, as had been previously quoted.

By early April Kemnade was beginning to question the usefulness of further minelaying sorties because of the effectiveness of Allied radar cover and the small size of the area available, which made sweeping easy. Nevertheless, such operations continued with Sousse, Ras al Koran and Cap Blanc being mined during the month. Occasional encounters with Allied coastal forces proved inconclusive despite their numerical superiority.

As May approached, the situation on land reached crisis point as far as Axis forces were concerned and by the 6th the base at Ferryville was already under artillery fire. German Naval Command Tunisia therefore ordered the demolition of the harbour while two boats of the 3rd Flotilla mined the entrance to Bizerta (causing the loss of the USN boom defence vessel *Redwing*). The rest of the flotillas were withdrawn to Porto Empedocle after a boat of the 7th Flotilla had evacuated the German Naval Staff Tunisia from La Goulette.

Back in Sicily, defensive minefields were laid off Porto Empedocle during May and, at the end of the month base personnel and stores of both flotillas were ordered to Marseilles, while Licata and Porto Empedocle were to remain forward operational bases.

Flotilla strengths at this time were:

3rd Flotilla

S30, *S35*, *S55*, *S57*, *S59* at Porto Empedocle (operational)
S36 at Augusta (non-operational)
S54, *S58*, *S60*, *S61* at Marseilles (non-operational)
S56 at Palermo (non-operational, sunk by air raid 28 February raised, sent to Toulon for repair but sunk by bombs there 24 December   1944)

7th Flotilla

S152, *S155*, *S156*, *S157*, *S158* at Porto Empedocle (operational)
S151 at Toulon (non-operational)
S153, *S154* at Augusta (non-operational)

Operations in the Sicilian Narrows during May and June were abortive and no boats were able to intervene in the Allied assault on Pantelleria because signals arrived 24 hours late. In fact, communications were proving a serious operational problem at the time. By mid-June the threat of a landing operation against Sicily prompted plans to evacuate base personnel and stores to the Italian mainland, Viareggio or Leghorn being proposed for the 3rd Flotilla and Salerno for the 7th. Relations with Italian forces, which were never good, were deteriorating rapidly and co-operation between the two light forces was often entirely lacking. Italian inefficiency resulted in the Germans having to control their operational forces from Rome for example, a factor which boded ill for a successful defence of Sicily.

On 6 July Allied aircraft bombed Porto Empedocle, obviously aware of its importance as a light forces base. *S59* was sunk and two other boats damaged. These air attacks drove out the 3rd Flotilla from the south coast base where they were ideally placed to interdict any assault, as no doubt was the intention. They put into Palermo on the northern coast where they were helpless to protect the island against the landings. By 12 July both the 3rd Flotilla (three boats) and 7th Flotilla (four boats) had been withdrawn to Salerno on mainland Italy; later it was announced that Vibo Valentia was to be the base for the Messina Straits and Salerno the other main base. An organizational change was also made at that time with the formation of the 1st S-boat Division (K.Kpt. Max Schultz) which comprised the two flotillas.

During July both flotillas operated patrols in the Messina Straits and had occasional, and usually inconclusive, encounters with Allied coastal forces, but serviceability was becoming poor. The 7th Flotilla, for example, had only two boats operational with six under repair at Toulon. This flotilla was no longer considered fit for long-range operations because their speed was too low for them to avoid the enemy in daylight. By the end of August the S-boat forces were scattered about the central Mediterranean: five boats of the 3rd and 7th Flotillas were operational at Cagliari (Sardinia), six boats were under repair at Toulon, two at Salamis (Greece), two at Taranto and two en route to Pola for repair. When Italy surrendered on 8 September, the main base was withdrawn to Viareggio and patrols were made unsuccessfully into the Bay of Naples. *S54* and *S61*, caught in Taranto at the time of the Italian collapse, hurriedly left harbour with an MFP, sowing mines as they did so. The minelayer HMS *Abdiel* fell victim to one of these mines on 10 September while attempting to land troops; casualties were very heavy among troops of the embarked 1st Airborne Division. *MMS70* may also have been a victim of these mines. The two S-boats passed unscathed into the Adriatic, having scuttled the MFP, and making for Venice. On 11 September they encountered the elderly 935-ton Italian gunboat *Aurora* off Ancona and sank her. In addition, an Italian transport and a merchant

vessel were captured. Nearing Venice that day, they ran into the Italian destroyer *Quintino Sella* (which had been under refit and hurriedly sailed for the south) some 30 miles south of Lido. Torpedoes sent the destroyer to the bottom in minutes. Then, on putting into Venice on almost empty tanks, they forced the surrender of the local garrison. It had been an eventful trip.

Allied forces landed on mainland Italy at Salerno on 9 September and secured a tenuous foothold. The sole German naval forces to oppose them consisted of the few S-boats of the 3rd and 7th Flotillas at Civitavecchia. Three of these sailed on 10/11 September to attack Allied shipping off the beachhead and encountered a convoy, SNF-1, escorted by US destroyers. This was actually an 'empty' convoy bound for Oran. In their attack, the S-boats hit the destroyer *Rowan* on the port quarter with a torpedo just as she had detected the Germans and opened fire. She went down in less than a minute after a huge explosion. Further sorties were made on subsequent nights but scored no success. This was hardly surprising in view of the few boats available, generally no more than four, until six became available from 24 September. The difficulties under which they operated were considerable: not only were torpedo servicing facilities rudimentary but oil was in short supply and base accommodation virtually non-existent. To add to the problems, communications

Above and right: Heavy gun support to coastal convoys was often provided by Artillerie-fahrprahm (MFP), converted from normal ferry barges. The photograph to the right shows *AF46*. (IWM above and WZB right)

were inadequate and grossly overloaded. Facing the S-boats was the whole might of the Allied naval forces, which included large numbers of British, American and Canadian MTBs, PTs and MGBs. By the beginning of October, on the other hand, the operational S-boats of the 3rd and 7th Flotillas at Nettunia numbered only six. A similar number were in dockyard hands, mostly at Toulon, over 500 miles away from the landing zone. Six more 3rd Flotilla boats were in the eastern Mediterranean, at Venice (four) and Salamis.

Despite the problems, continuous efforts were made to achieve some success, so far elusive. Thus a force of six boats sailed on 3 October to attack the Salerno Palermo-North African convoy route. Contact was indeed made with such a convoy but the destroyer escort drove off the attackers who could score no successes. Bad weather, a shortage of mines and the poor state of many of the boats all combined to render their efforts fruitless. Lack of adequate aerial reconnaissance further aggravated matters and attack was only possible if, for example, boats penetrated right into the Bay of Naples itself, a task for which the 7th Flotilla boats were not fast enough.

Nettunia was the only available forward base and by the end of October it was being so heavily bombed that it could only be used as a jumping off point.

By mid-November it had been decided to switch all S-boat operations to the Adriatic and abandon the west coast of Italy as far as this command was concerned. The 1st S-boat Division was henceforth to be based at Venice and the 3rd Flotilla was destined for the Aegean. Boats were to be withdrawn to Genoa and then transferred overland and via the River Po to the new base at Venice. Remaining in the west in mid-December were three boats of the 3rd Flotilla, of which only one was operational, eight boats of the 7th Flotilla (at Viareggio, five operational) and seven boats (ex-Italian and all non-operational) of the 25th Flotilla, itself not yet formed. By 21 December all the 7th Flotilla boats were unserviceable and, after a final minelaying sortie into the Bonifacio Straits on the same day, the last two boats of the 3rd Flotilla were withdrawn to Genoa in preparation for their overland transfer to the Adriatic. All S-boats had now been withdrawn from the Mediterranean, the 25th Flotilla having never officially been formed.

Above: *MGB 660* and *MGB 633* in Mediterranean waters. As can be seen from the photograph, these Fairmile 'D' boats were very heavily armed, 6pdr, 2pdr and 20mm weapons in manual and power-operated mountings being fitted. (IWM)

12. ADRIATIC AND AEGEAN OPERATIONS,1943-45

Until the collapse of Italy in September 1943, the only S-boats in this theatre were those making use of the dockyard facilities in ports such as Venice, Pola and Salamis. Now, as has been recounted, all S-boats were to be transferred into this area for operations. Repair of the six boats under refit in Adriatic ports in October was facilitated by the arrival in Venice of the maintenance unit from Pola on 16 October, but the transfer of boats from the Ligurian Sea was delayed by low water levels in the River Po. Consequently, sorties in the Adriatic during December were limited to those conducted by the two 3rd Flotilla boats currently operational. These included patrol and escort duties as well as an attack on the harbour at Vis. The main task, however, was to secure the vital communication and supply lines down the east coast of Italy as far as the current front line and to perform a similar duty along the whole of the Dalmatian coast of Yugoslavia. There were about eighteen German army divisions in the Balkans and the abysmally poor land communications in Yugoslavia, Albania and Greece plus the large numbers of resistance groups forced virtually all supplies onto the sea routes. Mindful of this, German forces had, by the autumn of 1943, captured all the most important Dalmatian ports except Split and occupied several of the more strategic offshore islands. To interdict the German supply traffic, the Royal Navy transferred a depot ship and two flotillas of MTBs (57th and 60th) plus two destroyer flotillas (mixtures of 'Fleets' and 'Hunts') to Brindisi, later moving to Bari from October 1943.

The state of the S-boat forces in the Adriatic at the beginning of January 1944 was as follows:

3rd Flotilla
S55, operational at Cattaro
S30, *S33*, *S36*, *S54*, *S61*, all non-operational in Adriatic ports
S57, *S58*, *S60*, dismantling at Genoa in preparation for transfer to Adriatic (*S56* had been paid off and broken up as ordered by SKL on 15 December 1943)

7th Flotilla
S151 to *S158*, all dismantling at Genoa for transfer to Adriatic

24th Flotilla
S601, operational in the Aegean
S603, serviceable at Salamis

The last named flotilla had been formed on 14 November 1943 at Athens under the command of Kpt.Lt. Meier and consisted initially of a mixture of ex-Yugoslavian Lürssen boats and ex-Italian MAS types. Of the initial establishment, *S511* (ex-*MAS522*) was quickly lost to air attack by Beaufighters on her first sea passage (to Leros on 4 December) while *S512* was in such a poor state that she was never commissioned. Of the other boats, *S601* to *S604*, the ex-Italian boats, these were all in need of repair and overhaul.

Early in January two boats of the 3rd Flotilla made sorties to the islands of Vis, Hvar, Vrac and Rogoznica on two occasions, sinking partisan schooners and engaging MTBs. However, after escorting a captured yacht into Korcula, the German force was attacked by fighter-bombers with the result that the yacht and *S55* were sunk. Some reinforcement for the Adriatic arrived at the end of the month when the 24th Flotilla was transferred to Corfu with the later intention of establishing its main base at Grado at the northern end of the sea. Their passage was not uncontested and the boats were shot up en route by aircraft. Other reinforcements had to wait for water levels on the Po to rise, eleven boats being held up at Piacenza for six weeks.

As a result of the paucity of forces available to him, the commanding officer of the 1st S-boat Division decided that successful offensive sorties against the Italian east coast would only be possible when adequate boats were available. His alternatives were: (a) mining and torpedo operation behind enemy supply lines; (b) defence of German supply lines; (c) combined operations with the army; (d) in the quieter months of April and May the 3rd Flotilla would attack large convoys reported off the African coast from a base in Crete. Group South approved these proposals and subordinated S.O. 1st S-boat Division to Admiral Adriatic. Bad weather and Allied air superiority soon curtailed activities however. Operational strength rose only slowly because of problems on the Po; even by mid-March the 3rd Flotilla (Palmanova) had only two boats operational (in Cattaro) while the 24th Flotilla (Grado) had two available, one at Corfu and the second at Pola. Apart from the ex-Yugoslav boats, most of this latter flotilla consisted of former Italian MS boats, captured while under construction at Monfalcone and still incomplete.

Lack of supplies also delayed the establishment of suitable operational bases at Cattaro and Dubrovnik; and the former was the only base available at the time. It was not surprising, therefore, that when the British captured Hvar on 23 March 1944, no operations were launched against them, as only one boat was serviceable in the area. At the end of March, Kpt.Lt. Wuppermann, S.O. 21st Flotilla, arrived to discuss the transfer of his flotilla to the theatre, on the face of it another welcome reinforcement, but this flotilla consisted of the small 'LS' and 'KS'-type boats. These packed a powerful punch but were very frail and weather-dependent. It was intended that they first operate from Corfu but by May this had been altered and their operational area was to be the Aegean.

Despite their small numbers (generally no more than four) the S-boats continued offensive action whenever possible, as on 1 May when two boats engaged two destroyers, believed to be Italian, preparing to bombard the Albanian coast. They were beaten off without result on this occasion. On the next night two boats attempted to escort the 12th R-boat Flotilla from Cattaro to Durazzo but were intercepted by Allied forces and had to turn back. Patrols and anti-partisan operations were carried out along the Dalmatian coast but without significant success. S54 struck a mine off Cape Leukas while on passage to Corfu but the heavily damaged boat was successfully brought into Patras for repair, although she was later considered irreparable.

By mid-May the boats were becoming more active, claiming the sinking of a 250-ton coaster in an action off Vis on the 10th as well as supporting operations by the Army and escorting R-boats in their tasks along the coast. Towards the end of the month, British landings on Mljet led to a sortie against traffic to the island and a clash with British destroyers in which the S-boats were driven off without achieving any success.

Five boats of the 7th Flotilla had now returned to service following their transfer from the west and on 24 May they began their move to the base at Split. This base was not yet fully equipped with the requisite services and facilities. On 14 May two boats of the 24th Flotilla, S622 and S624, were sunk during an air raid on Monfalcone before commissioning and two others, S623 and S626, were very badly damaged. The dockyard was wrecked, causing yet further delays. With some eight to nine boats of the 3rd and 7th Flotillas now available for operations, it was to be expected that some success could be achieved but this was not the case. There were various reasons for this, including the light and short summer nights, the activity of enemy air forces and the strong enemy naval forces now deployed. Allied forces could count on good

co-operation between naval and air units and their radar equipment put the German boats, which lacked any radar at all, at a complete disadvantage. Their only electronic gear was a few FuMB sets.

The 24th Flotilla, whose nominal strength was ten ex-MS boats with a current operational force of eight, saw little action because of the poor state of its boats, breakdown and fire being frequent occurrences with their petrol engines. After the attempted transfer of S601 and S603 to the Adriatic in January, when the boats were damaged by air attack and returned to Athens, this flotilla remained in two groups: one in the Adriatic, the other in the Aegean.

Such operations as were mounted by the 3rd and 7th Flotillas were mainly escort and anti-partisan sweeps, the latter aimed at the schooner traffic running guns and supplies. Some success was achieved in the latter task but only a minute proportion of the traffic was apprehended, about thirteen small craft being sunk or captured in May/early June 1944. On 12 June, however, four boats of the 7th Flotilla were intercepted off Hvar by British destroyers while escorting a convoy from the Drvenik channel to Zlaringe island. S153 was sunk by *Eggesford* and two other boats were damaged. This action prompted a demand for better radar detection equipment and the comment that the boats of the 7th and 24th Flotillas were too slow to be successful against the Allied destroyers operating in the area.

In a survey of the situation by the Senior Officer of the 1st S-boat Division, F.Kpt. Max-Schultz, it was anticipated that by August some twenty boats would be available at best, but of these only three or four were effective fast boats of the 3rd Flotilla. As far as operational prospects were concerned, boats could be used for screening purposes if they hugged the coast and might get the opportunity to launch attacks from ambush positions. The 7th and 24th Flotillas could attack from Dubrovnik, Split and Sibenik if the enemy were still concentrated in Italy and if his Dalmatian operations were confined to commando operations from Lissa (Vis). The task of the fast 3rd Flotilla boats would be to scare off the destroyers while the small and unreliable 'LS' boats of the 21st Flotilla (*LS7*, *LS9*, *LS10* and *LS11*) could be used effectively in the Otranto Straits which were being blockaded. It was all rather negative, perhaps not surprisingly so.

On 22 June Admiral Adriatic ordered the 7th Flotilla to supply an escort for the Croatian torpedo boat *T7* during the transfer from Sibenik to Jablanak. *T7* sailed from Sibenik on the night of 24 June escorted by *S157* and *S154*. Later that night, torpedo detonations were heard on the island of Coccoglari, which had presumably been aimed at *T7*. Enemy MTBs were then sighted and *T7* turned towards the coast but was taken under fire by the MTBs (which were of the 57th Flotilla). A counter-attack by the German boats was thwarted by the position of *T7* and they were driven off, leaving *T7* on fire, sinking some

Above: MTM-type explosive motorboat aboard a heavily armed ex-Yugoslav S-boat in the Adriatic. (WZB)

time later. Armed as they were with only a couple of 2cm guns, the ex-Dutch type S-boats were badly outgunned by the Fairmile 'D's with 6pdr weapons. However, at least two boats of this flotilla (*S151* and *S158*) had received 8.6cm RAG outfits and used them with success against pursuing MTBs. In respect of the *T7* operation, it is likely that her movements, or those of the S-boats, had been reported by partisans, thus accounting for the presence of reconnaissance aircraft. The need for an effective detection system was indeed pressing. Some boats currently had FuMB4 'Samos' but the improved FuMB7 'Naxos' was urgently required (FuMB9 Wanz G2 'Cuba' was in some boats by August).

Some success was achieved the following month, when the 7th Flotilla (*S156*, *S151*, *S155*, *S154*, *S157* and *S158*) were escorting a small convoy from Ploca to Korcula on the night of 23/24 July. Intercepted by MTBs off Pelje, a fierce action ensued in which *MTB 372* was sunk, but during the manoeuvring *S155* and *S154* were in collision and were damaged. In another operation on 25 July, this flotilla, with *S151*, *S155*, *S156* and *S157*, were acting as close escort to a small convoy consisting of the coaster *Vega* and two I-boats, when they were attacked by MTBs

off Kanetza Island. *Vega* was soon hit and on fire and *S151* was badly damaged. Seven torpedoes were fired by the German force without effect but gunfire hit at least one of the enemy boats, although none was lost. Once again the Germans were driven off and their charge sunk.

To the north, boats of the 24th Flotilla screened four minelaying sorties ('Iltis' 1 to 4) by *TA37*, *TA38* and *TA39* at the end of July and in August were engaged on escort duties down the Dalmatian coast. On 11 August three boats, *S621*, *S627* and *S628*, ran aground; all were towed off successfully but, *S628* was badly damaged. Yet another questionable reinforcement for the Adriatic arrived by rail on 27 July, when six boats of the 22nd Flotilla (diverted from transit to the Black Sea) reached Monfalcone. These were 'KS' boats of dubious usefulness (*KS11*, *KS18*, *KS20*, *KS24*, *KS31* and *KS32*). The flotilla had been formed at Eckernförde on 1 December 1943 but not despatched for operational duties until 26 June 1944 when it left Kiel by rail for the Black Sea. Although it reached Vienna on 26 June, there were transport difficulties, including problems in transitting Italian railway tunnels which was only possible after the overhead wires had been isolated. In view of their limited usefulness, the flotilla was eventually seconded to the 11 Sicherungsdivision and did not form part of the S-boat force. All six boats were serviceable at their base, Lignano, by 7 August but their torpedoes and equipment had yet to arrive from Constanza. The following day, Croatian personnel arrived for training, the decision having been made to turn the boats over to the Croatian Navy. The rest of the month was given over to training the Croats and although the torpedoes arrived on 20 August, no offensive sorties were conducted. On 5 September *KS20* exploded and burned out due to a spark from a gauge in one of her petrol tanks. Four days later the boats were officially handed over to the Croats and the flotilla ceased to exist as a Kriegsmarine unit. Croatian units proved less than reliable and in December, following the desertion of *KS5* (ex-*KS32*) to the partisans, the Germans repossessed the boats and dissolved the Croatian formation.

By August the situation in the Dalmatians was such that all base personnel were manning defensive positions against partisan attacks and it was feared that the bases themselves might have to be abandoned. In September British and partisan troops landed on the islands of Hvar and Brac, which together with the island of Vis allowed almost a stranglehold on the Axis supply routes by sea to its beleaguered bases at Dubrovnik and Split. Such S-boat operations as took place were mainly in connection with escorting small convoys to and from the few coastal towns and ports held by the Germans. On 17/18 August five boats of the 3rd Flotilla left Dubrovnik as escort to a small convoy. This was attacked by three MGBs (*MGB657*, *MGB658* and *MGB663*) of the 56th MTB Flotilla and a small coaster was set on fire and abandoned. The S-boats failed to drive off the enemy and were themselves forced to retire. The following night *S33*, *S58*, *S57*, *S60* and *S30* sailed as escort to a group of I-boats which had been sent to search for survivors of the previous night's attack and were once again intercepted by MGBs. *S57* received at least twenty 40mm hits in her engine rooms and was quickly reduced to a flaming shambles, being later scuttled to prevent capture.

The Senior Officer of the 21st Flotilla, based at Palmanova, assumed command of Adriatic operations on 1 September 1944. The forces at his disposal included:

3rd Flotilla	4 boats operational at Dubrovnik
	3 boats unserviceable
7th Flotilla	4 boats operational at Split
	3 boats unserviceable
21st Flotilla	5 boats operational at Athens
22nd Flotilla	3 boats operational at Lignano
	6 boats unserviceable
24th Flotilla	1 boat operational at Grado
	9 boats unserviceable

The effectiveness of the 22nd Flotilla has already been discussed; that of the 24th Flotilla is self-evident - it was disbanded on 13 October; while the 21st Flotilla's 'LS' boats were of little operational significance. Their last three boats, *LS8*, *LS9* and *LS11*, were scuttled in the yacht harbour at Phaleron on 10 October 1944 when the Aegean was evacuated. *LS10* joined the escort of a convoy bound for Piraeus and was sunk by air attack off Volos on 14 October. The personnel of the flotilla withdrew northwards by land, reaching Skopje on the 18th where they fell in with the 22nd Mountain Regiment; most of them were co-opted into the ground war except for a few lucky individuals whose S-boat experience was valuable enough for FdS to fly them back to Germany. The flotilla was officially disbanded on 15 December. Perhaps the only offensive sortie during this period was one in October against the Ancona supply routes; it was unsuccessful.

Advances by Allied forces up the east coast of Italy and the capture of further Dalmatian islands forced the Germans inexorably northwards until they were trapped in the upper end of the Adriatic. The British 8th Army had captured Rimini on 21 September, while on the Yugoslavian coast, all up to the approaches to Fiume had been recaptured, leaving only the Istrian peninsula in German hands. One more loss occurred at this time when, on 25 October, a force of six Mosquitoes attacked craft lying in Sibenik harbour. *S158* was virtually destroyed and the next night she was scuttled.

On 2 October 1944 Kpt.Lt. Müller (Captain *S3*) proposed that the two flotillas, the 3rd and 7th, be combined in the interests of manpower economy; Petersen concurred and the 7th Flotilla was disbanded on 9 October. On 4 October the last boats of the former 22nd Flotilla, *KS17*, *KS21* and *KS23*, were transferred to the Croats. In view of the limited possibilities remaining for operations in the Adriatic, German Naval Command, Italy was considering releasing the 1st S-boat Division for employment by FdS in the east but SKL refused to allow the division to leave the Mediterranean. Instead, the division was reorganized and on 1 December comprised:

1st S-boat Division - F.Kpt. Max-Schultz (Palmanova)
3rd S-boat Flotilla - Kpt.Lt. Schultz
1st Group: *S30*, *S33**, *S36*, *S58*, *S60*, *S61*
2nd Group: *S151*, *S152*, *S154*, *S155*, *S156*, *S157*
3rd Group: *S621*, *S623**, *S626**, *S627**, *S628**, *S629**

The 2nd Group was formerly the 7th Flotilla and the 3rd, the 24th Flotilla. Of these boats, all were operational except those indicated * and distributed between Venice, Pola and Trieste.

The first sortie under the new organization took place on 3 December 1944. Eleven boats of the 1st and 2nd Groups sailed to attack Allied forces that had been reported landing on Lussin. Due to a breakdown in communications the S-boats were unaware of a Kleinkampfverband sortie that night and the inevitable occurred. The explosive motorboats attacked the S-boats which were hard put to evade them undamaged. The reports of the landings on Lussin proved false but on 17

December *S156*, *S154* and *S152* had a spirited engagement with bombarding Allied forces while lying in that port. Weather continued to be a problem and forced frequent delays to operational schedules, adding to the difficulties under which the force laboured; in contrast, British surface and air forces were active from dawn till dusk. Under the circumstances therefore, when higher command suggested remanning the 'KS' boats, S.O. 1st S-boat Division was understandably less than enthusiastic. A few sorties with the Kleinkampfverbande took place and in another action on 4 January 1945 four boats made a sortie to Isto Melada, where *HDML1163* was taken by surprise and blown to pieces by a torpedo from *S33*.

On 10 January a serious incident occurred when, in the course of an operation by the 1st Group, *S33*, *S58* and *S60* ran aground on the island of Unie to the south-east of the Istrian peninsula. As the flotilla's own efforts to bring the boats off were unsuccessful, five boats of the 2nd Group stood by while *MFP1153* and *MFP1043* were despatched to make the attempt to tow them off. All attempts proved fruitless and the stranded boats were still ashore on 12 January. Efforts continued for the next few days but on the evening of 15 January an enemy aircraft made contact, although not making an attack. It was obvious that an attack would not be long in coming so all usable materials were taken off the boats and they themselves were destroyed by fire in the early hours of 17 January. According to other sources, January also saw the loss by bombing at Pola of *S154*, but the KTB does not mention this and she was certainly operational as late as 16 January. Of the boats of the 1st Group, only *S30*, *S36* and *S61* remained but on 6 February S36 and S61 collided in the course of an action and were both badly damaged and out of action for the remainder of the war. The 2nd Group now consisted of *S151*, *S152*, *S154*, *S155*, *S156* and *S157*. The 3rd Group remained virtually intact with *S621*, *S623*, *S626*, *S628*, *S629* and *S630*. All these boats were in the northern Adriatic. Of the four boats originally belonging to the 24th Flotilla which comprised the Aegean Group, *S601-S604*, all these had been paid off at Salonika on 18 September 1944 because of serviceability problems and were destroyed in air raids the following month.

Fuel shortages curtailed activities by the Adriatic boats as the end of the war approached, but several British coastal forces craft are believed to have been victim to S-boat-laid mines in this period. Finally, *S157* was sunk by partisan forces off Trieste on 1 May. Two days later, K.Kpt. Wuppermann brought *S30*, *S36*, *S61*, *S151*, *S152*, *S155* and *S156* across the Adriatic to surrender at Ancona, understandably not wishing his men to fall into the hands of the partisans. All the remaining boats of the 3rd Group appear to have been scuttled or abandoned at Pola or nearby.

13. BLACK SEA, 1942-44

The advance of German land forces into the Soviet Union during 1941 was rapid and once the armies reached the shores of the Black Sea in their drive towards the Caspian and its oilfields, some form of naval support was clearly going to become necessary. Romania, the Axis ally at the southern end of the front, had a coastline on the Black Sea and maintained a small navy comprising four destroyers, some minor vessels and a submarine with a small construction programme in hand. The Romanian Navy, however, was not only poorly trained despite all the efforts of a German Instruction Group; it was also vastly outnumbered by the Soviet Navy. The latter's Black Sea Fleet in 1941 comprised one battleship, six cruisers, about sixteen destroyers and 44 submarines, not counting many minor warships. If this fleet were allowed a free hand, the Axis army's southern flank would be totally at the mercy of its firepower as it attempted to advance around the northern littoral to Rostov on Don and further east. There was little that Germany could do to bolster her ally, other than send small offensive craft down the arterial European waterways in the same way as had been done for the Mediterranean. A much better transit route than the French rivers and canals used in the earlier case, the Danube was to prove a lifeline for supplies to and from the Black Sea. The only other sea route into the Black Sea was via the Dardenelles where Turkish neutrality was a constant problem. Nevertheless, disguised transports and auxiliaries did pass to and fro between the Aegean and Black Sea, until Allied diplomatic pressure forced the Turks to curtail use of the Straits in July 1944.

THE NORTHERN BLACK SEA

Above and right: Two views of the Bulgarian *S1* being handled by the heavy-lift boom of the freighter *Sofia* during her delivery to Bulgaria. (USN)

The vessels ordered to the Black Sea in 1941 included six Type II U-boats and a flotilla of S-boats - the 1st Flotilla (K.Kpt. Birnbacher). This was an undertaking of considerable ingenuity and engineering. The passage of the U-boats is outside the scope of this narrative but the difficulties can be imagined by comparison with the passage of the 1st Flotilla. Many other vessels such as MFPs and KFKs were also transferred subsequently and a relatively large building programme was put in hand in captured and Axis Black Sea shipyards. These did not however include S-boats.

The route taken by the S-boats, and other units transferred to the Black Sea, involved sailing under tow from Hamburg up the River Elbe as far as navigation permitted, which was Dresden. There the boats had to be hauled out of the water on a specially constructed slip where there was a makeshift junction with the Autobahn. At that point responsibility for movement was with the German-American Petroleum Co. (DAPG) which had arranged two Kuhlmeier eight-axle special transporters, equipped with spring webbing in which the boat hulls were suspended. Each trailer was hauled by four tractors with four more at the rear end for braking and steering. Each trailer weighed about 210 tonnes and travelled at about 5-8km/hr. The boats were despatched in pairs and ahead of each pair was sent a special team to clear obstacles and remove bridges, etc. In some cases there was only a few centimetres clearance under bridges. Using the autobahn network, the boats were transferred from Dresden to the Danube at Ingolstadt, a journey of some 450km, which took about 36 hours. The boats were returned to the water at Ingolstadt and were then towed down river to the

shipyard at Linz, where local personnel, assisted by a team from Lürssen refitted some of the disembarked equipment railed down from Germany. The tow continued down through Hungary and into Romania until the dockyard at Galatz was reached. There the main engines were re-shipped and the final leg of the journey was made under power to Constanza, where the remainder of the operational equipment was to be reinstalled. The timetable for the task extended from December 1941 to March 1942 (Ingolstadt) with arrival in the Black Sea of the first boats expected by June 1942. Winter icing on the Danube was a factor that dictated passage timetables.

By 1 June, two boats had arrived at Constanza, two were at Linz and two en route to Constanza. Four more boats (*S47*, *S49*, *S51* and *S52*) were being prepared in Vegesack and Kiel for transit. All six boats of the first group (*S26*, *S27*, *S28*, *S40*, *S72* and *S102*) were operational by mid-June, the flotilla having been subordinated to Admiral Schwarzes Meer (Black Sea) on 26 May. A few days later, on 2 June, *S26* and *S28* carried out the first sortie, when they participated in the battles for Sevastopol on the Crimea.

Their arrival was timely because up until then the Soviet Black Sea Fleet had been very active, causing extreme discomfort to Romanian units advancing up the coast by bombardments and the landing of marines behind the Romanian lines, as well as resupplying Sevastopol with troops and munitions. The Romanian destroyers were never employed on offensive operations and the submarine *Delfinul* carried only the odd patrol, so the Soviet fleet was entirely uncontested at sea. It was anticipated that the arrival of the experienced S-boat flotilla would change matters.

Colonel-General von Manstein's 11th Army launched its final attack on Sevastopol with a gigantic bombardment from artillery of all calibres at the beginning of June (in this assault, the biggest gun employed was the 800mm railway gun 'Dora', whose shells weighed 4,800kg). Into the cauldron that was Sevastopol sailed the Soviet fleet without regard for loss or damage.

On the night of 18/19 June, *S28*, *S40*, *S102* and *S72* made a sortie against the Sevastopol traffic and made contact with an enemy convoy escorted by destroyers. In a lively action, *S102* torpedoed and sank a freighter but no details of the identity or size of this vessel have come to light (as in all theatres where actions against Soviet forces took place, lack of access to Russian records prevents verification of claims).

Attacks against the Soviet destroyers running into Sevastopol on the nights of 23, 24 and 25 June by between two and five boats achieved no success, but on the night of 2/3 July a sortie by five boats encountered three Soviet motor gunboats of the MO24 type. These were armed with one or two 45mm guns and machine-guns and a fierce small-arms engagement took place. It appears that the Russians were caught by surprise, as one of their boats

Above: Two boats prepare to leave for their base at Iwan Baba after overhaul in Sevastopol. (Courtesy G. Behrens)

still had the covers on her forward gun, even at the time of her sinking. Two of the three MGBs were sunk but *S40* was badly hit about the port torpedo tubes, causing the explosion of an air vessel which resulted in severe hull damage and a fire in the engine room; she was out of action for months. There were several casualties aboard both her and *S28* in this action. By 3 July, however, the last of the Soviet ground resistance had been broken and the naval traffic into the port ceased.

In July the 1st Flotilla moved its base to Iwan Baba, near Feodosia and formerly a torpedo research establishment of the Red Navy. Feodosia had been captured by German troops as early as 3 November 1941, evacuated and recaptured again on 18 January 1942. At the time of this move, only four boats were operational. Their task was to escort and screen German supply traffic to and from the Crimea and to conduct offensive sorties towards the Caucasian coast. K.Kpt. Birnbacher was relieved by K.Kpt. Christiansen on 1 August. From Iwan Baba, sorties were made to Novorossisk and Tuapse on several occasions, in particular during the evacuation of the former port, but sinkings were few. *S102* torpedoed a freighter off Tuapse on 10 August and a tanker off Novorossisk on 31 August. *S28* sank *Zhan-Tomp* (1,988 tons) at the same time.

By September the focus of operations had moved to the Taman peninsula where the German armies were forcing the Russians further east across the River Kuban. Soviet warships began a new evacuation task, removing troops from the peninsula and transporting them to Novorossisk. In doing so, they presented a tempting target for the flotilla. On the nights of 2,3 and 5 September, *S102*, *S27* and *S28* operated against this traffic, reporting nineteen sinkings, but *S27* was hit and sunk on 5 September by one of her own torpedoes, a circle runner, with heavy casualties. In the middle of the month *S49* arrived at Iwan Baba, replacing *S27*, but only *S26* was operational with her at the forward base as *S28*, *S72* and *S102* had been sent back to Constanza for major engine overhaul. The survivors of *S27*'s crew had been sent up to Linz to man *S51* when ready. Iwan Baba was attacked several times by Soviet aircraft during this period, but no damage was done to the flotilla. In a sortie by *S26* and *S49* on 24/25 September, the sinking of two ships totalling 3,500 tons was claimed off Cape Idokompass and another of 1,500 tons on the night of 26/27 September by *S26*.

Both these operational boats now required overhaul and were transferred to Constanza where they joined the other three boats, *S28*, *S49* and *S102*, which had recently completed their overhauls. *S51* and *S47* were at Linz and *S52* was still on shore at Ingolstadt because of low water levels. Thus, on 1 October there were no boats in the operational areas, but on 12 October *S102*, *S49*, *S26* and *S28* sailed from Constanza for Iwan Baba and a return to

operational duties. Success was hard to come by however. On 22/23 October the four boats attacked the Soviet cruisers *Krasnyi Krym* and *Krasny Kavkaz* which were returning to Tuapse from Poti with large numbers of troops embarked, but their torpedoes missed. It was believed at the time that one of the cruisers had been hit. There were inconclusive clashes with Soviet light forces on occasions when both sides suffered casualties but no important actions took place in this period. The flotilla's strength was improved in a number of ways by the end of the year, one of which was the commissioning on 6 December at Constanza of the converted merchant ship *Romania*, giving welcome base facility support. *S52* and the now repaired *S40* had left Linz at last under tow for Galatz and FdS had begun to allocate 4cm Flak 28 guns to the flotilla, *S28* and *S72* being earmarked for the first fittings. Operational at Iwan Baba were *S28, S51, S72, S102*; *S26* and *S49* were at Constanza undergoing minor engine overhauls, while *S40, S52* and *S47* were classed as reserve boats and were without engines.

In the early hours of 4 February 1943, the Russians began a major attempt to recapture Novorossisk by landing in force at Myschako. The 1st Flotilla operated against this beachhead, sinking the 'Tral'-class minesweeper *Gruz (T403)* on 28 February and also the gunboat *Krasnaya Gruzya*. In March operations were carried out against Tuapse and the Myschako beachhead, when *S26* and *S47* damaged a tanker on 17 March and at the end of the month mines were laid off Myschako by *S72, S28, S47* and *S102*. During the following month, operations off the Myschako area continued with barges, pontoons and small craft being sunk by the S-boats. They in turn were subjected to air attack at Iwan Baba, several boats receiving damage. In May too the German-held harbour of Anapa was shelled by the Soviet Navy and the destroyers *Kharkov* and *Boiki* were attacked on this occasion by *S51, S49* and *S26*, but unsuccessfully. However, *S72* and *S49* sank two small craft off Sochi on 19 May.

At the beginning of June 1943, the flotilla strength comprised *S26, S49, S51, S52* and *S72*, operational at Iwan Baba, *S28, S40, S47* and *S102* non-operational at Constanza, and *S42, S45* and *S46* at Galatz en route to the Black Sea. The depot ship *Romania* lay at Sevastopol. The Kriegsmarine was not the only 'foreign' navy in the Black Sea, for the Royal Italian Navy had also despatched midget submarines and MTBs to protect their tanker traffic to the Romanian oilfields. They also gave a creditable performance in offensive operations, but by May 1943 Italy's desire to wage war in the east had

Left: Propeller shafts being overhauled in a Black Sea floating dock. (Courtesy G. Behrens)

Right: The depot ship Romania. (Courtesy G. Behrens)

Right: An S-boat alongside the depot ship *Romania* at Sevastopol in 1943/44. Note the destruction of the port and its facilities. (G. Behrens)

Above: An air raid on Iwan Baba, 11 March 1944. (Courtesy G. Behrens)

slackened and her naval forces were withdrawn. The boats of the 4th MAS flotilla were therefore turned over to the Kriegsmarine, which formed a new S-boat flotilla, the 11th, on 20 May 1943 with *MAS 566, 567, 568, 569, 570, 574* and *575*; these were renumbered *S501-S507* respectively. In command was Kpt.Lt. Meyer. Of these boats however, *MAS 574* had been badly damaged by bombs at Anapa and was only taken over provisionally. The acquisition of the MAS boats did little to boost the success of S-boats in the Black Sea because, like many other vessels obtained, captured or taken over from other powers, they were non-standard as far as the Kriegsmarine was concerned. Their machinery and equipment were unfamiliar and the provision of spares posed an acute problem. The transfer of this flotilla was handled directly between OKM and the Italians, with the result that take-over time was minimal and no inventories were checked and verified. Spares which were supposed to be present patently were not and according to one Italian engine fitter a train load of spares and stores had been sent back to Italy two weeks before the transfer took place. Not surprisingly, therefore, flotilla serviceability was low, never more than three or four boats being operational.

Operations were however launched from their base at Feodosia after training and familiarization had been completed on 1 June. Their task was patrol and A/S duties between Feodosia and Anapa, with the first taking place on 12/13 June, when action was joined with Soviet light forces without result. The following night more enemy vessels were seen but the flotilla commander did not make a direct attack because of the danger of the bow waves giving their position away while still outside the range of their Breda guns (the enemy were equipped with 45mm guns). Instead, he suspected that they were en route to bombard Anapa harbour and lay in wait for them, but to no avail. Either his interpretation was wrong or he had been spotted and they had withdrawn. Further patrols were carried out between July and September, the boats frequently finding that the Soviet Air Force was uncomfortably active. By now, the shortage of spares and the absence of all special tools made the smallest repair a major exercise and consideration was given to paying off two boats for cannibalization. In the event, it was decided to disband the flotilla in October 1943. Three boats (*S501*, *S506* and *S507*) were paid off on 20 October and laid up in Sevastopol, and the other four were attached to the 1st Flotilla as the 'MAS Group'. The flotilla staff and crews of the three laid-up boats were to be transferred to the Aegean for the 24th Flotilla. The boats retained (*S502*, *S503*, *S504* and *S505*) are recorded by Gröner as having been transferred to Romania on 20 August 1943, but in fact all four are last recorded as having been paid off at Linz on 6 November 1944.

To return to the activities of the 1st Flotilla, there were several engagements with Soviet coastal forces in June 1943 and mines were also laid off Gelendzik. While the sinking of three lighters totalling about 1,500 tons off the Caucasian coast was claimed, S102 fell victim to a mine to the south of the Straits of Kertch on 8 July. Russian air attacks were now mounting steadily in intensity, but so far no serious damage had been incurred by any of the boats. Off the Myschako beachhead, S51 and S26 each sank a lighter of about 400 tons on 24 July and in other actions against the traffic along the Caucasian coast, the flotilla claimed the sinking of three coasters, a gunboat and an MTB. Four sorties at the beginning of September were unsuccessful and while returning from one sortie on the night of 10/11 September, the boats were attacked by fighter-bombers and lost S46. Eleven more sorties were made during the month and on 27 September in an attack on the harbour at Anapa (now re-taken by the Russians), five ships estimated at more than 2,000 tons in total were torpedoed and sunk.

At the beginning of October, S45, S28, S42, S51 and S52 had an inconclusive encounter with the Soviet destroyers *Besposhchadny* and *Sposobny* which were en route to bombard Feodosia. However, the two destroyers and the flotilla leader *Kharkov* were sunk by air attack the following day. During November and December the flotilla was continuously in action against the Soviet traffic to their beachhead at Eltingen and the Kertch Straits but without any special results. The military situation in the Black Sea was by now becoming serious and to bolster the naval forces there, Dönitz ordered the despatch of six more S-boats to this theatre. Petersen, however, objected to this weakening of his main attack against the British east coast convoy routes and succeeded in obtaining a compromise. Only three new boats were to be despatched in November, the rest early in 1944. On 1 November the 1st Flotilla comprised S26, S28, S40, S42, S45, S47, S48, S49, S51, S52 and S72 with S502-S505 unmanned and in reserve. Of these, S26, S28, S42, S45, S47, S51 and S52 were operational at Iwan Baba, S40 was unserviceable at Linz and S49 and S52 were unserviceable at Iwan Baba. S505 was paid off and S502-S504 out of service at Nikolaiev (S501, S506 and S507 had been turned over to MAST Sevastopol).

Bad weather heralded the new year and in January only two anti- shipping strikes were carried out off the Caucasian coast and one minelaying sortie was made to Tuapse. There was little operational activity in February either, mainly because of weather conditions. However, in an operation against a suspected MTB base at Gelendschik, enemy boats were encountered offshore and four were claimed sunk in a brief action. The promised reinforcements, S131, S148 and S149, had been prepared for transfer in December but there were considerable delays in their transport to the south. The four boats of the MAS Group on the other hand had now been towed from Nikolaiev to Linz for overhaul and were at the latter by mid-December, no longer part of the flotilla's establishment.

By February the flotilla was operating in two groups,

S26, S42, S45 and S49 from Iwan Baba, and S28, S47 and S51 from Constanza. S40 and S52 were being fitted with armoured 'Kalotte' bridges at the time, while the new boats S131, S148 and S149 were at Constanza in the final stages of reassembly, delayed by missing parts.

S51 and S40 were damaged in a raid by eleven Ilyushin Il-2 and five Lavochkin LaGG-3 aircraft at Iwan Baba on 3 March, and on 11 March Iwan Baba was again attacked with two raids on the same day. In the first, by 22 Il-2s and about a dozen fighters, four boats were hit, one, S49 seriously. The second raid in similar strength damaged two boats, S28 badly. Both had to be sent to Constanza for repair but S49 was again damaged by air attack at Feodosia on 13 March while en route to the Romanian port. Despite these casualties, there were still six operational boats at Iwan Baba on 20 March. A week later, orders were given, in view of the situation, to prepare a base at Sulina. At the same time the Romanians closed down the vital dockyard at Galatz and began to evacuate its equipment, thereby depriving the Axis forces of an important repair facility. Representations by the Germans secured a partial rescinding of the order as the other available yards, Varna, Sevastopol and Constanza, were all overloaded.

Further difficulties to operations were caused by the opening of a campaign on 8/9 April by No. 205 Group, RAF, to mine the River Danube. Between this sortie and the last on 4/5 October, Liberators and Wellingtons dropped 1,382 mines in eighteen sorties, paralyzing river traffic which had hitherto carried virtually all the Romanian oil delivered to Germany. Taken in conjunction with a concurrent attack on rail systems in Eastern Europe, it can be appreciated that such activities had an enormous effect on Germany's ability to wage war in the Black Sea and adjacent theatres, in particular the transfer of minor war vessels south and equally the withdrawal of warships to Germany.

Only a single S-boat sortie was carried out in March (on the night of the 4th/5th), when two Soviet gunboats were encountered off the Caucasian coast. The new boats, S148 and S149, had now, at the beginning of April 1944, begun their working up but were not yet operational. All the operational boats, five in number, were at Iwan Baba from where one group was despatched to Odessa to evacuate the General Staff and the Naval Commander after the Soviet ground offensive had captured Nikolaiev on 28 March. Boats of the 3rd R-boat Flotilla beat them to it and transferred them to the S-boats at sea. These personnel were transferred to Burgas or Constanza. As a result of the Soviet offensive, the position of the German forces along the northern shore of the Black Sea was now critical. A major operation to evacuate Odessa was under way and after Soviet troops began an attack against the Crimea on 8 April, a similar evacuation of Sevastopol began on 12 April, involving all naval forces available. Boats of the flotilla provided flank screening for these evacuation convoys and came into action with Soviet

torpedo cutters. The base at Iwan Baba had become increasingly exposed to Soviet air raids of late, many boats receiving minor or splinter damage, and it was inevitable that in time losses would occur. Some dispersion of the boats was achieved, to Sevastopol and Balaclava, but with the evacuation of the Caucasian coast the base had eventually, in late April, to be blown up and evacuated. The flotilla now operated from Sevastopol and Constanza, patrolling and escorting the evacuation traffic, again having inconclusive clashes with Soviet light forces. Three operations were mounted in May, during one of which there was an engagement with Soviet MTBs. During the following month an average of ten boats were operational in Constanza but there are no details of their activities. No operations at all appear to have been carried out in July, when an average of eleven boats were operational.

It was now clear that the Black Sea had been lost. There were only two means of escape: through the Dardenelles or up the Danube. Turkish politics prevented the former and Soviet forces were close to cutting the Danube lifeline. Romania herself was tottering: Constanza had been bombed by the USAAF in June, the Romanian Army was in full retreat before the Russians and finally, on 20 August, the Soviet Air Force raided Constanza. Among the many vessels sunk were *S42*, *S52* and *S131*, while *S45*, *S47*, *S49* and *S51* were damaged. The previous day the base at Sulina had been bombed, sinking *S26* and *S40* and damaging *S72*, while *S148* was mined off Sulina on 22 August. Romania capitulated on 23 September 1944, then switched sides and declared war on Germany two days later. As a result, almost all the damaged S-boats were scuttled to prevent capture, but three, *S45*, *S47* and *S51*, put to sea and made for the Bulgarian port of Varna. Bulgaria was not at war with the Soviet Union but this did not prevent the country being overrun by the Red Army and, with nowhere else to go, the crews of these three remaining boats scuttled them at Varna on 29 August 1944.

Mention must also be made of seven further S-boats destined for the Black Sea. The first of these was the leading boat of a new Bulgarian order for six placed with Lürssen, to augment the two, *F1* and *F2*, which had been ordered and delivered before September 1939. This boat, *F3*, was requisitioned by Germany as *S1* and operated with the 2nd Flotilla in 1940 but, no doubt with an eye to Bulgaria's stance vis-a-vis the USSR, it was cleared for return to her original owners in 1941. She was transferred overland to Linz and had arrived there by June 1941. At the same time, Bulgaria's order was made up by the transfer of two former Dutch boats put into service by the Kriegsmarine as *S201* and *S202*. These had been rejected by the Kriegsmarine after trials and, as was often the case with sub-standard equipment, found their way to an allied power. These two boats were also at Linz with ex-*S1*. The Bulgarians were pressed to buy these two but as they had ordered a homogeneous flotilla were reluctant to take

Opposite page: *S40* after being damaged by aircraft in the Black Sea when a torpedo reservoir exploded. (Courtesy G. Behrens)

Right: Splinter damage to *S26* in the Black Sea. (Courtesy G. Behrens)

them. They were eventually persuaded that they had ordered them and paid RM750,000, including equipment and delivery but excluding torpedoes. Crews were despatched to Linz and the three boats left there on 27 June and made a leisurely passage down the Danube, reaching Braila on 25 August and finally arriving at Varna on 6 September. By that time both the ex-Dutch boats' engines had broken down and no spares were available. Subsequently the three Lürssen boats were used on convoy escort duties by the Bulgarians, but it is doubtful if the ex-Dutch boats ever became operational. Germany offered more of these hulls to Bulgaria but without engines. The Bulgarians expressed interest provided that German motors could be supplied and that 35kt could be guaranteed, but it is doubtful if anything came of the idea. Actually nine cases of Rolls-Royce motor spares had been discovered in a warehouse in Cherbourg in 1940, these having been supplied originally to equip the French boats *VTB23* and *VTB24*; there were also propeller and rudder sets for *VTB9* and *VTB11*.

Likewise, plans to construct S-boats in Bulgarian yards with German assistance came to nought due to lack of capacity, although these yards did turn out KFKs and MFPs. The Bulgarian order for six *S1*-type boats placed with Lürssen had been cancelled by the Kriegsmarine at the beginning of the war, with *S1* being put into service by the Germans. However, it would appear that neither Lürssen nor the OKM were happy with the reversion to the older type of boat as discussions were held on the subject in July 1940, the contractor stating that only four boats, not six, could be delivered by January-April 1941. They explained that in the same time four standard *S26* types could be built and perhaps they should be substituted, taking motors from reserve since S-boat-type motors were not now required for the first type XID U-boat. Their view prevailed and on 5 October 1940, *S2* to *S6* were stricken and replaced by *S70* to *S73* (the numbers *S2* to *S6* could be re-used because the original boats had been sold to Spain).

The other four boats were those agreed for transfer to Romania in 1944 (*S86*, *S89*, *S92* and *S98*). The imminent collapse of Romania caused this transaction to be stopped on 24 August that year.

By now all four boats had reached Linz and two (one of which was *S86*) were already afloat. On 29 August OKM ordered that all four boats be returned to the north, but FdS considered it unlikely that the two already en route between Linz and Sulina would ever get back. *S86* became a unit of the Danube Flotilla but was mined and damaged south of Km950 on 28 August. Despite this damage, she appears to have been successfully recovered from the Danube for she is recorded as being with the 1st S-boat Training Flotilla at Egersund in May 1945, as was *S89*. *S92* and *S98* were in the Flensburg-Mürwik-Glücksburg area with the 5th Flotilla at the same time, so all would appear to have been withdrawn safely to the north.

14. DEPOT SHIPS

As was the case with all minor warships, S-boats were to a large extent unable to look after themselves without a great deal of base assistance. On-board facilities for maintenance and repair were rudimentary or, more usually, completely lacking. This applied as much to personnel as to workshops, for there was little that could be accomplished in a boat of about 35m length and with a technical complement of perhaps six men. Certainly these men would be skilled in their trade and probably on occasion performed major feats of engineering cunning. Nevertheless, the achievement of operational serviceability over a long period required some form of base support. It is important to realize that not only was machinery endurance a factor but so also was human endurance. Living and recreational facilities were basic and it was not possible to endure long periods aboard without a marked decrease in morale and efficiency. Nor was it possible to store and victual such small craft for extended periods. Base facilities were therefore a necessity, but shore bases could not support boats that could be required to operate anywhere in a war theatre. The answer was the depot ship, equipped and stored to maintain and succour a flotilla of

Below: Boats of the 1st Flotilla alongside *Tsingtau* at Kiel in Reichsmarine days. (BfZ)

small craft wherever they might be required to operate.

The first support vessel used by the S-boat forces was the elderly tender *Nordsee* built originally as a merchant ship during the First World War. *Nordsee* served the 1st S-boat Half Flotilla from 1932 until 1934 when relieved by the first purpose-built S-boats depot ship, *Tsingtau*.

TSINGTAU

Named to commemorate the German enclave in China lost in 1914, this ship was ordered from Blohm und Voss on 2 August 1933 as their yard number 496. She was classified at the time as a Fleet tender (Flottentender B) to disguise her true role and so evade the restrictions of the Versailles Treaty (similar restrictions applied to the U-boat depot ship *Saar* - Flottentender A). *Tsingtau*'s displacement was 2,490 tonnes full load and she was of transverse framed construction, fully welded except for the longitudinal shell seams and the deck. Main propulsion consisted of two MAN four-cylinder four-stroke diesels totalling 4,100hp for a maximum speed of 17.5kt. She was fitted with stabilizers. Accommodation was provided for a ship's company of 145 plus further accommodation for 242 men of her S-boats and ten flotilla staff. On the hold deck in compartment VI was a torpedo store accommodating 24 spare torpedoes, from where a hoist brought them into the large torpedo workshop, extending across the full beam of the ship on the upper deck. Warheads and pistols were also stored in the hold, forward of the torpedo store. After receiving the warheads and being serviced, the torpedoes could be moved aft by trolleys on deck rails and thence transferred to the waiting S-boats by cranes. For self-defence the ship was armed with two single 8.8cm L/45 weapons in LC/13 mountings and four 2cm MG C/30 single guns. Laid down on 21 October 1933, the ship was named *Tsingtau* when launched on 6 June 1934. She ran acceptance trials on 22 September that year and commissioned under Kpt.Lt. Ruhland on 24 September 1934. Ruhland, something of an adventurer, had served aboard *Königsberg* in African waters during the First World War and following the loss of this ship, joined the land forces in German East Africa, with whom he saw much active service. *Tsingtau* ranged far and wide with her flotilla over Baltic and North Sea waters in the 1930s, except between February and March each year, her annual three-month refit period, usually at Deutschewerk, Kiel.

By the summer of 1935, the planned expansion of the U-boat force was beginning to have an effect on ship construction and finances with the result that the possibility of using *Tsingtau* as a submarine depot ship was considered. It was argued that as this ship had been designed to administer two S-boat half-flotillas (i.e., twelve boats), it might be feasible to reduce this to one and use the space gained to install charging equipment for U-boat batteries and also for rescue equipment. The suggestion was that *Tsingtau* could be used to administer the 1st U-boat Flotilla at Kiel. However, this would only be possible if a new, smaller depot ship were built for just six S-boats plus flotilla staff. Armed sufficiently well to fight off a surfaced U-boat - i.e., with two-10.5cm guns (plus 3.7cm and 2cm) - this vessel would have a speed of 20kt (declared) as an 'Exempt Ship'. Endurance was to suit Baltic and North Sea use, with stores and torpedoes as *Tsingtau*.

It was envisaged that one ship would be included in the 1935 programme and a second in the 1936/37 programme. This, however, was unrealistic and in September it was stressed that construction of a new U-boat depot ship was most urgent and that a second S-boat depot ship would have to wait. In the event, the U-boat depot ship problem was solved by the purchase of two merchant vessels in 1936 (which became *Donau* and *Weichsel*), while the S-boats were catered for in the manner to be described later.

Kpt.Lt. Hinzke relieved Ruhland on 23 February 1938 and remained in command on the outbreak of war. With the 1st S-boat Flotilla (Kpt.Lt. Stürm), *Tsingtau* supported operations in Polish waters until ordered with her charges to the west, arriving in Wilhelmshaven on 6 September. K.Kpt. Sachs relieved Hinzke on 30 November. A refit at Deutschewerk followed between 28 December 1939 and 31 January 1940, after which the ship left the control of FdT and was attached to the Inspector of Training as a cadet training ship. Kpt.z.S. Klinger assumed command on 13 February 1940 at a time when the severe winter's ice was greatly hampering all training and operation. On 9 March 1940 *Tsingtau* was placed under the command of Gruppe (West) and on the 14th transitted the Kiel Canal, bound for Wesermünde. She was now to be one of the many units committed to 'Weserübung', the invasion of Norway and Denmark. Loaded with troops, stores and ammunition, *Tsingtau* sailed with Group 4, tasked with the occupation of Kristiansand and Arendal. This was successfully accomplished, *Tsingtau* being responsible for the securing of several Norwegian warships, including *Gyller*, *Kjell*, *Kvik* and *Lyn*. After escorting *Gyller* and *Odin* to Kiel on 18 May, Kpt.Lt. Just took over as captain on 28 May and two days later *Tsingtau* returned to FdT control. When bases in France became available, all depot ships were ordered to complete with stores and ammunition to support an S-boat offensive in the Channel. *Tsingtau* therefore sailed for Rotterdam on 25 August where she remained for about a month and a half before returning to Brunsbüttel on 19 October. Her next task was to administer the newly formed 4th Flotilla at Swinemünde, which consisted of those older boats employed on training duties.

In June 1941 *Tsingtau* took over the 2nd Flotilla once more for operational duty in the Baltic in connection with the invasion of Russia, serving also in the Gulf of Finland for a period. Ob.Lt.z.S. Brandt assumed command in September but was relieved by Kpt.Lt. Freyer in November when the flotilla was ordered back to the

Channel theatre. However, the depot ship was reassigned to duty with the 5th S-boat Flotilla and served the needs of this training flotilla in Baltic waters. March 1942 saw her administering the 6th Flotilla which she took to Norwegian waters, relieving the 8th S-boat Flotilla. *Tsingtau* now brought the 8th Flotilla back to Germany, arriving in Kiel early in July, after which followed a dockyard refit until October.

By that time the construction of hardened S-boat shelters at the operational bases in the western theatre, which were fully equipped for maintenance and repair, had eliminated the need for depot ships with the operational flotillas. On the other hand, the expansion of the S-boat arm had led to a large training commitment, which resulted in the S-boat Training Flotilla being formed as soon as boats became available for it. Thus, on completion of refit, *Tsingtau* joined the Training Flotilla at Swinemünde in November 1942. Then at the beginning of April 1943, when sufficient boats had been brought to an acceptable level of training, the 9th S-boat Flotilla was formed and *Tsingtau* was attached to work the flotilla up for operational duty. Her C.O. was now SdF.Kpt.Lt. Jacobsen. This duty lasted until December 1943 when the ship joined the newly formed S-Booteslehrdivision, in which she remained until the end of the war. Ob.Lt.z.S. Kmetsch relieved Jacobsen in December 1943 when the former was posted to the new *Hermann von Wissmann* then nearing completion in Holland. As more boats joined the Training Division, three training flotillas were formed within it, of which *Tsingtau* looked after the 2nd Training Flotilla. This she took to Norwegian waters (Oslofjord) in June 1944 but at the end of hostilities the ship was back in the Baltic. Post-war she was employed with the German Minesweeping Administration before being broken up on the Tyne in the 1950s.

TANGA

When, during the 1930s, the Chinese were attempting to modernize their ramshackle army and navy, approaches were made to several European nations for the supply of arms, including naval vessels. To tap this possible market, Germany formed a trade consortium in 1935, known as HAPRO, with the object of securing orders from China for arms, one of whose successes was a contract for a complete flotilla of S-boats and a depot ship. This ship was ordered from the Neptun A.G. yard at Rostock in 1936, as a slightly enlarged version of *Tsingtau*, constructed to German Lloyd rules. The hull was laid down on 13 April 1937 and launched on 14 December 1937. By the time the ship had been completed however, the Sino-Japanese war had effectively prevented any chance of the Chinese taking delivery so Germany offered to purchase the vessel. This appears to have been agreed and acceptance trials were begun on 19 January 1939. Commissioned on 21 January under the command of Kpt.Lt. Benning, the ship was named *Tanga*. Her

availability solved a major problem for the S-boat force, for it had been proposed that *Tsingtau* be allocated for flak training duties and replaced by a converted merchantman, *Samoa*. This was obviously an unpopular solution so the new purchase was welcomed.

Tanga took over the 2nd S-boat Flotilla and operated mainly in the Baltic until the outbreak of war. At the beginning of 1940, the flotilla was ordered to Wilhelmshaven but severe ice and unreliable engines prevented any real operational employment of the S-boats. In dockyard hands during 'Weserübung', *Tanga* did not become operational again until the end of April 1940. In the summer of that year, preparations were made to support S-boat operations in the Channel and to that end orders were issued on 24 August for depot ships to be fitted out as base ships for service in foreign ports by 10 September and to be ready at Borkum or Emden for deployment from 12 September. *Tanga* was allocated to Ostend or Zeebrugge, *Carl Peters* to Cherbourg or Le Havre and *Adolph Lüderitz* to Ijmuiden as soon as the military situation allowed. *Tanga* was in fact ready at Wilhelmshaven on 1 September. In the event, the severity of the RAF raids on the Channel ports where 'Seelöwe' invasion barges were being assembled forced the Kriegsmarine to reconsider the deployment of larger vessels westward and *Tanga* remained at Wilhelmshaven, some distance from the flotilla she was supporting. Attachment to the 2nd Flotilla continued until March 1941, when the 6th Flotilla was taken over; this was a training flotilla. She remained attached to this formation until October 1941 then, following the assumption of command by Ob.Lt.z.S. Brandt in November, was placed at the disposal of Flag Officer (Cruisers) for use as a tender in Norwegian waters. Stationed at Kirkenes in Arctic Norway, the ship led an inactive and isolated existence as a W/T repeating station for both BdK and Admiral (Nordmeer) until she finally sailed for home in October 1942. After a refit at the Naval Yard at Kiel, *Tanga* joined the S-Booteslehrdivision (S-boat Training Division) as depot ship for the 2nd Training Flotilla. Kpt.Lt.d.R. Vessel assumed command in August 1944 but in November was reappointed to *Hermann von Wissmann*, after which Kpt.Lt. Jacobson took over briefly until Ob.Lt.z.S. Wortman was appointed in command. January 1945 saw *Tanga* acting as depot ship for the 11th S-boat Flotilla and in May 1945 she was taken over by the Allies. A period of service with the GMSA followed, until on 3 December 1947 the ship was allocated to the USA under the Tripartite Agreement. Of little direct interest to the US Navy, *Tanga* was sold to Denmark and on 20 June 1948 renamed *Aegir*. She subsequently had a long career with the Royal Danish Navy until decommissioned finally in January 1967 and was later broken up by Paul Bergsoe & Son on the island of Masnedo.

When in the mid-1930s the projected S-boat force was planned to reach 75 boats by 1945, the subject of further depot ships was given much discussion and the parameters of a new design were established. Certain of these parameters were dictated by the abilities of the yard earmarked for future depot ship construction - Neptun A.G. of Rostock. This yard had no experience in longitudinal construction, little experience of welding and few welders. It was therefore decided to build a design based on German Lloyd rules and of transverse non-welded construction. The following particulars were established:

Length (water-line)	105m
Length (overall)	112.8m
Beam	14.2m
Displacement	4.1m
Displacement (standard)	3,320 tonnes
Displacement (full)	3,660 tonnes
Weight Statement:	(tonnes)
Full Load	
SI	1,850
MI	500
MII	250
Guns	110
Torpedoes	60
Provisions	80
Fittings	100
Fuel	230
Lubricating oil	20
Boiler oil	40
Drinking water	360
Feed water	20
Reserve	40
Total:	3,660 tonnes

The size of workshops was to be the same as in *Tsingtau* except that the forge and coppersmith's shops were to be next to the general machine shop while the mechanical workshop on the upper deck was to be large enough to accommodate a boring machine and a small lathe. Stowage for 24 torpedoes and 30 warheads was to be provided in the hold deck. For these torpedoes, four regulating spaces were provided in weatherproof areas and four on the upper deck. Seventy-two depth-charges were to be stored and eight sets of depth-charge equipment for the S-boats. Accommodation for a total of 403 was required. The ship's own defensive armament was, as designed, two 8.8cm L/45s in single shielded C/13 mountings, one 3.7cm SKC/30 twin and four 2cm guns. Later the 8.8cm weapons were replaced by two 10.5cm SKC/33 twin mounting LC/37s.

Two ships were initially ordered from Neptun on 17 September 1936 as yard numbers S496 and S470. *Carl Peters* was laid down on 15 April 1938, launched on 20 February 1939 and began trials on 20 November that year. She was commissioned on 6 January 1940. *Adolph Lüderitz* was launched on 13 April 1939 and commissioned on 11 June 1940. Two further units were

projected. S-Bootesbegeitschiffe A, B and C were to have MAN diesels while D was to receive Blohm und Voss engines.

Before either of the two new ships had been launched, the Kriegsmarine once again ran into the old problem of yard capacity which, on 20 October 1938, forced the Flottenabteilung to state that the situation in ship building and especially engine construction made it necessary to postpone all warships not strictly necessary for front line use. This included depot ships and it was questioned whether *Tsingtau* and the four new orders were strictly needed. Four days later SKL noted that with 75 S-boats planned - i.e., for eight flotillas, four each in North and Baltic Seas - no reduction in the number of depot ships could be countenanced (each depot ship could handle 15 boats). Already, however, the congestion in the shipbuilding industry had resulted in the two ships ordered from Neptun having their planned completion dates postponed from October 1937/January 1938 to January/March 1939 and even these dates were not to be met. The purchase of the China depot ship (*Tanga*) in 1938, yard congestion and a re-evaluation of the numbers of S-boats to be built, led to the cancellation of the second pair of depot ships 'C' and 'D', which had been ordered as yard numbers S487 and S488 on 18 July 1938.

CARL PETERS

Carl Peters (K.Kpt. Hinzke) arrived at Kiel from Rostock on 10 January 1940 to assume responsibility for the 1st S-boat Flotilla. The flotilla commander and his staff transferred to the new ship from *Tsingtau* but the boat crews remained aboard the latter for the present because they needed to be near their boats and the depot ship still had sea trials to complete. On 14 March 1940 *Carl Peters* sailed for Cuxhaven where her flotilla joined on the 26th. April saw the ship participate in 'Weserübung' as a component of Group 3, the Bergen force, returning to Kiel on 17 May. By September, *Carl Peters* lay at Wilhelmshaven with the 1st S-boat Flotilla, prior to moving down-channel, and by the end of the year she was based at Rotterdam. On 9 January a move was made to Ijmuiden and subsequently the depot ship was based on occasion at Amsterdam, while her flotilla was operational in the North Sea. When the flotilla was ordered home for refit, *Carl Peters* followed and by 1 June was at Kiel. War with Russia saw the ship with her flotilla based at Abo in Finland until October, when the 1st S-boat Flotilla was ordered home to refit for duty in the Black Sea.

In April 1942, *Carl Peters* took over the 5th Flotilla which was engaged on training duties and was now under the command of Ob.Lt.z.S. Renthal. During the afternoon of 30 June the ship was damaged by a mine in Prorer Wik off Sassnitz; the mine was probably one of those laid by the RAF on the night of 9/10 June or 11/12 June. Compartments I and II were flooded, necessitating repairs at Kiel which extended until December. At that time, the

Above: *Carl Peters* with the S-Booteslehrdivision in 1943. (H. Büchting)

8th Flotilla were at Kiel preparing for a move to Norway and *Carl Peters* was ordered as their depot ship. By New Year's Day 1943, she had reached Trondheim and a month later Bodø. Her sojourn in northern waters lasted until June 1943, when transferred to the S-boat training flotilla at Swinemünde. In December she was allocated to the 21st S-boat Flotilla at Eckerneförde to assist in the work-up of these small 'LS' and 'KS', boats but in February 1944 she was back with an operational flotilla, the 6th at Reval in the Gulf of Finland. She returned to home waters in June, joining the S-boat Training Division at Swinemünde, responsible for the 3rd Training Flotilla. On 24 February 1945, she was damaged by an accidental torpedo explosion while lying off Sassnitz. She was finally sunk by uncleared mines in Geltingerbucht on 14 May 1945.

ADOLPH LUDERITZ

On completion, *Adolph Lüderitz* (C.O.Kpt.Lt. Möbes) took over the 3rd S-boat Flotilla and in the autumn of 1940 moved to the Low Countries and was based at Rotterdam. By May 1941 both depot ship and flotilla were back at Kiel and the following month were transferred to Pillau. Operations against Russia followed, in the Baltic islands and the Gulf of Riga. At the end of October, however, the 3rd Flotilla was ordered home, earmarked for transfer to the Mediterranean. K.Kpt. Erasmi now assumed command of *Adolph Lüderitz* under orders to move to Norwegian waters with the 8th Flotilla, and sailed from Kiel north-bound on 18 November 1941. Based in Arctic Norway at Semskefjord and Kirkenes, the depot ship supported her flotilla during their operations in these inhospitable waters. When the 8th Flotilla left for home in July 1942, *Lüderitz* took over the 6th Flotilla at Tromsø. By mid-August she was being employed as a W/T repeating station for U-boats in Northern waters for Admiral (Nordmeer), based in Semskefjord. Flag Officer (S-boats) could ill afford the loss of this ship, if only temporarily, so pressed for her return as soon as possible. Her relief, the elderly *Meteor*, did not reach Northern waters until January 1943 despite *Lüderitz* having reverted officially to FdS control on 4 September 1942. She sailed for home on 9 January 1943, survived a torpedo attack by the Norwegian submarine *Uredd* off Alesund on 17 January, and arrived at Kiel on 4 February, where a refit was begun. On completion of this refit in July, *Lüderitz* sailed to Gotenhafen and later moved to Swinemünde for duty with the S-boat Training Flotilla. On formation of the S-Booteslehrdivision, *Lüderitz* joined this command. In December 1943 Ob.Lt.z.S.Kr.O. Gauland relieved K.Kpt. Erasmi and remained with the ship until the final surrender.

Lüderitz moved to the Skaggerak in March 1944 based at Kalundenberg with the 1st S-boat Training Flotilla and from there to Soon in Oslofjord. In January 1945 the ship was at Copenhagen but moved north again later and was damaged by aircraft while in Jossingfjord on the afternoon of 14 April 1945. At the collapse she was at Egersund. After the surrender, *Adolph Lüderitz* was allocated to the USSR under the tripartite agreement and was subsequently renamed *Paysherd*.

The cancellation of depot ships 'C' and 'D' was eventually rectified as a result of the occupation of the Low Countries and France for a large number of vessels were captured, complete and building in those countries. Flag Officer S-boats secured two of these, then building at the John Cockerill yard in Antwerp. They had been ordered by Poland as the merchant vessels *Lewant II* and *Lewant III*, yard numbers 688 and 689. The former had gone afloat just before the Belgian surrender but the latter was still on the slipway. Both were requisitioned by Germany for conversion to large Sperrbrecher, but by the spring of 1942 little progress had been made and construction was suspended. They were later redesigned as depot ships but their completion was badly delayed, probably by a combination of this redesign, other priorities and Belgian indifference. As completed, these ships displaced 3,700 tonnes full load and betrayed their

mercantile origin by the single-shaft Burmeister & Wain 3,600hp diesel installation. Armament comprised three 10.5cm guns in single shielded mountings, the forward pair superimposed, six 3.7cm and ten 2cm guns. The Kriegsmarine renamed the vessels *Gustav Nachtigal* and *Hermann von Wissmann*. The former had been intended to take over the 5th S-boat Flotilla by July 1941 and the latter the 6th Flotilla by April 1941, so the delays to their completion were considerable.

HERMANN VON WISSMANN

The first of the pair to complete was *Hermann von Wissmann*, on 16 December 1943, under the command of Kpt.Lt.(S) and Lt.z.S.d.R. Jacobsen. She ran trials at Antwerp in December, then remained at that port until February 1944, moving to Kiel in early March. In July 1944 *Hermann von Wissmann* was with the S-Booteslehrdivision at Sassnitz but in the middle of that month was ordered to the Gulf of Finland as depot ship for the 5th Flotilla, being based at Helsinki. However, Finland's armistice with Russia in September forced her withdrawal, first to Baltischport (Paldiski in Estonia) and then Libau. In mid-October she was transferred to Gotenhafen, and then moved to southern Norwegian waters in November with the 4th Flotilla. In January 1945 the ship was at Bergen but only one boat of her flotilla was with her. By March she was at Stavanger, which she left in the early hours of 17 March bound for Jossingfjord. As the war drew to a close, she moved south, entering Farsund in the forenoon of 8 April en route for Aabenraa in Denmark.

Right: *Hermann von Wissmann* in the Kiel canal, probably post-war. (WZB)

Following the surrender, *Hermann von Wissmann* was taken over by the Royal Navy and renamed *Royal Herald*, but in October 1950 was transferred to Belgium and named *Kamina*. In Belgian service she was used as a troop transport until 1962 when she was re-rated as a Command and Logistic Support ship for minesweepers. She was finally removed from the effective list in September 1967.

GUSTAV NACHTIGAL

Commissioned for service on 13 May 1944 under the command of K.Kptd.dR. Bohm, *Gustav Nachtigal* had an extremely brief life. She moved from Antwerp to Rotterdam on 8 June for degaussing and having been successfully cleared the following day, prepared to sail to Germany. On 13 June she sailed from the Hook as part of a small convoy (the other vessel was the newly completed *Ammerskerk*, a 7,900-tonne merchant ship), escorted by units of the 5th Defence Flotilla and 7th Minesweeper Flotilla. In all, the escort comprised six R-boats of the 9th R-boat Flotilla, four units of the 7th Minesweeper Flotilla and units of the 13th and 20th Vp flotillas. The convoy reached Den Helder by dawn the following day, where it remained anchored during the daylight hours and did not resume passage until 2215 that night.

Dutch resistance and probably 'Ultra' intelligence had warned the British of the impending movement and a strike was launched by the Beaufighters of the North Coates and Langham Wings of RAF Coastal Command, plus ten Mustangs of Fighter Command. Of the Beaufighters, those of Nos. 455 and 489 Squadrons and part of No. 254 were armed with cannon for anti-flak duties, No. 236 Squadron's machines were armed with rocket projectiles and ten aircraft of No.254 with torpedoes. Six of the latter were detailed to attack *Ammerskerk* and the remaining four were to take *Gustav Nachtigal* as their target. This strike overwhelmed the Germans, the flak guns of the escorts quickly being silenced. Ten RP hits were claimed on *Nachtigal* and eight on *Ammerskerk*. The torpedo aircraft were just as successful, hitting both ships with two torpedoes each, out of nine torpedoes launched. *Ammerskerk* sank quickly, as did *M103*, part of the escort. *Nachtigal* was badly hit and by 1000 hours she was drifting in the Hubert Gat with her stern almost blown off and bottomed. It had proved impossible to tow her although the tug *Memmert* was present and more were called for. The commander of the 7th Minesweeper Flotilla, who had three ships standing by as flak defence, considered that the depot ship was salvageable if lifting craft could be sent. However, after another five hours it had still not been possible to get a tow under way and the condition of the ship was serious. All valuables, secret documents and part of the crew were taken off. Her stern up to the after 10.5cm gun was fractured and under water, compartments 1-5 were flooded up to the 'tween deck, compartment 6 had $4\frac{1}{2}$m of water and rising, while No. 7 bulkhead was damaged. Under these circumstances, it was hardly surprising that at 1630 hours *Gustav Nachtigal* sank in 16m of water at the entrance to the Hubert Gat.

15. THE SMALL BATTLE UNITS (THE K-VERBAND)

The abortive attempt by British 'Chariots' to cripple *Tirpitz* in October 1942 had alerted the Kriegsmarine to the threat of attack even while the battleship was seemingly inaccessible in her lair in the Norwegian fjords. Another abortive attack, this time using Welman craft to raid the port of Bergen, merely reinforced this threat, but even so the subsequent successful attack on *Tirpitz* by X-Craft in September 1943 came as a tremendous shock to the Germans. Taken in conjunction with the known achievements of the British and Italians in the Mediterranean using midget submarines and of their use by the Japanese, it is surprising that the Kriegsmarine made no effort to develop similar weapons until the close of 1943. Attempts had been made to interest the high command in a variety of unorthodox weapons by various individuals, both service and civilian as early as October 1941 when Dr. Dräger of the Lübeck based Drägerwerk submitted a paper to the OKM in which he proposed the construction of a number of midget submarine designs of up to 120 tonnes. The smallest of these had a tadpole-like hull for maximum underwater speed and most were to be powered by diesels using nitrogen injection, a technique known since before the First World War. Dräger foresaw the need to construct not hundreds but thousands of these craft using automobile mass-production techniques with large scale sub-contracting. His raison d'être for these craft was: (a) for defence against a British invasion of the European coast; (b) to augment and partially supplant Vp boats; and (c) for use aboard auxiliary cruisers.

In his view such diminutive units would be of great use in British coastal waters and in the Mediterranean, where their small size would make them difficult targets for aircraft. At the same time, this small size and consequent restricted field of view was no longer seen as a disadvantage because of new detection methods such as S-Gerat and GHG which could be installed in the boats. Dräger's ideas were not well received in naval circles, which was hardly surprising because in 1941 Germany was master of Europe and Britain was in no position to mount an invasion. On 22 January 1942 his ideas were finally rejected on several grounds.

However, it is of interest to note that, in February 1942, Admiral Wenneker, the German Naval Attaché in Tokyo, was requested to obtain details of the Japanese two-man midget submarines used in the attacks on Pearl Harbor and Sydney, for which purpose he was supplied with a list of 46 design questions to ask. Eventually permission was obtained from the Japanese authorities and Wenneker left for Kure on 3 April 1942. The following day both he and the Italian Naval Attaché inspected one of the Japanese craft, a Type A boat, and obtained answers to some but not all of his questions. Nothing appears to have come of this visit. That same month Dip. Ing. Adolph Schneeweisse of the OKM issued a note dealing with small U-boats and U-boat carriers in which he recorded that a study of KTBs and action reports had revealed that the enemy had so organized his convoy escorts that single U-boats stood little chance of successful attacks and that massed attacks which swamped the escort were the only answer. He quite correctly predicted that the current major successes being achieved off the coast of the USA were only temporary. He therefore proposed the construction of an 'Unterwassersturmboote' of about 10 tonnes displacement capable of 30kt which could be carried on the decks of larger U-boats, two on the Type XIC and three or four on a Type XB. His sketch design was rather similar to the later 'Biber', a one man boat armed with three F5 or two G7a or G7e torpedoes.

There appears to have been as little reaction to Schneeweisse's ideas as to those of Dräger. The Kriegsmarine, perhaps even more than the Royal Navy, was a traditionalist force and could see no use for anything but the normal large U-boats. Yet just across the North sea lay Scapa Flow, often packed with targets suitable for midget attack, despite the obvious improvements in booms and defences since the sinking of *Royal Oak*. Even closer were Portsmouth and Plymouth. It took the damaging of *Tirpitz* and the realization that the German Navy had little with which to oppose an Allied invasion across the Channel, which seemed more and more likely, to prod the high command into investigating the development of small attack craft, surface, submersible and submarine. It was decided to form a special command, known as the Kleinkampfverbände (K-Verband), or Small Battle Unit Command, to develop tactics and operate all such craft of this nature. Appointed in command was Helmut Heye, who at the time was serving on the staff of Marinegruppenkommando (West) with the rank of Konteradmiral. This officer has previously appeared in these volumes when in command of the heavy cruiser *Admiral Hipper*, following which he had served in various staff posts in both southern and northern Europe, including appointment as Admiral (Schwarzmeer) between September and November 1942. His tenure of command of the Kleinkampfverbänd commenced in April 1944 and lasted until the final surrender.

Meanwhile, recruitment of personnel began and a base was established at Timmersdorfer Strand on Lübeck Bay.Two of the X-craft which had been lost during the attack on *Tirpitz* had been salvaged (*X7* as early as 1 October 1943) and in January 1944 they were brought to Lübeck for examination; they were probably *X6* as well as *X7*. It was vital that a usable weapon be developed as quickly as possible. Any such weapon must, however, make no demands on the production of other armaments, particularly U-boats, and had to make use of as much existing material as possible. Thus the first attempts were based around conversions of the standard G7e torpedo, modified to allow manned control. This project was supervised by Stabs Ing. Mohr and developed at the

Torpedo Versuchs Anstalt (TVA) from December 1943. Mohr played a major part in the programme and undertook much of the testing himself. The name bestowed on the craft , 'Neger' was a play on his name (Mohr = Moor in English). It was not actually a submarine because it did not have the ability to dive, merely a small amount of positive buoyancy, sufficient to support an underslung G7e torpedo. After much experimentation in a very short time, what can only be described as a makeshift weapon became available. The pilot sat in a small cockpit under a plexiglass dome and propulsion was by an electric motor of the type used to drive torpedoes themselves. The 5-tonne boat had a speed of about 4kt and a range of around 30nm at 3kt. Some 200 of these craft were ordered, and they were the first to see action, off Anzio in April 1944. The TVA was scheduled to deliver 50 in May, Deutsche Werke and the TVA 50 each in June, and Deutsche Werke the last 50 in July. Fifty would constitute a flotilla with ten in reserve. One drawback to the design was the lack of a suitable compass - the prototypes used at Anzio had to navigate by the stars - and it was realized early on that the inability to submerge was a serious fault, but the initial attempts to incorporate a diving tank were unsuccessful. By the time that this feature had been

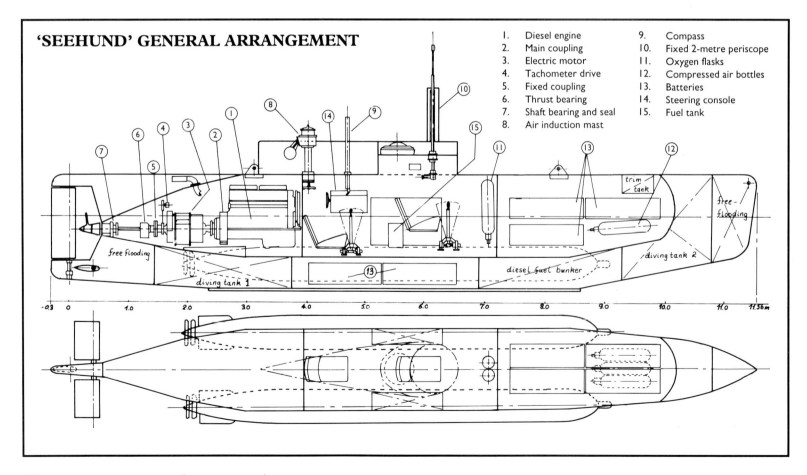

'SEEHUND' GENERAL ARRANGEMENT

1.	Diesel engine	9.	Compass
2.	Main coupling	10.	Fixed 2-metre periscope
3.	Electric motor	11.	Oxygen flasks
4.	Tachometer drive	12.	Compressed air bottles
5.	Fixed coupling	13.	Batteries
6.	Thrust bearing	14.	Steering console
7.	Shaft bearing and seal	15.	Fuel tank
8.	Air induction mast		

perfected however, around August 1944, the slightly longer craft had been renamed 'Marder', in which the diving tank was installed ahead of the pilot (the name 'Marder' was promulgated by the SKL on 21 July 1944, B.Nr1 Skl I Op 22659/44). The craft's diving endurance was very low and performance generally poor. Some 300 were constructed. Experiences during the invasion of Normandy had demonstrated that the ability to operate submerged was vital to success and survival, so the TVA developed the much larger 'Molch'. This still employed as many torpedo parts as possible, but displaced some 11 tonnes and had a longer but still torpedo-shaped hull from which two G7e torpedoes could be suspended, side by side. It was capable of about 50nm submerged at 5kt. Construction was mostly entrusted to Deschimag A.G. and about 390 were built. However, while undoubtedly an advance on previous types, the 'Molch' could hardly be described as satisfactory because the periscope had only limited arcs, depth control was difficult, no small gyro compass was available and the pilot had too much to do.The first craft was handed over on 12 June 1944 and thereafter construction was: June (3); July (38); August (125); September (110); October (57); November (0); December (28); January 1945 (32). Construction tempo was affected by the need to pressure-test every hull, air raids on Bremen and transport bottlenecks. Despite these numbers, 'Molch' was unsuccessful and saw only limited service.

The smallest actual submarine to achieve series production was named 'Biber', which had been developed from an idea suggested by K.Kpt. Bartels to Flenderwerft, Lübeck, following examination of the Welman craft captured at Bergen in November 1943. From a relatively crude prototype named 'Adam', a series production design was developed that displaced 3.6 tonnes. However, no suitable diesel engine was available and a petrol motor had to be used instead. This was a 32hp Opel Blitz lorry engine, which provided surface propulsion, while yet again a 13hp electric torpedo motor was installed for submerged travel. Surfaced range was 100nm at 6.5kt and 8.6nm at 5.3kt, plus 8nm at 2.5kt. Despite a diving depth of 20m, lack of compensating and trimming tanks meant that the boat could not be maintained at periscope depth and therefore attacks had to be carried out on the surface. Trimming the boat while under way represented a major problem and contributed to the excessive work load on the single crewman. Two G6e torpedoes could be carried, slung below the hull to port and starboard. Air raids on Kiel, which destroyed some components, failed seriously to affect the production rate, so the shipbuilding commission could report that the planned output of 200 by September would be achieved.

In 1944,, deliveries were as follows: May (3); June (6); July (19); August (50); September (117); October (73); November (56) = 324 boats.

The 'Biber', 'Neger', 'Marder' and 'Molch' were essentially makeshift stopgap weapons of limited potential,

having the single advantage of speed of construction. However, if the basic weapon is unsuccessful, the number available becomes academic. What was required was a true midget submarine, with good offensive potential and sufficient crew to operate it successfully. The first design to reach fruition was 'Hecht', designated type XXVIIA, which was intended to attach limpet mines to anchored ships. Propelled by a 12hp AEG torpedo motor, the boat was designed for purely submerged work, for which purpose a gyro compass had to be installed. This was very bulky equipment which cramped internal arrangements considerably. The mine charge weighed 800kg. After design work had been completed, the Chief of the Naval Staff demanded that 'Hecht' be able to carry a torpedo as an alternative, but because of the small displacement only torpedoes of negative buoyancy could be used. Hitler approved construction of 50 of this design on 18 January 1944 and on 9 March Germania was given an order for a prototype, followed on 28 March by an order for 52 production boats. In April it was decided to build large numbers of these boats and the numbers *U2111-U2300* were allocated, but in the event only 53 boats were completed - i.e., the original contracts. Deliveries were: May 1944 (2); June (1); July (7) and August (43). Not a successful type, 'Hecht' were used only for training purposes.

Almost in parallel with the 'Hecht' programme, the Construction Office was developing another design which was also given a true U-boat designation, Type XXVIIB, with diesel and electric propulsion and the ability to carry two torpedoes. Also investigated was a closed-cycle propulsion unit for this design but this remained in the development stage at the end of the war. The final design emerged with a 60hp Büssing lorry engine providing surface power and a 25hp AEG electric motor for underwater travel. It had most of the characteristics of the larger U-boats, being able to dive and trim at periscope depth. Two men formed the crew. Endurance was 270nm at 7.7kt (surface) and 63nm at 3kt (submerged), or 19nm at 6kt. On 30 July 1944 three prototypes were ordered from Howaldt at Kiel and plans were laid for large-scale production at a number of sites. At one stage in June 1944 it was envisaged that 1,000 of these boats, now known as 'Seehund', would be built at the rate of 70 per month. However, early in September Admiral Backenköhler, Chief of Naval Armaments, had to report that Dönitz would not agree to 'Seehund' production at the expense of Type XXIII construction; this was a sensible decision as the prospects for success of the new Type XXIII were far greater than those of the midget, despite packing the same offensive potential - two torpedoes. Nevertheless, Direktor Merker of the Main Ship Construction Committee pressed for trials to be completed as quickly as possible so that series production could begin within a short time. By October 1944 the plan called for 99 from Schichau, Elbing, 67 from Germania and thirteen from Klöckner, Ulm, in 1944. In 1945 Germania were to deliver a further

78 before turning over to Type XXIII boats; 45 a month were to be delivered from Schichau during 1945 plus 342 from Klöckner that year, a grand total of 994. As in the case of many other grand schemes at this period of the war, the reality fell far short of expectations. Raw material problems and shortages, labour difficulties, transport bottlenecks and conflicting priorities combined to reduce 'Seehund' production to 165; delivered as follows: 1944 - September (3), October (35), November (61), December (70); 1945 - January (35), February (27), March (46), April (8). Howaldt built three, Schichau (Elbing) 136 and Germania the rest. U-numbers were allocated from U5001 to U6351. Three of those on order from Schichau (from within U5350-U5484) and three from Germania (one from U5096-5119 and two from U5120-U5142) were scheduled to be fitted with 'Clothilde' closed-cycle diesels.

The final Small Battle Unit to be considered is 'Linsen', an explosive motor boat first developed by the Abwehr and employed by the Brandenburg Regiment. Their first use was an ineffectual attack on the Anzio bridgehead in April 1944, while still under Army control. After some political inter-service argument, these boats, of which 30 had been built, were later taken over by the K-Verband. With a length of 5.75m and powered by a Ford V8 petrol engine, these craft operated in threes, two explosive boats and one control boat. The former, packed with a 300kg (later 400 kg) charge in the stern, was piloted by a single crewman until the moment when the control boat took over by radio control. The boat operator then jumped overboard to be rescued by the control boat. Aboard the latter was the helmsman and two operators for the radio control. Once under remote control (by similar apparatus to the Army's 'Goliath' system), the crewless boats were directed towards the targets at 35kt. When the target was struck, the boats sank and the delayed action charge detonated with the effect of a ground mine. In September 1944 the construction programme envisaged 1,200 units, of which all but 200 were to be radio-controlled, the remainder being wire-guided. At that time deliveries in August totalled 144 with 281 planned for September. In service, the Navy found the original boats, of light spruce construction, too flimsy for open sea use and later built an improved and strengthened version of their own.

These 'Linsen' were operated by Naval Operational Commandos (MEKs) whose task, before they were taken over from Abwehr I, was reconnaissance and espionage. In the summer of 1944 this was still the case with MEK 20 at Cavella in Italy and MEK 90 at Dubrovnik, while MEK 71 at Toulon appears to have been a very shady unit indeed, connected with covert operations in Sardinia and possibly Corsica.

An indication of the high status, authority and independent nature of the Kleinkampfverbande is illustrated by the fact that MEK 71 was ordered by its superiors to investigate the possibility of acquiring one or more of the Type XXIII U-boats planned for construction at Toulon. According to their information, only two were actually under construction at the time (the summer 1944), but mass-production was expected to begin soon. When Skl got to hear of this scheme, they vetoed it completely: the Kleinkampfverband were not to be allowed any of the U-boats, nor were they to be able to build their own. They were, however, permitted to take over the former Italian 'CB' midget submarines, scuttled in September 1943, of which three were complete, four nearly so, six under construction and one under repair in the Adriatic. To transport them they were also allocated the submarines *Sparide* and *Murena* which had been refloated and could be made ready in about three months. As far as is known, nothing came of the idea although both boats and the submarine *Grongo* were towed to Genoa from La Spezia on 9 August. There all three were sunk in an air raid by the RAF on 9 September. There is no record of the 'CB' boats being used by the Germans but some were transferred to the Fascist Republican forces. The special operational units in existence in July 1944 were: MEK 20 (Cavalla); MEK 60 (Le Havre/Rouen); MEK 70 (Brest); MEK 71 (Toulon); MEK 75 (formed in February 1944 for Anzio); MEK 80 (Northern Italy) and MEK 90 (Dubrovnik). Later MEK 40 was formed in Denmark, MEK 65 in the Channel area and there may have been others, such as those intended for operations on the Danube and other eastern European rivers. Assault craft schools were established at Sesto Calende in Italy (Lehrkommand 600 and 601) and Stresa (602), as well as Frogmen Saboteur schools at Venice (Lehrkommand 700 and 701), Bad Tolz (702) and Valdagno (704). Their activities are outside the scope of this volume.

OPERATIONS

On the morning of 22 January 1944, Anglo-American forces landed at Anzio on the west coast of Italy, about 30 miles south of Rome. Although achieving initial surprise, the landing was not followed up quickly enough, so the German Army was able to contain the beachhead for some time. Weak but effective Luftwaffe forces had scored some success against bombarding Allied warships, whose gunfire support was vital to the break-out from the beachhead but there were no Kriegsmarine forces of any consequence available. Only the S-boats of the 1st S-Boat Division were in the area and their successes were negligible. By April the Allies had still failed to break out of the beachhead and there was a considerable concentration of shipping lying off - a tempting target if only the means could be found to attack it. It was decided that, despite the relatively under-developed state of the K-Verband equipment, this would be a suitable target for its men and craft. Accordingly, MEK 75 was formed with 40 'Neger' and despatched by rail early in April to Rignano, near Florence, where they arrived on 6 April. After some delay caused by difficulties in procuring heavy road transport, the unit finally arrived at Practica di Mare on the evening of 13 April and was

Above: A 'Neger' washed ashore at Anzio. The weapon lies on its side, its torpedo unfired. (IWM)

hidden in pine woods. There were immediate difficulties in locating a suitable launching spot because of the shallow beach gradient and, it was not until the night of 20/21 April that the first attack could be launched. After considerable effort by the men of the unit and with the somewhat reluctant assistance of some 500 soldiers, 23 of the 30 'Neger' were launched (Bekker states only seventeen). The attack proved a fiasco. Arriving to alerted defences at daybreak, at least four were sunk by gunfire or depth-charges and one was captured intact. Only thirteen returned from the sortie, which did not damage a single Allied ship, despite claims to the contrary. Almost immediately afterwards the unit was withdrawn to Germany. Thus ended the first sortie by the K-Verband in the Mediterranean, after which the total 'Neger' strength available to the Kriegsmarine was 29 units. There was however another small battle unit in the area, a 'Linsen' unit of the Abwehr which had secretly entrained in Germany on 24 March and moved to La Spezia without the knowledge of the Kriegsmarine. Inter-service arguments as to its deployment and control kept it out of action for the present however.

The K-Verband did not see further action until June 1944 when the Allies invaded Europe. As Germany's remaining destroyers and torpedo boats were kept well out of the invasion area by overwhelming Allied sea and air superiority, the only seaborne means of attack were the small battle units of the K-Verband, despite its still makeshift equipment. A unit of ten control and 24

explosive 'Linsen' under the command of K.Kpt. Kolbe arrived at Bolbec, east of Le Havre, on 19 June, moving to its forward base at Honfleur between 20 and 21 June. These were former Abwehr boats and as such not well suited to open water operations, but the Navy's own 'Linsen', with increased strength and greater fuel capacity, were not yet ready for service. The first attack was scheduled to take place on the evening of 25 June, when eight control and nine explosive boats were towed out by R-boats. However, one of the explosive boats ran alongside its tow and blew up, sinking the R-boat (*R46*) as well as two of the control boats. Despite this mishap the sortie continued, but bad weather wrecked all plans for the high seas swamped many of the boats and only two reached the release point. These failed to see any targets in the poor visibility and were eventually obliged to beach themselves. It was another fiasco. Two further attempts in June met with similar failure due to accidents and material failures, so that on 30 June Kpt.z.S, Böhme (formerly C.O. of *Z22* and *Z23* but now in command off all K-Verband units in France) was forced to report that the 'Linsen' were no longer serviceable and that 'Marder' were to be employed in future. Note that while Bekker refers only to 'Neger', the official records speak only of 'Marder' so that it is possible that popular usage was 'Neger' since this was developed first and that 'Marder' differed only in minor respects. Forty 'Marder' left Germany by rail on 13 June en route to Paris, the first group of 30 arriving at Trouville on the 28th before moving to Villers-sur-Mer, where they were hidden in Favrol Woods. The second group arrived at Pont L'Evéque on 5 July, reaching Favrol Woods the next day.

On 25 June one 'Biber' was despatched from Kiel via Aachen and Paris to Rouen, for an attack on the Caen Canal and Orne bridges, but by the time of its arrival the opportunity for this mode of attack had disappeared and frogmen were used instead. What happened to the 'Biber' is not known.

To return to the 'Marder', preparation of the launching sites (as in Italy) took a long time, so it was not until 5 July that the right conditions obtained for the first attack. Twenty-six 'Marder' were despatched, of which two returned prematurely with motor trouble. This attack claimed as sunk: one *Aurora*-class cruiser, two destroyers, one merchant ship and two LSTs, plus a cruiser, one destroyer and four other vessels damaged. The attack was claimed as a great success, despite the fact that fifteen of the attacking force failed to return. In fact, the only Allied losses were the British minesweepers *Magic* and *Cato*. Three nights later another attack by 21 craft achieved only the sinking of another minesweeper, *Plyades,* and damaged the old cruiser *Dragon* so badly, that she had to be added to the 'Mulberry' defences as a CTL. None of the 'Marder' returned.

Further sorties now depended on the arrival of reinforcements, of which 30 'Marder' were expected by 17 July and other types at the beginning of August. K Flotilla 211 (K.Kpt. Bastian), comprising 32 explosive and sixteen control 'Linsen', arrived at Houlgate by the beginning of August to complement the 'Marder', and 'Dackel' long-range torpedoes were to be used by the S-boat flotillas at the same time. On the night of 2/3 August a combined sea and air attack took place, involving one group of sixteen control and 28 explosive 'Linsen' and a second of 58 'Marder'. The Luftwaffe put in an air raid but the planned 'Dackel' attack at first light could not take place because of damaged port facilities. Parts of both 'Linsen' and 'Marder' groups failed to get away and only seventeen 'Marder' and ten control 'Linsen' returned to base. The attack caused chaos at the invasion beachhead but resulted only in the sinkings of the 'Hunt'-class destroyer *Quorn*, the trawler *Gairsay* and *LCT 764*. The transports *Fort Lac la Ronge* and *Samtory* were damaged. In addition, the old cruiser *Durban*, sunk as part of the 'Mulberry' breakwater was further damaged. At least six of the 'Marder' fell victim to the Spitfires of the 2nd TAF, while another was captured intact. It was yet another expensive failure.

In the attacks of 5/6 and 6/7 August only 'Dackel' were employed, but on 8/9 August another 'Linsen' attack by twelve control and sixteen explosive boats saw the loss of all but eight control boats for no return, despite claims for the sinking of nine ships including a destroyer. Further 'Dackel' operations on 9/10, 10/11 and 14/15 August caused damage to the 5,205-ton *Iddesleigh*, the elderly cruiser *Vindictive*, repair ship *Albatross* and a minesweeper.

'Marders' made another sortie on the night of 15/16

August when 53 were scheduled for launching. However, thunderstorms and inexperience resulted in only eleven setting out, of which seven returned prematurely. One ammunition ship was claimed sunk but no actual Allied losses were incurred. The last 'Marder' sortie took place on 16/17 August, when 42 put out from Villers-sur-Mer. Their only success was the sinking of the small auxiliary *Fratton* (757 tons) and one LCG (*831* or *1062*). Two torpedoes hit No.5 Gooseberry and another the previously damaged *Iddesleigh*. Only sixteen 'Marder' survived, returning to Le Havre because Villers-sur-Mer was no longer tenable as a base. Böhme and his staff also relocated to Le Havre.

By 4 September 'Dackel' operations were abandoned to conserve stocks for use in the North Sea and off the coasts of Belgium and Denmark. Then on 18 August 'Linsen' and 'Marder' units began to withdraw from the French

Above: A 'Biber' on trials, with camouflaged periscope. (IWM)

coast. Böhme and his staff moved to Amiens, while the 'Linsen' were despatched to Strasbourg for eventual transfer to the south of France. The 'Marder' were redeployed to Tournai in Belgium, which is inland on the River Scheldt near the Franco-Belgian border. The last of the 'Marder' crossed the Seine on 20 August, the same day that a fresh 'Marder' flotilla reached Rheims from Germany. As the 'Marder' did not have the range to reach the invasion area from Le Havre, it was decided instead to operate them from the Seine Bay, but the military situation soon prevented this and on 23 August they were ordered to the south of France.

It was still intended that the K-Verband continue operations against the invasion force, however, and on 21 August F.Kpt. Bartels left Germany with K Flotilla 261 (24 'Biber') en route for Tournai, moving to Fécamp between 23 and 27 August from where it was now planned to operate; Le Havre had by this time been evacuated. Fécamp was actually too far east to make an ideal base, but nevertheless on the night of 30/31 August 22 'Biber' were put into the water, although because of the destruction to harbour facilities, only fourteen got to sea (between 2130 and 2330 hours that night). High seas and strong gales caused twelve to abort the mission but the remaining two claimed a merchant ship and one minesweeper sunk (not confirmed by Allied records). Both returned safely. Fécamp was immediately abandoned, the 'Biber' and torpedoes destroyed and the flotilla was withdrawn to München-Gladbach, suffering some casualties en route. Böhme and his staff left for the same destination the next day, 1 September, marking the end of K-Verband operations on the French coast.

A 'Molch' flotilla, due to arrive at Tournai the same day as the 'Biber' flotilla, never reached the coast. Similarly, a fresh 'Linsen' flotilla which left Germany on 26 August for Fécamp was held at Brussels pending a decision on its future deployment. Eventually it was sent to München-Gladbach via Ghent for later use in the south of France. En route it suffered considerable losses in encounters with British armoured columns which must have been considerably surprised at the nature of their opponents.

It will have been noted that the various small battle units were grouped into flotillas, K-Flotille, which consisted of base staff and about 60 operating personnel. On 1 September these were organized and disposed as follows:

K-Flotille 211	'Marder'/'Linsen', Germany
K-Flotille 212	'Linsen' Ath, near Brussels
K-Flotille 261	'Biber', en route to Lübeck
K-Flotille 361	'Marder'/'Linsen', Germany
K-Flotille 362	'Linsen', Germany (ex-France)
K-Flotille 363	'Linsen', Baltic (ex-France)
K-Flotille 364	'Linsen', en route to Genoa from Tournai
K-Flotille 365	'Linsen', en route to Genoa from Baltic
K-Flotille 411	'Molch', en route to Genoa from Tournai
K-Flotille 412	'Molch', to leave Germany for Italy 10 September

There was a lull in K-Verband operations in northern Europe until 22 September when it was decided to base a 'Linsen' flotilla in Holland for operations against Allied traffic in the Scheldt and to support the German garrison at Dunkerque by sending in supplies. The first 'Linsen' arrived in Groningen by rail from Lübeck about 26 September. There was now a change in the command organization: Böhme was posted to Denmark and later Italy, to command K-Verband units in the southern theatre; while F.Kpt. Müsenberg assumed command of the area extending from Dunkerque to Hanstholm, including Heligoland and the Frisian Islands. On 5/6 October the first 'Linsen' sortie was made from the advance base at Flushing supported by MEK 60. One formation was to escort a supply run to Dunkerque, while the second of four groups would attack Allied minesweepers in the Scheldt. Matters did not go well, for two of the first group were sunk by their own harbour defence patrol, while force 5 winds and a heavy ground swell prevented any success against the minesweepers. Fourteen were driven ashore and destroyed, twenty more foundered and 26 returned to base. Later that day the flotilla was withdrawn to Rotterdam and thence via Groningen to Plön in Germany. Once again, the 'Linsen' had proved a complete and utter failure, yet the Germans persisted in their construction and use for a fresh flotilla of 60 boats became operational on 10 October, reaching Groningen on the 12th and Rotterdam two days later, from where they were despatched to Flushing by MFPs. All their subsequent operations against lock gates and harbour facilities in the Scheldt were accompanied by a conspicuous lack of success and heavy losses. The 'Linsen' flotilla held at Brussels was sent to Schartau near Lübeck to re-form for duty in the south of France but by 24 October found itself in Flushing, as did the 'Biber's from Fécamp, which arrived at Groningen via Schartau and East Jutland on 31 October. 'Linsen' made one more abortive sortie from Flushing on the night of 31 October/1 November, before that port too had to be abandoned.

It must by now have been evident to many that 'Linsen', 'Marder' and probably 'Biber' were expensive failures. There is some evidence that it was also becoming more difficult to obtain volunteers for the K-Verband and even Admiral Heye wrote, 'the only hope is for independent operations by selected crews and to keep the bulk on reserve for possible Allied landings in northern Holland'. Dönitz however would not hear of it for in his view the 'Biber' had especially good prospects and could not be left idle. At the time too consideration was given to airlifting K-Verband units into the Channel Islands but was discarded as impracticable. Twelve to fifteen flights by large and slow transport aircraft would have been necessary, using large quantities of scarce fuel, with the prospect of horrific losses in the face of total Allied air superiority. In any event, it had already been discovered that the existing weapons were not suitable against moving traffic and the navigational problems in the tides and races around the islands do not bear thinking about.

On 15 November 1944 the dispositions were as follows:

'Linsen'	36 at Den Helder	K.Flotiile
	36 at Scheveningen	212 and 214
	24 at Hellevoetsluis	
'Biber'	30 at Poortershavn	K.Flotille
		261, 262,
	39 at Groningen	263

Experimentation continued. 'Linsen' were adapted to carry BM 250 mines and 'Biber' were also being modified for minelaying as a result of their limited abilities against moving targets. Thirty GS mines (twenty magnetic/acoustic and ten magnetic/pressure) were despatched from Lübeck by rail for Groningen on 25 November for use by 'Biber' craft. Trials were expected to be concluded by 3 December. At the same time three patrol vessels and an R-boat group were attached for towing 'Biber' to the operational areas. The arrival of fresh 'Linsen', modified 'Linsen' with picked pilots and 'Molch' from Heligoland and Borkum (K.Flotille 1/412 and 2/412) made no difference at all to the success of operations. Bad weather prevented sorties until 17 December when 27 modified 'Linsen' were launched but only one reached the target area making an unsuccessful attack on a destroyer, and only ten boats returned. Even 'Dackel' operations were considered in the River Scheldt, using Siebel ferries modified to launch them. Two of these were fitting out at Wilhelmshaven and Rotterdam, while 50 'Dackel' were on hand at Den Helder; but nothing seems to have come of the idea.

In mid-December a comprehensive plan of attack was drawn up for the operation of K-Verband units in the Scheldt. Thirty 'Biber' would operate from Poortershavn and the special 'Linsen' from Hellevoetsluis. Thirty 'Molch' were to be prepared for use at Rotterdam in later sorties, when they were to be towed into action by units of the Rhein Flotilla. The initial assault was to be followed

Left: 'Biber' on road trailer abandoned during the withdrawal from Fécamp. (IWM)

up by thirty 'Biber' from Groningen and 'Linsen' from Hellevoetsluis and Scheveningen. The 'Linsen' at Den Helder were to participate after modifications at the end of December and those at Groningen were to be held in reserve. The 60 'Molch' expected from Heligoland would arrive at Assens by 22 December and would follow up operations of those from Borkum. Reinforcements expected from January 1945 included: 60 'Linsen' from Fedderwardsiel (Weser); 30 'Biber' from Norden (Ems); 30 'Biber' from Lübeck; and 60 'Molch' from Germany. Twenty-four 'Biber' and MEK 60 were held in readiness for the destruction of the Nijmegen bridges, a task for which a unit had been formed on 16 September, comprising six 'Linsen', three 'Marder' and ten Frogmen. In addition, the first 'Seehunde' were expected at Ijmuiden at the end of December.

All this concentration of force achieved little, for after further disasters the 'Linsen' were temporarily withdrawn. Eighteen 'Biber' sailed from Poortershavn and Hellevoetsluis on 22/23 December but were attacked by MTBs and lost four of their number while hurriedly slipping their tows. One ship, *Alan-a-Dale* (4,700 tons), was sunk but no 'Biber' returned. One had been mined on the way out, one returned with mine damage, and the remaining twelve, armed with mines and torpedoes, disappeared. None of the eleven despatched on 23/24 December, nor three sailed the next night, returned. In fact, up to the end of the year, 112 'Linsen' and 52 'Biber' had failed to return from operations. Morale in 'Biber' units especially must have been questionable. The combined strength of 'Biber' flotillas was now only seventeen, of which ten were operational. Sightings of 'Biber' by air and sea patrols were rare at this time and only eight were claimed by Allied units. The remainder

just vanished, probably victims of the stress of weather. The fourteen 'Biber' remaining at Hellevoetsluis were sent out on 27 December but while sailing, two torpedoes were accidentally fired in the lock, reportedly by the only boat not fitted with safety gear, installed as a result of the earlier accident. Eleven 'Biber' and two harbour defence craft were sunk. One of the craft which did sail (No. 90) was found drifting off North Foreland on 29 December by the minesweeper *Ready*, its pilot having been suffocated by petrol fumes, an ever-present hazard for the crewman.

It was now recommended by Flag Officer (North Sea) that 'Biber' operations be suspended but the Naval Staff disagreed because they considered their efforts vital. Dönitz at this time decreed the appellation 'Opferkämfer', literally 'suicide operations' for the 'Biber' pilots. Flag Officer (North Sea) made the caustic comment that since no 'Biber' had ever returned from an operation, their success could hardly be calculated!

In the meantime, the first six 'Seehunde' had left Germany by road on 24 December followed by daily batches of six more. At the end of the month there were twenty operational at Ijmuiden. Thus at the turn of the year, the K-Verband strength was:

Den Helder	21 'Linsen'
Ijmuiden	24 'Seehunde'
Scheveningen	33 'Linsen'
Rotterdam	20 'Biber'
	12 'Molch'
Hellevoetsluis	27 'Linsen'
Inland reserves:	
Amersfoort	60 'Molch'
Assen	30 'Molch'

Left *U 5329* (Lt.z.S Ulli Muller/
Lt. Ing. Jurgen Niemann) prior
to sailing on the 5th 'Seehund'
sortie, Saturday 3 February
1945. Note camouflage paint.
(Herr Schöne)

On New Year's day 1945, 'Seehunde' made their first sortie when seventeen sailed to attack Allied convoys off the Kwinte Bank. Only two returned to base after the operation but seven others beached themselves on the coast; some of them were recovered later. Of the remainder, one each was sunk by the destroyer *Cowdray* and frigate *Ekins*, one was beached at Domberg and a fourth was found abandoned by an MTB. The other four just disappeared. Only the naval trawler *Hayburn Wyke* was a victim of this operation. It was not an auspicious debut for the new weapon. Mishaps continued, one 'Seehund' capsized in the lock at Ijmuiden and another fired a torpedo inadvertently in the North Sea Canal, sinking a barge. However, ten reinforcements were sent from Wilhelmshaven on 13 January and 30 more were due to arrive later that month. A sortie by eight boats on the evening of 3 January was thwarted by bad weather, and on the 6th two sailed only to return with diesel troubles. The next actual sortie took place on 10 January when five 'Seehunde' left for patrol on the Kentish coast off Margate. Two returned early with defects, one more after depth-charging on 11 January, and only one of the last pair actually reached the operating area. After an abortive attack, this boat reached base safely but her consort was overcome by the weather and finally beached off the North Foreland. Foul weather also prevented a planned sortie

into the Scheldt by twelve 'Molch' on 10 January. Two days later all operations were suspended because of the bad weather. Thus on 20 January 1945 the K-Verband strength in Holland was:

'Seehunde'	26 at Ijmuiden
'Linsen'	27 at Den Helder
	33 at Scheveningen
	27 at Hellevoetsluis
'Molch'	30 at Rotterdam
	60 at Amersfoort
	60 at Zeist
	17 en route from Heligoland
'Biber'	20 at Poortershavn

When the weather improved, ten 'Seehunde' were able to sail in three groups on 21 January, four for Ramsgate, three to the North Foreland and the rest to the swept channel off Lowestoft. Of these, seven returned prematurely with defects while two sighted nothing on their patrol but returned safely. The last boat suffered a compass failure and found itself in the Thames Estuary where it unsuccessfully attacked a ship at 2330 hours on 22 January. Set northwards by the tides, unknown to the coxwain, the 'Seehund' was off Lowestoft by the 24th. There she was detected and attacked by *ML 153* but without effect. After sitting on the bottom for some time, the coxwain surfaced, unaware that the boat had now been set as far north as Great Yarmouth. Consequently, when steering east for home she ran aground on Scroby Sands. After two and a half days of unsuccessful efforts, the exhausted crew were forced to fire flares and were then taken off by the Trinity House vessel *Beacon*. This is a vivid illustration of the courage and fortitude of the K-Verband crews in the operation of their almost suicidal missions with such crude and unreliable equipment. This incident also alerted the British to the possible range of these craft.

Ice and cold weather continued to affect 'Linsen' operations in the latter half of January, while further 'Biber' sorties were as expensive as usual. Thus, of fifteen 'Biber' despatched from the Hook on 29/30 January, five returned with ice damage caused by collisions with floes and one sank from the same cause. One beached at Hellevoetsluis after 64 hours at sea, while the remaining six vanished without trace. There were no Allied claims for these. Once again the courage of these crews must be underlined; alone in freezing conditions and with little navigational assistance in a treacherous region, it is not surprising that casualties were very high.

The final 'Seehunde' sortie of the month was on 29 January when ten boats left Ijmuiden in two groups, one was bound for Margate, the second for the South Falls. Only two reached their billets, one of the craft making an unsuccessful attack; the remainder returned for various reasons.

There were no 'Molch' operations in January because the intense cold reduced the battery performance to such an extent that West Scheldt operations were not possible. Trials later showed that 55 miles was possible and therefore they could be used if towed as far as Goeree. Trials were also conducted using S-boats to carry 'Linsen' for extended sorties.

On 3 February the 'Molch' depot at Amersfoort was bombed by 2nd TAF Spitfires but none were damaged and on the same day nineteen Lancasters of No. 617 Squadron attacked the Poortershavn base with 'Tallboy' bombs which wrecked the facilities but did not damage the K-Verband units. However, destruction of the cranes prevented any 'Biber' sorties in February. Good dispersal of the 'Seehunde' also prevented losses during another attack on Ijmuiden. 'Seehunde' sorties continued on 5 February (eight boats), 10 February (ten boats) and 12 February (five boats). Only the last recorded any success, damaging the Dutch tanker *Liseta* (2,628 tons) from convoy TAM80 off the North Foreland. At least two boats were lost on these sorties and several were beached. The K-Verband considered that since only 30 per cent of 'Seehunde' were operational at any one time, some 80 were necessary at Ijmuiden to maintain attacks on the Thames-Scheldt convoys. It was expected that this figure would be reached by the end of March 1945, but it never was. Proposals to send 'Seehunde' into the Gulf of Finland in early January 1945 were vetoed by Dönitz on the grounds that all were needed in the West and he raised the priority of 'Seehunde' construction over all other coastal defence projects.

Because of the lack of success in the Scheldt, an attempt to use 'Seehunde' instead was made, combined with a 'Linsen' raid. Four 'Seehunde' put out on the morning of 16 February and fifteen 'Linsen' that night. Of the 'Seehunde', two vanished without trace, one attacked and missed a convoy of landing craft, then beached on return, while the last saw no targets and also went aground on return. The 'Linsen' were again a total failure. Since the more valuable 'Seehunde' were no more successful than the expendable 'Biber' and 'Molch', they reverted to open-water operations, and on 20 February three boats sailed for the Ramsgate area, four on the 21st for the South Falls and one more on the 23rd. All reached their billets, sinking *LST364* from convoy TAM 87 and the cable ship *Alert* (941 tons) east of Ramsgate. All boats returned, although one of them was attacked by Beaufighter 'J' of No. 254 Squadron east of Orfordness. During this period also, 'Linsen' and 'Molch' sorties were made, resulting in the loss of six out of fourteen of the latter. *ML588* and *ML901* each sank one and shore gunfire another. The rest vanished without trace. No damage was caused to Allied forces and an appreciation of the ineffectiveness of the K-Verband forces in the first two months of 1945 can be seen:

	sorties	losses	results
January			
'Seehunde	44	10	1 ship sunk (324 tons)
'Biber'/'Molch'	15	10	nil
'Linsen'	15	7	nil
February			
'Seehunde'	33	4	2 ships sunk (3,691 tons) 1 ship damaged (2,628 tons)
'Biber'/'Molch'	14	6	nil
'Linsen'	24	3	nil

However, the 'Seehunde' results appeared to be improving.

The organizational structure on 8 March 1945 was:

Viz.Adm. Helmuth Heye
Chief of Staff - F.Kpt. Frauenheim
1. K-Staff, (North) - F.Kpt. Mussenberg,
    HQ at Sengwarder
    Advance HQ at Rotterdam
    Depots at Groningen and Utrecht
5th K-Division, Ijmuiden
    2.K-Staff, (Norway) - Kpt.z.S. Beck, HQ Oslo
1st K-Division, Narvik

3. *K-Staff, (Skagerrak)* - F.Kpt. Brandi, HQ Aarhus

4. *K- Staff, (South)* - Kpt.z.S. Boehm, HQ Levico

6th K-Division, Pola

5. *K-Staff, (Special Duties)* - Kpt.z.S. Duwell, HQ
Kammer am Attersee
Set up for river operations in eastern europe

6. Training Establishments

Lehrkommando 350	'Marder'	Suhrendorf
Lehrkommando 400	'Molch'	Wilhelmshaven
Lehrkommando 250	'Biber'	Kleine Holewiek
Lehrkommando 300	'Seehund'	Neustad
Lehrkommando 200	'Linsen'	Plön
Lehrkommando 100	'Linsen'	?
Lehrkommando 600	Assault craft	List/Sylt
Lehrkommando 700	Frogmen	List/Sylt
Lehrkommando 900		?Sylt

In March ten 'Seehunde' sailed for the North Foreland (five on the 6th, three on the 9th, one on the 11th, one on the 16th) but scored no successes, losing four of their number; *MTB 675* sank one, *Torrington* two and Beaufighter 'F' of No. 254 Squadron one. Further air attacks on returning units were without result. During the same period, nine other 'Seehunde' sailed for operations off the coast of East Anglia (four on the 6th, one on the 9th, one on the 11th, one on the 16th and two on the 19th). One of these sank the 2,878-ton *Taber Park* from convoy FS1753 off Southwold, but one 'Seehund' was sunk by *MTB 394* on 22 March about 23 miles south-east of Great Yarmouth.

Meanwhile, further disaster overtook the 'Biber' units when, on 6 March, while preparing for a sortie, one pilot released his torpedoes in the basin at Rotterdam, the resulting explosion sinking fourteen of these craft and damaging nine others, with a consequent heavy loss of life. Nevertheless, eleven survivors sailed that evening to operate in the Scheldt. Yet again none returned. One was captured by an ML off Breskens the following day and four others were found abandoned on beaches at North Beveland, Domberg, Knocke and Zeebrugge, while one was sunk by shore gunfire off Westkapelle on 8 March. The other five just vanished.

Between 11 and 12 March a large combined operation was launched against the Allied supply line to Antwerp. Both S-boats and the K-Verband were involved. Of the latter, fifteen 'Biber' armed with torpedoes and mines, fourteen 'Molch' and 27 'Linsen' left Rotterdam and Hellevoetsluis to operate in the West Scheldt. Still success eluded them and losses were heavy: thirteen 'Biber', nine 'Molch' and sixteen 'Linsen', a total of 38 craft failed to return from the sortie. Of the 'Biber' and 'Molch', the following causes appear established for their losses:

2	Coastal Command Swordfish, pm 11 March off Schouwen Island
4	Naval MLs, forenoon 12 March off Westkapelle
1	2nd TAF Spitfires, pm 12 March off Walcheren
4	Shore batteries, Flushing and Breskens, pm 12 March
1	HMS *Retalick* 0328/13 north-west of Walcheren

There were also six losses from unknown causes of which some were certainly by air attack; RAF Coastal Command claimed one 'Seehund', three 'Linsen' and eight 'Biber/Molch' as a result of operations at that time. As the S-boat attack was equally unsuccessful, this was an expensive 36 hours for the Kriegsmarine and no further operations took place until 22 March when twelve 'Linsen' made a fruitless sortie to Ostend. On the night of 23/24 March sixteen 'Biber' sailed from Poortershaven for the Scheldt approaches armed with torpedoes and mines. As far as is known, no success was achieved, with only seven craft returning. Of those lost, one and a possible total of three were sunk by *Retalick* off Ostend, one by No. 254 Squadron Beaufighters off Goeree and one was seen abandoned on Schouwen Island. The fate of the other four is unknown.

Between 24 and 26 March four 'Seehunde' sailed for the coast of East Anglia and six for the Thames-Scheldt convoy route. This resulted in the sinking of two ships, the coaster *Jim* (833 tons) and the steamer *Newlands* (1,556 tons) but four boats failed to return. Off East Anglia, one was sunk by Beaufighter 'Q' of No. 254 Squadron and another by the corvette *Puffin*. The latter was so badly damaged, however, that she was declared a constructional total loss. Off North Foreland *HDML 1471* sank one and *ML586* another off Walcheren. Results for March 1945 were as follows:

	Sorties	Losses	Results
'Seehunde'	29	9	3 ships (5,267 tons) sunk
'Biber' and 'Molch'	56	42	3 ships (255 tons) sunk
'Linsen'	66	27	nil

By the beginning of April 1945, the Allied forces had almost completely encircled Holland, making reinforcement by road or rail impossible; even before that, Allied air superiority had made things very difficult. Only the 'Seehunde' were sufficiently seaworthy to make the passage from Wilhelmshaven. Heavy air raids on known K-Verband bases caused structural damage but no losses to boats so that on 8 April the strength in Holland comprised 29 'Seehunde' at Ijmuiden, 24 'Biber' at Rotterdam, 60 'Molch' at Amersfoort and 51 'Linsen' at Scheveningen/Hellevoetsluis. Four more 'Seehunde' reached Holland from Wilhelmshaven on 20 April and fourteen more by 1 May, plus two more from Heligoland. An average of 33 'Seehunde' were at Ijmuiden for the final weeks of the war of which only 50 per cent were operational.

All operations were held up by bad weather until 5 April when sorties began again, 36 patrols being made up to the end of the month. On the East Coast, north of the Thames, the cable ship *Monarch* (1,150 tons) was sunk off

Orfordness, but three 'Seeh_nde' were lost - one to Beaufighter 'U' of No.236 Squadron on 12 March off the Hook, one to the destroyer *Garth* on 14 March off Orfordness and a third on 29 March to the corvette *Shelldrake* south-east of Lowestoft. Of the nine boats working in the Scheldt, one torpedoed the small US Navy oiler *Y17* (800 tons) from TAC90 but Beaufighter 'P' of No. 236 Squadron accounted for a 'Seehund' off Walcheren, the shore batteries at Blankenberghe another on 18 April and one was found abandoned off Walcheren the following day. From 17 April, seventeen boats had sailed for the Dover-Dungeness area where one sank *Samida* (7,219 tons) and damaged *Solomon Juneau* (7,176 tons) from convoy TBC123, but *ML102* sank one midget submarine off Dover, another ran aground east of Calais and a third was sunk by Beaufighter 'W' of No. 254 Squadron. On 11 April another boat attacked convoy UC63B east of Dungeness, damaging *Port Wyndham* (8,580 tons) but this 'Seehund' or perhaps another boat was sunk by *MTB 632* that same day. Yet another fell victim to air attack off the Hook on 12 April and one more to Barracuda 'L' of No. 810 Squadron the following day in the same area.

'Biber' sorties were resumed on 9 April when five put out for the Scheldt armed with torpedoes and mines. Three were sunk by aircraft and one was mined. On 11 April two more set out for a mining sortie, from which only one returned, while on 21 April six more set out to lay mines. Of these, four returned but two vanished. In the last 'Biber' operation of the war in Dutch waters, four sailed from Rotterdam to lay mines, but only one returned.

'Linsen' operations continued again with the usual heavy losses, some of which were incurred on supply runs to the beleaguered garrison at Dunkerque at the hands of the frigate *Ekins*. The last 'Linsen' sortie of the war was on the night of 20/21 April, again a supply run to Dunkerque.

'Seehunde' operational sorties ceased on 28 April but they too were employed on the supply run to Dunkerque. One sailed at the end of April and three on 2 May. All reached their destination before the final surrender. The operations of the K-Verband in the North Sea can be summarized as follows:

	Sorties	Losses	Results
'Seehunde'	142	35	9=18,451 tons sunk
			3=18,354 tons damaged
'Biber'/'Molch'	102	70	7=491 tons sunk (mines)
			2=15,516 tons damaged
'Linsen'	171	54	nil

The K-Verband who operated in other areas, including Denmark and Norway. The first 'Marder' flotilla arrived at the Skaw on 1 September 1944, moving to Asaa ten days later. On 23 September a 'Seehund' flotilla was sent by rail to Aalborg and a 'Biber' flotilla the same day. Two days later a 'Biber' flotilla withdrawn from Fécamp via Lübeck was despatched to Denmark, and on 28 September Kpt.z.S. Boehm and his staff arrived to control all K-Verband operations in Denmark. There was at this period a strong belief that the Allies would invade Denmark or attempt to force entry into the Skagerrak, hence the build up of forces. Early in November 1944 the proposed

Right: 'Molch' abandoned on the airfield at Forus, Norway, in 1945. (IWM)

organization in Northern waters was as follows:

N Norway	60 'Biber'	Westfjorden/Lofoten
	60 'Marder'	
S Norway	60 'Molch'	Oslo/Kristiansand (S)
Denmark	60 'Biber'	Aarhus/Osterburg
	60 'Marder'	Asaa
	12 'Hecht'	Asaa
Heligoland	30 'Molch'	
Borkum	30 'Molch'	
Ems Estuary	30 'Biber'	
Fedderwardsiel	30 'Linsen'	

'Linsen' were also being sent to the west coast of Norway. By mid-December 1944, K Flotilla 216 with 60 'Linsen' were at Levanger in Trondheimsfjord, while K Flotilla 215 with a similar number of boats passed through Oslo on 20 December northward bound. One of their tasks was to seek out and destroy bases for British MTBs which were believed to exist at isolated islands along the coast. In the Baltic too, exercises were being planned between destroyers and 'Linsen' as late as January 1945, and even when the incomplete torpedo boat *T40* was towed out from Gotenhafen on 9 March 1945, part of her deck cargo included twelve 'Linsen'. Such adherence to a weapon known to be unsuccessful is difficult to understand. There was now a change in command when Böhme was posted to Italy with Kpt.z.S. Düwel taking over in Denmark and Kpt.z.S. Beck in Norway. The first 'Biber' flotilla to reach northern Norway was K Flotilla 265, which arrived at Harstad on 22 November, but a proposal to transfer 30 more (K Flotilla 263) from Kristiansand (S) to Bodø was not approved by Dönitz as they were required to augment the Skagerrak defences in conjunction with new radar installations at Kristiansand and Tromoy. There was only one operation launched by the K-Verband in northern waters and this was an imaginative and daring attempt on the Russian fleet off Murmansk, in the manner of those carried out by Italian and British midget submarines. Three U-boats were to sail from Harstad, each with two 'Biber' on deck, which would be launched forty miles off the target, the battleship *Archangelsk* (ex-*Royal Sovereign*) and any other important shipping. On completion of the attack, the 'Biber' would rendezvous with the U-boats, then scuttle. *U295*, *U716* and *U739* sailed from Harstad on 5 January, but en route first one and then another of the 'Biber' developed leaks in fuel systems, caused by the diesel vibrations of the U-boats. Although the operation was continued until well past North Cape, 'Biber' serviceability was now so poor that the senior officer had to abandon the mission.

In Denmark, Kpt.z.S. Düwel was now appointed to Army General HQ in connection with K-Verband operations on the Danube, Drau and Oder rivers, in view of the situation in the east. His successor was F.Kpt. Brandi. The organization in Scandinavia was now to be: one 'Biber' flotilla at Kristiansand (S), one 'Marder' flotilla at Norway (West Coast) and half a 'Linsen' flotilla. Provisional reinforcements were one new 'Marder' flotilla, an assault boat flotilla and a 'Marder' flotilla from Jutland on relief by 'Molch'. The 'Hecht' had been sent back to Germany and their crews retrained on 'Seehunde'. No action took place and on 29 March Dönitz agreed to the transfer of twenty 'Biber' from Narvik to South Norway, considering the ten 'Biber', 30 'Linsen' and 20 'Marder' remaining to be adequate. Units and materials were being sent to Norway until the end of the war, as shown by the fact that six 'Molch' were lost with the steamer *Hansa I*, together with half the pioneer equipment of that flotilla when the ship was sunk on 9/10 April (see *German Destroyers of World War Two*). However, the Allies had no need to invade Scandinavia and all these preparations were in vain.

Leaving aside special operations on the rivers of Eastern Europe, the other theatre where the K-Verbande were employed was the Mediterranean. As recounted earlier, the first special units to reach this area were the explosive boats of the Abwehr, but they did not mount their first operation until a sortie on 1 July 1944 from La Spezia. This was a total failure and they were withdrawn and taken over by the Navy. The 'Marder' of MEK175 were also withdrawn after the Anzio sortie. It was not until 26 August 1944, after the Allies had landed in the south of France, that new formations were despatched to the Mediterranean. These were the 60 'Marder' that arrived in Rheims on 20 August and were then withdrawn to Tournai before leaving for the south on 26 August. By 1 September the first group had arrived at Genoa and a flotilla of 'Molch' had started out from Gettdorf near Kiel, for the same destination. Fifteen 'Marder' arrived at San Remo, where a forward base was established, on 3 September, in order to attack the bombarding forces.

The first attack was launched on 5 September but only five boats sailed. Only one returned after an abortive attack on a French contre-torpilleur (heavy destroyer). By 7 September fifteen more had reached San Remo, giving a serviceable total there of 25. Meanwhile, 30 more 'Marder' had arrived at Verona as a reserve for operations on the west coast of Italy. A second attack took place on 9/10 September when fourteen 'Marder' sailed, but again losses were heavy for no return; only four got back to base. There were now only eleven units serviceable at San Remo and operations were suspended unless a suitable stationary target presented itself. Another 'Marder' flotilla reached Verona from Germany on 11 September, followed by the first group of 'Molch' on 13 September. The 'Marder' continued to Padua while twenty of the 'Molch' were sent to San Remo, the remainder (thirty) to Padua. The build-up continued with the arrival on 20 September of the 'Linsen' flotilla, withdrawn from France on 18 August, and half flotillas of 'Marder' and 'Molch' arrived at Verona on 18 and 20 September respectively. These latter were destined for the Adriatic, while the 'Linsen' later went to Ravenna. By 25 September there were ten 'Molch' and eighteen assault boats at San Remo and in a sortie that night, seven out of nine 'Molch' sent out failed to return, whereupon 'Molch' sorties were abandoned. 'Linsen' made their first and only sortie from Corsini on the night of 30 September / 1 October, transported by MFPs. No contact was made with Allied forces but bad weather resulted in only two control boats returning. The remainder of the flotilla was transferred to San Remo, where 48 arrived on 18 October. At the same time, the 'Marder' at Treviso were ordered to Savona, then diverted to Venice for overhaul and finally despatched to Trieste. There was now a lull in activities in the Ligurian Sea, until 18/19 November when fifteen 'Marder' sailed from San Remo to attack traffic off the coast; only seven returned. Finally, on 31 December, five more sailed to attack targets off Villefranche, of which only one was lost. The surviving boats were now withdrawn to Padua for transfer to the Adriatic.

The 'Linsen' at La Spezia made one sortie on 16/17 January, losing ten boats out of 33, and before the end of the month were withdrawn to Verona and thence to Lake Balaton in Hungary for Danube operations. In the Adriatic, operations were confined mostly to commando type raids and thus are outside the scope of this narrative. It is not believed that the 'Molch', 'Marder' and 'Linsen' participated widely, if at all. At the end of 1944 and early in the New Year, several minor commando-type raids were carried out by MEK71 from Pola, such as those on the night of 9/10 January 1945 when four S-boats ferried ten men and five folding boats of MEK71 to attack bridges and communications over the Tenna estuary on the coast of Italy, south of Ancona. This was successfully accomplished and on the same night other units of MEK71 attacked Allied forces in the port of Zara. A later attack on Zara using both S-boats and SMA boats of K. Flotilla 612 on the night of 18/19 January failed because the latter could not cope with the heavy seas. On instruction from Dönitz, trials began for the transport of 'Linsen' by the S-boats of the 3rd Flotilla, also then based at Pola. The 'Linsen' were in fact the Italian equivalent, the MTM or Motoscafi da Turismo Modificato, (Modified Tourist Motorboats), taken over by the Kriegsmarine and operated by K. Flotille 612. However, difficulties were experienced because the boats of the 3rd Flotilla were smaller than those used for the same purpose in the North Sea and it is uncertain if any such operations were mounted in the upper Adriatic.

In retrospect, it has to be said that all the effort expended on these weapons, both in men and materials, was never justified in terms of the results achieved. Indeed, given the nature of the generally poor designs available and the strength of Allied counter-measures, they could hardly be expected to do so. Certainly in the case of the Scheldt operations, Luftwaffe minelaying was far more likely to have closed the river, had sufficient resources been available. Similarly, the same result may well have been achieved by air-laid mines off Normandy, rather than the expensive K-Verband operations.

16. MINESWEEPERS

By the outbreak of the First World War in August 1914, the mine had been developed into a powerful weapon of both offence and defence, although it would probably be true to say that the latter use prevailed at the time. Germany, surrounded as she was by the shallow North and Baltic Seas, had seen the potential of this device and by 1914 the Kaisermarine's stocks numbered some 9,000 units of efficient design. That their role was seen as defensive is indicated by the fact that from 1905 until 1917 the Coastal Artillery Branch had been responsible for mining matters. However, two small cruiser-type minelayers had been completed in 1907-08, *Nautilus* and *Albatros*, although their speed of 20kt was a little on the

low side for offensive use. In addition, from the *Kolberg* class of 1909-11, all German cruisers were equipped for minelaying and two, *Bremse* and *Brummer*, were specifically constructed as such. Torpedo boats were also fitted for minelaying. Rather surprisingly, minesweepers were not included in pre-war programmes and it was not until 1914 that a class of purpose-built ships was put in hand. This was the 450-ton *M1* class of which, with modifications, some two hundred units were ordered. Not all of these were completed but some survived to take part in the Second World War. They were handy coal-fired ships designed for minesweeping, but like all such craft were useful for other tasks, such as escort duties. In 1917 a

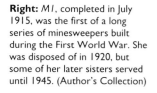

Right: *M1*, completed in July 1915, was the first of a long series of minesweepers built during the First World War. She was disposed of in 1920, but some of her later sisters served until 1945. (Author's Collection)

TYPE M35 GENERAL ARRANGEMENT

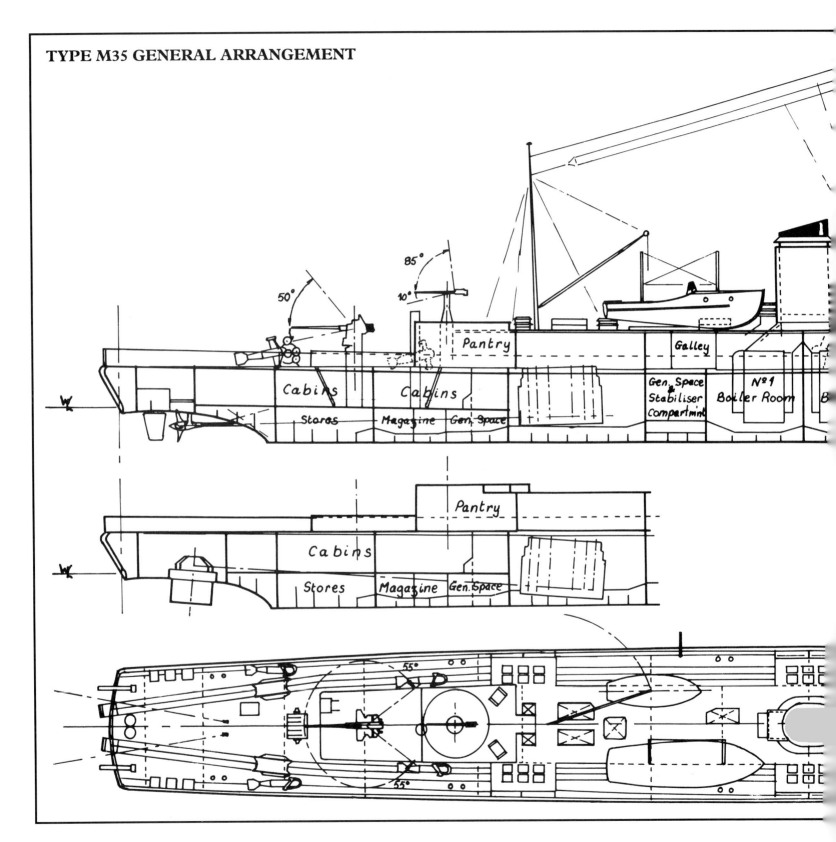

85°

50°

10°

Pantry

Galley

Cabins   Cabins

Gen. Space
& Stabiliser
Compartment

N°1
Boiler Room

W

Stores   Magazine   Gen. Space

Pantry

Cabins

W

Stores   Magazine   Gen. Space

55°

55°

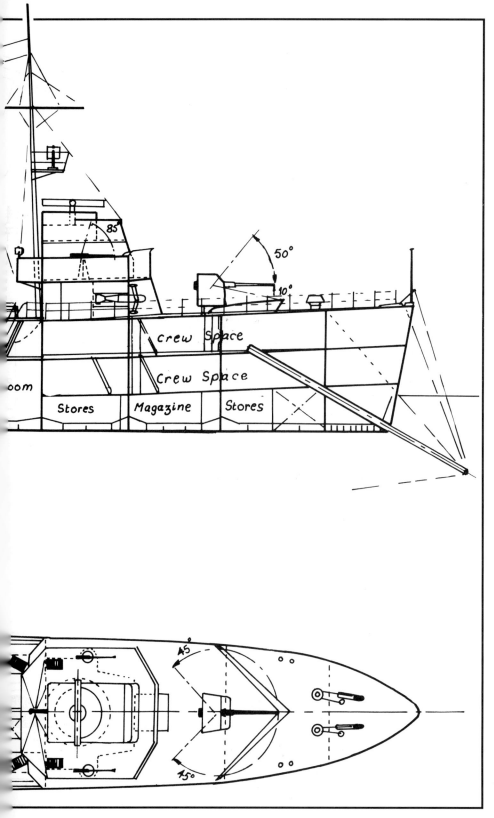

Crew Space

Crew Space

Stores | Magazine | Stores

...oom

85

50°

10°

45

45°

new class of shallow-draft minesweepers was designed, displacing only about 200 tonnes, and orders were eventually placed for more than sixty of these craft. The first FM-Boote to enter service was *FM3* on 13 February 1918 but the type proved unsatisfactory and as a result of new developments in minesweeping, construction was halted after nineteen boats had been completed. In fact, Germany had by then been defeated and many of the incomplete vessels were sold out for commercial use. Several ended up in minor foreign navies and one, *FM36*, completed after the war as a merchant ship, was taken over in 1941 by the Kriegsmarine in the Black Sea, where she served as the A/S vessel *Xanten*, later *UJ116*.

Until the end of the First World War, all mines were fired by contact means ('horns') except for shore-controlled defence fields - so that the method of sweeping was by wire and cutter, and the Kriegsmarine's sweepers had no other sweeping device available to them. It was therefore an unpleasant shock when, on 8 August 1918, the destroyer *V68* was mined and sunk off the coast of Flanders. *G95* also received light damage from another explosion but, despite minesweeping, no mines were found. Later *G41* was damaged by another explosion, the torpedo boat *A58* was sunk on 15 August and the next day a patrol vessel was also lost. Once again repeated sweeping failed to locate any mines and it was assumed that magnetic mines had been employed for the first time. No sweeping device became available to the Kaisermarine before the Armistice, but this was the only such field laid by the Royal Navy during the First World War because the mine in question, the Sinker Mk I (M), was not considered very successful! Apparently, on the first use of these mines, most detonated prematurely after 40 minutes (i.e., as soon as the safety-plugs had dissolved), but this defect was later remedied. The mines had been laid by the 20th Destroyer Flotilla.

The autumn of 1917 saw the removal of mine-warfare from Coastal Artillery control, with the formation of minesweeping and minelaying departments, but this was far too late and the Treaty of Versailles abolished this separation, placing them under the Torpedo Branch. The Reichsmarine was permitted to retain minesweepers, not least to clear up the huge numbers laid around German coasts during 1914-1918. From the spring of 1919 until the autumn of 1922, the 'volunteer-crewed' minesweepers of the 'provisional' Reichsmarine were active in the North Sea and Baltic coastal waters, as well as on the Murmansk coast surprisingly enough, clearing the minefields. This task absorbed virtually the whole of the meagre resources available in terms of men, materials and vessels and as a result prevented any immediate rebuilding of the fleet. As soon as it was possible to do so, the minesweeping service was run down and its resources were diverted elsewhere. Thirty-six 'M'-class ships entered service with the Reichsmarine but all of the 'FM' boats were sold out. These boats formed the backbone of the minesweeping force between the wars and it fell to minesweepers to make the first official post-war visits by German naval vessels to foreign ports (Gothenburg, Memel and Frederikshaven) after the formation of the new 1st Minesweeper Half Flotilla in late 1924 (*M113, M122, M136* and *M145*).

With the passage of time, a number of these vessels were converted to tenders and depot ships or for other subsidiary uses. Thus by the late 1930s only fifteen were available for service as minesweepers. In the meantime, the Boom Experimental Command (Sperrversuch-kommando, or SVK) had been covertly formed in 1922, and in 1930 separate minelaying and minesweeping commands were re-established. This was followed in 1933 by the formation of the Boom Defence School (Sperrschule). Only one half flotilla of minesweepers was kept active. In 1932 this comprised *M66, M98, M109, M111, M126, M132* and *M146*, commanded by Kpt.Lt. Ruge, who was to spend much of his career in minesweepers and later became C-in-C of the re-formed German Navy, the Bundesmarine, in the 1950s.

In December 1935 plans for a second half flotilla to be formed on mobilization were discussed. For this purpose it was necessary to employ those boats which had been given extra beam to enable them to carry the 10.5cm SKL/45 gun in a C/06 MPL mounting. The boats in question were *M89, M102, M110, M122, M126, M81* and the unmodified *M85*. Because of treaty limitations, there had been no guns available to arm the minesweepers any earlier.

By now there was clearly a need to replace these elderly ships and a new design was prepared: the Type 35, which was considerably larger than the older M15 type, displacing 894 tonnes. Its hull was divided into twelve watertight compartments, with fourteen main bulkheads and was of mixed welded and riveted construction; butts were welded and seams double-riveted. Plate thickness was 5-9mm. There was no continuous double bottom but a longitudinal bulkhead ('Wallgang') extended from the skin plating to the upper deck between frames 21.5 and 45.5. This was welded oil- and watertight. The main machinery was a twin-shaft reciprocating steam layout with two oil-fired La Mont high-pressure boilers, the latter paired in a single boiler room. Output was 3,500hp and gave a designed maximum speed of just over 18kt. *M1* and *M2* were unusual in that they had Voith-Schneider propellers. Equipped primarily with wire sweeps for contact mines, the large sweep deck aft accommodated a powerful winch together with the floats, kites and otters required for the task. On the extreme stern were the usual M/S davits to handle the sweeping equipment. The Type 35's armament comprised a single, shielded 10.5cm SKC32 forward and aft, together with (as designed) one 2cm MG C/30 aft and one in each bridge wing. The 10.5cm guns were served by electric ammunition hoists with ten rounds per gun in ready-use lockers. Control was exercised by a simple rangefinder on the navigating bridge. The ships were also equipped for minelaying and could carry up to 32 EMC mines or an equivalent weight of

other types. The mine rail length was 75.6m; when minelaying, the ships could not use their sweep gear. During the Second World War minelaying was to be an important part of these vessels' duties in all theatres in which they were deployed. The mine rail length permitted the carriage of 60 EMC mines (or 38 if the after gun was to remain operational) but stability considerations restricted the load to 32 EMCs. Two depth-charge throwers were fitted to port and starboard at shelter deck level aft of the boat. They were fitted for, but not initially with, S Geräte. Individual ships were slightly altered internally to perform various duties within a minesweeping flotilla: for example, as leader, flotilla engineer officer, supply officer, Dan layer, medical officer, etc. Externally the main differences were the three variations in handling the heavy motor boat - derrick, gantry or simple davits. In addition, the Type 35s were equipped as torpedo servicing ships (Torpedoklarmachenboote) with the necessary air compressor and boom for lifting torpedoes. Their main sweep was the specially developed Scherdrachengerate, or SDG, similar to the British Oropesa sweep for contact minesweeping. Not until 1939 was an influence sweep available despite the much earlier development of a magnetic mine by Germany.

Twelve ships were authorized under the 1935 programme but only nine were ordered on 22 November that year, spread equally between three yards. The machinery contracts went to Rheinmetal-Borsig or Wumag-Gorlitz for some boats (i.e., *M1, M7* and *M12* respectively). *M1* was laid down on 9 July 1936 and the last, *M9*, on 20 March 1937. Meanwhile the remaining three units were ordered on 1 September 1936, one from each yard, *M12* being laid down on 4 October the following year. Building schedules were delayed considerably by the need to make alterations to completed boats at the expense of those yet to be finished. Thus *M2, M6, M9, M11* and *M12* suffered in this respect, while as early as June 1938 *M1-M4* were being delayed by late deliveries of pipe work. Twelve further units were ordered on 3 March 1937 under the 1936 programme with the same yards except that Flenderwerft, Lübeck, got one extra vessel at the expense of Oderwerk, Stettin. Because of the yard congestion referred to in earlier volumes, this programme was also delayed and *M24* was not laid down until 31 July 1939.

By November 1938, after the first units had been delivered to the Kriegsmarine (*M1, M4* and *M7*), it had become apparent that the ships were turning out heavier than planned - by 80 tonnes in fact. The exact breakdown of this growth is not known in detail but weapons accounted for 15 tonnes, while the machinery foundations had been strengthened and S Geräte fitted in place of KDB. The designed endurance of 2,000nm had not been achieved (in common with all contemporary Kriegsmarine designs) and in fact was only 1,500nm. Stability was reduced and influence minesweeping equipment as well as the compressor could not be fitted. In view of these

shortcomings, the Construction Office proposed making the hull longer and beamier, with increased draft or freeboard (or both). The optimum draft was 2.25m, which would at the same time increase the effectiveness of the S Geräte. Increasing the hull dimensions would allow bunkerage to be raised by 20 tonnes and therefore go some way towards attaining the original designed radius. There was a need to reduce construction work - therefore all would receive Voith-Schneider propellers - and as a result of the increase in generator capacity demand from 30kW to 200kW, the length of the engine room had to be increased by 1m. In December 1938 the

Marinekommandoamt agreed to an increase in length of 2m with a *reduction* in beam to be agreed with the Construction Office after tank towing tests. Draft was to be 2.15m and freeboard increased by 10cm. All were to receive the Voith-Schneider propellers. As partial weight compensation, the 3.7cm gun was deleted and a 2cm substituted. If any weight reserve remained, it was to be used to strengthen the skin plating. This sub-class was to be known as 'Minensucher Type 38'.

By March 1939 the Construction Office reported that, because of the stability problems on the M35 type, it would not now be possible to fit the boats for torpedo

regulating duties as there was no space for the compressor. This had to be deleted because of the need to fit influence sweeps, the KfRG, which necessitated a transformer in No. 2 generator space and a consequent increase in the length of that space. When the Type 38 design had been finalized, its overall length had been increased by nearly 3m and the beam by 0.5m. This increased the full load displacement by 908 tonnes from the 874 of the original Type 35 design. However, the desired 20 tonnes increase in bunkerage was not achieved, only an additional 12 tonnes. The twelve ships ordered on 4 May 1938 (*M25* to *M36*)were built to this design.

The result of these design modifications, and the delays referred to earlier, was that only eleven ships (*M1-M11*) had commissioned by the outbreak of war with Poland on 1 September 1939. An additional factor was the relatively complicated nature of the type's construction which extended building times; *M24*, for example, was not commissioned until February 1941, a construction period of nineteen months. To reduce building time, the design was therefore simplified internally and modified in the light of service experience when the first batch of war programme ships were ordered, on 19 September 1939, followed by a second batch on 27 September. This amended design was known as Type 39 Mob and incorporated modified framing in the bows, a reduction of deadwood aft and the fitting of bilge keels. The war programme extended the number of yards involved from three to ten, with ships numbered up to *M260*, but there were huge gaps in this sequence and in the event only 69 units were built, the last of which was commissioned as late as March 1943. Even before the war, there had been problems in yard allocation. In October 1938 it was anticipated that boats up to *M45* could be ordered in 1939 without serious problems arising, and if Danziger

Waggonfabrik could be used, further vessels could be built. Oderwerk, scheduled to join the destroyer programme, could produce three minesweepers per year if taken off destroyers (in fact this yard never did build destroyers, and was eventually put into the U-boat programme but built only a few later Type VIIC boats). On the other hand, Stülcken could build ten anti-submarine escorts (UJ) at the expense of eight sweepers, which it was suggested could be split between Kiel dockyard (two ships) and Deutsche Werft Hamburg (six).

During wartime service, the armament of these minesweepers was augmented by more flak guns as their coastal employment in areas of high enemy air activity rendered them very vulnerable. As early as June 1941 it had been proposed that the after 10.5cm gun be replaced by a twin 3.7cm, but this was not universally agreed and it was suggested that a better solution would be to have half the boats with this layout and half with it reversed, i.e., with the twin 3.7cm forward. *M101*, *M36* and *M255* were to prove this layout. From about late 1942 vessels employed in the Channel received a 2cm vierling in place of the after 2cm single and had the bridge wing mountings replaced by twins. Some received a 3.7cm/M42 automatic instead of the vierling and most had two MG151s as well. Some were intended for use as 'Kampfboote' conversions, with heavier armament (i.e., one vierling, four twin 2cm, two MG151s, one 7.3cm Föhn rocket-launcher and four 8.6cm RAG M/42 launchers but it is not known which, if any, of the type actually received this armament.

From late 1939, the new influence sweep, the Kabelfernraumgerät or KFRG, became available in two versions: (F) for shallow water and (T) for deep water. This comprised two non-buoyant electric cables supported by floats and was similar to the British 'double O' rig. Swept path was 150m with 40m electrodes depth and

towing speed 9kt. It required the additional fitment of a 60kW pulse generator. At the same time, the ships themselves had to be fitted with degaussing equipment to enable them to sweep with a good degree of safety. However, by May 1940, while all new 'M' boats had degaussing cables and there were transformers available, the switchgear was makeshift as the designed gear was not yet available. Thus the 1st Flotilla was due to be dealt with during the current (May) refit, the 2nd Flotilla was already fitted, but the 3rd Flotilla was to be fitted 'eventually' at Lübecker Flenderwerft (British use of magnetic mines began in April 1940). Already the inexorable growth had begun - common to all minesweepers of all nations as the war of weapon and counter-measure continued. In 1940, following the capture of the Low Countries where there arose a special requirement to sweep in very shallow water, a new sweeping rig was extemporized using captured searchlight cabling. This was developed as the Schleppspulgerät (SSG), a magnetic loop type with a towing speed of 6kt. Magnetic firing had been complemented with acoustic firing mechanisms by the Kriegsmarine as early as 1940, so that when Britain began to employ acoustic mines in 1942, there was a sweeping device ready. This was the Geräuschboje-Turbine (GBT) in which the action of the body moving through the water caused a hammer action to operate and simulate the noise of a merchant ship's propeller.

The Type 35/37 minesweepers could also, when required deploy another type of magnetic minesweep, developed originally for shallow water use by the Danish Navy. This was the Hohlfernraumgerät (HFG), essentially an electromagnet in a long float of 12m, 15m and 24m lengths (the latter for fleet sweepers). Acoustic mines could also be swept with the Knallkorpergerät (KKG) which was an explosive sweep employing charges dropped into the water at regular intervals. As with the explosive cutter fitted to wire sweeps, this explosive device was sometimes unpredictable and therefore unpopular with the crews. To operate their influence sweeps, the Type 35 and 40 minesweepers required a 65V, 500A generator for KFRG/M250/4R, 2R or 2M and needed an extra 115V, 175A set to operate the SSG/N or HFG/24.

As far as electronic warfare was concerned, fitment was limited to FuMB passive radar detectors as the radar sets (planned for flotilla leaders only) never materialized. FuME was also scheduled to be fitted but how far this progressed is not known.

The Type 35 minesweepers had not been particularly well received by the Fleet and inevitably comparisons were made with the elderly but useful and robust 'M16' type. This was not altogether surprising as the Naval Staff had already seen fit to make modifications to the design, and it was only to be expected that those who commanded the ships at sea would find further faults.

In the opinion of the Fleet, the new ships were satisfactory for all minesweeping tasks in coastal waters; they were more seaworthy than the older 'M16' types and were faster. However, they were not fast enough to operate with the Fleet (which was in any case a task of the F-Boote). Their range, quoted as 1,000nm at 17kt, was insufficient and the comprehensive gunnery outfit, carried at the expense of minesweeping space, was another source of criticism. Torpedo recovery fittings were a peacetime luxury and should be landed to improve minesweeping gear. The major criticism concerned their machinery, which was seen as unnecessarily complicated, bearing in mind the need for the use of reserve personnel in wartime. This it was alleged led to breakdowns due to errors, the 2nd Flotilla being quoted as always having one boat out of seven out of service despite only six months in commission. The older boats of the 1st Flotilla were said to be even worse.

It would appear that a letter sent by Konteradmiral Stohwasser, Flag Officer Minesweepers (East), to the Construction Office in October 1939 triggered off a new design investigation. This letter was the result of Stohwasser being informed that the Nobiskrug yard, when asked by the OKM if they could accommodate construction of Type 35 minesweepers, replied in the negative, because the Type 35s were too complicated. The OKM had therefore notified the yard that their only alternative would be minesweeping trawlers. Nobiskrug then informed the OKM that construction of a trawler type would take about six months while an old 'M16' type would only need four months and cost less. At the same time, the 'M16' type had a 2kt speed advantage and 3m less draft. These building times seem to be extremely optimistic, even unrealistic.

One of the factors influencing Stohwasser and his colleagues at BSO, Gruppe (Ost) and Gruppe (West) was the complicated nature of the Type 35's machinery. War had meant the calling up of reservists, many of whom had no experience of this type of propulsion, with the result that, because of the lack of training and errors, 30-40 per cent of all 'M35' sweepers were unserviceable at any one time. All the commanding officers urged a return to the old type minesweepers; trawlers were not a good substitute, as the Boom Defence Command pointed out, bearing in mind experience gained during the First World War.

The Construction Office replied to the SKL on 23 October to the effect that they were unsure whether trawlers could in fact be dispensed with and that they did not agree that the old minesweepers could be built faster than trawlers. The first 'old' ship to be built would take far longer in their opinion, added to which there were no plans in existence. Moreover, they could not accommodate the new minesweeping gear. If new plans were to be drawn up with the old-type machinery, there would be an inevitable drop in speed. Finally, the suggestion of 30-40 per cent unserviceability with the 'M35' type was strongly refuted.

This prompted SKL to request that FdM(W), Gruppe (W) and Flottenkommando forward details of operational availability for the 'M35'-type sweepers (and the F-Boote) under their command and comment on the usefulness of the old M-Boote, and also state what could be deleted from the old M-Boote design while still retaining a useful ship. SKL had already acknowledged to the Construction Office and Marinekommandoamt that the number, type and abilities of the sweepers was unsatisfactory and that it was understandable that Stohwasser wished to improve

Below: These two Type 35 boats show differing shields to their forward guns. Note also the tactical symbols and flotilla leader's pennant. (BfZ)

matters. However, if the Construction Office believed that an 'old' design could not fulfil the tasks required, even at the expense of 2kt and gave no faster building time, SKL saw little merit in proceeding. It was impossible to stop trawler conversion as long as there were insufficient regular minesweepers.

Admiral Saalwächter at Gruppe (West) agreed with Stohwasser that old-type designs were superior to trawlers, but what was needed, he believed, were large numbers of quickly-built regular minesweepers which could be built in all yards. This ruled out the Type 35. Reciprocating machinery was simple, reliable, good for about 15kt and would suit reserve personnel manning. Armament could be reduced to one 10.5cm or 8.8cm with two 2cm. A/S equipment could be dispensed with but a gyro compass was necessary. Overall, the main advantage over the Type 35 was the simple machinery; whether coal- or oil-firing was employed could be investigated. The 40 or so Type 35 ships programmed would suffice for A/S and minesweeping duties.

The Construction Office, while agreeing with both Saalwächter and Stohwasser on a number of points, stressed that so far the only agreed advantage of the old 'M' type was its simple machinery, and they continued to refute the suggestion that the machinery shipped in the Type 35 was unreliable. On the contrary, lubrication and bearing service was better in the latter and only the serving of the combined manoeuvring and throttle valves when running at high powers under circumstances where the propellers might race needed vigilance. So far, in fact, the machinery had survived overloading and mistakes well. At the beginning of December 1939, the Marinekommando-amt informed the Construction Office and other interested parties that the question of a new design was being examined but that the 'M35' type would be continued. Broad design requirements laid down for the new Type 40, as it was designated, were:

Tasks : Minesweeping and A/S in Baltic and North Sea
Design : Good seaworthiness, robust and simple bilge keel required

Minesweeping: As Type 35 but:
(i) Bow protection gear
(ii) KfRG
(iii) Degaussing
(iv) Some fitted as Dan-layers
(v) No minelaying ability
(vi) No depth-charge throwers
(vii) Six single depth-charge traps (for twelve DCs)

Armament: 1 - 10.5cm (not HA), 100rpg
2 - MG C/30, 4,000rpg
1 - 1.5m range finder
S Geräte, KDB and NHG

Machinery: Coal fired old style machinery (18kg/cm^3)

All auxiliaries steam-driven
Endurance and speed at least as good as the old type
Coal 120 tonnes minimum

The Construction Office's sketch design for the new ship showed a small increase in size over the Type 15 but with a better hull form. As a result, speed would not suffer, due to the better lines, and would be about 15kt. Compared with the Type 35, hull construction involved only a third of the work for the earlier design, while the machinery could be built in half the time. The yard question was then examined. Norderwerf was occupied up to 1942 with four seaplane-tenders for the Luftwaffe (*Karl Meyer*, *Max Stinsky*, *Immelmann* and *Boelcke*). Unterweser could build eight minesweepers per year. Nobiskrug had four trawlers on order and four catapult barges for the Luftwaffe, after which they could, from 1941, build five, later eight, ships per year. Meyer (Papenburg) had a light vessel to complete and could from July 1941 deliver one ship every three months; while Elsfleth could build one ship every three months from December 1940.

In general, the various commands approved the design, but with further comments on the armament, the use of coal-firing, the need for all or only some with S Geräte, equipment etc. By-mid January 1940 tank towing tests had been completed. These demonstrated that the lines were good and that a maximum speed of 16.6kt could be expected, with a continuous speed of 16.3kt. The Construction Office recommended the installation of an exhaust turbine, used on trawlers for years, to increase speed to 17.3kt. This brought the speed almost up to that of the Type 35, with better range:

Speed	M35	M40 with turbine	without turbine
10kt	2,200nm	4,100nm	4,000nm
14kt	1,400nm	2,250nm	1,900nm
17kt	1,000nm	1,400nm	-

There were no supply problems with the turbine and in the event of failure, it could be disconnected. Now the Type 40 had virtually the same abilities as the Type 35, involved half the building content but had twice the range. Seventy-nine Type 35s were on order or under construction and with the abilities of the Type 40 so improved, even the Construction Department now questioned the continuance of the Type 35.

During January Raeder requested that the 2cm guns be replaced by two 3.7cm SKC/36s, but this gun was not available so an interim solution of one 2cm forward and one twin 2cm aft was proposed. However, the Weapons Office pointed out that the 2cm Dop L/C37 had not been prove and could not be in production before 1941, leaving the ship with the original two 2cm guns. Finally, at the beginning of February, the Marinekommandoamt agreed to the installation of the exhaust turbine and to cease production of the Type 35 boats after 69 units, then

TYPE M40 GENERAL ARRANGEMENT

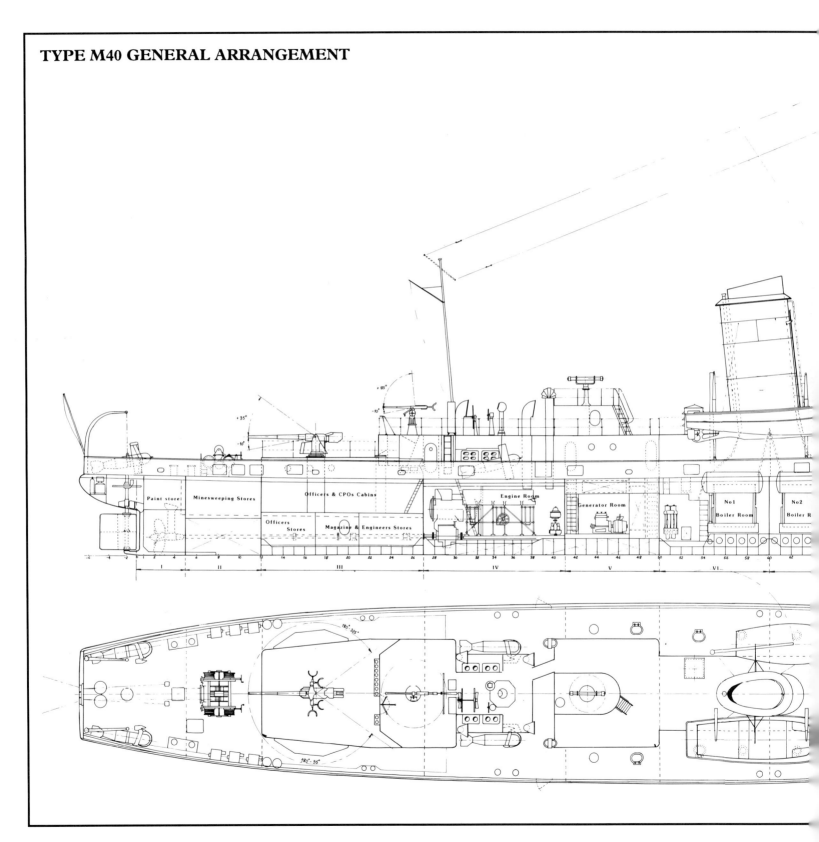

Paint store | Minesweeping Stores | Officers & CPOs Cabins | Engine Room | Generator Room | No1 Boiler Room | No2 Boiler R

Officers Stores | Magazine & Engineers Stores

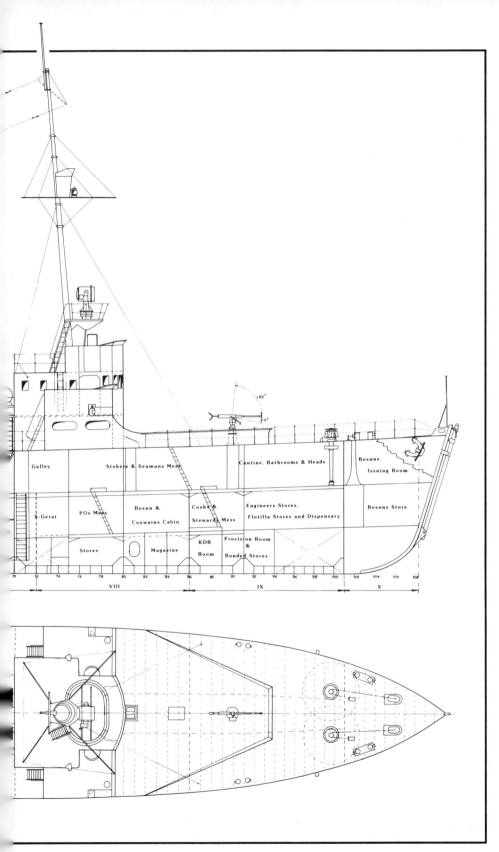

Galley

Stokers & Seamans Mess

Cantine, Bathrooms & Heads

Bosuns
Issuing Room

S-Gerat

POs Mess

Bosun &
Coxwains Cabin

Cooks &
Stewards Mess

Engineers Stores,
Flotilla Stores and Dispensary

Bosuns Store

Stores

Magazine

KDB
Room

Provision Room
&
Bonded Stores

VIII

IX

X

switch to the Type 40, using the freed capacity for U-boat construction. The ten cancelled boats were at Schichau (four) and Deutsche Werft (six).

The demand on yard capacity in Germany with the increased rate of U-boat construction led to consideration of placing orders in occupied countries, of which the two obvious choices were France and the Netherlands. In the event, no minesweepers were ordered from French yards but Dutch yards eventually delivered sixty Type 40 ships - almost half the total to reach service. The first orders were placed on 3 September 1940, with the first keels being laid in April 1941. The programme ended with the last ships being completed in July 1943, the Type 40 Construction Groups having been dissolved on 28 June at Rotterdam Droogdok, 29 June at Nederlands Droogdok and 30 June at Gusto. Much of this work was widely sub-contracted, as the following table shows:

	M422	M423	M427	M495	M496
Hull	Wilton	Wilton	Wilton	Gebr.Pot	Gebr.Pot
Boilers	Wilton	Wilton	Wilton	Stork	Rott.DD
Engines	Stork	Wilton	AMF	AMF	Stork
Exhaust	Deschi-	Deschi-	CEMP	Stork	Stork
Turbine	mag	mag			

AMF = Arnhemsche Machinen Fabrik, Holland

CEMP = Companie Electro Mechanique de Paris

The Type 40 design displaced only 775 tonnes full load against the M35's 870 tonnes, with a correspondingly shorter but marginally more beamy hull, which was transversely framed of ST42 steel. Frame spacing was between 0.42 and 0.55 m. There were sixteen main bulkheads of which the watertight ones divided the hull into ten watertight compartments. These were on frames 5,12, 27, 41, 50, 60, 72, 86 and 101. Between frames 27 and 70, a longitudinal wing bulkhead ('Wallgang') extended from the bottom shell plating to the upper deck. Bilge keels were fitted from frames 41 to 63. The two boilers were housed in separate spaces, compartments VI and VII, separated from the engine room in compartment IV by the generator space and coal bunkers. Senior rates were berthed aft in a triple cabin in compartment III where there was also a double cabin for officers and a mess space. Petty officers and junior rates were berthed forward. On the upper deck, various cabins in the deck-houses accommodated washrooms and heads for the officers, as well as the minesweeping stores (after deckhouse frames 23-30). Amidships were cabins for the engineer officer and commanding officer (40-50) while below the bridge (frames 70-80) were the transformer room, offices, bow protection gear and provisions. At bridge level were the radio office and chart room.

The main machinery was simple with two Schultz low-pressure boilers and two three-cylinder triple-expansion engines giving a total 1,800hp, to which had been added

Bauer-Wach exhaust turbines of 450hp each. This had been agreed in February 1940. Two 20kW generators were shipped, each in its separate space in compartment V. Total coal bunker capacity was 142.3 tonnes, mainly stowed in the wing spaces. Maximum speed was a little over 17kt and endurance 1,200nm at full speed.

Armament comprised one unshielded 10.5cm SKC/32U gun in a U-boat-type LC/36 mounting aft on frame 27, one 3.7cm SKC/36 in a Flak LC/36 mounting on the half deck forward of the bridge and two single 2cm C/38s aft. Two MG34s were also carried. They were fitted with S Geräte on the 'tween deck amidships, frames 71 - 74. The hydrophone office was located between frames 86 and 89, with the KDB equipment in the hold. The echo-sounder and NHG were fitted in the chart-house. A medium-scale A/S outfit was carried, comprising four depth-charge throwers and reloading equipment, together with six single depth-charge traps; 36 depth-charges were generally carried. This armament was subject to change as the war progressed, with a 2cm Vierling usually replacing the aftermost 2cm initially. Later 2cm LM44 twins were fitted where singles remained and an extra 2cm was fitted forward of the bridge. There were complaints from sea about the 10.5cm gun which was a low-angle weapon when what was most frequently required was an HA gun - as the Type 35 sweepers had. Thus, the ultimate aim was to rearm these ships with one 10.5 SKC/32gE, two 3.7cm Flak M42s in a twin mounting LM42, one 3.7cm Flak M42 in a single mounting and six 2cm (1 x 4, 1 x 2),

together with two MG151 machine guns. Twelve EMC mines could be carried by some units, contrary to the original intention. It was planned to equip leaders with radar but it is uncertain how far this ever progressed.

Above: *M254* showing a twin 3.7cm mounting aft. (WZB)

Left; *TS4* converted from a standard Type 40 minesweeper for duty with the Torpedo School. Note tubes on the forecastle and the derrick aft. (BfZ)

Right: A Type 40 boat is commissioned. Note the paucity of flak guns. (WZB)

Below: A Type 40 boat in distinctive camouflage. Note the 'Sumatra' FuMB aerials and the Vierling. (WZB)

The first ship to complete, *M381* in August 1941, was subjected to an extensive period of trials, in particular to prove her machinery. Test-bench trials ashore at Deschimag and Stettiner Oderwerke had shown results better than anticipated, but performance at sea was obviously the crucial test. One of the aspects given detailed evaluation was the type of coal required for best results. The boiler design needed a short-flame coal for optimum performance, but there were considerable doubts that this would be regularly available in all the intended operational areas. It was also recognized that the calibre of engine-room personnel was likely to be relatively low. This led to some experimentation with (a) short/medium-flame coal and (b) long-flame coal, to establish their suitability for this class of ship. Accordingly, *M381* ran trials out of Kiel on 8 May 1942, using the latter variety of fuel, but because of mining was unable to proceed beyond the Kiel light-vessel. 1,700ihp was achieved at 220rpm and despite the short run it soon became evident that this type of coal was unusable on military grounds. Even at low speeds, a red glow was visible at the funnel top and uptakes suffered damage. At higher speeds, smoke and flames issuing from

Above and opposite: Two more Type 40 camouflage schemes; both ships lacking all electronic gear. (WZB)

the funnel were highly dangerous and at night conspicuously visible. Later that month the OKM stated that the boilers and machinery of the Type 40 minesweeper had, by demand of the Fleet at sea, been designed similar to the old First World War 'M' class with economy improvements conferred by an exhaust turbine - a statement that sounds defensive, as if the new class was already being criticized. Trials showed that 15.4kt could be achieved on 220rpm with no sweep gear out and 17kt at 257rpm for a brief period only. Continuous sweeping at 11kt on 200rpm could be maintained. Endurance at 8kt without the exhaust turbine was 2,813nm and 2,760nm at 11kt using the turbine - nowhere near the predicted figures quoted earlier.

Minelaying, predominantly by the RAF and aimed at U-boat training areas in the Baltic, together with the need to secure a coastline extending from Kirkenes in the Arctic to Bayonne on the Spanish border by way of the Baltic, placed a tremendous strain on the Kriegsmarine's minesweeping resources. Much of the sweeping, as in the Royal Navy, was performed by requisitioned trawlers, and a large trawler construction programme had been put in hand in yards in the Reich and occupied territories; by August 1941, for example, only 43 'Fleet' sweepers (actually a definition not used by the Kriegsmarine) had entered service, although only three of them had been lost since the beginning of the war. However, losses were only part of the problem, for many ships were badly damaged by aircraft and mine, putting them out of service for considerable periods and tying up dockyard facilities. There were other problems too and the M35 programme proceeded fitfully; deliveries reached only four per month on three occasions and despite the large M40 programme, it was not until the first six months of 1942 that large numbers of new ships began entering service. The M40 type performed well enough but its armament was subject to some criticism, its 10.5cm gun being only a low-angle weapon whereas in the M35 type the gun was high-angle and two were carried. Shortages of raw material, in particular copper, caused 27 Type 40 boats to be suspended in 1942, but this figure was later reduced to twelve. Neptun (Rostock) produced a modified design in 1942 to meet criticism and new demands, by lengthening the hull to accommodate a second 10.5cm gun forward, this design being known initially as 'Minensuchboote 42', later amended to 'Minensuchboote 43'. By April 1943 six boats which had been ordered on 26 November 1942 were listed as Type 43, these being *M268/269* (yard numbers 376/377) at Atlaswerke, *M331/332* (yard numbers 436/437) at Lübeck and *M390/391* (yard numbers 253/254) at Elsflether.

The pressing need for more minesweepers led to the 1943 programmes taking a somewhat different course, because in June of that year Schichauwerft-Königsberg were requested by the OKM to investigate how many slipways in their eastern yards would need to be prepared to build 58 minesweepers per year. Despite close investigation, Schichau eventually had to report that this plan was not feasible, mainly because of the shortage of shipyard workers in East Prussia, together with difficulties in material supply and procurement. They proposed a different solution to the problem and on 12 June 1943 this was deemed feasible by the OKM. A week later a revised proposal was put forward: construction was to be by prefabrication methods, reducing yard work that needed shipbuilding skills to the minimum, while transferring all engineering and prefabrication work out to non-shipbuilding concerns - the objective being to produce one ship a week. It was proposed that the ship be made up of seven separate sections: (1) stern, (2) engine room with generators, (3) boiler room, (4) midships, (5) bows, (6) bridge and (7) superstructure. Schichau themselves would allocate six workshops for the construction of sections at Königsberg. Five weeks were estimated for construction to launching, two weeks for fitting out and one week for trials. Current construction of M40 minesweepers at Königsberg was taking about 30½ weeks to completion, so that the new method would reduce construction time by 74 per cent!

Meanwhile, the Shipbuilding Commission had rationalized the number of ship types under construction by ordering that the new sweeper would also be capable of performing torpedo-recovery and A/S duties, resulting in the cancellation of the Torpedofangboote Type 43 *TF25-39* and the Kriegs U-Jager *KUJ26-42*. In all, some 140 ships of the same basic design could now be ordered at one time, aiding the prefabrication case, because automobile or aircraft production line techniques could be employed. In September 1943 the Shipbuilding Commission directed that a new organization, Inginierburo (Ost), be formed at Königsberg, tasked with producing all the necessary alterations, amendments and drawings to produce the Type 43 design by the prefabricated method. To reach programme targets, some 30,000-40,000 drawings had to be prepared in three to four weeks. It was also decided to produce a full-scale prototype for trials, which after all tests would be commissioned into service. However, further calculation of man-hours required revealed that Schichau themselves could only produce about 45-50 per cent of what was needed, and it became evident that other minesweeper yards would have to be called in to the programme to produce sub-sections. These were to be rail-transportable and complete with all piping, cabling and services. Tolerances and weld shrinkage were perceived as possible problem areas and special instruction manuals were prepared for issue to the various sub-contractors.

There was a further factor for consideration. By 1943 there were serious shortages of raw material in the Reich and every effort had to be made to reduce the use of certain materials. Thus Dr. Merker of the Shipbuilding Commission directed Ingenieurburo (Ost) to reduce the boat's weight by about 63 tonnes, which at the same time presented stability problems. This in turn led to a number of detailed changes to the design:

(a) Increase in beam by 0.3m
(b) Reduction of construction displacement from 683 tonnes to 668 tonnes
(c) Slight alteration in the bottom design
(d) Increase in sheer forward by 700mm
(e) Increased flare of the bows
(f) Rearrangement of the double bottom spaces
(g) Switch from transverse to longitudinal construction

These measures gave a weight saving of 53 tonnes per ship, plus a further 7 tonnes obtained by reducing operational equipment, and resulted in a saving of 6,720 tonnes of material from a yearly programme of 112 ships - i.e., enough for an extra twelve ships per year.

The Type 43 now differed from the Type 40 in several respects: greater length (5.5m), more beam (0.5m) and heavier armament (2 x 10.5cm). Ammunition stowage for the 10.5cm weapons was quadrupled. Perhaps more important, the new boat could quickly be fitted for other duties as mentioned earlier: for example as a U-Jäger with extra depth-charges sufficient for seven full 21 DC patterns or as a minelayer with 24 mines. As a Torpedofangboot, racks for seventeen practice torpedoes were provided with associated derrick and reduced armament. All vessels were also to be fitted for, and 50 per cent of them with, two 53.3cm torpedo tubes in the waist to port and starboard. The additional weight of tubes, torpedoes and director was 7 tonnes, to be compensated for either by landing two paravanes, 20 depth-charges and four throwers or by landing a further two paravanes or six more depth-charges for extra weight compensation. Deliveries of the torpedo version were eventually reduced to 24 from Königsberg plus nine more in the Black Sea.

The ship's steam plant was also changed, the Schultz boiler being replaced by a Wagner boiler, and the generating capacity was increased to 200kW due to operational demands (two 80kW diesel-generators for minesweeping plus two of 20kW for ship's supply). Boiler efficiency was increased by fitting superheaters and feedwater pre-heaters; the resulting lower exhaust temperatures reduced the 'red-hand' effect so evident in the Type 40 and gave a 15 per cent increase in fuel efficiency. However, the main engines remained the same as those in the Type 40. Much attention was paid to economy in cabling and wiring; valves, lamps, pipework and other components were rationalized and copper was replaced by cast steel wherever possible. These measures did much to reduce the man-hours necessary in construction.

Orders had already been placed for Type 43 minesweepers in the non-prefabricated version on 26 November 1942. Some of the earliest of these were: *M268* and *M269* by Atlaswerke (yard Nos. 366 and 367); *M331* and *M332* by Lübecker Maschinenbau (yard Nos. 436 and 437); and *M390* and *M391*, Elsflether (yard Nos. 253 and 254), these having been originally ordered as Type 40 units in October 1941. Later it was decided, probably for reasons of clarity, not to use the vacant number blocks in the Type 40 sequence but to number the new design from *M601* upwards. Orders were therefore placed on 26 November 1942 as follows:

M601 - M604, A.G. Neptun, Rostock (yard Nos. 535-538)
M661 - M667, Elsfletherwerft (yard Nos. 253 -259)
M751 - M752, Lübecker Maschinenbau (yard Nos. 436-437)

Further orders placed on 7 May 1943, were for:
M621 - M628, Atlaswerke, Bremen (yard Nos. 376-383)
M641 - M646, Unterweser (yard Nos.?)
M681 - M684, Norderwerft, Hamburg (yard Nos.?)
M701 - M708, Rickmerswerft, Wesermünde (yard Nos. 247-254)
M731 - M734, Nobiskrug, Rendsberg (yard Nos. 532-535)

TYPE M43 GENERAL ARRANGEMENT

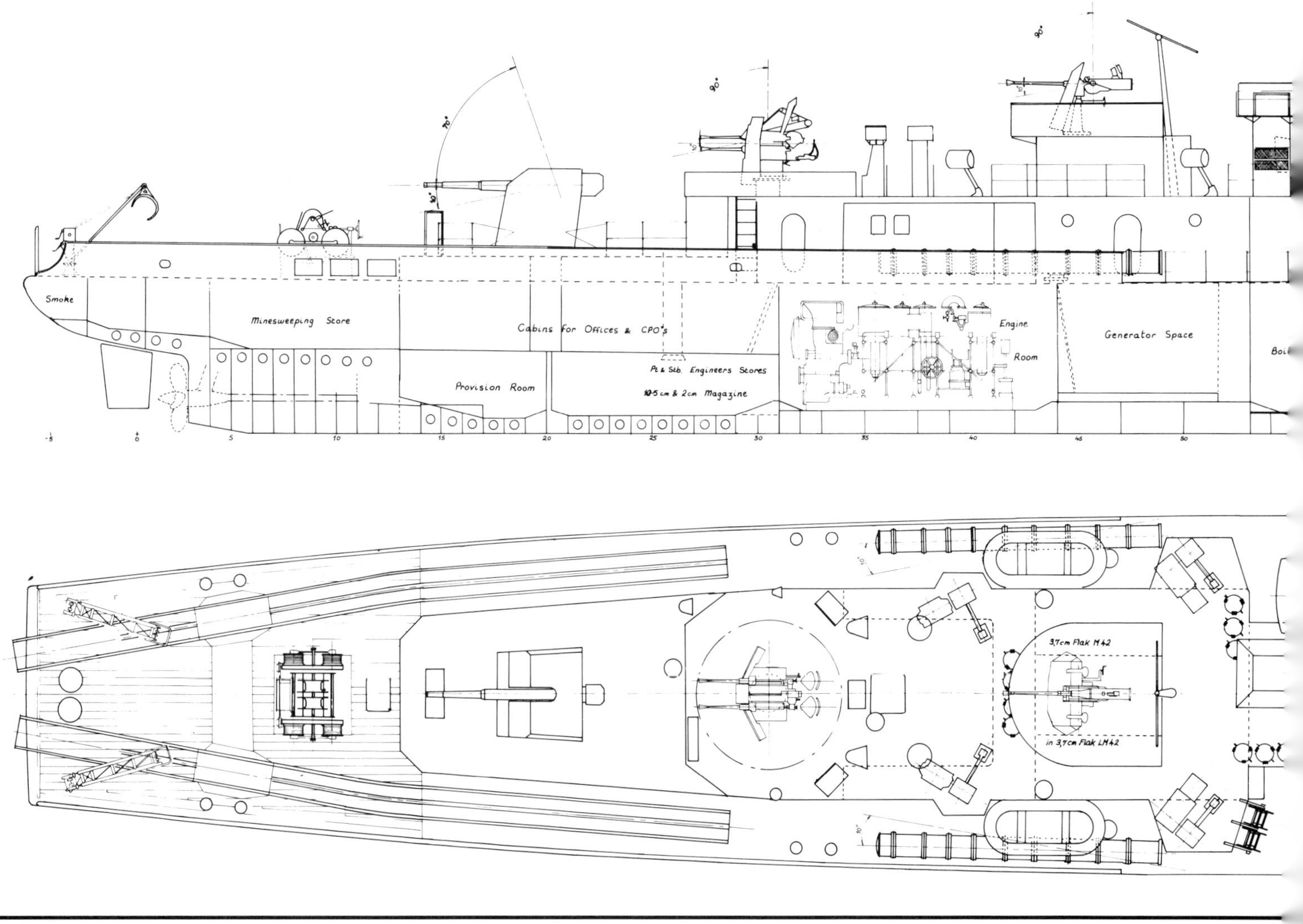

Smoke

Minesweeping Store

Cabins For Offices & CPO's

Engine Room

Generator Space

Boi

Provision Room

Pt & Stb. Engineers Stores

10·5 cm & 2cm Magazine

3·7cm Flak M42

in 3·7cm Flak LM42

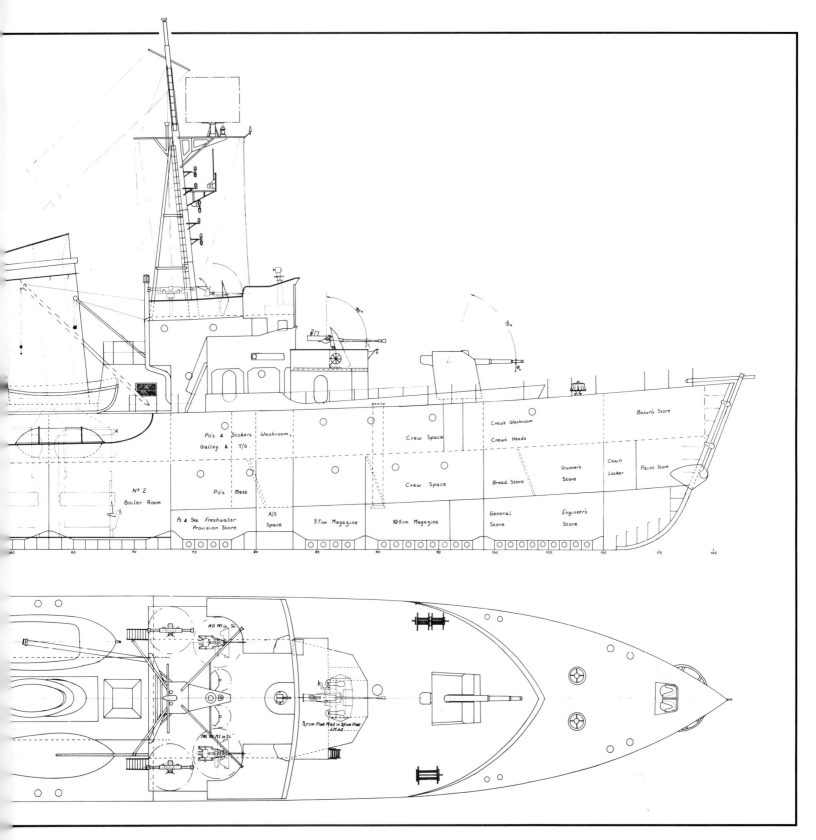

Po's & Stokers Washroom,

Galley & T/S

Crew Space

Crew's Washroom

Crew's Heads

Bosun's Store

N° 2
Boiler Room

Po's Mess

Crew Space

Gunner's
Store

Chain
Locker

Paint Store

Pt & Stb Freshwater
Provision Store

A/S
Space

3·7cm. Magazine

10·5cm. Magazine

Bread Store

General
Store

Engineer's
Store

MG 151 in SL

3·7cm Flak M42 in 3·7cm Flak
L.M.42

MG 151 M1 in SL

M771 - M773, Lindenau, Memel (yard Nos. 89-91)

M781 - M783, Meyer, Pappenberg (yard Nos. 435, 446-447)

M791 - M792, Ottenser Eisenwerke, Hamburg (yard Nos.?)

However, the switch to mass-production methods led to the cancellation of all the above units in 1944 (16658/44) with the exception of *M601-M604* and *M661-M667*. The latter group must also subsequently have been transferred from Elsflether.

Thus the four original units at Neptun (*M601-M604*) ordered on 7 May 1943 were augmented by a further 62 units (*M605-M666*) ordered on 4 December 1943 also from Neptun, plus 66 more (*M801-M866*) from Schichau, Königsberg, which had not originally been part of the 1943 minesweeper programme. In addition, *M1000-M1009* were ordered from Korneuberg at Vienna for service in the Black Sea, but because of the situation there these orders were transferred to Toulon in the south of France and finally, on 29 September 1944, re-ordered from Neptun, Rostock, as *M667-M675*. The ships on order at the end of November 1944 were of the following sub-types:

Minesweepers: *M601-M610, M641-M662, M801-M811, M840-M854*
Torpedo Recovery Vessels: *M611-M640*
Torpedo Armed: *M812-M827, M855-M864*
U-Jäger: *M828-M839*
Not specified: *M663-M675, M865, M866*

The mass-production principle was a sound one but by the time that this new minesweeper programme was under

Above: An unidentified Type 43 boat. This design reintroduced the forward 10.5cm gun. (BfZ)

way, the RAF had done a great deal to destroy or disrupt Germany's industrial infra-structure, particularly transport and communications. This had a considerable effect on the M43 programme and also on the Type XXI and XXIII U-boat programmes. Thus by Christmas 1944 only seven ships had been launched by Neptun, of which only two had been commissioned. Schichau had put six hulls afloat, but only one of these had been commissioned. Meanwhile, minesweeper losses had begun to rise alarmingly - 29 ships in August 1944 alone. After reaching a peak of 173 minesweepers completed in April 1944, the remainder of

Below: Two Type 43 boats at Cuxhaven in May 1945. (IWM)

the year saw no fewer than 60 ships sunk or surrendered, a loss rate which was impossible to sustain. No further trawlers could be requisitioned from civilian sources because their catch was now vital to the population and the naval trawler programme was small (and, in any case, already a casualty to the M43). Thus the Type 43 programme assumed major importance, especially as it was indirectly linked with U-boat training.

Sub-contractors to Schichau were Oderwerke (Stettin), Stettiner-Vulkan, Lübecker Maschinenbau and Nobiskrug (Rendsburg), with additional assemblies being supplied by Schichau's own factories at Prappeln and Königsberg. Neptun was serviced by Atlas (Bremen), Rickmerswerft (Wesermünde), Unterwesser (Bremen) and Norderwerft (Bremen). Parts were also being supplied from as far away as Holland, which by late 1944 was a problematical source to say the least. Delay was inevitable and on 17 December, during a conference at Schichau, the matter was discussed in detail. *M801* had been delivered but the man-hours put into her were 360,000 compared with 200,000 estimated target; *M601* at Rostock needed 320,000 man-hours. Since these ships were both prototypes, this was only to be expected, but the final building target was 170,000 man-hours. *M802* was expected to be delivered at the end of December, which was just achieved, but the four ships for January (*M803-M806*) had been launched virtually as empty hulls. There was a great shortage of pipework, W/T doors and hatches, valves, etc, and it was stated that some 60 couriers were out and about endeavouring to obtain the missing parts. Those that could not be obtained, including some for *M806* (a January ship), were having to be fabricated at Königsberg; while of the February batch, there was no material at all for winches in Königsberg for ships *M809* onwards. As far as *M808* was concerned, of the 2,700 parts required for the three sections, only 1,300 had been delivered; and of these, only 600 had been built in. Engine deliveries were also late.

By the end of the year, *M806* and *M807* lay empty afloat, with *M808-M810* still in the section hall. A similar picture emerged at Neptun, for only eleven boats had been completed at this yard by the war's end, to add to five from Schichau. Several of these were incomplete in many respects, lacking items of equipment no longer available, and a couple of ships sailed virtually direct from the yard to surrender. The degree to which the Higher Command ignored the realities of the situation at the beginning of 1945 was no different for minesweepers than it was for U-boats and other vessels, for as late as 1 February they were forecasting the completion of *only* 50 of the Type 43 ships (out of the 141 planned), when only 16 ships were afloat. Six days later the Russians overran the Königsberg shipyards. Two flotillas re-formed with the Type 43 minesweeper, the 12th and 2nd, while the new 6th Flotilla never entered service.

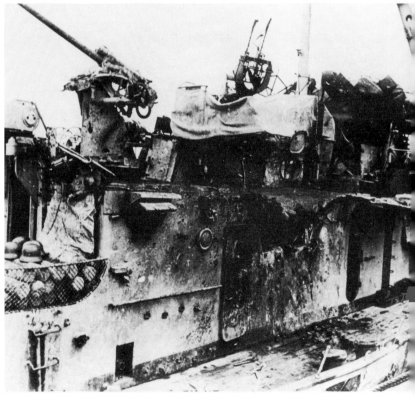

17. MISCELLANEOUS VESSELS

GRILLE

Projected as a State yacht and 'Aviso' under the designation 'Flottentender C', this attractive vessel was funded under the 1933 programme. Ordered from Blohm und Voss on 21 August 1934, her keel was laid down 1 June 1934, after which construction progressed so rapidly that she was launched on 15 December the same year. Acceptance trials were commenced on 19 May 1935 and the ship was commissioned the following day under the command of K.Kpt. Brinckmann (later to command *Prinz Eugen*). Displacing 3,430 tonnes full load, *Grille* was powered by one of the new high-pressure steam plants then being developed by the Kriegsmarine. This comprised a twin-shaft geared turbine installation with four Benson boilers with superheaters operating at 100kg/cm². Her designed top speed was 26kt on 26,400hp. The hull was longitudinally framed and almost fully welded. Internal sub-division by fourteen main watertight bulkheads gave a high degree of integrity and was designed to allow full flooding of any three adjacent compartments without the upper deck going under.

The designed armament comprised four 12.7cm SKC/34 single guns in MPLC/34 mountings, together with four 3.7cm SKC/30s in two twin LC/30 mountings and four 2cm Flak 30 single weapons. Provision was also made for six depth-charge traps and twelve depth-charges. However, the initial armament shipped was two 10.5cm Ubts/Tb.L/45 guns in LC/16 single mountings, one twin 3.7cm and two 2cm guns. The ship was also equipped for minelaying (one of her wartime tasks was considered to be the mining of French Biscay ports) and could accommodate any of the following mine types: EMA (200), EMB(186), EMC I (132), EMC II (130), UMA (170), FMB (228), FMC (128), RMA (120) and RMB/C (152), or a combination of any of these. If a full mine load was embarked, all double-bottom bunkers and water tanks had to remain full for stability reasons.

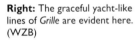
Right: The graceful yacht-like lines of *Grille* are evident here. (WZB)

On trials the ship was found to have good seaworthiness characteristics and was unusually dry forward thanks to the graceful sheer and curve of the bows. However, the high superstructure made the ship very sensitive to the wind and with a beam wind she heeled like a yacht. During her trials, *Grille* touched bottom off Heligoland, severely damaging the hull and reducing her speed considerably. Other problems were experienced with the high-pressure boilers because of frequent catastrophic tube failures.

In service, *Grille* was soon used for state occasions. On 26 August 1935 for example, Adolf Hitler, the heads of the three armed services and Argentinian dignitaries came aboard for a few days. On 7 November that year the new Kriegsmarine ensign was hoisted, which same flag was flown at half mast on 25 November following the death of Admiral Jellico. *Grille* passed into dockyard control at Blohm und Voss on 5 December for refit and did not return to service until 17 April 1936. In the meantime the death of King George V on 28 January had been honoured by her flags (*Grille*'s log is full of flag ceremonies). Machinery trials in the Elbe followed between 17 and 21 April, then a few days more out in the North Sea, before the ship returned to Blohm und Voss for further work which lasted until 10 May.

Grille now sailed around the Skaggen bound for Kiel, where on 26 May she hosted Admiral Raeder for a review of the fleet. Hitler and his staff boarded *Grille* once more on 28 May for another fleet review the next day. After a 21-gun salute from *Admiral Graf Spee* off Laboe in Kiel Fjord, Hitler and his entourage went ashore. In June the Führer was aboard again with Field Marshal von Blomberg (the War Minister) and others at Wilhelmshaven, while Kiel Week and the 1936 sailing Olympics saw her presence at that event, during which Hitler put in yet another visit to his state yacht. In July *Grille* sailed east and on the 5th ran speed trials on the Neukrug mile, reaching 25.285kt on 383rpm; 26kt was attained with 410rpm and 16kt on one shaft at 290rpm. October saw *Grille* on a visit to Norway carrying von Blomberg, during which the ship called at Hammerfest, Tromsø and Narvik.

Annual refit at Blohm und Voss followed between 3 November 1936 and 22 March 1937, at which time the idea of converting her to diesel propulsion with no extra weight penalty was discussed. Four layouts were studied: (a) three supercharged four-stroke engines per shaft; (b) high-speed double-acting two-stroke engines (as per *Nürnberg*) - i.e., MAN 7Z 32/44,600rpm; (c) M9 Z 42/58 nine-cylinder engines (*Graf Spee*) in a direct-drive configuration; and (d) twin-shaft system, four motors per shaft driving via Vulkan couplings. (d) was the favoured option but nothing came of this project.

In May 1937 *Grille* conveyed Field Marshal von Blomberg to Southampton, returning to Wilhelmshaven on the 20th; von Blomberg went ashore on 22 May. Her next voyage was to Iceland. Admiral Commanding (Baltic) came aboard and hoisted his flag on 28 June, after which *Grille* sailed for northern waters. Continuous machinery trials were carried out in open sea conditions before the ship spent four days (2 to 5 July) in Reykjavik. Ports in Norway were visited on the return and *Grille* arrived in Kiel on 10 July. In October 1937 a cruise was made to Funchal and Ponta Delgade before the annual refit at Blohm und Voss between 31 January and 22 March 1938.

On 7 May 1938 Brinckmann (now Fregattenkapitän) was posted to the Marinewehramt and her former first officer, K.Kpt. von der Forst, assumed command of *Grille*. He in turn was promoted to F.Kpt. on 1 October that year. As the likelihood of war grew, *Grille* was placed under the command of Flag Officer (Panzerschiffe) and, wearing his flag, lay at Wilhelmshaven on 1 September 1939 loaded with 130 EMC mines in preparation for laying the defensive 'West Wall' mine barrage. Between 3 and 7 September she participated in five major minelaying operations with cruisers and destroyers before being ordered back to the Baltic on 10 September. Towards the end of the month the ship arrived at Swinemünde and on 1 October sailed for mercantile warfare patrol north of the islands of Oland and Gotland, which lasted until the 3rd. A second patrol was made between 7 and 10 October in the Aaland Sea towards the northern end of the Baltic. Further patrols were carried out between 13 and 16 October and 24 to 28 October in the same area. A short machinery overhaul followed at Deutschewerke, after which another three-day patrol began on 28 November. December saw a similar routine with a patrol between the 15th and 19th, but on 9 January 1940 *Grille* collided with the small steamer *Axel*, which sank. Repairs to *Grille* lasted until the first week of February. On 21 February the ship started a routine refit at Deutschewerke, Kiel, which extended until 7 May. *Grille* therefore missed 'Weserübung' and was ordered instead to the Gunnery Training School at Sassnitz. However, she made a brief foray to Wilhelmshaven with *Köln* between 13 and 23 May, participating in a minelaying sortie in the North Sea on the 19th. On 5 July the Training Command was formed with *Grille* as part and her new C.O., K.Kpt. Poske (appointed on 1 July), in command. She was now experiencing trouble with her engines, suffering an explosion in No. 2 boiler room, and spent August at Blohm und Voss for this to be rectified. After that she transitted the Kiel Canal on 5 September and arrived at Ostend on 9 September for possible duty in connection with Operation 'Seelöwe'. Persistent air raids forced her withdrawal to Rotterdam on 21 September where she lay in readiness until 26 October when withdrawn to the Baltic once more (K.Kpt. Lanz had assumed command of the ship on 16 October). Based at Kiel as part of Minenschiffe Gruppe (Nord) from 26 November, she was transferred back to the Gunnery School on 28 December.

The invasion of Russia in June 1941 required her operational services once more. Shortly before that, at the end of May, *Grille* had been ordered to equip and fit out

BREMSE PROFILE AND PLAN SHOWING SKETCHED ALTERATIONS

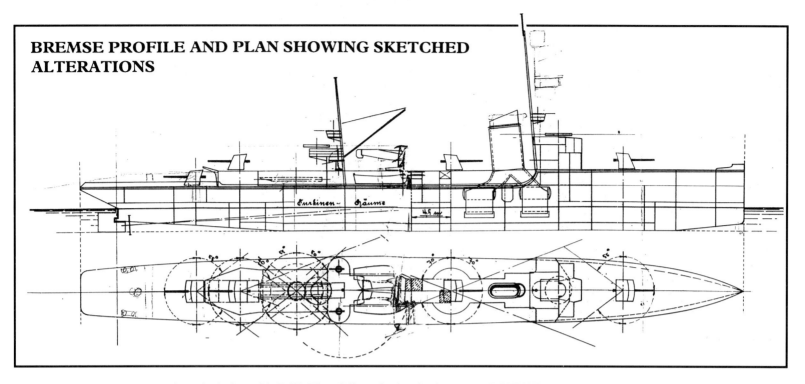

for minelaying with BdK (Flag Officer Cruisers) who was in charge of the seagoing side of 'Barbarossa'. However, on 4 June it had still not been decided if the ship could be spared from her important duties with the SAS. Eventually *Grille* was ordered to join the minelaying force and between 19 and 21 June assisted in the laying of the barrages 'Wartburg I-III' between Oland and Memel with *Preussen, Versailles* and *Skaggerak*. In August *Grille* operated briefly from Turku in Finland before returning to Swinemünde on 17 August for Gunnery School duties. A further proposal to employ her as an escort for the Norwegian ore traffic was vetoed on the grounds of her importance to the Gunnery School and the fact that she was in need of a refit.

Her refit party was actually formed on 23 February 1942 and the ship paid off at Kiel on 23 March. The refit lasted six months, with *Grille* re-commissioning on 24 August 1942 under the command of Kpt.Lt. Just. After working up, *Grille* was ordered to Northern waters and on 1 October sailed from Kiel for duty as flagship of Admiral (Nordmeer) and as a mine transport. She arrived at Narvik on 6 October and remained in northern Norwegian waters until the end of the war. During this period *Grille* never went to sea but acted merely as a stationary base ship at the ore quay with only very occasional shifts of berth, such as that on 24 July when she moved to Ankenes.

Allocated to Great Britain in 1946 under the Tripartite Agreement, *Grille* was sold into civilian service that year and after many changes of ownership finally arrived at Bordenstown, New Jersey, USA, on 20 April 1951 for breaking up.

BREMSE

Towards the end of the 1920s the question of replacing the elderly gunnery training tender *Drache* had come up for discussion. *Drache*, built in 1908, was long past her prime, being some 20 years old, slow at 11 to 13kt and did not meet current requirements for training gun captains, gunnery officers or towing targets. The old cruisers and torpedo boats were no better, but with the advent of the new 'K'-class cruisers and the modern Type 23 and 24 torpedo boats, something better was required. Tenders were outside the limitations of the Treaty of Versailles, save only that any armament had to be provided from existing stocks; so that there was no legal reason why Germany should not proceed with an ' Ersatz Drache'. The basic requirements of the design were as follows:

(a) Sufficient speed to allow realistic gunnery practice (i.e., about 27/28kt)
(b) Modern cruiser/destroyer armament and fire-control system
(c) An elevated fire control platform
(d) Good accommodation space for trainees
(e) Splinter protection for the crew when towing targets
(f) Sufficient speed and power for towing targets

Because of the speed demanded, the new design was estimated to require a displacement of about 1,450 tonnes, compared with *Drache*'s 800 tonnes. The original design in fact corresponded more to a fully combatant scout and did not conform to the prescribed requirements above. It

Above: *Bremse* before reconstruction. (WZB)

would appear that the intention was to produce a fighting warship disguised as a tender. On a displacement of 1,450 tonnes, the ship was armed with four 15cm guns, two 50cm torpedo tubes, two AA guns and a seaplane. Geared steam turbines in a twin-shaft arrangement formed the propulsion unit. Ten years later a design of this nature would not have passed muster as anything but a destroyer, but in 1928 there were no single-funnelled destroyers. Nevertheless, the offensive capabilities of such a design were so obvious that politics came into play because of the need to be seen to be observing the requirements of the Versailles Treaty.

Consequently, the Construction Office was ordered on 1 October 1928 to amend the design considerably. There was only to be one gun aft, the quarterdeck and stern were to be fitted for towing and a winch was to be shipped. The torpedo tubes were deleted and boats added in their place. The funnel was not to resemble that of a destroyer and was to be vertical if possible. The simple pole foremast was to be replaced by a tubular tower with a 3m rangefinder/spotting top with searchlight and accommodation for four to six trainees. Protection was required for the upper deck and 'Wallgang'; this latter feature was vetoed on 18 December 1928. Eventually the steam turbine arrangement was abandoned for diesels, the extra exhaust uptakes requiring a second funnel where the seaplane would have been housed. The move to diesels was motivated by their economy, producing double the action radius of a steam layout, immediate availability of power and economy of manning. In addition, it was intended that the installation provide design and operating data for the new diesel machinery to be installed in the first of the Panzerschiffe, *Deutschland*. However, because of delays, this proved impossible. Originally the ship was to have received four two-stroke double-acting MAN M6Z 42/58 3,100bhp engines, two per shaft, but the final machinery installation of 'Ersatz Drache' consisted of eight

two-stroke double-acting MAN M8Z 30/44 diesels developing a total of 28,400bhp, coupled four to each shaft through Vulkan gearing. Her designed top speed was 29kt for one hour, 27kt continuous and on trials she made 29.1kt.

On 9 September 1929 the order for the construction of the new vessel was placed with the Naval Yard at Wilhelmshaven, where the hull was laid down on 22 April 1930. Christened *Bremse* on the occasion of her launch on 24 January 1931, the ship was commissioned on 14 July 1932. As completed, *Bremse* was armed with with four 12.7cm SKC/25 guns in single shielded mountings, one forward, one amidships and two aft; the superfiring arrangement of the after guns was retained despite earlier objections. These guns had originally been intended for the Type 23 torpedo boats but had not been shipped because of political objections. Light armament comprised two twin 3.7cm SKC/30 mountings and two 2cm MGC/30 guns as planned, but it is doubtful if the 3.7cm were ever fitted and 2cm were carried instead. No torpedo armament was fitted, although the ship was equipped for minelaying and could accommodate 102 EMC mines or 132 UMAs or 156 EMAs or a combination of various mines up to the same equivalent weight.

From joining the fleet until the outbreak of war, *Bremse* came under the orders of the Naval Gunnery Inspectorate and was attached to the ship's Gunnery School at Kiel. In service problems were experienced with stability, and *Bremse* was taken in hand before the war for modifications which considerably altered her appearance and at the same time reduced top weight. The tubular foremast with its heavy spotting top and rangefinder was removed and replaced by a simple pole mast. In addition, the prominent cowls were removed from both funnels, the forward funnel was cut down in height and the casings modified.

The outbreak of war found *Bremse* still in the Baltic (under the command of K.Kpt. Forschner), where she was involved in a minor collision with *Leipzig* off Kiel on 7 November. Her initial tasks were escorting troop convoys and minelayers and mercantile warfare patrol in the southern Baltic. In the course of the latter, numerous ships were intercepted and stopped but *Bremse* carried no sea boats at davits, which made the despatch of boarding parties a slow process. By early 1940 *Bremse* had been transferred to Naval Command Group (West) for operations in connection with the invasion of Norway. Accordingly the ship entered the Kiel Canal on 10 March 1940 and arrived at Wilhelmshaven the following day. There she remained for the rest of the month and was still there at the beginning of 'Weserübung'. For this operation, *Bremse* was attached to Group 3 under the command of Konteradmiral Schmundt, tasked with the occupation of Bergen. Also part of the same group were the light cruisers *Köln* and *Königsberg*, two torpedo boats and some S-boats. Schmundt was none too pleased at having this slow vessel with his group (he also had the depot ship *Carl Peters*, a modern vessel but of only 23kt maximum). To safeguard against their having problems, the commander of the 61st Infantry Division, whose troops were taking passage in the group, was requested to load only non-essential men and equipment aboard these two ships. Then in the event of their having difficulties, they could be diverted to Oslo and railed up from there. *Bremse* was actually due for a machinery overhaul and for the present was capable of only 23kt; her diesels had run over twice the scheduled hours.

On 4 April Forschner attended a Captains' conference about the forthcoming operation and the following day was advised of the landing date - 9 April. Troops were loaded on the 7th and *Bremse* moved into the lock, together with the two cruisers, three-quarters of an hour before midnight. On the 8th, at 0400, all three ships sailed. After meeting the remainder of the units of Group 3, Schmundt pressed on and the following day entered Norwegian coastal waters, bluffing his way past the Norwegian patrol vessels. Off Kvarven the shore batteries opened fire, missing *Köln* but a hit in the bows of *Bremse* caused some damage to the forecastle and there were twelve killed and wounded among the embarked troops. *Königsberg* however, was badly hit. By mid-morning all the troops had been landed successfully. *Köln* sailed for home soon afterwards, leaving the damaged *Königsberg* (sunk by Fleet Air Arm Skua dive bombers the next day) and *Bremse*. The latter remained to assist in mopping up the various minor Norwegian naval units left in the area which included a couple of old torpedo boats. One of these, *Stegg*, dating from First World War and armed with two 3in guns and four torpedoes, was caught by *Bremse* in Hardanger Fjord and sunk at Heroysund on the 20th. On the same day the ancient *Tyr* was taken at Uskdal; this was an old Rendel gunboat dating from 1887 (!) currently being used as a minelayer. At Uskdal, *Bremse* also sank *Smart*, a 122 ton ex-mercantile patrol vessel.

In the early hours of 30 April *Bremse* ran aground and had to sail to Stavanger to repair the damage and refit, remaining in drydock until 6 August. By autumn she had returned to Kiel, where she was held in readiness for a feint operation in connection with 'Sealion' until the latter was postponed. On 30 October she sailed once more for Norway. However, while lying at anchor at Frederikshaven on 1 November, *Bremse* was rammed by the NDL-owned merchant vessel *Donau*, receiving damage to her bows in the forward compartments. Once again she moved into the dockyard and landed all her ammunition preparatory to beginning repairs; she was docked between 9 and 16 November. *Bremse* finally sailed for Oslo on 26 November and from there on the 29th to Stavanger where she arrived the next day. However, her troubles continued and on 2 December she ran aground in Faafjord, causing the starboard shaft to seize. The port shaft and propellers were also damaged and some leaks sustained. After being refloated, *Bremse* was towed to Bergen on the 4th, escorted by the old torpedo boat *Zack* (ex-Norwegian *Snogg*). Then on 7 December, towed by the tugs *Jason* and *Herkules*, she left for Stavanger, where she was repaired at the Rosenbergwerft, not beginning post-repair trials until 17 June 1941. During this time K.Kpt. Forschner was relieved by K.Kpt. von Brosy-Steinberg. Following repair the ship returned to Germany.

Bremse sailed for the third and last time to Norway on 6 July 1941, escorted by the torpedo boats *Kondor* and *Falke*. She reached Stavanger the following day, Trondheim on the 9th and, crossing the Arctic Circle on the 10th, reached Tromsø the same day. On 16 July she sailed escorting the hospital ship *Meteor* and, joined by the M.V. *Bretagne* from Honnigsvaag, convoyed the former to Hammerfest, then moved up to Kirkenes. For the rest of the month, *Bremse* escorted convoys between Kirkenes and Hammerfest. However, on 30 July she was in Kirkenes when an air raid took place. This had been launched from the aircraft carrier *Victorious* and consisted of twenty Albacores of Nos. 827 and 817 Squadrons, FAA, and Fulmars of No. 809 Squadron. In a disastrous attack, during which eleven torpedo-bombers and two fighters were shot down, none of the torpedoes hit *Bremse*. The Germans lost one Ju 87 and one Bf 110, the crew of the latter being rescued by *Bremse*. Convoy operations between Kirkenes, Hammerfest and Tromsø continued with the odd exercise in between, such as that on 6 August when she was despatched to rescue the crew of a ditched Do 18 flying-boat. After a long search, the aircraft was located, the crew rescued and the flying-boat towed into port. On 20 August while en route from Kirkenes to Tromsø, *Bremse* reported a submarine just east of North Cape. Twelve depth-charges were dropped without noticeable result. There were submarines operating there, British as well as Russian, for *Trident* and *Tigris* were both based on Murmansk at the time. The next day *Trident* fired four torpedoes at *Bremse* but these do not seem to have been noticed by the German ship.

On 6 September *Bremse* was senior officer of a small

convoy, consisting of the 3,101-ton transport *Barcelona* and the 6,418-ton *Trautenfels* loaded with 1,500 troops of the 6th Mountain Division and their equipment. Other escorts included the trawlers *Nordlicht* and *UJ1701* and the R-boat *R162*. Another trawler, the *Vp Friese*, had been detached because of her inadequate speed, *UJ1203* being ordered to take her place. The latter's subsequent movements are not clear and it would seem that she had not officially joined the escort at the time of the action to be described.

Meanwhile, far to the north, the British cruisers *Nigeria* (Capt. J.G.L. Dundas) wearing the flag of Rear Admiral Vian and *Aurora* (Capt. W.G. Agnew) had participated in the evacuation of Spitzbergen and the destruction of its installations. After oiling from *Oligarch*, Vian moved to the south of Spitzbergen to arrive at the northern limit of the evening German air reconnaissance from north Norway as late as possible. This position was reached at 1400 hours on 6 September. From there he intended to strike south to arrive at a point 4nm west of Nordkyn at 0030 on the 7th. Increasing speed to 29kt, the two British cruisers pressed on to the south through the Barents Sea, passing Bear Island and closing the northern Norwegian coast in rising seas. A north-easterly gale was blowing and a heavy swell from the east made passage conditions uncomfortable. Darkness set in at about 2230 hours and low cloud obscured the moon. Cold and drizzle squalls added to the misery of the watch on deck. Under the prevailing conditions, Vian considered it unlikely that a visual landfall could be expected on Svaerholtavet and was therefore using his radar to probe his way inshore, assisted by soundings (the depth shoaled steeply from 150 fathoms to 100 around Nordkyn). At 0103 the British squadron altered course to 240° and reduced speed to 20kt in order to sweep the sound. Twenty minutes later, *Nigeria*'s radar obtained contacts ahead, assumed to be land, range 5,000 yards. *Aurora* was at this time in station 5 cables astern of

the flag. Vian brought the squadron round to starboard to clear the coast but while doing so, lookouts suddenly reported a blurred object off the port bow, bearing 250°. The high rate of change of bearing and the poor weather conditions made difficulties for the director, but then other contacts were reported and it became clear that the previous radar contact had not been land but ships. About three minutes had elapsed since this first contact and action stations were closed up in both cruisers.

The ships intercepted by Admiral Vian's force were of course the *Bremse* convoy which had left Hammerfest sailing via Honnigsvaag bound for Kirkenes. At the time of their interception, the German ships were transitting the entrances to Porsanger and Lakse Fjord, from where they had to leave the shelter of the islands and make an open sea passage around Nordkyn. The British cruisers had made a passage of 200 miles under poor conditions and by coincidence had arrived off Nordkyn at exactly the same moment as the most valuable German convoy for some time. The obvious inference is that it was no coincidence at all and that Vian's force had been directed south for just such a purpose. True the area of interception was one of the most favourable, being the start of the convoy's open water passage, but the interception of such an important troop convoy leads to the suspicion that either Norwegian resistance elements had reported its progress or, more probably, that 'Ultra' had been responsible.

Be that as it may, the two forces had now made contact. The German convoy was disposed with *UJ1701* in the van, followed in line ahead by *Trautenfels* and *Barcelona*, the two transports. The patrol vessel *Nordlicht* was on the port beam of the leading transport and *R162* on the starboard beam of *Barcelona*. *Bremse* zigzagged to port off *Barcelona*. Of the escort, only *Bremse* with her 12.7cm (5in) guns could offer any defence against surface forces, for the remainder of the escorts were converted trawlers or in the case of *R162* a motor minesweeper. On

Below: *Bremse* after reconstruction. (WZB)

the other hand, the two British cruisers had a total of eighteen 6in guns and sixteen 4in guns, as well as AA guns. However, the weather conditions and close-quarters nature of the engagement negated much of this British advantage, for there is little doubt that if the cruisers had been able to stand off and fight the action, the German convoy would not have survived. Of course, the British cruisers might well have been caught themselves by the Luftwaffe had conditions been better.

The action which followed was confused in the extreme with neither side quite sure of what the other force was doing or composed of. In fact, the Germans seemed to be more aware of what was happening than the British but the loss of *Bremse*, her log and a good part of her crew meant that a reconstruction of events from the German point of view is also difficult.

To return to the ships, *Nigeria* checked her starboard turn on confirmation of the contacts as enemy, opening fire at 0129. She then sighted what was classified as a destroyer or torpedo boat wearing the pennant number A03 off her port bow and crossing close across the cruiser's bows. *Nigeria*'s directors were still groping for the original target sighted (a trawler?) and did not hear the order to shift target to this new ship. Agnew in *Aurora* ordered his Torpedo Officer to fire torpedoes at the trawler first sighted, but then also saw the vessel wearing A03 and ordered his 6in onto her. He opened fire at 0129 also and used his pom-poms as well. Because of the noise of gunfire, the order to fire torpedoes was not heard and the opportunity was lost. Just before fire was opened a large transport was seen in the mist but quickly disappeared.

There was of course no destroyer-type vessel with the German convoy and it is probable that this was in fact *Bremse* whose two funnels may have confused the British lookouts; she was however positively identified later. *Bremse*, at the start of the action, was making 18kt and sighted the two cruisers off her starboard bow, closing at a range of about 2,000m. As a result of her zigzag pattern, *Bremse* now found herself with the cruisers between her and the convoy and therefore altered course to run parallel with them. *Bremse* increased speed to 24kt and made smoke as both sides opened fire. Meanwhile, the convoy and its close escort had turned to starboard to seek safety within the fjords as *Bremse* got off a sighting report. On receipt of this by Gruppe (Nord) and Admiral (Polarküste), all coastal convoys were halted and the 6th Destroyer Flotilla, lying at Kirkenes, was ordered to immediate notice but not sailed pending clarification of the situation.

Nigeria passed close under the stern of A03 (*Bremse*?) and turned away to port to avoid any torpedoes. Both cruisers engaged with 6in and close-range weapons at pointblank range, scoring many hits. *Aurora* alone fired 20 rounds of 6in and 104 of 2pdr. As their target disappeared into the smoke, the cruisers swung round 180° to follow her. Their turn had only just been completed and course

steadied on 090 when, at 0134, another warship was sighted close on *Nigeria*'s starboard side, steering for *Aurora*. This ship was identified as an 'F'-class escort sloop wearing pennant number I30. However, this was almost certainly *Bremse* again, having reversed course in the smoke. She passed between the two cruisers, so close in fact that *Aurora* was forced to make a violent alteration to starboard to avoid a collision, and was hotly engaged by both cruisers at a range of only 100m. *Nigeria* fired three 6in broadsides, claiming one hit, and *Aurora* many rounds of 4in and pom-pom, claiming hits on the enemy's bridge. The situation aboard *Bremse* at the time cannot be precisely ascertained, for although there were some survivors' reports, there is no accurate timescale to them. Her midships gun had been unserviceable from the start of the action and it is likely that she had by now sustained some structural damage and casualties. *Aurora* claimed a hit amidships with 'Y' turret at 0140, which caused an explosion, reportedly stopping the enemy ship. Meanwhile, *Nigeria* entered the smoke screen only to have her bows severely damaged at 0137 by what was thought to have been a submerged wreck.

Here we have yet another mysterious aspect of this action, for *Bremse* was still afloat according to the British report of proceedings and it was to transpire later that no other German ship was sunk. The damage to *Nigeria* extended from the forefoot up to the main deck and aft to the anchor hawse holes. The intriguing question is what caused the damage? It would seem that it was not *Bremse* that was rammed, nor was any other German ship. The damage itself was remarkably similar to that suffered by *Nürnberg* when torpedoed by *Salmon* in 1939. *Nigeria* emerged from the smoke to see another target, this time actually identified as *Bremse*, and in another close-range action claimed further hits. *Bremse* herself was thought to be engaging *Aurora* at the time. The German ship turned away and an explosion like a torpedo hit was seen aft. This explosion, also taken as a torpedo by the German crew, occurred on the port quarter in compartments II and III, wrecked the steering and disabled both after guns. *Bremse* was now in a bad way, listing but still manoeuvrable after a fashion as long as she had way on. Only the forward gun was still serviceable.

The cruisers now engaged what were reported as trawlers at 0144, one of which was taken to be that sighted at the start of the action. Hits were claimed but it cannot be established just what target this was, or whether it was a ship at all. After this brief respite, *Bremse* was sighted once more and engaged by *Aurora* with five broadsides, hitting with three of them, before crawling away to the north and disappearing. Then after opening fire on yet another unidentified target, with daylight breaking, the two cruisers disengaged and returned through rising seas to Scapa, where they arrived on the 10th, having suffered only superficial damage.

Bremse was now listing badly. All her guns were out of action, the after control position and wardroom were wrecked, the after 2cm guns on the deckhouse knocked out and the quarterdeck fittings destroyed. As the forward gun was hit, the forward 2cm also stopped firing and Brosy-Steinberg ordered abandon ship. Confidential books were ditched and cutters and rafts were launched before *Bremse* finally went down.

A rescue operation by *VP1701*, *VP1706*, *UJ124*, *Nordlicht* and *R162* rescued 37 survivors but the C.O. was not among them. The destroyers were never sailed to support her and *Bremse* went down fighting a gallant action alone, effectively preventing the cruisers from getting at their prime target, the transports.

It is interesting to note that both the British and Germans considered *Bremse* to have suffered a torpedo hit. No British ship fired any torpedoes and none of the German ships were equipped with torpedoes. The damage to *Nigeria*'s bows is unexplained but the question is posed: could the hit on *Bremse* and *Nigeria*'s damage have been caused by torpedoes? If so, from whom? Is it possible that a Soviet submarine was responsible, one which perhaps never returned to base to report her actions.

GELEITBOOTE

With the completion of the new Panzerschiff *Deutschland*, the question of providing a screening force came under discussion in the mid-1930s. These deliberations led eventually to the construction of a class of escort vessels designed specifically as the close escort for Panzerschiffe, it being considered that the role of the existing torpedo boats and the new destroyers was to act as an outer screen. The staff requirements for the new vessel envisaged a speed of about 28kt - their charges were only capable of 26kt, an excess judged sufficient in view of their close-support role. Designed tasks included fast search minesweeping ahead of the formation, for which a combination of good speed, shallow draft and reasonable radius of action was required. Anti-aircraft and anti-submarine duties were also to be part of the new ships' role.

The final design had a displacement of 712 tons (standard) which was declared as 600 tons in order to put the ships in the 'Exempt Vessels' category and avoid problems with Clause 8a of the London Naval Treaty of 1930 which placed no restrictions on vessels under 600 tons. In several areas the design was of an experimental nature, particularly in machinery where the new high-pressure steam turbines were adopted. The hull also showed some novel features, one of which was the so-called 'Staukiel' under the transom. This was a wedge shaped appendage designed to reduce stern squat at speed and was also incorporated into the new Type 34 destroyers. In service, however, this led to unfavourable hull stresses and was eventually eliminated.

The machinery installation was, unusually for a small ship of this period, arranged on the unit principle with boiler rooms and turbine rooms alternating. Ideally the machinery should have been a diesel installation for compatibility with operations in consort with the Panzerschiffe, but to obtain 28kt with the diesels of this era was impossible in a small vessel, given the bulk of such machinery. It appeared that the only alternative was the new high-pressure steam plant then under development. As a result, all except two of the ships received a pair of Lamont boilers operating at 450°C and 113 kg/cm² pressure. *F7* and *F8* were given Velox-type boilers operating at 480°C and 72kg/cm². In fact, this machinery was to prove one of the major shortcomings of the class and the Velox boiler in particular was never used again.

Armament comprised two 10.5cm SKC/32 weapons in single shielded MPL C/32 mountings forward and aft, the latter on the shelter deck so as to leave the quarterdeck clear for minesweeping. Two twin L/C30 mountings for 3.7cm SKC/30 guns were fitted amidships and two single 2cm MG C/30 guns were fitted in the bridge wings. Depth-charges were carried and the class could also be fitted for minelaying, being able to accommodate 62 EMA or 50 EMC mines or larger numbers of lighter mines such as the FMB if required.

The design was officially designated 'Flottenbegleiter' or fleet escort, thus confirming its role as Panzerschiffe escort, and a series of ten vessels was projected, known as Flottenbegleiter A-K. The first order placed was for *F7* and *F8* (yard Nos. B498 and B499) on 22 January 1934, with Blohm und Voss, followed by a second order with Germania at Kiel on 17 November 1934 for six units, *F1*-*F6* (yard Nos.526 to 531). The final pair, *F9* and *F10* were ordered on 24 August 1934 with the Wilhelmshaven Naval Yard (yard Nos.126 and 127); in this case the contract was for the hulls only, the machinery being contracted to Blohm und Voss. *F1* was laid down on 2 August 1934 and

Below: *F7* lying at Oslo in May 1940. Note the degaussing coil and the absence of 3.7cm guns. (Author's Collection)

completed in December 1935, while the final ship to complete, *F10*, joined the fleet rather belatedly in March 1938. No further ships were built, although a projected force of seventeen was originally envisaged (ten minesweepers were built instead).

On entering service, these ten vessels formed the 1st (K.Kpt. Weiss) and 2nd (F.Kpt. Lucht) Geleitflotille comprising *F1*, *2*, *5*, *6*, *9* and *10*, and *F3*, *4*, *7* and *8* respectively. Both flotillas were based at Kiel. It soon became apparent that all was not well with the design and service at sea quickly demonstrated major problems with the class. By the autumn of 1937 a report was given to Flag Officer (Panzerschiffe), (FdP), which detailed a number of criticisms. Seaworthiness was generally acceptable but the bridge was very wet because of spray, a problem which was later reduced by alterations to the fore-ends. The speed was inadequate for high-speed minesweeping except in flat, calm conditions, and above sea state 4 the ships were unable to sweep effectively. It should be noted that Frahm active stabilization was fitted but because of the vessels' limited stability this was later removed, presumably because misuse could capsize a ship under extreme conditions. Without stabilization however, they were unsteady flak platforms even in good weather. Endurance was poor, a common complaint in Kriegsmarine designs of the period. There were some good points: A/S performance was acceptable, provided that a sufficient speed margin was available above their charges. FdM actually saw their best use as fast minesweepers for 14-18 kt merchant ships, so long as their machinery did not fail them, but F.Kpt. Rüge was hopeful that time and experience would improve reliability of the machinery.

During the following month, a further report from Rüge, this time to Konteradmiral Boehm (BdA), expressed the view that a new design was required as recent exercises had highlighted the need for fast minesweepers. In Rüge's opinion, a class of ten should be constructed, with eight for operations in the North Sea and the other pair for use as senior officers tenders in the North and Baltic Seas. This would allow the existing F-boats to be transferred to the less exposed Baltic command where, in addition, range was of less importance; it had been discovered that despite the use of redundant stabilizer spaces for extra bunkers, oil stowage was barely sufficient for three days at 50/60 tonnes per day on a bunker capacity of 174 tonnes.

In the light of their disappointing performance, Boehm felt obliged to redefine their role to the Flottenkommando and FdM. They were to be used as fast escorts and fast minesweepers but could not be considered satisfactory because they lacked the speed endurance and seaworthiness required. Nevertheless, in the absence of anything better, they had to be used. He considered that speed could be increased by reducing the armament, complement, superstructure and boats, but new construction would be the best solution. Any new design

should have the following criteria: 28kt with sweeps out; draft not exceeding 2.5m; two single 10.5cm guns with adequate fire control; and three single 2cm or two with one 3.7cm twin. Twelve ships would be needed.

This request was forwarded to the OKM. The 1937 exercises had shown that the F-boats were incapable of screening the Panzerschiffe but they could be used as minesweepers. No more were to be built and it was considered unlikely that a successful design could be achieved on less than 600 tons. OKM had concurred with a suggestion that they be replaced by the older Type 23 and 24 torpedo boats, which would land the after gun, torpedo tubes and rangefinder to augment their M/S and A/S outfits. However, the problems experienced by the new Type 35 torpedo boats prevented the older type from leaving front-line service and nothing came of the idea. Finally, in December 1937, a further critical report assessed them as follows: Fast escort - Too slow for fleet purposes. Endurance poor. Seakeeping inadequate. Machinery unreliable. Minesweeping - Useful but draft too great. Flak defence - Too lively a gun platform. A/S - Good but no detection gear fitted.

During the 1938 exercises only two out of ten boats were available at the beginning because of yard overhauls and even later only a maximum of six were available at any one time, with frequent breakdowns. These exercises showed the F-boats to be useless as dan-layers because of poor manoeuvrability and for the same reason they were unsuitable for paired sweeping. On the other hand, they were useful for search sweeps with ORG and OGG and could use 250-300m sweeps at speed remote from base for similar purposes. As for A/S duties, by the summer of 1939, some vessels had begun to receive S-Geräte detection equipment and in mid-July *F7* to *F10* were put at the disposal of the U-boat school at Neustadt for a trials programme. *F9* failed to participate because of the old bogey - she was undergoing an engine overhaul. For two days not a single contact was obtained, until eventually *F8* obtained one at 400m in a depth of 10m! On 20 July *F7* and *F10* gained good echoes at about 2,200m but could not detect the boat at periscope depth. The general opinion was that the equipment was not front-line operational, it had defects and required skilled operation - not an entirely unexpected outcome.

In view of the problems associated with this class of ship, it proved futile to attempt to keep two flotillas operational and the 2nd Flotilla was therefore disbanded. Some units were now diverted to other duties, *F3* being paid off for conversion to a senior officer's tender on 28 October 1938 and *F6* the following day for similar purposes. This was carried out at the Wilhelmshaven Naval Yard and involved the sides being plated in to the stern to provide additional accommodation, the landing of the 10.5cm gun and both twin 3.7cm mountings, the latter being replaced by single 2cm weapons. The hull was lengthened by about 5m mainly by alteration of the bows. In April 1939 *F1*, *F2*, *F4* and *F5* were paid off for conversion as well, the first as a senior officer's tender, the rest for TRV duties. Thus in July 1939 the intended future deployment of the F-boats was as follows:

F1 to re-commission on 11 October 1940 as senior officer's ship, FDM (Ost)
F2 to re-commission on 1 October 1939 as a Torpedo Recovery Vessel
F3 to re-commission as *Hai* for Flag Officer U-boats (East)
F4 to re-commission on 1 October 1940 as a TRV with the 12th U-boat Flotilla
F6 to re-commission on 15 July 1939 as *Königin Luise* for FdM (W)
F7 to join the 5th U-boat Flotilla as a TRV
F5, *F8*, *F9* and *F10* were to form a training flotilla for the Anti-Submarine School (UAS).

War in September 1939 disrupted these plans and delayed their completion. At that time only four units (*F7* to *F10*) were actually in commission as escorts with the Geleitflotille under the command of F.Kpt Pindter in Baltic waters. Employed initially in connection with the attack on Poland, when several submarine hunts were made, they were transferred to the Heligoland Bight on 6 September after Britain had entered the war. There followed a period of A/S sweeps, escort duties and other tasks in connection with the laying out of the 'Westwall' mine barrage, interspersed with frequent visits to dockyards for engine and boiler repairs. *F9* became a casualty on 13 December when escorting the damaged light cruiser *Leipzig* into Wilhelmshaven. She was struck by a torpedo from the submarine *Ursula* and sank quickly amid explosion of her boilers and depth-charges.

By now it was apparent that the F-boats could not be considered fit for operational duty and although *F5* joined the flotilla early in 1940, there were few occasions when more than one or two ships were fit for duty. Consequently FdM was determined to get rid of them and, in addition to the defects and shortcomings reported in earlier years, he now listed the absence of bilge keels, cracks in the shell plating, a tendency to roll wildly, and above all, constant mechanical breakdown. If they were to be of any use, the bows would have to be rebuilt, the hull stiffened with an external strake and the boiler and auxiliary problems thoroughly investigated. As far as the boilers were concerned, Rüge recommended a reduction in pressure as had been done with *F1* and *F6*. This appears to have been done, to 64kg/cm² in fact. On receipt of this catalogue of defects, BSN recommended that the whole class be transferred to the Baltic and replaced by the 1st Minesweeper Flotilla. SKL while agreeing that they be replaced, did not concur with their movement east and instead noted that the Maierform company were to be consulted with regard to improving the bow form and lines. *F10*, scheduled for refit at the end of January 1940, was selected as the prototype hull. However, a few days after this decision, the Marinekommandamt pointed out that only four vessels were available to the Geleitflotille as the remainder were being converted to other tasks. This

Above: *F2* was converted to a torpedo recovery vessel. Photos of her are rare.

Left: *F1*, converted to a senior officer's tender, in Norwegian waters. (WZB)

was too few to form an operational flotilla and it was proposed that it be disbanded instead. SKL reconsidered the matter in this light and after finding that *F10* would tie up dockyard facilities for three months or more, at the expense of the U-boat and auxiliary cruiser programmes, decided to cancel the refits on 12 February. The Geleit Flotilla was formally disbanded on 1 April 1940, on which date *F2*, *F7*, *F8*, and *F10* were transferred to the 1st U-boat Training Flotilla at the disposal of Flag Officer (U-boats) for TRV and escort duties. For the former task, rails and trolleys for three torpedoes were required on each beam and, if possible where still fitted, the stabilizer gear was to be removed. A torpedo regulating shop was to be fitted on each beam. Other modifications included the landing of one power boat, the fitting of bilge keels and some hull stiffening. Two standards of armament were envisaged, one for TRV duties, the other for escort duties. For the former only two single 2cm MG C/30 guns were specified, on the original 10.5cm positions. Those classed as escorts would land the forward 10.5cm but retain the 3.7cm and 2cm weapons. *F7* was already in hand but FdU stressed the urgency of the programme. On 1 August 1940, *F2*, *F5*, *F7*, *F8*, and *F10* joined the newly formed 25th U-boat Flotilla, which was also a training formation.

F7 and *F8* saw brief service in southern Norwegian waters in April and May 1940, but this was their last operation for several years, apart from a brief consideration by SKL for their use (with others of the class) in connection with operation 'Seelöwe', the invasion of England. As their armament had been greatly reduced for TRV duties and their general training level was poor, this was not proceeded with and they remained in the Baltic on subsidiary duties. With their reduction to other non-front-line tasks, the subsequent service career of these ships is a little patchy, but the following details are known: *F1* was renamed *Libelle* on 23 May 1941 and re-commissioned at Königsberg on 5 June under the temporary command of Kpt.Lt. Quaet-Faslem. There is some doubt whether the name *Libelle* was confirmed as the ship was invariably referred to as *F1* in official records. She was allocated as a tender to Flag Officer (Destroyers), FdZ, and from May 1942 spent some time in Norwegian waters, moving north with *Lützow*. Stationed at Bogen Bay, Narvik, she was briefly employed on escort duties before having to return home for machinery overhaul. She was ordered to Trondheim on 26 August and thence to Kiel where she arrived on 4 September. On 15 September she moved to Wilhelmshaven, while the focus of destroyer operations remained in French waters. In June 1943 *F1* returned to Wesermünde and thereafter served in Baltic waters until 1944 when FdZ was made responsible for the Skaggerak. *F1* remained in this area until surrendered at Copenhagen in May 1945, having been renamed *Jagd* on 15 January. Allocated to the USA in 1946, she served with the GMSA until scrapped in France in 1947.

F2 spent the war attached to the 23rd and 25th U-boat Flotillas at Danzig after re-commissioning on 6 April 1940

under the command of Kpt.Lt. Schwallsh as a TRV. Initially she was armed with one 10.5cm but this was later removed. In June 1944 she (together with *F4*, *F5* and *F7*) was ordered from Admiral (Eastern Baltic) to MOK (Nord) for service with the 5th Sicherungsdivision, and in April 1945 the 5th Escort Flotilla was formed with *F2*, *F4*, *F7*, *F8* and *F10*. After surrender, *F2* was allocated to Britain and laid up in Scapa Flow where she foundered at her moorings on 30 December 1946. The wreck was purchased for salvage by Metric Engineering in 1967.

F3 was re-commissioned on 5 March 1940 with the name *Hai* instead of the intended *Königin Luise*. It had been intended that she act as a tender for Flag Officer (Torpedo boats), replacing the destroyer *Leberecht Maass*, but in April 1940 the OKM decided that the elderly tender *Jagd* be allocated to FdT, much to the latter's disgust. Instead, the ship was employed as a tender for FdM (Ost) in 1940 and later FdM (Nord), seeing service in the Baltic, Gulf of Riga and Gulf of Finland during 'Barbarossa' when she received bomb splinter damage on 28 July 1941. She was also attacked in Kotka Bay by aircraft on 24 June 1942. Her armament comprised one 10.5cm UTO Flak L/45 on a UbTbts LC/16 mounting, one twin 3.7cm and two 2cm C/38. She also saw service with the 14th Sicherungsflotilla and after refit at Königsberg, returned to service as a tender for Admiral (Eastern Baltic). Withdrawn west in the face of the advancing Soviet forces, *Hai* was sunk by rocket-firing Typhoons of the 2nd Tactical Air Force off the Belts on 3 May 1945.

F4 re-commissioned at Stettin on 1 August 1940 under the command of Ob.Lt.z.S. Klunder as a trials vessel for the SVK and TVK, in which capacity she remained until the dire shortage of escort vessels in 1944 saw her transfer to the 7th Minesweeper Flotilla in the North Sea. She was earmarked for minelaying duties in the Little Belts in connection with 'Barbarossa' in June 1941, after a refit at Kiel, but the inactivity of the Soviet fleet rendered this duty unnecessary. Allocated to Britain in 1946, *F4* was laid up at Lyness until handed over to the British Iron and Steel Co. on 12 January 1949 for breaking up.

F5, after re-commissioning on 18 December 1939 at Königsberg, served for most of the war with the 23rd and 25th U-boat Flotillas at Danzig. Her armament was reduced to two twin 3.7cm and one single 2cm C/38. In 1944 she too joined the 7th Minesweeper Flotilla and by January 1945 was at Wilhelmshaven but later returned east and, on the evening of 29 January, detonated an RAF-laid magnetic mine in the Copenhagen-Swinemünde swept channel. She suffered heavy damage aft in compartments I-III but remained afloat. The buoy-layer *Main* got a line aboard and attempted to tow *F5* back to Swinemünde but the latter fouled a wreck, capsized and sank with the loss of 65 of her crew.

F6 finally re-commissioned on 20 September 1939 as a tender and, renamed *Königin Luise*, was the only vessel of the class to participate in 'Weserübung'. She acted as the senior officer's ship of FdM (West) in command of Group 10, charged with the occupation of Esbjerg and Nordby in Denmark. Thereafter she saw service with the 4th Sicherungsdivision, 4th R-boat Flotilla and 6th UJ Flotilla, operating extensively on the Atlantic and Channel coasts of occupied France. In the autumn of 1944 *K_nigin Luise* was refitting at Rotterdam and in October was towed to Borkum as part of convoy 1291 (this is almost certainly the 'Narvik'-class destroyer referred to on page 220 of Peter Scott's book *The Battle of the Narrow Seas*). *F6* was eventually sunk by B-24 Liberators of the US 8th Air Force at Wilhelmshaven on 30 April 1945.

F7 served most of the war with U-boat Training Command, 23rd and 25th U-boat Flotillas, before being ordered to MOK (Nord) in June 1944. She served thereafter with the 7th Minesweeper Flotilla and was eventually ceded to the USSR in 1946. Under the Red Flag, the ship was renamed *V214* and served in the Baltic at Ventspils during the 1950s. From the spring of 1956 she was renumbered *V25* but her final disposal is unknown.

F8 spent a brief period at Oslo in May 1940, then saw the remainder of the war out with U-boat Training Command. She saw some brief action during the hunt for the Soviet submarine *L21* after the latter had achieved some success against German shipping in 1945. Ceded to the USA after the war, *F8* was eventually broken up by Hendrik Ido at Arnbecht, Holland, in 1950.

F10 was also attached to U-boat Training Command for most of the war but was employed on escort duties in the eastern Baltic by 1944, and in June of that year formed part of the escort for *Prinz Eugen* during the latter's deployment to the Aaland Islands. Non-operational at Frederikshaven in January 1945, *F10* was allocated to the USA in 1946 and scrapped with *F8* at Arnbecht.

BRUMMER

The construction of *Brummer* was another step towards the replacement of all the elderly vessels left to the Reichsmarine as a result of the Treaty of Versailles. In this case, the vessel to be replaced was the flak training ship *Fuchs*, formerly a Type 15 minesweeper completed in 1919. Consequently the new ship was known during the design period as 'Artillerieschulboot Ersatz Fuchs'. Like her earlier consort *Bremse*, the new vessel was to serve a number of purposes apart from her main training role. The most important of these was as a test-bed for the main machinery installation of the new Type 34 destroyers. For this purpose, a high-pressure twin-screw turbine layout was specified, giving the 3,000-ton full load displacement ship a maximum speed of 23kt. For her main designed role, she was provided with a mixed gunnery outfit to allow sea-training of gun crews on the most common heavy flak weapons then in service with the Navy. Initially these comprised twin 8.8cm SKC/32 guns in twin LC/32 mountings in Nos. 1 and 4 positions, with two single 8.8cm Flak L/45s in MPL C/13 shield mountings on the shelter decks forward and aft (Nos. 2 and 3 guns). Two twin 3.7cm SKC/30 mountings were shipped to port and starboard amidships, while four to six 2cm MG C/30s completed the gunnery outfit. She was also fitted for minelaying but could accommodate nowhere near the 450 mines attributed to her in most reference books; in fact, she could carry no more than 86 EMC I mines or at most 150 of the lighter FMB type.

Below and opposite page: Two views of *Brummer* showing different armament. (WZB)

Nevertheless, with her all-round outfit, lacking only torpedoes, this vessel obviously had the makings of a useful multi-purpose warship. In time of war she could be employed as a gunboat, escort or minelayer. Her role as a machinery test-bed was, however, rather reduced because eight of the Type 34 destroyers, for which similar machinery was intended, had been ordered before a contract was placed for 'Ersatz Fuchs'. It was not until 24 August 1934 that Deschimag A.G. at Bremen received the order for this ship, her keel being laid on 27 December that year. Construction proceeded rapidly and the ship was launched on 29 May the following year, named *Brummer* and commissioned barely seven months later, on 12 December. This allowed a twelve-month trials period before the first destroyer, *Leberecht Maass*, commissioned; but the fact remained that by the time any useful experience had been gained with *Brummer*, many of the destroyers were far too advanced to benefit much. Consequently they were to suffer from machinery problems throughout their service lives (see *German Destroyers of World War Two*). In the years leading up to the outbreak of war in September 1939, *Brummer* continued in her training role, with her armament being altered to suit current needs. Thus by July of that year her outfit was as follows:

  2 x 8.8cm SKC/32 in twin mounting LC/32 (No. 1)
  2 x 10.5cm SKC/33 in twin mounting LC/31 (No. 4)
  1 x 10.5cm SKC/32 in MPL C/32 (No. 2)

1 x 10.5cm SKC/32 in experimental Flak LC/35 (No.3)
Plus four 3.7cm and six single 2cm guns.

With war approaching, the SKL were considering how best to equip her for active duty, for which purpose a homogeneous gunnery outfit was obviously a high priority. Various options were considered, including the use of some or all of the heavy flak outfits from 'K'-class cruisers under refit (i.e., *Karlsruhe*). Stability was a problem and work needed to be done to establish just what extra armament could be accommodated, especially in view of the need to allow 125 tonnes deck load when used as a minelayer. The proposals included eight 10.5cm SKC/33s in four twin 8.8cm LC/31 mountings (or twin 10.5cm LC/37 mountings), or eight 8.8cm SKC/32 guns in four twin mountings. In the end the outfit proposed was:

  4 x 8.8cm SKC/32 in two twin LC/32 (or 10.5cm LC/37)
  4 x 10.5cm SKC/33 in two twin LC/31 mountings
  8 x 3.7cm SKC/30 in four LC/30 twins
  6 x 2cm MG C/30 singles

When war with Poland broke out, *Brummer,* under the command of F.Kpt. Leithauser, was operating in the Pommeranian Bight in Baltic waters. Her first warlike operation was a minelaying sortie on 2-4 September, when a mere 27 FMC mines were laid in the Gedser narrows; otherwise her routine was barely affected by the outbreak of hostilities. F.Kpt. Gebauer assumed command on 28 November and was pleased to receive orders in December that his ship was to participate in mercantile warfare patrols after a quiet three months. *Brummer* sailed on her first patrol on 14 December, which lasted until the 20th when she returned to Swinemünde. A second patrol lasted from 28 December to 4 January 1940 but by this time a refit was pending. At the end of the month she was prepared for dockyard hands and sailed to Stettin escorted by an ice-breaker. *Brummer* started her refit at Stettiner Oderwerk, which lasted until she was undocked on 4 March. Almost immediately, on 8 March, she received orders to transfer to Gruppe West, moving in preparation to Swinemünde on 14 March. Five days later she sailed for Kiel, arriving there on 21 March, having encountered problems with ice. There seems to have been some indecision as to what use to make of the ship, for after a week in Kiel *Brummer* was ordered back to Swinemünde and on 1 April rated once again as a Flak Training Ship. Barely three days had elapsed before orders were received to proceed to the west with all despatch and on 5 April she secured at Cuxhaven. Yet again no operational orders were forthcoming despite her C.O.'s enquiries, *Brummer* being merely designated as a reserve ship for the 'Weserübung' operation.

Brummer lay at Cuxhaven until 12 April when she was ordered back east again and the following day was ordered from Kiel to Frederikshaven where she was to embark troops bound for Norway. On the evening of 14 April, the ship arrived in the Danish port and took on board 409 troops, including a battalion staff. The torpedo boats *Jaguar* and *Falke* embarked 150 men each, while *F5* took 100. All sailed at 2030 hours that evening, steaming a direct course for Oslofjord because of the submarine dangers. *Karlsruhe* had already been torpedoed and sunk and *Lützow* badly damaged by British submarines while returning to Germany following their participation in 'Weserübung'. *Brummer*'s squadron arrived safely in Oslo the following forenoon, disembarked their troops and sailed for home the same evening.

At 2115 hours, *Jaguar*, leading the squadron, fired five white signal rockets, raised the submarine alarm and dropped depth-charges while the remainder of the group pressed on. Then at five minutes after midnight, *Brummer*'s port lookout reported torpedoes off the port quarter. Gebauer immediately ordered hard a starboard, with the result that two torpedoes passed harmlessly across the bows but a third struck the ship abreast No. 1 gun. The explosion of this torpedo touched off the forward magazine and the resultant double explosion blew away all forward of No. 2 gun, which itself hung down at a drunken angle. The whip of the explosion threw everyone down on the deck and broke off the top mast and searchlight. Gebauer himself was catapulted down to the boat deck and injured. By the time that he had returned to the bridge, he found the engines still rung on full ahead and ordered them stopped. *Brummer* was now settling

down by the bows with a list to port. All unnecessary crew members were taken off by *F5* while the damage control parties made valiant efforts to save the ship. All efforts were in vain, for by 0600 her list had approached 40deg, whereupon the last men were taken off by *Jaguar*. *Brummer* eventually went down in 110 metres at 0750 that morning.

Her assailant had been the British submarine *Sterlet*, which was to last little longer than her victim. On 18 April this boat was depth-charged and sunk with all hands by the A/S vessels *UJ125*, *UJ126* and *UJ128*.

U-JÄGER

The question of constructing a specialized anti-submarine vessel, or U-Jäger, exercised the Naval Staff's mind towards the end of the 1930s with the result that, by early April 1938, the design of a convoy escort was being discussed. The primary function of such a vessel was to be anti-submarine (U-J) and A/A (Flak) defence with the subsidiary tasks of fleet screening and offensive A/S patrol work. Displacement was not to exceed 1,000 tonnes, draft was to be less than 2.5m if possible, continuous speed 20kt and endurance 2,500nm at 15 kt. Armament was to comprise: two triaxial twin flak dual-purpose mountings (with fire control facilities forward and aft); two 3.7cm and four MG C/30 lighter weapons; four depth-charge throwers, two trainable throwers and 60 depth-charges. Machinery was to be of a simple minesweeper type arrangement. Another proposal envisaged no fewer than four twin flak mountings, 25kt continuous speed and an endurance of 3,000nm at 15kt! These latter were obviously too ambitious and a few days later, on 27 April, the Construction Office was asked to detail the possible dimensions and abilities of a design based broadly on the Type 35 minesweeper using the same machinery, armed with two 10.5cm guns and fitted with GHG, KDB and presumably S-Geräte, having a draft of 3.5m. A comparison with a pure 'UJ' design of 1,700 tonnes was requested. Early in May the Construction Office reported that the hull dimensions would have to be 68m x 9m x 3.5m, compared with 66m x 8.3m x 2.1m for an M35 design, with the result that the construction displacement was increased to 1,060 tonnes (cf., 731 tonnes for M35). Given the same armament - i.e., two 10.5cm guns - and similar machinery for an endurance of 3,000nm at 12kt, speed would be 2kt less than the M35. However, 16kt was unacceptable for an anti-submarine vessel in the view of those involved. Accordingly, a second draft was prepared with the following dimensions: 73m x 9.5m x 3.5m (1,250 tonnes). Reciprocating engines developing 5,100hp for a speed of 18kt were to be used; endurance was to be 3,000nm at 10kt and 1,900nm at 12kt; while armament was to comprise two 10.5cm, one 3.7cm and two MG C/30 guns.

The project section was against a specialized 'UJ' vessel of such large dimensions and preferred an 'M35' suitably equipped for the task. Raeder was also interested in improving the design and as a result of his stimulus, the Marinekommandoamt detailed some of his questions in August 1938. On the subject of speed, discussions with U-boat men had established that, faced with a destroyer or torpedo boat, a U-boat would dive. On the other hand, faced with an unknown vessel, a U-boat would not risk closing it on the surface. Thus 19kt would be sufficient for a U-Jäger provided that a U-boat's submerged speed was still low. As usual, Raeder was interested in increasing the gun outfit and requested consideration of: (a) one twin heavy flak forward; (b) one twin forward and a single astern; and (c) twins forward and aft. However, the Construction Office calculated that these designs would have displacements of 1,255, 1,345 and 1,435 tonnes respectively, with a loss in speed of a quarter to a half a knot. The general consensus was that (c) was preferred, the lower speed being acceptable for a design which could outgun a U-boat and act as a good flak ship for slow convoys of valuable ships.

On 17 August Raeder asked if a suitable U-Jager could be developed from the F-boat but the answer was in the negative because this type's draft was too low and its machinery very noisy. The General Office preferred the larger design with four 10.5cm guns but Raeder disagreed, considering that this vessel would itself have to be escorted. The following day, however, the Marinekommandoamt requested an immediate estimate of the costs for four vessels armed with two twin 10.5cm guns and requested details of possible construction yards and building times. It was eventually agreed to order four ships and Raeder instructed that they were to be 'experimental

vessels for detection equipment'. Contracts for the four vessels, *UJ1* to *UJ4*, were placed with Stülcken at Hamburg on 11 November 1938 as their yard numbers S747 to S750. Completion dates ranged from 20 May 1941 to 15 February 1942.

For some reason Raeder wished to disguise the true purpose of these vessels and on 12 January 1939 ordered their designation to be changed to 'gunboats', or Kanonboote. Henceforth they appeared in building records as *K1* to *K4* or *KB1* to *KB4* (as 'Kanonboote 38'). On completion, *KB1* was to join the SVK and on 1 October the 2nd Gunboat Flotilla was to form with *K2-K4*. In the spring of 1942 it was anticipated that the 1st Flotilla would form with *K5-K7* plus three more by the autumn of 1944.

By the spring of 1939 there were demands for design changes, in particular to the main machinery, currently a reciprocating steam installation capable of 18.5kt maximum, and 18kt continuous. The call for this to be increased to 7,000hp was not accepted by the Construction Office because it would require a redesign. A combined reciprocating/turbine layout would be complicated and bulky, while a turbine layout could not be made quiet enough. There were also proposals for diesel engines. In a further discussion about powerplants on 1 June 1939, the various types were examined, it being stated that the current design with steam reciprocating engines could not give more than 18.5kt maximum. Direct-drive turbines, turbines with fluid drive with Föttinger transmission ('too complicated'), geared steam turbines ('two years development for couplings - not guaranteed') and diesels were all discussed, none of which

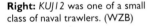

Right: *KUJ12* was one of a small class of naval trawlers. (WZB)

met everyone's agreement. It was only agreed that the existing plant be used for the first seven units, but it soon became clear that yard capacity and shortage of raw materials would be a critical factor at a time when yards were full to bursting with the Kriegsmarine's expansion programme. To waste resources on ships whose functions could quite adequately be performed by minesweepers and auxiliary craft was out of the question and as a result the whole programme was cancelled in 1940. Later, in its place, a programme of naval trawler construction was begun, an adaptation of a civilian design and designated 'Kriegs U-Jäger'. This displaced some 970 tonnes full load and was armed with one 8.8cm, one 3.7cm and numerous 2cm guns as well as a heavy depth-charge outfit. The main propulsion was a simple triple-expansion engine with an exhaust turbine, driving a single screw; coal-firing was employed. Twenty units were ordered on 24 May 1941 from four different yards: Unterweser (*KUJ1-6*); Nobiskrug, Rendsburg (*KUJ7-12*); Meyer, Papenburg (*KUJ13-18*) and Ottensereisenwerke (*KUJ19 and 20*). Shortage of materials and labour, coupled with other, higher priorities, led to the suspension of *KUJ4-6, 9-12, 16-20* and *23-25* in 1942 for a period. Thus, despite the simplicity of their design, it was not until April 1943 that the first ship (*KUJ13*) entered service. Deutsche Werft received orders for *KUJ21-25* (and took over that for *KUJ19/20* on 14 August 1943) and there were plans to construct up to 40 of these vessels. However, the M43 minesweeper design was modified to perform A/S duties among other tasks with the result that *KUJ18-20, KUJ24* and *KUJ26-42* not completed or never ordered.

MEHRZWECKBOOTE (MZ BOATS)

In an attempt to rationalize the wide variety of naval vessels employed on coastal defence and escort duties, the OKM in March 1943 laid down a requirement for a multi-purpose escort designed for series construction. This was to be able to undertake gun and flak defence of convoys, particularly in the Channel, have an A/S capability, good turning circle and also be fitted with torpedoes for opportunity attacks on worthwhile targets. This latter requirement seems to have stemmed from demands earlier in the war for an R-boat equipped with torpedoes for use against destroyer attacks on convoys. Simplicity and ease of construction were to be the main features of the design, which was intended as a cheap replacement for trawlers, VPs, etc. In its final form, this displaced 290 tonnes (332 tonnes full load), the welded steel hull being 51.75m overall with a beam of 7.2m. Propulsion was provided by a single Deutz six-cylinder four-stroke diesel of 1,000hp for a maximum speed of 14kt. However, with a rearrangement of the internal longitudinal bulkhead, the design allowed for the later installation of twin-shaft machinery, possibly steam in place of diesel. Bunkerage was 17.5 tonnes, giving a range of 1,000nm at 14kt. The armament comprised two 8.8cm KM41s in single Flak LM41

mountings, one each forward and aft, at frames 39.5 and 8.5; a single 3.7cm Flak M42 on frame 34.5 ; and eight 2cm weapons (2 x LM44 and 1 Vierling 2cm 38/43). Whip and hoist ammunition supply was provided with 24rpg ready-use shells for the 8.8cm, 140rpg for the 3.7cm and 400rpg for the 2cm. Two G7a torpedoes were carried in fixed tubes in the bows in the same manner as the S-boats. The ship was fitted for minesweeping (SDG, GBT, KKG) and the shipping of 36 EMC mines was being investigated. For A/S purposes, a medium 'UJ' outfit was fitted. Gunnery fire control was restricted to one 1.5m rangefinder and one 'Torpedobrückennachtzielapparat' or bridge torpedo night sight.

A series of twelve ships (*MZ1* to *MZ12*) was planned, with the prototype *MZ1* being ordered from H.C.Stülcken and Sons at Hamburg on 24 May 1943 as their yard number 816. *MZ1* was laid down on 12 October 1943. In the meantime *MZ2-MZ12* had been ordered from G.H.H Rheinwerft at Walsum on 5 June 1943, but as this yard was becoming heavily involved in the MFP programme, the contract was transferred to Flenderwerft, L_beck, on 13 December 1943, becoming their yard numbers 371 to 381. In turn, because this yard also had a commitment to the U-boat programme, the contract was transferred to Stülcken at Hamburg on 29 July 1944. As a result of this indecision, the keels of *MZ3* and *MZ4* were not laid until 22 November 1944 and that of *MZ2* until 2 December 1944. *MZ1* was launched on 16 April 1944 and commissioned for the 11th Vp Flotilla under the command of Ob.Lt.z.S. (Kr.O) Adolph Klein on 29 August the same year. The other three units made little or no progress, partly because of air raids but also as a result of the teething troubles experienced by the lead ship. They remained on the slipways at the end of the war, and on 17 April 1946 the British Authorities ordered the hulls to be broken up.

MZ2 and subsequent ships were intended to be constructed on the prefabrication method, the hull being divided into six sections or 'Baugruppe'. These were : Section 1, stern to 300mm forward of frame 5; Section 2, to 300mm aft of frame 11.5; Section 3, to 300mm forward of frame 22.5; Section 4, to 300mm aft of frame 30.5; Section 5, to 300mm forward of frame 41.5; and Section 6, 300mm forward of frame 41.5 to bow. The keel extended from frame 6.5 to the bow and there were two longitudinals either side of it and two stringers on each beam. The skin, varying in thickness between 4mm and 7mm, was stiffened by 70mm x 5mm flat longitudinals. Main bulkheads were of 9mm plate.

When *MZ1* was inspected by Dr. Diederichs on 28 April 1944, shortly after her launch, he commented favourably on the design of the vessel. She was then awaiting the delivery of her main engine and other items of equipment, but was expected to complete by June. At the time of this inspection , the designed A/S outfit was only three single depth-charge traps on each beam which, as Diederichs pointed out, was poor for a vessel to be fitted

Right: *MZ1* remained unique. Note the torpedo tube aperture. (WZB)

Below: Amidships detail view of *MZ1*. (WZB)

with S-Geräte. He recommended two throwers each side with a depth-charge stowage of 80 if possible. This was considered a couple of months later when the SKL were discussing the suitability of various types, including both 'MZ' and R-boats for anti-submarine tasks. The former had the necessary hull space and strength to ship a medium 'UJ' outfit with sufficient depth-charges, but it was thought that the noise and vibration from the engine might be a problem. At a conference on this subject held on 27 June it was decided that, after completion of acceptance trials, *MZ1* would receive an S-Gerät with a fixed hull dome, the set being fitted in the chart house. A medium 'UJ' outfit consisting of four throwers, six single traps and 64 depth-charges was to be shipped. On the other hand, *MZ2* to *MZ12* were not to receive a 'UJ' outfit so as not to delay completion. From *MZ13* on, a full 'UJ'

outfit was to be carried. The medium 'UJ' outfit described above is however that listed for *MZ2* upwards according to the Bauvorschrift (Waffenanlange) for these units.

At the beginning of September 1944 it was further considered whether the 'MZ' boat, designed for coastal escort duties, could also be adapted to replace some if not all of the AFPs (Artilleriefafhrprahm) - or Landing Craft (Gun) - which were employed to defend local convoys in all theatres from gun attacks. These were conversions of the ordinary cargo Marinefahrprahm, the first of which were *F520* and *F290*, ordered by the SKL on 6 December 1943 at Elsflether Werft. The former was accepted on 8 January 1944 and the latter on 19 January. Conversion costs were RM247,392. The armament of both types was similar, but the 'MZ' had more speed although less armour (only a 20mm 'Wallgang' as opposed to a 20-40mm waterline belt and 100mm concrete over magazine spaces). The 'MZ' would be a better sea boat without the disturbing tendency of the AFP to capsize when bombed. As usual, the problem was yard capacity, for by this time Dutch and Belgian yards had been lost while home yards could only deliver 28 AFPs by June 1945 and eleven 'MZ' boats. As the 'MZ' boats were more complex to build, this proposal foundered as conditions in the Third Reich dissolved into chaos.

The service career of *MZ1* is poorly recorded. Some sources indicate that she was with the TEK at Kiel from October 1944 to January 1945, then with the SEK also at Kiel until February. She is recorded as being part of a convoy between Wesermünde and Wilhelmshaven with units of the 11th Vp Flotilla and arriving at Cuxhaven on 13 January 1945. By April the ship was attached to the EKK at Eckernförde and reportedly became a British prize in May 1945. The strange fact is that this ship does not appear in any Allied lists of captured or surrendered vessels and her real fate remains unknown.

R-BOATS (RAUMBOOTE)

For inshore minesweeping and local escort duties, a considerable programme of motor minesweepers was put in hand from 1930 onwards. The first of these, *R1*, was funded under the 1929 programme and ordered the following year from Lürssen under the guise of a fast diesel tug. This boat displaced about 43 tonnes and was powered by MWM diesels for a speed of 13 knots. A similar vessel, *R2*, was ordered from Abeking & Rasmussen on 16 August 1930 as a 'C/F Boat'. However, this craft received Maybach diesels. Between 1930 and 1934, a series of sixteen boats was put in hand, orders being placed on 15 August 1931 for *R3-R5*, on 30 November for *R6* and *R7*, on 2 June 1932 for *R8* and on 21 June 1933 for the remainder, *R9-R16*. Unlike the S-boat programme, R-boat construction was shared between three yards, although Lürssen built only *R1* and *R8* and thereafter concentrated on S-boats. The R-boats were of composite wood and light metal construction, with displacement gradually increasing to 52.2 tonnes for *R9-R16*. *R6* and *R7* received Linke-Hoffmann diesels and *R8* DWK motors with Voith-Schneider propellers. All had a raised forecastle and were armed with a single MG C/30 gun. They were equipped for both contact and (later) magnetic minesweeping and could alternatively be used as minelayers, being able to carry up to six mines.

In 1934 a larger design was introduced, known as a medium R-boat, whose displacement increased to 120 tonnes. Craft of this type had a flush-decked hull and all were powered by MAN motors with Voith-Schneider propellers. Four were ordered as *R17-R20* on 18 July 1934, three of which were built by Abeking and Rasmussen (*R18-R20*) and one by Schlichting at Travemünde. Except for their ability to ship six to eight mines because of their larger size, these ships' capabilities in their main role were similar to those of the earlier vessels. Four further slightly enlarged versions were ordered on 25 November 1935 from the same yards in the same proportions, *R24* going to Schlichting. Once again all were fitted with Voith-Schneider propulsion. This larger hull in *R17-R24* allowed a 2cm gun forward and aft.

The next series of boats, of which six units (*R25-R30*) were ordered on 29 December 1936, two (*R31* and *R32*) on 29 August and eight (*R33-R40*) on 24 September 1937, were slightly shorter, less beamy and had a greater draft than the preceding series. All received MWM motors with normal propeller drive.

Below: *R4*, Note the hull lines and lack of weapons or mine-sweeping gear. (WZB)

This page: Dazzle painting was frequently employed on R-boats. (Author; WZB)

The years leading up to the outbreak of war saw further orders placed for another sixteen boats, *R41-R48* on 10 December 1938 and *R49-R56* in June 1939. These boats were all to the *R21* design but with MWM reduction geared motors and Voith-Schneider propellers.

By 1 September 1939, 40 out of these 56 boats had been commissioned. After the outbreak of hostilities, new orders were placed for a total of 53 boats, of which *R57-R72* were contracted to Abeking & Rasmussen on 2 October 1939 and *R73-R88* on 29 December. The remainder were placed with a new yard, Burmester at Burg Lesum, which replaced Schlichting on their transfer to the S-boat programme. Two batches were ordered from Burmester, *R151-R158* at the same time as the order for *R57* and *R159-R166* when *R73* was ordered. The boats ordered from this company were of the *R25* type but with supercharged diesels, while those from Abeking & Rasmussen were of the *R21* type.

Further orders were placed throughout the war for these very useful maids of all work, two new variations being introduced. One was the *R218* Type, a boat of increased displacement (Grosser R-Boot), 165 tonnes full load, initial contracts being placed on 29 June 1942. These boats had a top speed of 25kt, were powered by MWM diesels of 2,500hp, and their increased size permitted a 3.7cm gun to be added to their armament. Further orders were placed in 1943-44 but only 75 boats out of the 226 contracted for reached service, some only in the last months of the war.

The other type was the so-called escort R-boat, or 'Geleitraumboote', developed as a result of demands emanating from Group (Nord) in November 1940 for a more offensive vessel for employment in the Baltic, Norway and off Britain's east coast. SKL, however, were unenthusiastic, pointing out that for a displacement of over 120 tonnes, wood was not considered a suitable construction medium and that the use of steel would make impossible demands on shipbuilding capacity. For the required speed of 25kt, it was calculated that 4,000hp would be necessary and although 1,400hp Germania U-boat engines were available, three of these were estimated to give a speed of 22.5kt, below that demanded. Using 2,100hp Germania diesels would push up the displacement to 300 tonnes for a top speed of 23.9kt. S-boat engines were unsuitable because of the operational requirements of the GR-boat. Altogether, SKL saw no point in considering the matter further and advised Group North to that effect in March 1941.

Nevertheless, orders were placed for such a design with Abeking & Rasmussen on 25 September 1941, when 20 boats were contracted, *R301-R320*, a change of plan possibly influenced by the outbreak of war with the Soviet Union in June that year. These boats displaced 189 tonnes full load but retained the composite wood/light metal construction. Main propulsion was three MWM motors totalling 3,750hp for a maximum designed speed of 25kt, but in practice they were pushed to make 23.5kt.

Armament comprised one 3.7cm Flak M42, six 2cm in LM44 twin mountings and one single 2cm, plus two single MZ43 trainable torpedo tubes.

By April 1942 their construction had already been suspended, probably as a result of the expulsion of the Red Fleet from the open waters of the Baltic and official disinterest in the type. Group West now began to express interest in these boats and pressed for the suspension to be lifted. In reply, SKL pointed out that there was a shortage of raw materials and that construction of this boat would be at the expense of normal R-boats. It was recognized that there was a need for fast, well-armed escorts in the West, but it was felt that a better solution would be to modify normal R-boats under construction and arm them with one 3.7cm and three 2cm guns, accepting a slight loss in speed. This could be done within a short period - i.e., from the summer of 1942. Group West agreed reluctantly but regretted the drop in speed. Thus, while the suspension of *R301-R320* was eventually lifted, *R313-R320* were later cancelled in December 1943 and *R321-R400* were never ordered.

R-boats served in all operational theatres from Arctic Norway to the Black Sea. Only a brief resumé of their activities can be given here:

1ST R-BOAT FLOTILLA: Poland 1939, 'Weserübung' Group 5 1940, Channel 1940, Baltic 1941, Gulf of Finland 1942-44, Baltic 1945.

2ND R-BOAT FLOTILLA: North Sea 1939-40, 'Weserübung' Group 10 1940, Channel 1940-44. Disbanded 15 August 1944; re-formed 15 January 1945, Baltic.

3RD R-BOAT FLOTILLA: Poland 1939, North Sea 1940, Channel 1940-41, Black Sea 1941-44. Re-formed 1 March 1945, Baltic.

4TH R-BOAT FLOTILLA: North Sea 1939-40, Channel 1940-44, Norway 1944-45.

5TH R-BOAT FLOTILLA: Baltic 1939-40, Norway 1941, Gulf of Finland 1941, North Norway 1941-45.

6TH R-BOAT FLOTILLA: Mediterranean 1941-45.

7TH T-BOAT FLOTILLA: Channel theatre 1940, North Norway 1941-45.

8TH R-BOAT FLOTILLA: North Sea and Channel 1942-44.

9TH R-BOAT FLOTILLA: Holland 1942-45

10TH R-BOAT FLOTILLA: Channel 1942-44.

11TH R-BOAT FLOTILLA: Baltic, Holland, Channel 1939-40.

12TH R-BOAT FLOTILLA: Channel 1942-43, Mediterranean 1943-45.

13TH R-BOAT FLOTILLA: North Sea 1943-45.

14TH R-BOAT FLOTILLA: Channel 1944, Baltic 1944-45

15TH R-BOAT FLOTILLA: Baltic 1944-45.

16TH R-BOAT FLOTILLA: Norway 1944-45.

17TH R-BOAT FLOTILLA: Baltic 1944-45.

21st R-boat Flotilla: Central Norway 1943-45.

30th R-boat Flotilla: Black Sea 1943-44.

Left: *R108* showing the deck layout. (WZB)

Right: An R-boat en route for the Black Sea. (WZB)

APPENDICES

I. TECHNICAL DATA: S-BOATS

S1
Displacement: 51.6 tonnes (full load); 39.8 tonnes (standard)
Length: 26.85m (oa)
Beam: 4.37m (max.)
Draught: 1.40m (max.)
Machinery: 3-shaft Daimler-Benz BF2 petrol engines; 2,700hp = 34.2kt (max.); 7.1 tonnes petrol = 350nm at 30kt
Armament: two 53.3cm torpedo tubes (2 × 1); one 2cm MgC/30
Crew: 12

S2–S5
Displacement: 58 tonnes (full load); 46.5 tonnes (standard)
Length: 27.94m (oa)
Beam: 4.46m (max.)
Draught: 1.45m (max.)
Machinery: 3-shaft Daimler-Benz BF2 petrol engines; 3,000hp = 33.8kt; 7.5 tonnes petrol = 582nm at 22kt
Armament: two 53.3cm torpedo tubes (2 × 1); one 2cm MgC/30
Crew: 12

S6
Displacement: 85 tonnes (full load); 60.4 tonnes (standard)
Length: 32.36m (oa)
Beam: 5.06m (max.)
Draught: 1.36m (max.)
Machinery: 3-shaft MAN L7 19/30 diesel engines; 3,960hp = 32kt (max.); 10.5 tonnes diesel fuel = 600nm at 30kt.
Armament: two 53.3cm torpedo tubes (2 × 1); one 2cm MgC/30
Crew: 12

S7–S13
Displacement: 86 tonnes (full load); S10–S13, 92 tonnes; 75.8 tonnes (standard)
Length: 32.36m (oa)
Beam: 5.06m (max.)
Draught: 1.36m (max.); S10–S13, 1.42m max.
Machinery: 3-shaft MAN L7 19/30 (S7–S9) or Daimler-Benz MB502 (S10–S13) diesel engines; 3,960hp =
36.5kt (S7–S9); 35kt (S10–S13); 10.5 tonnes diesel fuel = 600nm at 30kt
Armament: two 53.3cm torpedo tubes (2 × 1); one 2cm MgC/30
Crew: 18

S14–S17
Displacement: 105.4 tonnes (full load); 92.5 tonnes (standard)
Length: 34.62m (oa)
Beam: 5.26m (max.)
Draught: 1.67m (max.)
Machinery: 3-shaft MAN L11 diesel engines; 6,150hp = 37.7kt (max.); 13.3 tonnes diesel fuel = 500nm at 32kt
Armament: two 53.3cm torpedo tubes (2 × 1), 4 torpedoes; one 2cm MgC/30
Crew: 18

S18–S25
Details as for S14–S17 except for:
Machinery: 3-shaft Daimler-Benz MB501 diesel engines; 6,000hp = 39.8kt (max.); 13.3 tonnes diesel fuel = 700nm at 35kt

S30–S37, S54–S61
Displacement: 100 tonnes (full load); 78.9 tonnes (standard)
Length: 32.76m (oa)
Beam: 5.06m (max.)
Draught: 1.47m (max.)
Machinery: 3-shaft Daimler-Benz MB502 diesel engines; 3,960hp = 36kt; 13.3 tonnes diesel fuel = 800nm at 30kt
Armament: two 53.3cm torpedo tubes (2 × 1), 4 torpedoes; one 2cm MgC/30
Crew: 24

S26–S29, S38–S53, S62–S133, S159–S166
Displacement: 112 tonnes (full load); 92.5 tonnes (standard)
Length: 34.94m (oa)
Beam: 5.28m (max.)
Draught: 1.67m (max.)
Machinery: 3-shaft Daimler-Benz MB501 diesel engines; 6,000hp = 39.0kt (max.); 13.5 tonnes diesel fuel = 700nm at 35kt; (later supercharged to 7,500hp = 41kt as MB511)
Armament: two 53.3cm torpedo tubes (2 × 1), 4 torpedoes; two 2cm MgC/30 or C/38
Crew: 24

S139–S150, S167–S169, S171–S227, S229–S260
These boats differed from the S26 type only in having a 1m longer hull and the installation of supercharged MB511 engines on completion

S170, S228, S301–S425, S701–S825
Displacement: 121 tonnes (full load)
Length: 34.94m (oa)
Beam: 5.28m (max.)
Draught: 1.67m (max.)
Machinery: 3-shaft Daimler-Benz MB511 diesel engines (S701–825); 3-shaft Daimler-Benz MB518 diesel engines (others); 9,000hp = 43.6kt; 15.7 tonnes diesel fuel = 780nm at 35kt
Armament: two 53.3cm torpedo tubes (2 × 1), 4 torpedoes except S701–825 four 53.3cm torpedo tubes (4 × 1), 4 torpedoes; six 3cm (3 × 2). These guns were never available, three one 3.7cm or 4cm Flak 28 Bofors, three 2cm (1 × 2, 1 × 1)

S501–S507, S510, S512–S513
Displacement: 29.4 tonnes
Length: 18.7m
Beam: 4.70m
Draught: 1.50m
Machinery: 2-shaft Isotta-Fraschini BM183 petrol engines; 2,300hp = 44.1kt (max.); 3.9 tonnes petrol = 350nm at 42kt; (plus two auxiliary motors for cruising)
Armament: two 45cm torpedoes; one 2cm Breda
Crew: 13
(There were detail differences between these ex-Italian boats, MAS 566–570, 574–575, 551, 553–554, which were completed between April and October 1941)

S601–S604
Displacement: 61 tonnes (full load); 51 tonnes (standard)
Length: 28.0m (oa)
Beam: 4.46m (max.)
Draught: 1.51m (max.)
Machinery: 3-shaft Daimler-Benz BF2 petrol engines; 3,000hp = 33.0kt (max.); 5.8 tonnes petrol = 265nm at 33kt; (plus 100hp cruising motor on centre shaft)

Armament: two 55cm torpedo tubes (2 × 1), 2 torpedoes; two 2cm Breda; later fitted with German-pattern 53.3cm tubes

Note: These were the ex-Yugoslav *Velebit*, *Dinara*, *Triglav* and *Rudnik*

S621–S630
Displacement: 70 tonnes (full load); 67.5 tonnes (standard)
Length: 28.0m (oa)
Beam: 4.3m
Draught: 1.75m
Machinery: 3-shaft Isotta-Fraschini ASM183 petrol engines (ASM185 in *S629*); 3,300hp = 31kt (4,500hp =

35kt, *S629*); 8.1 tonnes (7.2 tonnes *S629*, *S630*) petrol
Armament: two 53.3cm torpedo tubes (2 × 1), 4 torpedoes; two 2cm Breda
Crew: 19
Note: Former Italian MS boats

KM1–KM36
Displacement: 18–19 tonnes (full load); 15–16 tonnes (standard)
Length: 15.95m (oa)
Beam: 3.5m (max.)
Draught: 1.1m (max.)
Machinery: Two BMW 6 petrol engines; 1,300hp = 30/32kt

Armament: Four TMB mines; one Mg39; as *KS* boat: two 45cm fixed stern tubes; 1 mg
Crew: 6

LS1–LS34
Displacement: 13 tonnes (approx.)
Length: 12.5m (oa)
Beam: 3.46m (max.)
Draught: 0.92m (max.)
Machinery: Two Daimler-Benz MB507 petrol engines; two Junkers 6-cylinder diesels (*LS1*, 2, 5, 6); 1,500hp = 34/40.9kt
Armament: two 45cm fixed torpedo stern tubes; one 2cm
Crew: 7

II. CONSTRUCTION AND FATES: S-BOATS

Number	Commissioned	Fate
S1	7.8.30	Numbered *UZ(S)16* until 31.3.31, then *W1* until 16.3.32. Stricken 10.12.36 and sold to Spain as *Badajoz*. Renamed *LT13* 1939.
S2	22.4.32	Stricken 10.12.36 and sold to Spain as *Falange*. Destroyed by fire at Malaga, 18.6.37.
S3	27.5.33	Stricken 10.12.36 and sold to Spain. Damaged beyond repair while being unloaded at Cadiz 10.2.37. Never commissioned.
S4	20.6.32	Stricken 10.12.36 and sold to Spain as *Requeté*. Renamed *LT11* 1939. Stricken 3.46.
S5	14.7.32	Stricken 10.12.36 and sold to Spain as *Oviedo*. Renamed *LT12* 1939. Stricken 4.46.

(Note that these five boats were not officially stricken from the Kriegsmarine until after the arrival of the first pair at Ferrol)

Number	Commissioned	Fate
S6	23.11.33	Sold to Spain 1937 as *Toledo*. Renamed *LT14* 1939. Stricken 1942.
S7	10.10.34	To UK 1945. Scuttled in North Sea 2.5.46.
S8	6.9.34	To Fast A/S group 11.9.40. Hulked by 5.45. Scuttled at sea 17.5.45.
S9	12.6.35	To Fast A/S Group 5.8.40. TVA from 5.4.41. To USA 1945. Scuttled in North Sea 2.5.46.
S10	7.3.35	To 55th and 51st Vp Flotillas from 3.42. To USA 1945. To Norway 7.47 but not put into service.
S11	3.8.35	To 55th and 51st Vp Flotillas from 3.42. To USSR 1945.
S12	31.8.35	Renamed *V5504* 4.42. To USA 1945. Scuttled in North Sea 2.5.46.
S13	7.12.35	Renamed *V5510* 3.42. Later to 51st Vp Flotilla. To UK 1945.
S14	12.6.36	To Fast A/S Group 1.8.40. Renamed *V5509* 1941. Lost 1944.
S15	27.2.37	To Fast A/S Group 16.9.40. 55th and 51st Vp Flotillas from 1941. To USA 1945. Transferred to Denmark 7.47 as *T46*.
S16	22.12.37	To Fast A/S Group 8.8.40. 55th and 51st Vp Flotillas from 1941. To USSR 13.2.46.
S17	18.3.38	Badly damaged by heavy seas off Heligoland 4.9.39 and paid off.
S18	14.7.38	Converted to fast tug 1942. Renamed *Herold* 22.2.43. Sunk by air attack off Laland 5.5.45.
S19	6.10.38	To UK 1945. Expended as target.
S20	21.3.39	To UK 1945. Sold out.
S21	19.12.38	Sunk at Boulogne 21.6.40. Raised and recovered 26.5.42. To USA 1945. Transferred to Norway 7.47 (not recorded

Number	Commissioned	Fate
		by R.Nor.N. Historical Dept.)
S22	16.5.39	Disposed of by burning 1946.
S23	15.7.39	Mined off N. Foreland 12.7.40 and sank in tow.
S24	18.9.39	Paid off 24.6.41. To USSR 15.1.46.
S25	5.12.39	Paid off 28.6.41. To UK 1945. Sold out.
S26	21.5.40	Sunk by Soviet aircraft off Sulina 19.8.44.
S27	5.7.40	Sunk by own torpedo off the Taman Peninsula 5.9.42.
S28	1.9.40	Damaged by Soviet bombing at Constanza 20.8.44 and scuttled 25.8.44.
S29	28.11.40	Sunk in action with MGBs in North Sea 29.3.43.
S30	23.11.39	Surrendered at Ancona 3.5.45.
S31	28.12.39	Mined off la Valletta 10.5.42.
S32	15.3.40	Mined off Dungeness 21.6.40.
S33	23.3.40	Stranded on Unije 10.1.45. Wreck destroyed by *MTB 698* 16.1.45.
S34	30.4.40	Disabled off Malta by shore batteries 17.5.42 and wreck sunk by Bf 109s the next day.
S35	19.5.40	Mined NW of Bizerta 28.2.43.
S36	14.6.40	Paid off after collision with *S61*, then surrendered at Ancona 3.5.45.
S37	11.7.40	Mined and sunk off Orfordness 12.10.40.
S38	8.11.40	Sunk off Thames Estuary by *Campbell* and *Garth* 20.11.40.
S39	8.2.41	Sunk in air raid on Le Havre 15.8.44.
S40	22.2.41	Sunk by Soviet aircraft off Sulina 19.8.44.
S41	1.3.41	Collided with other S-boats in Channel 19.11.41 and sank in tow.
S42	16.3.41	Burnt out on slip during Soviet air raid on Constanza 20.8.44.
S43	28.3.41	Mined and sunk north of Dagö 27.6.41.
S44	19.4.41	Sunk by USAAF 8th AF during raid on Kiel 25.7.43.
S45	28.4.41	Damaged in Soviet air raid on Constanza 20.8.44. Scuttled at Varna 29.8.44.
S46	22.5.41	Sunk by Soviet fighter-bombers off Feodosia 11.9.43.
S47	13.6.41	As for *S45*.
S48	20.6.41	To USA 1945.
S49	11.7.41	As for *S45*.
S50	25.7.41	To USSR 15.1.46.
S51	8.8.41	As for *S45*.
S52	22.8.41	Sunk during Soviet air raid on Constanza 20.8.44.
S53	6.9.41	Rammed and sunk by *S39* off the East Coast 20.2.42.
S54	9.8.40	Mined off Cephalonica and paid off 8.9.44. Scuttled 31.10.44.
S55	23.8.40	Sunk by aircraft west of Korkula 10.1.44.
S56	20.9.40	Bombed and sunk at Palermo 28.2.43. Raised and trans-

Number	Commissioned	Fate
		ferred to Toulon. Sunk by bombing while under repair 24.11.43.
S57	30.9.40	Sunk in action with MGBs between Dubrovnik and Korkula 19.8.44.
S58	18.11.40	Stranded on Unije 10.1.45 and destroyed by MTBs 16.1.45
S59	27.11.40	Sunk by air attack at Porto Empedocle 6.7.43.
S60	20.12.40	As S58.
S61	1.2.41	Damaged in collision with S36 during action. Paid off at Pola. Surrendered at Ancona 3.5.45.
S62	19.9.41	Transfer to Finland cancelled. To UK 1945.
S63	2.10.41	Rammed and sunk by Mackay off Cromer 25.10.43.
S64	2.11.41	Transfer to Finland cancelled. To USA 1945. To Norway 7.47 as B-94, Lyn. Stricken 1950 and scrapped.
S65	16.6.42	To USSR 15.1.46.
S66	21.6.42	Destroyed in RAF Bomber Command raid on Le Havre 15.6.44.
S67	19.3.42	To UK 1945. Later bought by Italian Navy.
S68	1.7.42	To USA 1945. To Denmark 7.47 as T62, Viben.
S69	21.12.41	To UK 1945. Sold out.
S70	11.12.41	Mined and sunk in the Channel 5.3.43.
S71	11.1.42	Sunk in action with Garth and Montrose off Lowestoft 17.2.43.
S72	3.2.42	Scuttled off Constanza 23.8.44 after being damaged by Soviet aircraft off Danube estuary 19.8.44.
S73	19.2.42	Paid off at Kiel 3.5.43. Sold to Spain 6.43 as LT21.
S74	27.3.42	Scuttled in North Sea after being damaged by Beaufighter of 254 Sqn. off Texel 5.11.43.
S75	9.4.42	Sunk by Typhoons of 56 Sqn. and Spitfires of 118 Sqn. off Ijmuiden 5.3.43.
S76	1.5.42	To USA 1945. Transferred to Norway 7.47. Cannibalized and stricken 2.50 (not recorded by R.Nor.N. Historical Dept.).
S77	9.5.42	Damaged in action off Ostend 25.7.43 and scuttled.
S78	3.6.42	Sold to Spain 6.43. Renamed LT22.
S79	27.6.42	To USA 1945. Transferred to Denmark 7.47 as T58. Renamed Musvaagen 1951. Broken up 10.55.
S80	10.7.42	Mined and sunk off Viborg 1.9.44.
S81	28.7.42	To USSR 4.1.46.
S82	21.8.42	To USSR 15.1.46.
S83	7.9.42	Proposed transfer to Finland cancelled. To UK 1945.
S84	19.9.42	Destroyed in RAF air raid on Le Havre 15.6.44.
S85	7.10.42	To USA 1945. Transferred to Norway 7.47 as B95, Storm. Transferred to Denmark 1951 as Tranen. Casualty 27.6.63 and stricken 1963.
S86	15.10.42	Transfer to Romania stopped 1944. To USSR 4.1.46.
S87	4.11.42	Foundered after bombing by Swordfish of 819 Sqn. off Ostend 20.5.44.
S88	20.11.42	Sunk in action with MTB607 off Cromer 25.10.43.
S89	28.11.42	Transfer to Romania stopped 1944. To UK 1945.
S90	10.12.42	Still operational 9.9.44. Fate unknown.
S91	22.12.42	Damaged by air attack on Le Havre 2.8.44. Sunk off Fécamp by MGBs after emergency repairs 25.8.44.
S92	14.1.43	To UK 1945. Sold.
S93	4.2.43	Sunk in air raid on Ijmuiden 26.3.44. Raised 7.7.44 and broken up.
S94	18.2.43	Collided with S128 and sank during action with MGBs east of Lowestoft 23.2.44.
S95	28.2.43	To UK 1945.
S96	11.3.43	Rammed and sunk by ML145 east of Lowestoft 25.9.43.
S97	25.3.43	To USA 1945. Transferred to Denmark 7.47 as T63, Ravnen. Broken up 1962.
S98	10.4.43	To USA 1945. Transferred to Norway 7.47 as B96, Kvikk. Stricken 2.50.
S99	17.4.43	Transfer to Finland cancelled. To USSR 4.1.46.
S100	5.5.43	Destroyed by air raid on Le Havre 15.6.44.
S101	30.11.40	To USSR 4.1.46.
S102	30.12.40	Mined and sunk south of Kerch Straits 8.7.43.
S103	9.2.41	Sunk off Mummark by 2nd TAF Typhoons 4.5.45.
S104	27.3.41	Mined and sunk in Channel 9.1.43.
S105	4.5.41	To UK 1945.
S106	6.6.41	Mined and sunk off Dagö 27.6.41.
S107	6.7.41	To USA 1945. Transferred to Denmark 7.47 as T52, Gribben. Broken up 1960.
S108	14.8.41	Disposed of by burning 1946.
S109	14.9.41	To USSR 4.1.46.
S110	19.10.41	To USSR 15.1.46.
S111	11.12.41	Foundered in tow of MGB88 after capture during action in North Sea 15.3.42.
S112	28.1.42	Scuttled at St. Peter Port 5.45.
S113	14.3.42	To USSR 1945.
S114	23.4.42	Sunk by air attack on Le Havre 2.8.44. Raised and broken up.
S115	30.5.42	To UK 1945.
S116	4.7.42	Paid off after mishap in Elbe estuary 1.45.
S117	8.8.42	Was to have been transferred to Finland. To USA 1945. Transferred to Norway 7.47 as B97, Tross. To Denmark 1951 as Herjan.
S118	14.9.42	To USSR 14.1.46.
S119	22.10.42	Collided with S114 and sank during action in Channel 8.3.43.
S120	5.12.42	To UK 1945.
S121	14.1.43	Sunk by Whirlwinds of 263 Sqn. in L'Aberwrach harbour 11.8.43
S122	21.2.43	To USA 1945. Transferred to Denmark 7.47 as T64.
S123	19.3.43	To USSR 4.1.46.
S124	15.4.43	Sold to Spain on completion. Renamed LT23.
S125	16.5.43	Sold to Spain on completion. Renamed LT24.
S126	12.6.43	Sold to Spain on completion. Renamed LT25.
S127	10.7.43	To USA 1945. Transferred to Denmark as T56, Isflugen. Broken up 10.55.
S128	27.8.43	Sunk in collision with S94 during action off Lowestoft 23.2.44.
S129	24.9.43	Caught fire during bombing raid on Ijmuiden 26.3.44 and scuttled to avoid explosion. Raised 6.4.44 and scrapped.
S130	21.10.43	To UK 1945 and commissioned for trials as P5130. Sold to West Germany 7.3.57 as UW10.
S131	5.1.44	Burnt out during Soviet air raid on Constanza 20.8.44.
S132	10.12.43	To USSR, 16.1.46.
S133	31.12.43	To USA 1945. Transferred to Denmark 7.47 as T54.
S134	29.5.43	Sold to Spain on completion. Renamed LT26.
S135	29.5.43	To USSR 4.1.46.
S136	10.6.43	Sunk in action with Sioux, Duff and Krakowiak off Barfleur 11.6.44.
S137	6.7.43	Sunk by USAAF 8th AF B-17s in raid on Kiel 29.7.43.
S138	20.7.43	Sunk during RAF raid on Le Havre 15.6.44. Raised 8.44 and scrapped.
S139	1.8.43	Mined and sunk off Cap Barfleur 7.6.44.
S140	7.8.43	Mined and sunk off Cap Barfleur 7.6.44.
S141	20.8.43	Sunk in action with La Combattante off Isle of Wight 12.5.44.
S142	3.9.43	Destroyed in RAF air raid on Le Havre 15.6.44.
S143	17.9.43	Destroyed in RAF air raid on Le Havre 15.6.44.
S144	1.10.43	Sunk by aircraft at Le Havre 30.7.44.
S145	8.10.43	Scuttled at Brest 18.9.44.
S146	22.10.43	Destroyed in RAF air raid on Le Havre 15.6.44.
S147	5.11.43	Sunk in actin with La Combattante north of Cherbourg 25.4.44.
S148	5.1.44	Mined and sunk north of Sulina 22.8.44.
S149	5.1.44	Burnt out during Soviet air raid on Constanza 25.8.44. Wreck scuttled 28.8.44.
S150	4.12.43	Destroyed in RAF air raid on Le Havre 15.6.44.
S151	19.12.41	Badly damaged off Korkula by British destroyer 11.7.44 but brought into Pola. Surrendered at Ancona 3.5.45.

Number	Commissioned	Fate
S152	31.3.42	Surrendered at Ancona 3.5.45.
S153	19.4.42	Sunk in action off Hvar with *Eggesford* 12.6.44.
S154	10.6.42	Sunk by air raid on Pola (18, 20 or 21.1.45?)
S155	19.7.42	Surrendered at Ancona 3.5.45.
S156	5.9.42	Surrendered at Ancona 3.5.45.
S157	8.9.42	Sunk by grenades west of Trieste 1.5.45.
S158	9.9.42	Disabled by Mosquitoes at Sebenico 25.10.44 and scuttled 26/27.10.44.
S159 to *S166*: Ordered 11.7.42 but suspended 4.42.		
S167	17.12.43	Sunk in collision in the southern North Sea 22.2.45.
S168	23.12.43	To UK 1945. Sold out.
S169	8.1.44	Sunk in RAF raid on Le Havre 15.6.44.
S170	11.2.44	Still operational 15.1.45. Fate not known.
S171	11.1.44	Destroyed in RAF raid on Le Havre 15.6.44.
S172	18.2.44	Destroyed in RAF raid on Le Havre 15.6.44.
S173	25.2.44	Destroyed in RAF raid on Le Havre 15.6.44.
S174	3.3.44	To USA 1945. Transferred to Norway 7.47 as *Rap*. Broken up 2.50.
S175	11.3.44	To USSR 15.1.46.
S176	17.3.44	Sunk off Humber in action with MGBs 7.4.45.
S177	30.3.44	Sunk off Humber after collision during action with MGBs 7.4.45.
S178	6.4.44	Sunk by Beaufighters of 143 and 236 Sqns. off Boulogne 13.6.44
S179	19.4.44	Sunk by air attack together with *S178* 13.6.44.
S180	28.4.44	Lost on German minefield in the Molengat 15.1.45.
S181	5.5.44	Sunk by Beaufighter 'G' of 236 Sqn off Texel 21.3.45.
S182	12.5.44	Rammed and sunk off Cap d'Antifer in action with *MTBs 412* and *430* 27.7.44
S183	19.5.44	Sunk in action with MGBs west of Dunkerque 19.9.44.
S184	26.5.44	Scuttled after being damaged by shore batteries off Dover 5.9.44.
S185	3.6.44	Sunk in action with MGBs north of Dunkerque 23.12.44.
S186	23.6.44	Destroyed in raid on Wilhelmshaven by USAAF 8th AF B-24s 30.3.45.
S187	10.2.44	Destroyed in RAF raid on Le Havre 15.6.44.
S188	1.3.44	Destroyed in RAF raid on Le Havre 15.6.44.
S189	31.3.44	Sunk by aircraft with *S178* and *S179* 13.6.44.
S190	22.4.44	Foundered in Seine Bay after action damage 23.6.44.
S191	18.5.44	Sank after collision with *S301* in Fehmarnsund 7.5.45.
S192	7.6.44	Sunk in action with MGBs west of Ostend 23.12.44
S193	28.6.44	Destroyed in USAAF raid on Ijmuiden 10.2.45.
S194	19.7.44	Still operational at 23.1.45. Fate unknown.
S195	28.6.44	To USA 1945. Transferred to Norway 7.47 as *E3*, later *B-93*, *Kjekk*. Transferred to Denmark as *Lommen* 1951.
S196	3.7.44	To UK 1945.
S197	10.7.44	To USA 1945. Transferred to Denmark as *T59*, later *Raagen*.
S198	15.7.44	Sunk by RAF Bomber Command at Ijmuiden 15.12.44.
S199	21.7.44	Sunk by gunfire of Tongue Sand Fort 23.1.45.
S200	3.8.44	Sunk west of Dunkerque after collision with *S701* during action with MGBs 19.9.44.
S201	28.7.44	Scuttled in S-boat base at Kiel 3.5.45.
S202	8.8.44	Sunk by collision with *S703* in North Sea 8.4.45.
S203	13.8.44	Sunk in collision with *R220* off Lindesnes 9.11.44. Raised and refitted. Sunk NW of Texel by air attack 21.3.45.
S204	19.8.44	To UK 1945. Sailed to England 1.46
S205	28.8.44	To UK 1945. Sailed to England 1.46.
S206	31.8.44	To USA 1945. Transferred to Denmark 7.47 as *T55*, later *Hoegen*. Sunk in collision 11.9.57.

Number	Commissioned	Fate
S207	19.9.44	To UK 1945. Transferred to Denmark 30.7.48 as *T61*, later *Skaden*.
S208	28.9.44	To UK 1945. Commissioned as *MTB5208*. To Bundes-marine 12.3.57 as *UW11*.
S209	21.10.44	To USSR 1945.
S210	27.9.44	To USA 1945. Transferred to Norway 18.7.47 as *Snar*. Stricken 2.50.
S211	1.10.44	To USSR 15.1.46.
S212	11.10.44	To UK 1945. Commissioned as *MTB5212*.
S213	4.1.45	To UK 1945. Broken up 7.45.
S214	8.12.44	To USSR 4.1.46
S215	1.12.44	To UK 1945. Sold out 1947/48.
S216	27.12.44	To USA 1945. Transferred to Denmark as *T53*, later *Havoernen*. Broken up 1958.
S217	30.1.45	To UK 1945. Sold out 1947/8.
S218	18.1.45	To USA 1945. Shipped over 5.11.45.
S219	9.8.44	To USSR 15.1.46.
S220	27.8.44	Sunk in action with *Seymour* NW of Ostend 2.3.45.
S221	10.9.44	To UK 1945. Sold out 1947/48.
S222	23.9.44	To USSR 4.1.46.
S223	29.10.44	Mined and sunk in North Sea off Ostend 8.4.45.
S224	17.11.44	Sunk by bombs at Wilhelmshaven 2.45 (but note no major raids on this target by either USAAF or RAF in February).
S225	1.12.44	Shipped to USA 5.11.45.
S226	27.2.45	Sunk by air attack (2nd TAF?) east of Fehmarn 6.5.45.
S227	.44	To USSR 4.1.46.
S228	19.4.45	To UK 1945 and broken up.

Contracts for *S229* to *S260* were cancelled or abandoned.

Number	Commissioned	Fate
S301	31.1.45	Sunk in collision with *S191* Fehmarnsund 7.5.45.
S302	12.2.45	To USA 1945. Transferred to Norway 7.47 as *E1*, later *Blink*. Transferred to Denmark as *Falken*. Stricken 1961.
S303	24.2.45	To UK 1945. To Norway 7.47 as *E2*. Renamed *Brand* 1948. Transferred to Denmark as *Taarnfalken* 1950.
S304	9.3.45	To UK 1945 and broken up 1946.
S305	29.3.45	To USA 1945. Transferred to Denmark 31.7.47 as *T57*, later *Jagtfalken*. Scrapped 1962.
S306		Incomplete at war's end. To USA. Later transferred to Denmark 31.7.47 as *T57*, later *Glenten*. Broken up 1961.
S307		Incomplete at war's end. To UK 1945.

Contracts for *S308* to *S328* and boats up to *S425* were cancelled or abandoned. Seven incomplete hulls sent to UK were lost (scuttled?) in North Sea, including *S311* and a further fourteen were broken up.

Number	Commissioned	Fate
S701	3.7.44	Badly damaged in collision with *S199* 23.1.45. To USA 1945 and sold to Dutch owners 1951.
S702	30.7.44	Sunk after colliding with *S200* during action west of Dunkerque 19.9.44.
S703	30.8.44	Sunk after colliding with *S202* during action in North Sea 8.4.45.
S704	2.10.44	To USSR 15.1.46.
S705	22.10.44	To UK 4.1.46 and sold.
S706	31.10.44	Shipped to USA 30.1.47.
S707	4.12.44	To USSR 15.1.46.
S708	19.2.45	To USSR 15.1.46.
S709	.45	To USSR 29.3.46.

S710 to *S825* remained incomplete, had been abandoned or their contracts cancelled at the time of the capitulation. One boat believed completed as a fishing vessel by the Poles post-war.

III. TECHNICAL DATA: MINESWEEPERS

Minensuchboote 35/39Mob
Displacement: *M1–M24*, 874 tonnes (full load); 772 tonnes (standard); *M25* up, 878 tonnes (full load); 775 tonnes (standard)
Length: 68.10m (oa), *M1–M24*; 68.40m (oa), *M25* up
Beam: 8.70m (max.)
Draught: 2.65m (max.)
Machinery: 2-shaft reciprocating engines*; 2 Wagner or Lamont boilers; 3,000hp = 18.3kt; 117.6 tonnes oil fuel = 810nm at 18kt; *M1 & M2* Voith-Schneider propulsion
Armament: two 10.5cm SK C/32gE in MPL C/32; one 3.7cm SK C/30; two 2cm MG C/30; 28 to 32 mines
Flak later augmented to: one 3.7cm Flak M42; four 2cm MG C/38 in twin mountings; two Mg 151
(There were many variations in service – see main text.)
Boats intended for conversion to 'Kampfboote', of which none can be identified, were to receive: two 10.5cm SK C/32gE; one 3.7cm Flak M42; one 2cm Flak 38 Vierling (1 × 4); eight 2cm Flak 38 in four LM42 mountings; two Mg 151; one 7.3cm Föhn; four 8.6cm R.Ag. M42
Crew: 107

Minensuchboote 40
Displacement: 775 tonnes (full load); 543 tonnes (standard)
Length: 62.30m (oa)
Beam: 8.90m (max.)
Draught: 2.82m (max.)
Machinery: two triple-cylinder triple-expansion engines with Bauer Wach exhaust turbine; two coal-fired Schultz Marine boilers; 2,400ihp = 17.2kt; 162 tonnes coal = 1,200nm at 17kt
Armament: one 10.5cm Utof L/45; two 2cm Mg C30 later augmented by one 3.7cm SK C/30 forward;
Final intended outfit: one 10cm SK C/32 gE; two 3.7cm Flak M42 in twin LM42 mounting; one 3.7cm Flak M42 in single mounting; one 2cm Vierling (1 × 4); two 2cm Mg C/38 in twin LM44 mounting; two Mg151
Torpedo School Training Boats received: one 3.7cm SK C/30U; one 2cm Vierling (1 × 4); two 53.3cm torpedo tubes (2 × 1)
'Kampfboote' were armed: two 10.5cm SK C/32gE (2 × 1); three 4cm Flak 28 Bofors (3 × 1); four 2cm Mg C38 in LM44 twin mountings; two Mg151; eight 8.6cm R.Ag.M42
Some Minensuchboote 40 were fitted for minelaying, 12 EMC or similar.
Crew: 74 (minesweeper), 80 (with Staff), 71 (TS)

Minensuchboote M43
Displacement: 821 tonnes (full load); 582 tonnes (standard)
Length: 67.75m (oa)
Beam: 9.0m (max.)
Draught: 2.68m (max.)
Machinery: as Minensuchboote 40 except 136 tonnes coal
Armament: two 10.5cm SK C/32gE (2 × 1); two 3.7cm Flak M42 (2 × 1); one 2cm C38 Vierling (1 × 4); two Mg151; 24 mines
Torpedo Versions: two 53.3cm MZ43 trainable torpedo tubes (2 × 1); Fangboote (TRV) only: one 3.7cm Flak M42; one 2cm C38 Vierling (1 × 4); two Mg151
Crew: 90 (minesweeper), 95 (UJ), 66 (Fangboote)

IV. CONSTRUCTION AND CAREERS: MINESWEEPERS

Number	Ordered	Laid Down	Launched	Completed	Builder	Yard No.
Minensuchboote 35/39Mob						
M1	22.11.35	9.7.36	5.3.37	1.9.38	(a)	S710
(1, 4) Sunk by aircraft of Coastal Command in Nordby fjord near Bergen 12.1.45.						
M2	22.11.35	15.7.36	15.4.37	25.2.39	(a)	S711
(2, 4) Sunk by Beaufighters of 144, 455 and 489 Sqns. in Fedjefjord 11.4.45.						
M3	22.11.35	6.11.36	28.9.37	10.12.38	(a)	S712
(1) Transferred to USSR 15.11.46.						
M4	22.11.35		16.10.37	10.4.38	(b)	787
(1, 5, 6) To USA 1946. To France 9.10.47. Stricken 7.8.48 and hulked.						
M5	22.11.35		16.10.37	14.1.39	(b)	788
(1) Sunk by mine laid by HM s/m *Porpoise* off Ramsoyfjord 18.6.40.						
M6	22.11.35.	22.2.37	8.1.38	6.6.39	(b)	789
(2) Mined and sunk off Lorient 23.10.41.						
M7	22.11.35	17.10.36	29.9.37	31.10.38	(c)	242
(1) To USSR 15.11.46						
M8	22.11.35	17.10.36	29.9.37	11.1.39	(c)	243
(1) Torpedoed and sunk by *MTBs 234, 244, 241* and *232* off the Hook 14.5.43.						
M9	22.11.35	20.3.37	16.11.37	5.5.39	(c)	244
(2) Paid off 23.8.44. To USA 1946. To France 9.10.47 as *Somme*. Paid off 8.3.60.						
M10	1.9.36		9.8.38	30.5.39	(a)	S718
(2) Torpedoed and sunk by *MTB 353* 3nm off Dunkerque 14.3.44.						
M11	1.9.36	15.1.38	23.8.38	7.8.39	(b)	788
(2) Sunk SW of Feiestein 6.6.40 by mine laid by HM s/m *Narwhal*.						
M12	1.9.39	4.10.37	6.8.38	21.8.39	(c)	249
(2) To USA 1946. To France 9.10.47. Accommodation hulk at Lorient.						
M13	3.3.37	14.5.38	28.2.39	7.9.39	(a)	S727
(2) Sunk in German minefield off R. Gironde due to steering problem 31.5.44.						
M14	3.3.37	16.8.38	25.4.39	1.12.39	(a)	S728
(1) Mined and sunk off Swinemünde 3.5.45.						
M15	3.3.37	6.3.39	4.9.39	22.2.40	(a)	S729
(1, 3) Sunk in USAAF bombing raid on Hamburg 20.3.45.						
M16	3.3.37	2.5.39	15.11.39	1.6.40	(a)	S730
(1, 3) Badly damaged by bombs at Kotka 4.11.43. Towed to Kiel. Further damaged by bombs 20.3.45. Scuttled off the Skagen 18.5.46.						
M17	3.3.37	29.7.39	17.1.40		(b)	803
(1, 3) Paid off at Rochefort 22.8.44. To USSR 15.11.45.						
M18	3.3.37	16.9.39	19.3.40		(b)	804
(1, 3) Scuttled at Deutsche Werke, Kiel, while under repair 5.45.						
M19	3.3.37	28.10.39	8.5.40		(b)	805
(3, 1) Damaged by air attack on Kiel 9.4.45 and beached.						
M20	3.3.37	10.9.38	16.6.39	11.12.39	(c)	K257
(1) Sunk by Soviet aircraft in Narva Bay 20.7.44.						
M21	3.3.37	10.9.38	6.9.39	18.4.40	(c)	K258
(2) Paid off 23.8.44. To USA 1946. To France 9.10.47. Accommodation ship at Lorient.						
M22	3.3.37	20.1.39	20.3.40	30.7.40	(c)	K259
(3) Scuttled in Kiel Canal at Achterwehr 7.5.45.						
M23	3.3.37	20.1.39	11.7.40	26.10.40	(c)	K260
(5, 6, 7) Mined and sunk at Pernau 11.7.41. Raised and recommissioned 22.4.43. To UK 1945.						
M24	3.3.37	31.7.39	12.10.40	22.2.41	(c)	K261
(8) To UK. To France 9.10.47 as *Ailette*. Paid off 22.11.56. To Bundesmarine 28.2.57						

Number	Ordered	Laid Down	Launched	Completed	Builder	Yard No.

as *Wespe*. Scuttled in North Sea 25.10.73.

M25	4.5.38	25.9.39	19.3.40	16.11.40	(a)	S741

(2) Scuttled in western France 9.44.

M26	4.5.38	13.11.39	21.5.40	21.12.40	(a)	S742

(8) Sunk by air attack off Cap de la Hague 14.5.42.

M27	4.5.38	20.11.39	20.11.40	10.2.41	(a)	S743

(8) Mined and sunk in Gironde Estuary 11.8.44.

M28	4.5.38	29.12.39	29.7.40	22.5.41	(a)	S744

(8) Paid off at St. Nazaire 16.1.45. To UK 1945. To France as *Meuse* 9.10.47. Finally paid off 14.1.57.

M29	4.5.38	2.10.39	18.5.40	4.9.40	(b)	813

(3, 1) To USSR 15.11.45.

M30	4.5.38	16.10.39	1.6.40	31.10.40	(b)	814

(3, 1) To USSR 20.11.45.

M31	4.5.38	1.11.39	13.7.40	19.12.40	(b)	815

(5, 6) Torpedoed and sunk by Soviet MTBs off Honningsvaag 21.10.44.

M32	4.5.38	15.11.39	24.8.40	8.3.41	(b)	816

(7, 8) To USA 1945. Sold as merchantman. Broken up at Ghent 1950.

M33	(4.5.38)	12.6.41	1.4.42	18.12.42	(d)	433

(7) To UK 1945. Used as accommodation ship.

M34	(4.5.38)		7.8.42	26.6.43	(d)	434

(8) To USSR 3.2.46.

(*M33* and *M34* were Flenderwerft, Lübeck, orders S278 and S279, transferred 20.1.41)

M35	4.5.38	9.11.40	6.9.41		(e)	1437

(5, 6) To USA 1945. To France 9.10.47 as *Bapaume*. Stricken 23.7.52.

M36	4.5.38	21.12.40	2.1.42		(e)	1438

(1, 4) Sunk by RAF Beaufighters (2nd TAF) in Kattegat 4.5.45.

M37	19.9.39	15.7.40	12.10.40	16.6.41	(f)	366

(1) Sunk by Soviet MTBs in Narva Bay 4.6.44.

M38	19.9.39	4.5.40	28.2.41	13.12.41	(f)	367

(2, 6) To UK 1945. To France as *Oise* 9.10.47. Stricken 24.2.58.

M39	19.9.39	25.10.40	8.8.41	5.5.42	(f)	368

(6, 7) Torpedoed and sunk by *MTB354* and *361* off Ouistreham 24.5.44.

Further construction was planned to *M50* at one ship per four months but it is not known what the intended yard allocation was. *M50–M55* were allocated to Schichau (Königsberg) at 6 October 1939. *M56–M80* were to complete at the rate of one ship every six weeks.

M81	19.9.39	20.12.40	17.7.41		(d)	427

(4, 5, 6) To USA 1945. To France 9.10.47 as *Laffaux*. Paid off 22.1.56. To West Germany 28.3.57 as *Hummel*. Paid off 5.10.63.

M82	19.9.39	23.3.41	17.11.41		(d)	428

(6, 7, 21) To UK 1945. Sold BISCO and arrived Blyth for scrapping 3.5.48.

M83	19.9.39	5.6.41	9.3.42		(d)	429

(6, 7) Sunk in action with *Ashanti* and *Piorun* off Jersey 14.6.44.

M84	19.9.39	3.9.41	9.6.42		(d)	430

(6) Damaged by ground mines 25.4.44. Scuttled in dock at Le Havre 11.8.44 while under repair.

M85	19.9.39	6.12.41	18.9.42		(d)	431

(6) To UK 1945. To France as *Yser* 9.10.47. Paid off 21.12.56 and transferred to West Germany as *Brummer* 12.2.57. Broken up 1974.

Orders for *M86–M100* were not placed.

M101	27.9.39	15.3.41	22.9.41		(g)	229

(4) Sunk in collision with mercantile *Levante* off Marflese Light House near Namsos 25.11.42.

M102	27.9.39	1.8.41	28.4.42		(g)	230

(6, 7) To UK 1945. Sold BISCO and arrived T. W. Ward (Grays) for scrapping 24.5.48.

M103	27.9.39	3.12.41	6.8.42		(g)	231

(7, 21) Sunk by Beaufighters of 236, 254, 455 and 489 Sqns. in Ems estuary, 15.6.44.

M104	27.9.39	1.4.42	7.11.42		(g)	232

(7) To UK 1945. Sold BISCO and arrived T. W. Ward (Grays) for scrapping 10.5.48.

Rickmers were also allocated *M105* and *M106* but these may not have actually been ordered. Further construction plans called for the completion of ships up to *M130* at the rate of one every 2½ months.

M131	19.9.39	20.12.41	31.8.42		(h)	79

(7) To UK 1945. Sold BISCO and arrived T. W. Ward for scrapping at Grays 24.5.48.

M132	19.9.39	25.6.40	7.4.41	20.1.42	(h)	80

(1, 4) Torpedoed and sunk by HMS/m *Sceptre* off Eggeröy 20.9.44.

M133	19.9.39	31.10.41	3.8.42	26.3.43	(h)	81

(6) Irreparably damaged by a torpedo from *MTB748* off Cotentin Peninsula 14.6.44. Scuttled at St. Malo 6.8.44.

M134–M150 were never ordered but planned for completion at one ship per three months.

M151	19.9.39		19.10.40	5.5.41	(b)	829

(3, 4) To USSR 15.11.45.

M152	19.9.39		16.11.40	30.6.41	(b)	830

(2, 8) Mined and sunk off Gironde 23.7.43.

M153	19.9.39	12.4.40	4.1.41	1.9.41	(b)	831

(2, 7) Sunk in action with *Melbreak*, *Wensleydale* and *Glaisdale* off Ushant 10.7.43.

M154	19.9.39	15.6.40	3.5.41	1.11.41	(b)	832

(5, 6, 7) To USSR 13.2.46.

M155	19.9.39		19.7.41	27.1.42	(b)	833

(1, 6, 7) To USSR 15.11.45.

M156	19.9.39		4.10.41	28.4.42	(b)	834

(6, 7) Damaged in action with *Tantaside*, *Talybont*, *Brissendale*, *Wensleydale* on 5.2.44, then sunk by Typhoon of 266 Sqn. at L'Aberwrach 6.2.44.

M157–M200 were never ordered but planned to complete at the rate of one boat per month.

M201	19.9.39	20.1.40	18.5.40	20.12.40	(i)	494

(5, 6, 7) Mined and sunk in Irben Straits 10.7.41. Raised and repaired. To UK 1945. Sold BISCO and arrived T. W. Ward (Grays) for scrapping 10.5.48.

M202	19.9.39	3.40	29.9.40	15.2.41	(i)	495

(5, 6) To USA 1945. To France 9.10.47 as *Craonne*. Stricken 27.6.51.

M203	19.9.39	15.4.40	29.9.40	3.6.41	(i)	496

(1, 4) To USSR 15.11.45.

M204	19.9.39	19.5.40	21.12.40	24.8.41	(i)	497

(1, 4) To USSR 15.11.45.

M205	19.9.39	4.10.40	3.5.41	4.11.41	(i)	498

(5, 6, 7) To USA 1945. To France 9.10.47 as *Belfort*. Paid off 22.11.56 and transferred to West Germany 28.2.57 as *Biene*. Paid off 20.9.63. Broken up 7.74.

M206	19.9.39	4.10.40	5.5.41	21.12.41	(i)	499

(6, 7) Damaged by bombs 6.8.44 and scuttled at St. Malo 14.8.44.

M207–M250 were never ordered but were planned for completion at one ship per month.

M251	19.9.39	12.1.40	12.7.40	16.12.40	(j)	285

(5, 6) To USA 1945. To France as *Péronne* 9.10.47. Stricken 27.6.51.

M252	19.9.39	28.3.40	27.9.40	15.2.41	(j)	286

(5, 6) To USA 1945. To France as *Ancre* 9.10.47. Paid off 28.7.60.

M253	19.9.39		23.11.40	21.4.41	(j)	287

(5, 6) To USA 1945. To France as *Vimy* 9.10.47. Paid off 22.11.56. Sold to West Germany 12.2.57 as *Bremse*. Stricken 5.10.63.

M254	19.9.39		17.2.41	16.6.41	(j)	288

(8) To USSR 3.2.46.

M255	19.9.39		1.4.41	11.10.41	(j)	289

(4) To USSR 15.11.45.

M256	19.9.39	20.3.41	31.5.41	19.1.42	(j)	290

(1, 2, 6, 8) Damaged by aircraft off Cap de La Hague and foundered in Cherbourg 15.5.42. Raised and recommissioned 5.44. To USSR 29.11.45.

Further construction of this type was projected up to at least *M262* [sic] but no orders were placed because the Type 40 had been substituted.

Minensuchboote 40

M261	8.10.40	10.4.42	10.9.42		(f)	369

(21, 27) To UK 1945. Transferred to Norway 19.11.47 but scrapped.

M262	8.10.40	25.6.42	31.12.42		(f)	370

(28) Scuttled at Bordeaux 25.8.44.

M263	8.10.40	17.12.42	18.5.43		(f)	371

(10) Sunk in action with *Bellona*, *Tartar*, *Ashanti*, *Haida* and *Huron* off the Ile d'Yeu 6.8.44.

Number	Ordered	Laid Down	Launched	Completed	Builder	Yard No.
M264	5.6.41		19.5.43	21.9.43	(f)	372

(10, 11) Sunk by Beaufighters of 144, 404, 236 and 254 Sqns. off Heligoland 18.7.44.

| M265 | 5.6.41 | | 21.9.43 | 15.1.44 | (f) | 373 |

(6, 8, 29) To USSR 28.12.45.

| M266 | 11.10.41 | | 18.3.44 | 15.8.44 | (f) | 374 |

(30) Sunk by RAF at Kiel 26.8.44. Raised. Sunk by B-24s of USAAF 8th AF 11.3.45.

| M267 | 11.10.41 | | 13.6.44 | 8.3.45 | (f) | 375 |

(6, 29) To USSR 20.11.45.

M268	11.10.41					376
M269	11.10.41	Re-ordered as Type 43		26.11.42	(M621–623)	377
M270	11.10.41					378
M271	8.10.40		.42	30.1.43	(g)	233

(28) Sunk by air attack at Pauillac (Gironde) 5.8.44.

| M272 | 8.10.40 | | .42 | 26.3.43 | (g) | 234 |

(9) To UK 1945. To Norway 19.11.47 but broken up.

| M273 | 8.10.40 | | .43 | 15.5.43 | (g) | 235 |

(9) Sunk in action with *Bellona*, *Norfolk*, *Onslow*, *Orwell* and *Onslaught* off Egersund 11.1.45.

| M274 | 8.10.40 | | .43 | 12.6.43 | (g) | 236 |

(9) Scuttled (reason not known) in Scheldt Estuary 5.9.44.

| M275 | 25.4.41 | | 25.5.43 | 4.9.43 | (g) | 237 |

(10) To UK 1945. To France 7.7.47 as *Ancre*. Paid off 8.12.47.

| M276 | 25.4.41 | | .43 | 30.10.43 | (g) | 238 |

(9) Scuttled (reason not known) in Scheldt Estuary 5.9.44.

| M277 | 5.6.41 | | 25.11.43 | 5.2.44 | (g) | 239 |

(8) To UK 1945. To France 1946. Paid off and hulked 7.4.48.

| M278 | 5.6.41 | | 25.1.44 | 20.4.44 | (g) | 240 |

(25) Completed as *TS4*. To USA 1945. To West Germany as *Seestern* 15.8.56. Paid off 14.1.60.

| M279 | 11.10.41 | | 4.7.44 | 21.10.44 | (g) | 241 |

Completed as TS9. To USSR 20.11.45.

| M280 | 11.10.41 | | | | (g) | 242 |

As *TS14*, remained incomplete at capitulation. Broken up.

M281–M290 were never ordered.

| M291 | 8.10.40 | 1.5.42 | 27.3.43 | 5.8.43 | (h) | 82 |

(11, 30) To USSR 24.11.45.

| M292 | 8.10.40 | 15.8.42 | 19.6.43 | 24.11.43 | (h) | 83 |

(8) Sunk by Mosquitoes of 235 and 248 Sqns. in Gironde Estuary 21.8.44.

| M293 | 8.10.40 | | .43 | 26.4.44 | (h) | 84 |

(29) Sunk by Mosquitoes of 143, 235, 248, 333 and 404 Sqns. in Kattegat 2.5.45.

| M294 | 5.6.41 | | 4.3.44 | 28.8.44 | (h) | 85 |

(25) To USA 1945. To West Germany 15.8.56 as *Seepferd*. Paid off 14.1.60.

| M295 | 5.6.41 | | .44 | — | (h) | 86 |

(25) Transferred to Pillau for completion. Scuttled incomplete at Gotenhafen 1945. Later raised and became Polish mercantile *Panna Wodna*.

| M296 | 11.10.41 | | — | — | (h) | 87 |

Construction probably abandoned at end of 1944. Blown up on slip 1945.

| M297 | 11.10.41 | | — | — | (h) | 88 |

This ship, renamed *TS15*, reordered from Atlaswerke (Bremen) 4.12.43 as yard No. 376. Type 43? Construction probably abandoned.

M298–M300 were never ordered.

| M301 | 8.1.40 | 27.8.40 | 9.4.41 | 11.10.41 | (k) | 298 |

(22, 29) Sunk by Halifax of 502 Sqn. off Aarhus in Kattegat 4.5.45.

| M302 | 8.1.40 | 28.11.40 | 26.7.41 | 18.4.42 | (k) | 299 |

(22) To UK 1945. To Norway 19.11.47 but never in service.

| M303 | 8.1.40 | 1.5.41 | 29.12.41 | 5.9.42 | (k) | 300 |

(22) Sunk by Soviet MTBs *TKA205* and *TKA219* off Kyberg 11.10.44.

| M304 | 8.1.40 | | 30.4.42 | 17.11.42 | (k) | 301 |

(28) Mined in Gironde 18.8.44, then scuttled at Bordeaux 25.8.44.

| M305 | 8.1.40 | | 20.10.42 | 15.2.43 | (k) | 302 |

(21) Capsized and sank off Brüsterort in storm 17.1.45.

| M306 | 8.1.40 | | 19.12.42 | 4.5.43 | (k) | 303 |

(9) To UK 1945. To Norway 19.11.47 but never entered service.

| M307 | 8.1.40 | | 16.3.43 | 11.10.43 | (k) | 304 |

(10, 11) Sunk by Beaufighters of 144, 404, 455, and 489 Sqns. off Langeoog 21.7.44.

M308–M320 were never ordered.

| M321 | 19.2.40 | | 29.3.41 | 19.9.41 | (b) | 835 |

(22) To UK 1945. To Norway 19.11.47 but never entered service.

| M322 | 19.2.40 | 23.9.40 | 31.5.41 | 6.12.41 | (b) | 836 |

(22) To UK 1945. To Norway 19.11.47 but never entered service.

| M323 | 19.2.40 | 23.11.40 | 9.8.41 | 11.6.42 | (b) | 837 |

(21, 27) To UK 1945. To Norway 19.11.47 but never entered service.

| M324 | 19.2.40 | 20.1.41 | 20.9.41 | 28.11.42 | (b) | 838 |

(21, 23) To USSR 26.10.45.

| M325 | 8.10.40 | 10.5.41 | 31.10.42 | 18.5.43 | (b) | 839 |

(28) Sunk by air attack at Pauillac (Gironde) 5.8.44.

| M326 | 8.10.40 | 12.5.41 | 30.1.43 | 23.10.43 | (b) | 840 |

(9) To UK 1945. To Norway 19.11.47 but never entered service.

| M327 | 8.10.40 | 3.11.41 | 12.6.43 | 4.3.44 | (b) | 841 |

(11, 21, 27) To USA 1945. Later transferred to USSR.

| M328 | 8.10.40 | 16.6.42 | 12.6.43 | 18.8.44 | (b) | 842 |

(25) To USA 1945. To Italy 20.7.49 as *Antilope*. Broken up 1959.

| M329 | 11.10.40 | | 25.8.43 | 24.3.44 | (d) | 434 |

(8, 11, 27) Sunk at Wilhelmshaven by USAAF 8th AF B-24s 30.3.45.

| M330 | 11.10.40 | | 7.2.44 | 21.10.44 | (d) | 435 |

(25) Completed as Kampfboot. To USSR 1945.

| M331 | 26.11.42 | | — | | (d) | 436 |

Ordered as Type 43 but later cancelled and replaced by *M751*.

| M332 | 26.11.42 | | — | | (d) | 437 |

Ordered as Type 43 but later cancelled and replaced by *M752*.

M333–M340 do not appear to have been ordered.

| M341 | 19.2.40 | 28.9.40 | 10.6.41 | 19.4.42 | (i) | 500 |

(21, 25) To USSR 1945.

| M342 | 19.2.40 | | 11.6.41 | 7.6.42 | (i) | 501 |

(21, 25) To USSR 1945

| M343 | 19.2.40 | 15.10.40 | 6.12.41 | 20.9.42 | (i) | 502 |

(21, 24) Sunk in action with *Ashanti* and *Piorun* off Jersey 14.6.44.

| M344 | 19.2.40 | 15.10.40 | 13.12.41 | 14.12.42 | (i) | 503 |

(28) Scuttled at Rochefort 23.8.44.

| M345 | 8.10.40 | 15.5.41 | 27.6.42 | 24.1.43 | (i) | 504 |

(28) Torpedoed and sunk by 415 Sqn. Hampden off Calais 18.5.43.

| M346 | 8.10.40 | | 27.6.42 | 18.4.43 | (i) | 505 |

(9) Torpedoed and sunk by Soviet submarine *S56* off Gamvik, Tanafjord, 17.7.43.

| M347 | 8.10.40 | 4.7.41 | 7.11.42 | 4.7.43 | (i) | 506 |

(10, 11) Sunk by Beaufighters of 144, 254, 455 and 489 Sqns. off Schiermonikoog 28.8.44.

| M348 | 8.10.40 | 4.7.41 | 7.11.42 | 19.9.43 | (i) | 507 |

(9, 11, 30) To USSR 15.10.45.

M349–M360 were never ordered.

| M361 | 19.2.40 | 20.9.40 | 5.3.41 | 6.8.42 | (e) | 1494 |

(22) To UK 1945.

| M362 | 19.2.40 | 20.12.40 | 1.4.41 | 26.10.42 | (e) | 1495 |

(21, 27) To UK 1945. To Norway 19.11.47. To Denmark 1952 but broken up.

| M363 | 19.2.40 | | 31.5.41 | 5.1.43 | (e) | 1496 |

(28) Mined in Gironde 17.8.44, then scuttled at Bordeaux 25.8.44.

| M364 | 19.2.40 | | 9.8.41 | 4.3.43 | (e) | 1497 |

(9) To UK 1945. To Norway 19.11.47 but never entered service.

| M365 | 8.10.40 | | 25.7.42 | 20.4.43 | (e) | 1509 |

(9) To UK 1945. To Norway 19.11.47 but never entered service.

| M366 | 8.10.40 | | 5.9.42 | 11.6.43 | (e) | 1510 |

(10) Sunk by Beaufighters of 236 and 404 Sqns. at St. Nazaire 8.8.44.

| M367 | 8.10.40 | | 23.12.42 | 5.7.43 | (e) | 1511 |

(10) Sunk by Beaufighters of 236 and 404 Sqns at St. Nazaire 8.8.44.

| M368 | 8.10.40 | 19.2.42 | 15.2.43 | 14.8.43 | (e) | 1512 |

(11, 22) Damaged in collision with U-boat NE of Lindesnes, then mined and sunk 15.4.45.

| M369 | 5.6.41 | 19.2.43 | 18.6.43 | 21.9.43 | (e) | 1550 |

(27) To USSR 1945.

Number	Ordered	Laid Down	Launched	Completed	Builder	Yard No.
M370	5.6.41	1.3.43	17.7.43	3.11.43	(e)	1551

(8) Badly damaged by Beaufighters of 236 Sqn. off Royan and beached 12.8.44.

Number	Ordered	Laid Down	Launched	Completed	Builder	Yard No.
M371	5.6.41		31.7.43	15.12.43	(e)	1552

Completed as *TS1*. To USA 1945. Later sold out commercially.

M372	5.6.41		25.9.43	2.2.44	(e)	1553

Completed as *TS3*. Sunk by Soviet aircraft off Swinemünde 12.5.44.

M373	11.10.41		30.11.43	15.5.44	(e)	1579

Completed as *TS5*. To USA 1945. Sold out commercially.

M374	11.10.41		18.12.43	27.6.44	(e)	1580

Completed as *TS6*. To USA 1945. Sold out commercially. Broken up Ghent 1950.

M375	11.10.41		10.3.44	25.7.44	(e)	1455

Completed as *TS8*. To USA.

M376	11.10.41		19.4.44	23.8.44	(e)	1456

Completed as *TS10*. Sunk by Soviet aircraft off Hela 11.4.45.

M377	11.10.41		27.6.44	17.10.44	(e)	1457

Completed as *TS11*. To USSR 1945.

M378	11.10.41		.44	—	(e)	1458

As *TS13*, towed incomplete to Rostock. To USSR 1945.

M379	11.10.41	.44	—	—	(e)	1459

Destroyed on slip 1945.

M380	11.10.41	.44	—	—	(e)	1460

Destroyed on slip 1945.

(It will be noted that the yard numbers of *M375* to *M380* are out of sequence. However, *M377* and *M378* are also listed in official documents as yard numbers 387 and 388, with orders dates of 12.10.43. This yard numbering was the new sequence at Königsberg for the Type 43 design and it may well be that *M375* to *M380* were all re-ordered on 12.10.43 as yard numbers 386 up, having been transferred from other yards.)

M381	8.1.40	24.5.40	15.2.41	9.8.41	(l)	244

(22) Torpedoed and sunk by HMS/m *Venturer* off Kristiansand (N) 12.2.45.

M382	8.1.40		28.6.41	20.12.41	(l)	245

(22) Torpedoed and sunk in Ravnefjord north of Molde, Norway, by R.Nor.N. MTB715 31.1.45.

M383	8.1.40		22.11.41	20.6.42	(l)	246

(21) Sunk by Beaufighters of 455 and 489 Sqns. north of Spiekeroog 13.8.44.

M384	8.1.40		12.9.42	19.12.42	(l)	247

(28) Scuttled at Nantes 11.8.44.

M385	8.1.40		.43	17.5.43	(l)	248

(10) Sunk in action with *Mauritius*, *Ursa* and *Iroquois* off Les Sables d'Olonne 15.8.44.

M386	8.10.40		1.7.43	9.10.43	(l)	249

(11, 29) To USSR 15.10.45.

M387	8.10.40		.43	11.2.44	(l)	250

Completed as *TS2*. Scuttled at Lübeck 2.5.45.

M388	11.10.41		22.2.44	22.7.44	(l)	251

Completed as *TS7*. To USA 1945. To West Germany as *Seehund* 17.7.56. Stricken 4.1.60.

M389	11.10.41		22.7.44	20.12.44	(l)	252

To USA 1945.

M390–M396 were originally ordered on 26.11.42 as Type 43 ships from Elsflether as yard numbers 253 to 259, of which the first two were renumbered *M661* and *M662*. Numbers up to *M400* would also have been included. All were cancelled when the Type 43 construction became prefabricated.

M401	3.9.40	24.3.41	4.4.42	30.11.42	(m)	229

(23) To USSR 26.10.45.

M402	3.9.40	24.3.41	4.4.42	3.1.43	(m)	230

(24) Sunk by RAF Bomber Command Lancasters at Boulogne 15.6.44.

M403	3.9.40	21.4.41	15.9.42	27.2.43	(m)	231

(25, 29) Bombed and sunk SE of Anholt by Halifax of 502 Sqn. 19.4.45.

M404	3.9.40	21.4.41	14.10.42	26.3.43	(m)	232

(26) To UK 1945. To France 1948. Stricken 7.8.48.

M405	3.9.40	21.4.41	14.11.42	29.4.43	(m)	233

(27) To USSR 15.10.45.

M406	28.9.40	21.4.41	30.12.42	2.6.43	(m)	234

(29) To USSR 15.10.45.

M407	28.9.40	23.6.41	15.2.43	19.6.43	(m)	235

(30) To USSR 15.10.45.

Number	Ordered	Laid Down	Launched	Completed	Builder	Yard No.
M408	28.10.40	26.6.41	25.3.43	3.7.43	(m)	236

(10) To UK 1945. To France 1948. Stricken 7.8.48.

M409/M410 were never ordered.

M411	3.9.40	8.5.41	22.8.42	29.10.42	(n)	418

(23) To USSR 26.10.45.

M412	3.9.40	8.5.41	6.9.42	9.12.42	(n)	419

(24) Ran aground during German raid on Granville 9.3.45 and blown up by crew.

M413	3.9.40	24.5.41	26.10.42	13.1.43	(n)	420

(25) Sunk by Soviet aircraft in Narva Bay 21.7.44.

M414	3.9.40	28.5.41	9.11.42	9.2.43	(n)	421

(27) Torpedoed and sunk by Beaufighters of 236 and 254 Sqns. NW of Frisian Islands 17.5.43.

M415	28.9.40	23.7.41	16.1.43	15.3.43	(n)	422

(29) To USSR 20.11.45.

M416	28.9.40	23.7.41	13.2.43	7.4.43	(n)	423

(30) Sunk in action with *Kent*, *Bellona*, *Myngs*, *Zambesi*, *Verulam* and *Algonquin* off Egersund 12.11.44.

M417–M420 were not built, although *M417* may have been ordered from De Schelde on 28.9.40.

M421	3.9.40		29.11.41	10.9.42	(o)	677

(23) Mined and sunk off Kolberg on an RAF-laid field 13.2.45.

M422	3.9.40		6.8.42	28.10.42	(o)	678

(24) Sunk by RAF aircraft of 236 and 404 Sqns. at St. Malo 4.8.44.

M423	3.9.40		18.10.42	29.11.42	(o)	679

(23, 25) To USSR 26.10.45.

M424	3.9.40		18.10.42	22.12.42	(o)	680

(26) Sunk by air attack at St. Malo 4.8.44. Raised post-war and scrapped.

M425	3.9.40		18.10.42	31.1.43	(o)	681

(27) To USSR 20.11.45.

M426	28.9.40		18.10.42	5.3.43	(o)	682

(29) Sunk by Beaufighters of 236, 254, 255 and 489 Sqns. off Kristiansand (S) 12.9.44.

M427	28.9.40		18.10.42	14.4.43	(o)	683

(30) Sunk in action with *Kent*, *Bellona*, *Verulam*, *Myngs*, *Algonquin* and *Zambesi* off Rekkefjord, Norway 13.11.44.

M428	28.9.40		18.10.42	29.5.43	(o)	684

(10) Sunk by Beaufighters of 236 and 404 Sqns. at St. Nazaire 8.8.44.

M429/M430 not built although allocated to Wilton.

M431	3.9.40	18.4.41	7.3.42	29.9.42	(p)	284

(23) To USSR 4.11.45.

M432	3.9.40	19.4.41	7.3.42	27.10.42	(p)	285

(24) To UK 1945. To France 10.47 as *Suippe*. Stricken 15.6.53.

M433	3.9.40	16.4.41	11.4.42	21.11.42	(p)	286

(25) Sunk by aircraft from *Implacable* in Vegafjord 27.10.44.

M434	3.9.40	23.4.41	11.4.42	23.12.42	(p)	287

(26, 27) To UK 1945. To France 10.47. Stricken 7.8.48.

M435	3.9.40	26.5.41	27.6.42	8.2.43	(p)	288

(27) Sunk by Beaufighters of 455 and 489 Sqns. NE of Ameland 14.5.44.

M436	28.9.40	31.5.41	27.6.42	6.3.43	(p)	302

(22, 29) To UK 1945. To Norway 19.11.47.

M437	28.9.40	29.5.41	27.6.42	28.4.43	(p)	303

(30) To USSR 24.11.45.

M438	28.9.40	4.6.41	27.6.42	10.6.43	(p)	304

(10) Sunk by Beaufighters of 236 and 404 Sqns. at St. Nazaire 8.8.44.

M439/M440 were not built.

M441	3.9.40	9.4.41	19.6.42	26.11.42	(q)	552

(23) To USA 1945. To West Germany 17.7.56 as *Seelöwe*. Stricken 4.1.60.

M442	3.9.40	15.5.41	17.8.42	31.11.42	(q)	553

(24) To UK 1945. To France as *Marne* 10.47. Stricken 19.6.57.

M443	3.9.40	26.6.41	15.9.42	1.2.43	(q)	554

(23, 25) To USSR 28.12.45.

M444	3.9.40	16.7.41	30.11.42	4.4.43	(q)	555

(26) Sunk by mines and air attack off Brest 14.8.44.

Number	Ordered	Laid Down	Launched	Completed	Builder	Yard No.
M445	3.9.40	5.5.41	12.12.42	8.5.43	(q)	556

(29) Sunk by USAAF bombing raid on Hamburg 31.12.44.

Number	Ordered	Laid Down	Launched	Completed	Builder	Yard No.
M446	3.9.40	10.6.41	3.2.43	8.6.43	(q)	557

(30) To USSR 20.11.45.

M447–M450 were not built although projected for construction at P. Smit.

Number	Ordered	Laid Down	Launched	Completed	Builder	Yard No.
M451	3.9.40		24.12.41	4.1.43	(r)	796

(25) Stranded north of Porkkala-Kallaboa during storm 30.1.44. Wreck blown up 31.1.44.

Number	Ordered	Laid Down	Launched	Completed	Builder	Yard No.
M452	3.9.40		19.12.42	7.2.43	(r)	797

(24) To UK 1945. To France 10.47 as *Aisne*. Stricken 7.4.52.

Number	Ordered	Laid Down	Launched	Completed	Builder	Yard No.
M453	3.9.40		15.12.42	20.3.43	(r)	798

(25) To USA 1945. Broken up at Ghent 3.49.

Number	Ordered	Laid Down	Launched	Completed	Builder	Yard No.
M454	9.10.40		.43	10.5.43	(r)	799

(26) To UK 1945. To France 10.47. Stricken 7.8.48.

Number	Ordered	Laid Down	Launched	Completed	Builder	Yard No.
M455	28.9.40		7.12.42	11.6.43	(r)	800

(29) Sunk by air raid on Hamburg 30.7.44. Raised 26.8.44. Sunk again by bombs at Cuxhaven 4.45.

Number	Ordered	Laid Down	Launched	Completed	Builder	Yard No.
M456	28.9.40		3.3.43	2.7.43	(r)	801

(30) To USSR 3.3.46.

M457/M458 were never ordered.

Number	Ordered	Laid Down	Launched	Completed	Builder	Yard No.
M459	3.9.40	7.5.41	31.7.42	7.12.42	(s)	97

(25) Sunk by Soviet aircraft in Narva Bay 10.4.44.

Number	Ordered	Laid Down	Launched	Completed	Builder	Yard No.
M460	3.9.40	8.5.41	31.7.42	6.2.43	(s)	98

(25) To USA 1945. To West Germany as *Seeigel* 30.8.56. Stricken 29.1.60.

Number	Ordered	Laid Down	Launched	Completed	Builder	Yard No.
M461	3.9.40	10.5.41	24.10.42	25.3.43	(s)	99

(27) To USSR 20.11.45.

Number	Ordered	Laid Down	Launched	Completed	Builder	Yard No.
M462	9.10.40	25.5.41	27.1.43	7.5.43	(s)	100

(29) Sunk by Beaufighters of 236, 254, 455, and 489 Sqns. NE of Skagen 12.9.44.

Number	Ordered	Laid Down	Launched	Completed	Builder	Yard No.
M463	28.9.40	28.5.41	17.2.43	3.7.43	(s)	101

(28) Scuttled at Bordeaux 25.8.44.

M464–M466 were never ordered.

Number	Ordered	Laid Down	Launched	Completed	Builder	Yard No.
M467	3.9.40	17.4.41	9.1.42	31.10.42	(t)	675

(23) To USSR 4.11.45.

Number	Ordered	Laid Down	Launched	Completed	Builder	Yard No.
M468	3.9.40	2.4.41	9.7.42	3.12.42	(t)	676

(23) Mined and sunk west of Namsos 12.8.44.

Number	Ordered	Laid Down	Launched	Completed	Builder	Yard No.
M469	3.9.40	2.4.41	9.7.42	6.1.43	(t)	677

(27) Torpedoed and sunk by *MTB458* NW of Vlieland 4.7.44.

Number	Ordered	Laid Down	Launched	Completed	Builder	Yard No.
M470	28.9.40	3.4.41	21.10.42	27.2.43	(t)	678

(29) To USSR 29.11.45.

Number	Ordered	Laid Down	Launched	Completed	Builder	Yard No.
M471	28.9.40	3.4.41	21.10.42	12.4.43	(t)	679

(27) Sunk by rocket attack from Beaufighters of 143, 236, 254, 455 and 489 Sqns. in Marsdiep, Den Helder, 25.9.44.

M472–M474 were never ordered.

Number	Ordered	Laid Down	Launched	Completed	Builder	Yard No.
M475	3.9.40	2.5.41	29.8.42	23.12.42	(u)	783

(24) To UK 1945. To France 1947. Stricken 21.8.48.

Number	Ordered	Laid Down	Launched	Completed	Builder	Yard No.
M476	3.9.40	25.6.41	3.10.42	20.3.43	(u)	784

(26) To UK 1945. To France 1947. Stricken 7.8.48.

M477–M482 were never ordered.

Number	Ordered	Laid Down	Launched	Completed	Builder	Yard No.
M483	3.9.40	11.1.41	16.5.42	1.12.42	(v)	902

(24) Sunk by Whirlwinds of 263 Sqn. south of Alderney 15.6.43.

Number	Ordered	Laid Down	Launched	Completed	Builder	Yard No.
M484	28.9.40	31.3.41	25.8.42	20.1.43	(v)	903

(27) To USSR 15.10.45.

M485 was never ordered.

Number	Ordered	Laid Down	Launched	Completed	Builder	Yard No.
M486	3.9.40	8.3.41	3.12.41	3.12.42	(w)	238

(26) Sunk in action with *Bellona, Tartar, Ashanti, Huron* and *Iroquois* SW of St. Nazaire 6.8.44.

M487/M488 were never ordered.

Number	Ordered	Laid Down	Launched	Completed	Builder	Yard No.
M489	3.9.40	5.41	28.8.42	15.4.43	(x)	905

(30) Torpedoed and sunk by Norwegian MTBs *712* and *722* (54th Flotilla) off Mosterhaven 23.12.44.

M490–M494 were not ordered although projected for construction at Smit & Zoon.

Right: Detail view of the bridge layout of a 1st Flotilla boat in 1940. (G. Behrens)

Number	Ordered	Laid Down	Launched	Completed	Builder	Yard No.
M495	3.9.40		4.9.42	11.3.43	(y)	888

(26) To UK 1945. To France 10.47. Broken up.

M496	28.9.40		12.1.43	7.6.43	(y)	889

(30) To USSR 24.11.45.

Minensuchboote 43

M601	7.5.43		31.8.44	22.11.44	(i)	535

(12) To UK 1945. Sold BISCO and arrived Middlesbrough for scrapping 20.4.48.

M602	7.5.43		21.10.44	14.12.44	(i)	536

(12) To UK 1945. Scrapped.

M603	7.5.43		2.11.44	31.12.44	(i)	537

(12) To UK 1945. Scrapped.

M604	7.5.43		10.11.44	18.1.45	(i)	538

(12) To UK 1945. Sold BISCO and arrived on the Tyne for scrapping 28.3.48.

M605	4.12.43		13.12.44	3.2.45	(i)	539

(12) To UK 1945. Sold BISCO and arrived Ward (Grays) for scrapping 17.3.48.

M606	4.12.43		20.12.44	20.2.45	(i)	540

(2) To USA 1945. Broken up at Ghent 1950.

M607	4.12.43		20.12.44	16.3.45	(i)	541

(2) To USA 1945. Sold out commercially. Various owners, still in service 1982.

M608	4.12.43		20.1.45	20.3.45	(i)	542

(2) To USA 1945. Sold out commercially. Various owners, still in service 1982.

M609	4.12.43		29.1.45	27.3.45	(i)	543

(2) To UK 1945. Sold BISCO and arrived Newcastle for scrapping at Dunston 17.2.48.

M610	4.12.43		27.2.45	5.10.45	(i)	544

To USA 1945. Broken up at Ghent 1950.

M611	4.12.43		12.3.45	.45	(i)	545

(2) To USA 1945. To West Germany 18.8.56 as *Seeschlange*. Stricken 13.2.60.

M612	4.12.43		23.3.45	1.4.45	(i)	546

To UK 1945. Sold BISCO and arrived Ward (Grays) for scrapping 17.3.48.

M613–M616 were probably scuttled incomplete at Rostock, while *M617–M633* remained as sections in the assembly shop. Many further units also remained incomplete as less advanced sub-assemblies in contractors' works.

M801	4.12.43		9.9.44	3.12.44	(e)	390

(12) To USA 1945. To Italy as *Gazella* 20.7.49. Stricken 1967.

M802	4.12.43		29.9.44	4.1.45	(e)	391

(12) Sunk at Kiel by USAAF 3.4.45. Wreck partly demolished 15.12.45. Finally dispersed by depth-charges 20.5.46.

Number	Ordered	Laid Down	Launched	Completed	Builder	Yard No.
M803	4.12.43		19.10.44	17.1.45	(e)	392

(12) To USA 1945. To Italy as *Daino* 20.7.49. Stricken 1966.

M804	4.12.43		1.11.44	23.1.45	(e)	393

(12) Bombed and sunk at Mönkeberg, Kiel, by USAAF 8th AF B-24s 11.3.45.

M805	4.12.43		9.11.44	26.1.45	(e)	394

Sunk by USAAF 8th AF B-24s at Kiel 11.3.45. Wreck demolished 17.12.45.

M806	4.12.43		21.11.44	.45	(e)	395

To UK 1945, not fully fitted out. Scraped on the Tyne 28.3.48.

M807	4.12.43		13.1.45	—	(e)	396

Towed to Rostock 99% complete 1.45. Fell into Russian hands 5.45.

M808	4.12.43		.45	—	(e)	397

Towed to Rostock 99% complete 1.45. Fell into Russians hands 5.45.

As with the *M601* series, many ships remained incomplete in sections, sub-assemblies and parts, of which *M809–M813* were in the final assembly shop 88% to 45% finished. Of the orders placed with Kornneuberg at Vienna, little progress was made before the situation in the Black Sea theatre forced the transfer of these contracts to Deutche Werke at Toulon. By then, however, this was unrealistic and the transaction was merely a paper one.

Key to Builders:
(a) H. Stucken (Hamburg)
(b) Oderwereke (Stettin)
(c) Flenderwerft (Lübeck)
(d) Lübecker Maschinen-Ges (Lübeck)
(e) Schichau (Königsberg)
(f) Atlas-Werke (Bremen)
(g) Rickmerswerft (Wesermünde)
(h) Lindenau (Memel)
(i) Neptun (Rostock)
(j) Deutsche Werft (Hamburg)
(k) Unterweser
(l) Elsflether Werft (Elsfleth)
(m) Rotterdam DD
(n) De Schelde (Vlissingen)
(o) Wilton-Fijenoord (Schiedam)
(p) Nederlandsche Sch. (Amsterdam)
(q) P. Smit (Rotterdam)
(r) Gusto (Schiedam)
(s) Nederlandsche D. (Amsterdam)
(t) v.d. Giessen (Krimpen)
(u) j. & K. Smit (Kinterdijk)
(v) Boeles (Slikkerveer)
(w) Verschure (Amsterdam)
(x) L. Smit (Kinterdijk)
(y) Gebr. Pot (Bolnes)

Notes:
(1) Figures in paranteheses indicate flotillas to which these ships belonged.
(2) The transfer of boats to Norway post-war appears to have been merely an administrative measure for flotillas clearing mines from Norwegian waters and not a transfer to the Royal Norwegian Navy.

V. TECHNICAL DATA: KLEINKAMPFVERBAND

	'Hecht'	'Seehund'	'Biber'	'Molch'
Displacement, m³, (+weapons)	11.83	14.9	6.25	11.01
Displacement, m³, (−weapons)	9.47	12.3	3.65	8.40
Length, m (oa)	10.39	11.86	9.03	10.78
Beam, m	1.70	1.68	1.57	1.82
Pressure hull dia. (max.) m	1.30	1.28	0.96	1.16
Diving depth, (max.), m	50	30	20	40
Motor type		LD 6cyl Diesel	25lt 6cyl Petrol	
Manufacturer		Bussing	Opel	
Rating		60hp	32hp	
Revolutions		1,400rpm	2,400rpm	
Electric motor type	AV76	AW77	GL231/7.5	GL231
Manufacturer	AEG	AEG	SSW	SSW
Rating	12hp	25hp	13.3hp	13hp
Revolutions	1,300rpm	1,040rpm	1,450rpm	551rpm
Batteries, number	5–8	8	3	12
type	8MAL210	7MAL210	13T210	13T210
Periscope	ASRC14A	SRC16	SRC15	SRC15
Fuel		0.46t	0.11t	
Surface speed (max.)	5.7kt	7.7kt	6.5kt	4.3kt
Submerged speed (max.)	6.0kt	6.0kt	5.3kt	5.0kt
Surfaced range (max.)		270 at 7.7	100 at 6.5	50 at 2.9
Submerged range (max.)	38 at 4	63 at 3	8.5 at 5.3	50 at 3.3
Armament	1 Torpedo/Mine	2 torpedoes	2 torpedoes	2 torpedoes
Crew	2	2	1	1

(Source: Hauptangaben Klein-U-Boote, Stand 25.7.44. Potsdam WO4-12359)

REFERENCES AND BIBLIOGRAPHY

OFFICIAL SOURCES

German War Diaries (Kriegstagebücher)
(a) Commands: Gruppe Nord; Gruppe West; Führer der Torpedoboote (FdT); Führer der Schnelleboote (FdS); 1st Schnellbootdivision: 1st, 2nd, 3rd, 4th, 5th, 6th, 7th, 8th, 9th, 10th, 11th, 21st, 22nd, 24th S-Bootes-flotille; 2nd S-Bootesschulflotille, Geleitflotille
(b) Ships: *Tsingtau, Tanga, Carl Peters, Adolph Lüderitz, Hermann von Wissmann, Bremse, Brummer, Grille*

Documents-German
Freiburg Archives: TS189/19415; TS360/2471; RM20/995; RM20/1560; RM20/1578; RM53/2; RM53/3; RM20/221; RM7/1203; RM7/1201; RM7/1252; RM7/1208; RM7/1220; RM20/1615
Potsdam Archives: W-04/23315; W-04/6104; W-04/3727; W-04/12396; W-04/22752; W-04/17732; W-04/16844; W-04/12243; W-04/13011; W-04/4248; W-04/12359

Documents-British
Naval Historical Branch: PG44182; PG32120; NID 24/107/45; M. Div.401; FDS 65/54
Public Records Office: ADM1/19388; ADM189/131; ADM199/261; ADM199/422; ADM199/629; ADM199/645; ADM199/784; ADM2240; ADM199/2241; ADM199/2327; ADM219/121; ADM223/28; ADM223/29; ADM226/64; AIR27/954; AIR41/47; AIR41/48; AIR41/73

PUBLISHED SOURCES

Anon, *British Vessels Lost at Sea 1939–45* (Stephens, 1976)
Barker, R., *The Ship-Busters* (Chatto & Windus, 1957)
Beaver, Paul, *E-Boats and Coastal Craft* (PSL, 1980)
Behrens, G., *Die Geschichte der 1. Schnellbootsflotille 1931–1945* (Behrens, 1989)
Bekker, C. D., *The K Men* (Kimber, 1955)
Brown, D., *Warship Losses of World War Two* (Arms & Armour Press, 1990)
Cooper, B., *The Buccaneers* (Macdonald, 1970)
English, J., *The Hunts* (World Ship Society, 1987)
Foch, H., *Fast Fighting Boats* (Nautical Pub. Co., 1978)
Freeman, Roger. A., *The Mighty Eighth War Diary* (Arms & Armour Press, 1990)
Gerdau, Kirt., *Kampfboot M328* (Koehlers Verlag, 1989)
Gröner et al., *Die deutschen Kriegschiffe, Band 2* (Bernard & Graef, 1983)
Halley, James. J., *The Squadrons of the RAF* (Air-Britain, 1988)
Hervieux, P., *The S-Boat War in the West 1941/42* (Warship)
Hummelchen, G., *Schnellboote* (Warship Profile 31, 1974)
Kühn, V., *Schnellboote im Einsatz* (Motorbuch Verlag, 1986)
Middlebrook, M., and Everitt, C., *The Bomber Command War Diaries* (Penguin, 1990)
Ostertag, R., *Deutsche Minensucher* (Koehlers Verlag, 1986)
Rohwer, J., and Hummelchen, G., *Chronology of the War at Sea, Vols. I and II* (Ian Allan, 1974)
Roscoe, T., *US Destroyer Operations in World War 2* (NIP, 1953)
Roskill, S., *The War at Sea, Vols. I to III* (HMSO)
Rössler, E., *The U-Boat* (Arms & Armour Press, 1981)
Scott, Lt.Cdr. P. *The Battle of the Narrow Seas* (Country Life, 1945)
Schneider, G.-D., *Vom Kanal zum Kaukasus* (Koehlers Verlag, 1982)
Whitley, M. J., *The Type 43 Minesweepers* (Warship 27 & 28), *Marine Artillerie Leichter* (Warship 29), *Kriegsfisch-kutter* (Warship 39), *The loss of Bremse* (Warship 41), *The F-Boote* (Warship 45)

INDEX

ADDENDA TO THE OTHER VOLUMES IN THIS SERIES

GERMAN DESTROYERS OF WORLD WAR TWO

The following additional information came to hand, courtesy of Herr Reinhard Hoeisel, too late for inclusion in the second edition of that book. As it is likely that readers of *German Coastal Forces of World War Two* will have also read or purchased the companion *Destroyer* work, this new information is inculded here.

Type 41 Torpedo Boats

Name	Laid Down	Launched
T37	14.8.43	29.4.44
T38	11.10.43	17.6.44
T39	8.11.43	22.7.44
T40	27.12.43	2.9.44
T41	21.2.44	Not launched
T42	27.3.44	Not launched
T43	23.5.44	Not launched
T44	29.6.44	Not launched

GERMAN CRUISERS OF WORLD WAR TWO

Page 47: Tabular data refers to the ship as a heavy cruiser, not a carrier.

Page 48/49: The Building Party standing by the ship at Deschimag was disbanded on 30.6.43, but Hitler had sanctioned the use of her 20.3cm turrets for coast defence purposes on the Western Front as early as 26.8.42.

Scuttling of *Seydlitz*: It would appear that the scuttling of *Seydlitz* was not known to the higher command, as on 14.3.45 Admiral (Eastern Baltic) asked who had given the orders. Naval Officer Commanding (East Prussia) replied that on the afternoon of 25 January 1945 the Naval Harbourmaster at Königsberg received orders that in view of the grave military situation locally, the demolition of the ship was to be put in hand to prevent her seizure by the Russians. After obtaining instructions from C-in-C Armed Forces (Königsberg), this was carried out on the night of 28/29 January under the impression that the enemy were already in the suburbs. Demolition was by means of five 50kg charges hung over the side and not by torpedo warheads. Tugs had actually been ordered to prepare to move *Seydlitz* to Putziger Wik on 22 January but this had to be postponed by MOK (Ost) on the 23rd because the captain of *Leipzig* had commandeered the icebreaker *Ostpreussen*. The demolition of the ship cannot have been very thorough, as she was reported seen by PRU aircraft under tow southeast of Hango in the entrance to the Gulf of Finland on 10.10.46. If this report is correct, she was probably canibalized as spares for the ex-*Lützow*.

Page 71: The mounting referred to in line 11 was in fact a 2cm Vierling.

Page 113: *Furious* did have six Skuas of No. 801 Squadron and *Argus*, also present, two Swordfish of No. 825 Squadron. Attempts were made to arm the Swordfish for a strike while the Skuas shadowed *Hipper*, but the enemy was driven off by the cruisers before this could be done. Why a standing air patrol was not mounted is not clear.

Page 141: Penultimate line LH column; Delete *T17*, should read *T7*.

Page 159: LH Col. Line 19. Construction Stand by Party appointed 18.10.43. Ship recommissioned 30.4.44.

Page 160: During her refit *Köln* was to receive two Föhn rocket-launchers. The ship paid off on 5.4.45, when the majority of the crew joined the fortress guard at Kiel. Preparations were made for her demolition on 4/5.5.45. *Emden* had been hit by four incendiaries on 12.3.45 which caused no damage below the armoured deck. She was hit again, in No. 3 boiler room, on 3.4.45 and finally damaged by hits and near misses on 13.4.45, after which she was beached.

Page 162: *Leipzig* was in action against tank concentrations and gun batteries in the Danzig area during the forenoon of 10.3.45, firing 100 rounds. That same evening she engaged targets west of Zoppot while anchored off Gotenhafen and on 17.3.45 gave gunfire support in the Gdynia area. She had been ordered west on 14.3.45 but remained on fire support duty in the east until her ammunition was expended on 22.3.45. She arrived in Aabenraa in the evening of 29 March, loaded with 700 wounded and refugees, having experienced submarine and air attacks en route.

Page 169: *Königsberg* ordered 28.3.25; *Karlsruhe* 21.5.26; *Köln* 2.3.26; *Leipzig* 25.10.27.

GERMAN CAPITAL SHIPS OF WORLD WAR TWO

Page 12: *Zähringen* paid off at Gotenhafen, 6.11.44. She appears to have been raised following the raid on 18.12.44 as she was used as a block ship across numbers 4 & 10 basins on 31.3.45. *Hessen* was mined off Swinemünde and badly damaged on 23.6.43 but made port under her own power with three compartments flooded.

Page 73: SKl/Ob.d.M gave orders on 30.10.41 for the carrier to be moved to Gotenhafen by the tug *Atlantik*.

Page 76: A Construction Party was appointed to *Graf Zeppelin* on 1.2.43 and disbanded on 12.6.43.

Page 111: *Schleswig–Holstein* was laid up at Gotenhafen until 4.11.40 when she sailed for Kiel. *Schlesien* was laid up until 24.11.40.

Page 209: *Schlesien* had been ordered to Flensburg on 14.3.45 but was retained in the east, bombarding targets in the Zoppot area on 13 and 17 March. She was in action again from Gdynia on 18.3.45 but the following day received orders to be ready for transfer west by pm on the 20th at the latest. She duly sailed from Gotenhafen for Swinemünde on the 20th, only to have these orders countermanded just before midnight. She did not reach Swinemünde until the forenoon of the 22nd with 1,150 wounded and refugees, sailing again a couple of hours later.